MW00991809

WITHDRAWN

THE MAGNA CHARTA SURETIES, 1215

The Barons Named in the Magna Charta, 1215
and Some of Their Descendants
Who Settled in America
1607-1650

By FREDERICK LEWIS WEIS, Th.D.
and Arthur Adams, Ph.D.

THIRD EDITION

With Additions and Corrections By
WALTER LEE SHEPPARD, JR., M.S.

Baltimore
GENEALOGICAL PUBLISHING CO., INC.
1982

First Edition: Boston, 1955
Second Edition: Baltimore, 1964
Third Edition: Baltimore, 1979, 1982
Copyright © 1979
Genealogical Publishing Co., Inc.
Baltimore, Maryland
All Rights Reserved
Library of Congress Catalogue Card Number 79-89349
International Standard Book Number 0-8063-0866-4
Made in the United States of America

To

The Fellows of the American Society of Genealogists
whose greatest care in the exercise of their
profession is accuracy and integrity;
and especially to those Fellows
who have helped to make this book possible.

A. A.   F. L. W.

PREFACE TO THE THIRD EDITION

The reader will, perhaps, be curious as to the history of this work. The
Rev. Dr. Frederick Lewis Weis had done outstanding work on the early families of
Lancaster, Massachusetts, much of which is in manuscript and now in the collections of the American Antiquarian Society in Worcester. He followed this with his
now standard series on the Colonial Clergy of the thirteen original colonies, available in reprint. He then became interested in pre-Colonial pedigrees, and in 1950
published his well known Ancestral Roots of Sixty Colonists Who Came to New England (2nd edition, with some changes, the following year, additions and corrections
in 1956), which when released was the best work of its kind available, and which
has been further improved in corrected editions since. Unlike other similar publications, in Ancestral Roots evidential citations gave the source of each statement.

In 1951 Dr. Weis was elected a Fellow of the American Society of Genealogists.
In 1952 he published a Supplement to Ancestral Roots, and thereafter started collec-
ting material toward the present book. Most of the work had been completed by the
time The American Society of Genealogists met in Montreal in the fall of 1955, and
he brought the manuscript with him on the plane on which he was seated next to the
President of the Society, Dr. Arthur Adams, and to whom he showed it. In an un-
selfish effort to compliment Dr. Adams, he asked him to allow his name to be added
to the title page, and Dr. Adams consented. Though Dr. Adams' name was
given priority, those of us who knew both men, and the way in which the manuscript
was prepared, have no doubt that the real author was Fred Weis, and Fred Weis
alone should receive the credit. Dr. Weis, in further compliment to the Society,
refrained from copyrighting the volume so that, as he told the Fellows at the next
meeting, we would all be free to reprint the book or any part of it as we wished, and
that this was a gift to all of us from him.

Like other similar works, The Magna Charta Sureties is composed of an inter-
locking collection of pedigrees from many sources. Dr. Weis had limited his earlier pedigree collections to New England, the area that he knew well. With The Magna Charta Sureties he decided to include immigrants to all the original thirteen colonies. To do this he relied on the competence of those who worked in these other
geographic areas. Unfortunately, he did not require documentation of the pedigrees
which were submitted to him, perhaps because he trusted his contributors, perhaps
because the facilities for verifying the pedigrees were not available to him where he
lived in retirement at Dublin, New Hampshire, perhaps because in his later years he
was unwell, and travel for him was difficult. At all events, when this work appeared
in early 1955 it contained many more errors than did his earlier volumes and, unlike Ancestral Roots, omitted most references. In 1964 the Genealogical Publishing
Company decided to do a new printing of the work, and at the request of Dr. Weis,
and his wife, the present writer agreed to collect all the corrections that had been
noted at that time, and to enter them by hand in a clean copy of the work, which
was then reproduced as the second edition. This second edition has been exhausted for
some years, and this present edition, the third, is now totally re-set, dropping some
generations that were in error, incorporating many new lines and a great many corrections in the old ones, and adding references in many places where they had previously been omitted.

The reader should note that not all lines have been verified, nor do the nota-
tions of corrections in a line indicate that all other generations have been checked
and found to be correct. All compiled pedigrees in any book, including this one, are
subject to copying or typographical errors no matter how careful the author, editor,
or printer may be, and should be used with caution. Even though we believe this to
be one of the most carefully compiled and most accurate books in this field, the user
should verify all statements and dates with source material before transferring them
to a lineage blank for application for membership in an hereditary society, or before
incorporating them into a published genealogy. If any errors are noted we ask that
the reader communicate them to the undersigned.

The writer's thanks are due to correspondents, too numerous to identify, who
have sent corrections in the text of the first edition, and of the corrected reprint, or
who have drawn attention to hidden errors or mis-statements. Where appropriate,

v

lines appearing in this edition for the first time are credited to their authors. However, there are three persons who deserve special and particular thanks and recognition: William Addams Reitwiesner of Silver Spring, Maryland, Gary Boyd Roberts of Boston, Massachusetts, and Dr. David M. Foley of Augusta College, Augusta, Georgia. Mr. Reitwiesner has been my right hand in verifying references, in catching mis-statements and conflicting data, and his eagle eye has located not only errors, but corrections that should be made. Mr. Roberts has willingly helped in researching alternate lines where the ones appearing in the first edition had come into question or were found in error, and has done yeoman work in correcting many lines. Dr. Foley, besides supplying corrections to the first edition, has provided most of the Scottish lines that appear for the first time in this volume, and has promptly responded to all questions asked of him. Without their assistance this volume would still be in the formative stages.

Walter Lee Sheppard, Jr., FASG
923 Old Manoa Road
Havertown, PA 19083

AN INTRODUCTION TO THE MAGNA CHARTA

The Magna Charta (or Carta) is generally considered to be the cornerstone of Anglo-Saxon law, since it is the earliest agreement between sovereign and subject (i.e. the noble class) on the rights of both parties — that is, what each can do, and the limitation of powers. In addition, the Great Charter set up watchdogs for both sides: twenty-five men representing the barons, which twenty-five signed for the barons and were sureties for the baronial performance, and the friends of the king, who were named in the Charter.

The story of the Charter and the study of its wording and provisions fills many books. The reader may perhaps find the most interesting and useful of these to be a nineteenth-century work by Richard Thomson entitled An Historical Essay on the Magna Carta of King John, published in London in 1828. At the head of each page is a shield of arms of a person who was in some way related to the Charter or the events surrounding it, and these arms are indexed in tables beginning on page xvii. The text of the Charter is given, accompanied by essays on content, but of primary interest to the users of the present volume are the extensive biographical notes on the Sureties, and on those individuals mentioned in the text of the Charter, or connected with it. This book runs over 600 pages.

Of the twenty-five Sureties only seventeen have identified descendants. Four had no known surviving issue; the issue of one died out in the third generation, and of another in the fourth. Nothing whatever is known of William de Hardell and his family. The twenty-fifth, Richard de Percy, left only an illegitimate son, Henry, to whom he gave the manor of Settle (Yorks). Henry is known to have had a son Alexander, but further information about this line is lacking, and since Henry surrendered his manor of Settle to his cousins, efforts to learn more by land records have been unsuccessful. All of the first seventeen are represented in the pedigrees which follow.

For the convenience of the users of this book the editor has provided two tables, each with footnotes, to supply lineage information, one on the Sureties, the other on those persons who appear as friends of the King. Though there is some overlap between this work and Ancestral Roots, much of the material here supplied is different, and the two books may be used together.

THE TWENTY-FIVE SURETIES OF THE MAGNA CHARTA

Richard de Clare, Earl of Clare
William de Fortibus, Earl of Aumale (1)
Geoffrey de Mandeville, Earl of Gloucester (2)
Saher de Quincy, Earl of Winchester
Henry de Bohun, Earl of Hereford
Roger Bigod, Earl of Norfolk
Robert de Vere, Earl of Oxford
William Marshall, the Younger (2)
Robert fitz Walter of Dunmow
Gilbert de Clare
Eustace de Vesci (3)
William de Hardell, Mayor of London (4)
William de Mowbray
Geoffrey de Say
Roger de Mumbezon (or Mont Begon) (2)
William de Huntingfield
Robert de Ros of Hamlake
John de Lacy, Constable of Chester, Baron of Holton
William de Albini of Belvoir
Richard de Percy (5)
William Malet
John fitz Robert
William de Lanvallei

Hugh Bigod, later Earl of Norfolk
Richard de Muntfitchet, Baron of Stanstead (2)

---

(1) known issue extinct after 3rd generation
(2) no known issue surviving
(3) known issue extinct after 4th generation
(4) nothing known of him or his family
(5) no legitimate issue. He had an illeg. son, Sir Henry de Percy, who held the
market and fair and manor of Settle (Yorks), who had a son Alexander who held
land in Arram, par. of Leconfield. Descendants may exist. GEC X p. 452.

PERSONS NAMED IN THE PREAMBLE OF MAGNA CHARTA AS ADVISORS OF KING JOHN

Clerics

Stephen de Langton, Archbishop of Canterbury
Henry, Archbishop of Dublin
William, Bishop of London
Peter, Bishop of Winchester
Joceline, Bishop of Bath and Glastonbury
Hugh, Bishop of Lincoln
Walter, Bishop of Worcester
William, Bishop of Coventry
Benedict, Bishop of Rochester
Pandulph, the Pope's subdeacon and familiar (Papal Legate)
Almeric, Master of the Knights Templar in England

Nobles

William Marshall, Earl of Pembroke
William Longespee, Earl of Salisbury
William, Earl of Warren (and Surrey)
Alan of Galloway, Constable of Scotland
Warin fitz Gerold (1)
Hubert de Burgh, Seneschal of Poitou
Peter fitz Herbert
Hugh de Nevil
Matthew fitz Herbert
Thomas Basset
Alan Basset
Philip de Albini
Robert de Roppel
John Marshall of Hengham
John fitz Hugh.

---

(1) known issue extinct in 3rd generation

COLONISTS WHOSE ANCESTRY IS DISCUSSED

Anne Rich, wife of Col. Francis Willis	Virginia	60*
Capt. John Boteler (line unsatisfactory)	Maryland	61#
Thomas Boteler (line unsatisfactory)	Maryland	61#
Elizabeth Boteler	Virginia	61#
wife of Col. William Claiborne (unsatisfactory)		
Sir Richard Everard, Bt.	North Carolina	62
Gov. Charles Calvert, 3rd Lord Baltimore	Maryland	63
John Fenwick	New Jersey	65
John Fenwick	South Carolina	65
Thomas Ligon	Virginia	66
(much new material, research continuing)		
John Norwood (evidences lacking)	Maryland, North Carolina	67#
Henry Norwood	Virginia	68
Sir William Berkeley, Gov.	Virginia	69
Rev. Edward Foliot	Virginia	70
Col. William Randolph	Virginia	71
Rev. Hawte Wyatt	Virginia	72
Mary Bourchier, wife of Jabez Whitaker	Virginia	73
George Burroughs	Massachusetts	74
Richard Kempe	Virginia	75
Edmund Kempe	Virginia	75
William Fairfax	Virginia	76
George Constable	Connecticut	77
Elder William Wentworth	New Hampshire	78
(early part of line, earlier editions, faulty, alternate supplied)		
Herbert Pelham	Massachusetts	80
Penelope Pelham	Massachusetts	80
wife of Gov. Richard Bellingham		
Christopher Wetherill	New Jersey	81
Joseph Bowles	Maine (Massachusetts)	82
Dep. Gov. Francis Willoughby	Massachusetts	83
Hon. William Asfordby	New York	84
Sir Grey Skipwith	Virginia	85
Col. George Reade	Virginia	86
Dep. Gov. Roger Ludlow	Massachusetts	88
Sarah Ludlow, wife of Col. John Carter	Virginia	88
Gabriel Ludlow	New York	88*
Sir Thomas Lunsford	Virginia	88A*
Col. Roger Harlakenden	Massachusetts	89#
(part of line, earlier editions, void, alternate supplied, 89A)		
Gen. Hugh Mercer	Pennsylvania	91B*
Gov. Robert Barclay	East New Jersey	92
Sir Patrick Houstoun, Bt.	Georgia	92A*
Dr. John Irvine	Georgia	93
Rev. John Oxenbridge	Massachusetts	94
John Coke	Virginia	94A*
Elizabeth Bosvile	Massachusetts	95
wife of Col. Roger Harlakenden		
Capt. Thomas Southworth (unsatisfactory)	Massachusetts	96#
Obadiah Bruen	Massachusetts, New Jersey	97
Rev. Peter Bulkeley	Massachusetts	98
Elizabeth St. John, wife of Rev. Samuel Whiting	Massachusetts	98
Martha Bulkeley, wife of Abraham Mellowes	Massachusetts	98
Frances Bulkeley, wife of Richard Welby	Massachusetts	98
Elizabeth Bulkeley	Massachusetts	98
wife of Richard Whittingham and Atherton Haugh		
Olive Ingoldsby, wife of Rev. Thomas James	Massachusetts, Connecticut	98
Capt. Jeremy Clarke	Rhode Island	100
Col. Walter Aston	Virginia	101
Edward Carleton	Massachusetts	102
Elizabeth Coytmore	Virginia	103
wife of Capt. William Tyng		
Sarah Kenrich, wife of Ralph Eddowes	Pennsylvania	104
Joshua Owen	New Jersey	105
Lucy Legh, wife of Col. Alexander Rigby	Maine (Massachusetts	106

Capt. Henry Batte	Virginia	109
Gov. Robert Brooke	Maryland	110
Grace Chetwode, wife of Rev. Peter Bulkeley	Massachusetts	111
Anne Lovelace, wife of Rev. John Gorsuch	Virginia	113#
(alternate 113A is satisfactory, and includes Sir William Lovelace)		
John Prescott	Massachusetts	116#
(still not proven, unsatisfactory)		
John Throckmorton	Rhode Island	117
Richard Wodehull (or Woodhull)	New York	118#
(unsatisfactory)		
Elizabeth Marshall, wife of Thomas Lewis	Maine (Massachusetts)	120
Rev. John Davenport (broken line)	Massachusetts	122#
(original line incorrect, replace with 122A, correct)		
Capt. Thomas Bradbury (line unacceptable)	Massachusetts	123#
Col. Richard Lee	Virginia	124
(line has been questioned, see articles in Va. Gen.)		
Gov. William Leete	Connecticut	128
Sir Thomas Josselyn (line unacceptable	Maine (Massachusetts	133#
Capt. Charles Barham	Virginia	134
Samuel Appleton	Massachusetts	137
Alice Freeman	Massachusetts	163
wife of John Thompson, Robert Parke		
Edward Fitz Randolph	New Jersey	164

---

* New colonists added in this edition.
\# Lines from previous editions, now unacceptable as they appeared previously.
See also notes on such lines which have been altered to make them acceptable.

The editor has retained old, unacceptable lines in most cases, and has not re-numbered lines where generations were omitted or entered in error. The reason for retaining the old numbers is to make clear to the user which lines (those that may have been cited in pedigree or lineage blanks) require correction or deletion, and why the changes are necessary. Strange as it seems, genealogists for heredi-tary societies often blindly copy earlier pedigrees that have been submitted, with the result that the same errors appear time and time again. It is the editor's hope that retaining the numbers will make such errors more visible.

NOTE TO THE READER

Mr. Frederick W. Sawyer, III, 137 Mallard Drive, East Hartford, Connecticut 06118, a computer scientist, has developed a program for locating all generations in all lines ancestral to any individual, particularly to all the colonists named in An-cestral Roots, and can produce a print-out which lists and identifies them numerically. Except for his system such a study is a tedious and time-consuming matter. The system is, of course, equally applicable to Magna Charta Sureties. If you would like to determine all of the ancestors appearing in this book for any of the many colonists included in these lines, you may find it of advantage to communicate with Mr. Sawyer, who will provide such a print-out for any colonist, in either book, for a set fee.

ABBREVIATIONS

adm. - admitted
ae. - aged
aft. - after
als. - alias
A. M. - Master of Arts
ante - before
app. or appt. - apparently
b. - born
B. C. L. - Bachelor of Canon Law
B. D. - Bachelor of Divinity
bef. - before
betw. - between
bp. - baptized
Bt. - Baronet
c. - circa, about
cf. - compare
cit. - work cited, citato
Clay - Extinct and Dormant Peerages
   of the Northern Counties
Co. or co. - county
coh. - coheir
Col. Topo. et Gen. - Collectanea
   Topographica et Genealogica
CP - Complete Peerage
cr. - created
C. V. O. - Companion of the Royal
   Victorian Order
d. - died
DAB - Dictionary of American Biography
dau(s). - daughter(s)
D. D. - Doctor of Divinity
disp. - dispensation
div. - divorced
DNB - Dictionary of National Biography
d. s. p. - decessit sine prole, died
   without issue
d. s. p. legit. - died without legitimate issue
d. s. p. m. - died without male issue
dtd. - dated
d. v. p. - died within father's lifetime
d. y. - died young
E. S. - Stammtafeln zur Geschichte
   der Europäisch Staaten by Wilhelm Karl, Prinz von Isenburg
EYC - Early Yorkshire Charters by
   Farrer and Clay
ff. - following
fl. - flourished
Gen. - The Genealogist
gen(s). - generation(s)
Gen. Mag. - Genealogists' Magazine
gr. - granted
granddau. - granddaughter
GS - gravestone
h. - heir

Harl. Soc. Publ. - Harleian Society
   Publication
H. C. - House of Commons, Harvard
   College
HCS - Historical Collections of Stafford-
   shire
husb. - husband
ibid. - in the same place
Inq. p. m. - inquest (or inquisition) post
   mortem
I. p. m. - see Inq. p. m.
J. P. - Justice of the Peace
j. u. - jure uxoris, rights of wife
k. - killed
K. B. - Knight of the Bath
K. G. - Knight of the Garter
Knt. - Knight
lic. - license
liv. - living
LL. D. - Doctor of Laws
loc. cit. - place cited
m. - married
M. A. - Master of Arts
matric. - matriculated
M. C. - Magna Charta
M. D. - Master of Divinity
ment. - mentioned
Mich. - Michaelmas
Misc. Gen. et Her. - Miscellanea Genea-
   logica et Heraldica
M. P. - Member of Parliament
N. - name not known
NCHN - New County History of Northumberland
NEHGR - New England Historical and
   Genealogical Register
NGSQ - National Genealogical Society
   Quarterly
nr. - near
N. S. or n. s. - new series
NYGBR - New York Genealogical and
   Biographical Record
ob. - died
occ. - occurs
op. cit. - work cited above, opere citato
p. - page
P. C. - Privy Council
perh. - perhaps
PMHB - Pennsylvania Magazine of History
   and Biography
pr. - proved or probated
pres. - presumed
prob. - probably
Psh. - Parish
pub. - published
purch. - purchased
q. v. - quod vide, which see
ref(s). - reference(s)

Reg. Great Seal - Registrum magni
    sigilli regum Scotorum
Rot. - Rolls, rotalus
s. - son
sett. - settled
sh. - shortly
SP - The Scots Peerage
s.p. - without issue (see d.s.p.)
suc. - succeeded
summ. - summoned
suo juris - in his (or her) right
surv. - survived
TAG - The American Genealogist

ult. - ultimo
unkn. - unknown
unm. - unmarried
VCH - Victoria County Histories
VHM - Virginia Historical Magazine
vol. - volume
wid. - widow
y. - young (see d.y.)
Yorks PRS - Yorkshire Archaeological
    Society Public Record Series
yr. - younger
yrs. - years
yst. - youngest

MAGNA CHARTA SURETIES

Line 1

1. WILLIAM D'AUBIGNY (157-3), b. aft. 1146, Lord of Belvoir, co. Leicester, succeeded, 1167/8, d. 1 May 1236, Magna Charta Surety, 1215; m. (1) Margery, dau. of Odinel de Umfreville; m. (2) Agatha Trusbut. (See Nichols, Leicestershire II, 27.)

2. WILLIAM D'AUBIGNY (by first wife), Lord of Belvoir; m. (1) Albreda Biset; m. (2) Isabel, b. 1233/5, living 1285. (CP XI, 96, note c; Farrer, E.Y.C. I, 460-462).

3. ISABEL D'AUBIGNY (by second wife), d. 15 June 1301, of Belvoir Castle; m. betw. 5 June 1243 and 17 May 1244, SIR ROBERT de ROS (117-3), of Helmsley and Belvoir, M.P., 1261, 1265, d. 17 May 1285. (CP XI, 95).

4. WILLIAM de ROS, b. c. 1255, d. (pres. betw. 12 May and 16 Aug.) 1316, 1st Lord Ros of Helmsley, M.P., 1295-1316; m. bef. 1287, Maude de Vaux, dau. of John de Vaux. (CP XI, 96).

5. WILLIAM de ROS, of age 1316, d. 3 Feb. 1342/3, 2nd Lord Ros of Helmsley, M.P.; m. bef. 25 Nov. 1316, MARGERY de BADLESMERE (33-7). (CP XI, 98).

6. THOMAS de ROS, 3rd son, b. Stoke Albany, 13 Jan. 1336/7, d. Uffington, 8 June 1384, of Helmsley, M.P., 1362-1384, 4th Lord Ros; m. lic. 1 Jan. 1358/9, Beatrice Stafford, d. Apr. 1415, dau. of SIR RALPH de STAFFORD, K.G. (136-6) and MARGARET de AUDLEY (28-6), d. Apr. 1415, wid. Maurice, Earl of Desmond. (CP XI, 100).

7. SIR WILLIAM de ROS, K.G., b. c. 1368, of Belvoir, d. Belvoir, 1 Sept. 1414, M.P., 1394-1413, Treasurer of England, 1403-1404, K.G., 1403, 6th Lord Ros; m. lic. 9 Oct. 1394, MARGARET de ARUNDEL (121-9), d. 3 July 1438. (CP XI, 102).

8. MARGARET de ROS, living 1423; m. c. 1415, JAMES TUCHET (12-11), Lord Audley, b. c. 1398, d. 23 Sept. 1459, M.P., 1421-1455. (Generations 2 to 8: CP XI, 90-103; I, 340).

9. ANNE TUCHET, d. 1503; m. SIR THOMAS DUTTON (96-11) of Dutton, d. 23 Sept. 1459.

10. ANNE DUTTON, d. 22 Oct. 1520; m. c. 11 July 1463, SIR THOMAS MOLYNEUX, KNT. (25-11), d. 12 July 1483.

11. SIR WILLIAM MOLYNEUX, of Sefton, b. 1481, d. 1548; m. (1) Jane Rugge, dau. of Sir John Rugge of Shropshire.

12. SIR RICHARD MOLYNEUX, KNT., of Sefton, d. 3 Jan. 1568/9, Sheriff of Lancashire, 1566-1568; m. (1) Eleanor Radcliffe, dau. of SIR ALEXANDER RADCLIFFE (129-11), of Ordsall, q.v.

*   *   *   *   *   *

Balance of line appearing in earlier editions is cancelled.

*   *   *   *   *   *

Line 2

4. WILLIAM de ROS (1-4); m. Maud de Vaux. (CP XI, 97).

5. AGNES de ROS, d. sh. bef. 25 Nov. 1328; m. c. 25 Apr. 1298, Pain de

Tybetot, 1st Lord Tybetot, b. 11 Nov. 1279 or 24 June 1281, slain at the battle of Bannockburn, 1314, son of Sir Robert de Tybetot and Eve, dau. of Pain de Chaworth.
(CP XI, 97, note m; XII (2), 94).
     6. JOHN de TYBETOT, b. 20 July 1313, d. 13 Apr. 1367; m. (1) as her 2nd
husband, Margaret de Badlesmere, b. 3 Dec. 1344 - 4 Dec. 1347, dau. of Bartholomew de Badlesmere and MARGARET de CLARE (33-6).
     7. SIR ROBERT de TYBETOT (see 149A-7), bp. 11 June 1341, d. 1372; m. by
Trinity, 13 Apr. 1372, MARGARET DEINCOURT (74-8), q.v.

Line 3

     1. ROGER BIGOD (155-2), b. c. 1150, d. bef. 2 Aug. 1221, Steward of England,
2nd Earl of Norfolk, Magna Charta Surety, 1215; m. Ida. (CP IX, 586-589).
     2. HUGH BIGOD (155-3), d. Feb. 1224/5, 3rd Earl of Norfolk, Magna Charta
Surety, 1215; m. 1207, MAUD MARSHAL (148-2), d. 27 Mar. 1248. (CP IX, 589-
590).
     3. SIR HUGH BIGOD, yr. son, d. Nov. 1266, Chief Justice of England, 1257-
1260; m. (1) Joanna, dau. of Robert Burnet; m. (2) Joan de Stuteville, dau. of Nicholas de Stuteville and DEVORGILLA OF GALLOWAY (139-1), sister of Alan of Galloway. (DNB II, 486; CP IX, 590, note c, and below under Roger, 6th Earl; C. T.
Clay, Early Yorkshire Charters IX, The Stuteville Fee, 1952, pp. 18-23).
     4. SIR JOHN BIGOD, KNT. (son by second wife), of Stockton, co. Norfolk,
b. bef. 1266, dead 1306, heir to his brother, Roger Bigod, 6th Earl of Norfolk; m.
Isabel, d. 1311 (not heir to title, which vested in the crown).
     5. SIR ROGER BIGOD, KNT., d. 17 Apr. 1362, of Settrington, co. York; m.
Joan.
     6. JOAN BIGOD; m. 1358, Sir William de Chauncy, Knt., baron of Skirpen-
beck, co. York, 1399, and of Stepney, co. Middlesex, son of Sir Thomas de Chauncy. (Gens. 4-6, Yorkshire Arch. Jnl., vol. 32, pp. 180-190, 201).
     7. JOHN CHAUNCY, of Stepney, d. 22 Feb. 1444/5; m. Margaret Giffard,
dau. of William Giffard of Samford, Essex, and of Gedleston, co. Hertford.
     8. JOHN CHAUNCY, ESQ., d. 7 May 1479, of Pishobury Manor, Sawbridge-
worth; m. Anne Leventhorpe, d. 2 Dec. 1477, dau. of John Leventhorpe, Esq., one
of the executors of the will of King Henry V.
     9. JOHN CHAUNCY (89A-9), of Sawbridgeworth, d. 8 June 1510; m. Alice
Boyce, dau. of Thomas Boyce.
     10. JOHN CHAUNCY, of Pishobury Manor, d. 4 June 1546; m. Elizabeth
Proffit, d. 10 Nov. 1531, dau. of John Proffit, of Barcomb, co. Suffolk, and widow
of Richard Mansfield.
     11. HENRY CHAUNCY, of New Place Gifford's, d. 14 Apr. 1587; m. Lucy,
d. 25 Apr. 1566.
     12. GEORGE CHAUNCY, of Yardley-Bury, co. Hertford, d. 1625/7; m. (2)
after 1582, Anne (Welsh) Humberton, dau. of Edward Welsh, of Great Wymondley,
co. Hertford, and widow of Edward Humberton.
     13. THE REVEREND CHARLES CHAUNCY, B.D., b. 5 Nov. 1592, d. Cam-
bridge, Massachusetts, 19 Feb. 1671/2; 2nd President of Harvard College, 1654-
1672; m. 17 Mar. 1630, Catherine Eyre, bp. 2 Nov. 1604, d. 23 June 1667, dau. of
Robert Eyre of New Sarum, Wiltshire. The Rev. Messrs. ISAAC CHAUNCY, M.D.,
BARNABAS CHAUNCY, A.M., NATHANIEL CHAUNCY, A.M., and ISRAEL CHAUN-
CY, A.M. were their sons.

Line 4

     1. ROGER BIGOD, M.C. (3-1); m. Ida.
     2. HUGH BIGOD, M.C. (3-2); m. MAUD MARSHAL (148-2, 155-3).
     3. ISABEL BIGOD; m. (1) Gilbert de Lacy, d. 1230, of Ewyas Lacy, Trim and
Weoberley, son of Walter de Lacy, Lord of Meath, and Margaret de St. Hilary; m.
(2) after 1230, Sir John Fitz Geoffrey, d. 23 Nov. 1258, of Shere, Farnbridge, etc.,
Justiciar of Ireland, 1245-1256, son of GEOFFREY FITZ PIERS (160-3), Earl of
Essex and Aveline de Clare. (CP IX, 590, note c; XII (2), 370; V, 433-4 & note e
p. 433 & note a p. 434).

4. MAUD FITZ JOHN (by the 2nd husband), bur. 7 May 1301; m. (1) Gerard de Furnivalle, of Sheffield, co. York, d.s.p., bef. 18 Oct. 1261; m. (2) bef. 1270, William de Beauchamp, b. 1237, bur. 22 June 1298, 9th Earl of Warwick. (CP XII (2), 368-70; Sanders, Baronies, 10-11 & note 7, p. 10).

5. ISABEL de BEAUCHAMP, d. by 30 May 1306; m. (1) Sir Patrick de Chaworth, d. by 7 July 1283, Lord of Kidwelley, Wales, son of Patrick de Chaworth; m. (2) by 1286, Sir Hugh le Despenser, b. 1 Mar. 1260/1, hanged 27 Oct. 1326, Earl of Winchester, son of Hugh le Despenser and Aline Basset. (CP VII, 400; IV, 262; Sanders, 125).

6. MAUD de CHAWORTH (by the 2nd husband); m. as 1st wife bef. 2 Mar. 1296/7, Henry Plantagenet, Earl of Lancaster, b. c. 1281, d. 22 Sept. 1348, son of Edmund Plantagenet and Blanche of Artois, and grandson of King HENRY III (161-13) of England and Eleanor of Provence. (CP VII, 396-401). He m. (2) as 2nd husb., Alix, dau. of John de Joinville.

7. JOAN PLANTAGENET, d. 7 July 1349; m. JOHN de MOWBRAY (63-5), q.v. (CP VII, 401, note b; Clay, 140).

8. ALIANORE MOWBRAY, d. by 18 June 1387; m. as his 3rd wife, bef. 23 July 1358, ROGER de la WARRE (56-7), q.v.

9. JOAN de la WARRE, d. 24 Apr. 1404; m. (1) Ralf de Welyngton, d.s.p. 16 Aug. 1382; m. (2) by 24 May 1384, Sir Thomas West, b. 1365, d. 19 Apr. 1405, 3rd Lord West, son of Sir Thomas West and Alice Fitz Herbert. (CP XII (2), 520).

10. SIR REYNOLD de WEST, 6th Lord de la Warre, b. 7 Sept. 1395, d. 27 Aug. 1450; m. (1) bef. 17 Feb. 1428/9, Margaret Thorley, d. bef. 24 Nov. 1433, dau. of Robert Thorley, of Thynbest, Cornwall, and Anne Lisle; m. (2) by 19 Nov. 1443, Elizabeth Gleyndour, d. 1 Sept. 1452. (CP IV, 152-154).

11. SIR RICHARD WEST, 7th Lord de la Warre, b. c. 28 Oct. 1430, d. 10 Mar. 1475/6; m. bef. 10 June 1451, Katherine Hungerford, d. 12 May 1493, dau. of Sir Robert Hungerford, Lord Hungerford, and Margaret Botreaux. (CP IV, 154).

12. SIR THOMAS WEST, K.G., 8th Lord de la Warre, b. 1457, d. 11 Oct. 1525; m. (1) Elizabeth Mortimer, dau. of Hugh Mortimer and Eleanor Cornwall; m. (2) Eleanor Copley, dau. of Sir Roger Copley and Ann Hoo. (CP IV, 155).

13. SIR GEORGE WEST (by second wife), of Warbleton, Sussex, d. Sept. 1538; m. Elizabeth Morton, dau. of Sir Robert Morton of Lechlade, co. Gloucester. (CP IV, 158).

14. SIR WILLIAM WEST, b. by 1520, d. Wherwell, 30 Dec. 1595, "disabled of all honours" by Parliament, 1 Feb. 1549/50, cr. 1569/70 Baron Delaware; m. (1) bef. 1555, Elizabeth Strange, dau. of Thomas Strange of Chesterton, co. Gloucester; m. (2) Anne Swift, d. aft. 6 Oct. 1611. (CP IV, 158).

15. SIR THOMAS WEST (by 1st wife), 2nd Lord Delaware, b. c. 1556, d. 24 Mar. 1601/2, M.P., 1571-1593, Knt., 7 Dec. 1587; m. 19 Nov. 1571, ANNE KNOLLYS (80-15). (CP IV, 159).

16. ELIZABETH WEST and PENELOPE WEST (See Line 80.)

16. GOVERNOR THOMAS WEST, b. 9 July 1577, d. at sea en route to Virginia, 7 June 1618; A.M., Queen's Coll., Oxford, 1605; M.P., Knight, 3rd Lord Delaware, Governor of Virginia, Mar. 1610-1611. (CP IV, 160),

16. GOVERNOR FRANCIS WEST, b. 28 Oct. 1586, d. Feb. 1633/4; came to Virginia, 1608; Captain; Governor of Virginia, 1627-1629.

16. GOVERNOR JOHN WEST, b. 14 Dec. 1590, d. c. 1659; member of the Governor's Council, Virginia, 1631-1659; Governor of Virginia, 1635-1637.

16. NATHANIEL WEST, b. 30 Nov. 1592; d. Virginia, 1623/4.

Line 5

4. MAUD FITZ JOHN (4-4), d. 1301; m. (2) bef. 1270, William de Beauchamp.

5. GUY de BEAUCHAMP, b. 1278, d. Warwick Castle, 12 Aug. 1315, 10th Earl of Warwick; m. (2) bef. 1309/10, Alice de Toeni, d. sh. bef. 8 Jan. 1324/5, dau. of Ralph de Toeni. She was wid. of Thomas de Leyburn, d. sh. bef. 30 May 1307; she m. (3) William Zouche, Lord Zouche de Mortimer. (CP VII, 638; XII (2), 370-2; XII (1), 774, note j).

6. THOMAS de BEAUCHAMP, K.G., b. prob. 14 Feb. 1313/14, d. Calais, 23 Apr. 1369, 11th Earl of Warwick, K.G., 23 Apr. 1349; m. 1337, KATHERINE de MORTIMER (17-7, 147-6). (CP XII (2), 372-4).

7. PHILIPPA BEAUCHAMP, d. bef. 6 Apr. 1386; m. bef. 1 Mar 1350/1, SIR

HUGH STAFFORD, K.G. (136-7), b. in or bef. 1342, d. Rhodes, 16 Oct. 1386, M.P.,
1371, Earl of Stafford. (CP XII (2), 177-9; XII (1), 177).
    8. KATHERINE STAFFORD, d. 8 Apr. 1419; m. bef. 23 Nov. 1383, Sir Mi-
chael de la Pole, b. by 1367, d. Harfleur, 18 Sept. 1415, 2nd Earl of Suffolk, son of
Michael de la Pole, Earl of Suffolk, 1385, d. 1388, and Katherine Wingfield. (CP
XII (2), 441-2; XII (1), 441).

           *   *   *   *   *   *

Thomas de la Pole of Grafton Regis was younger brother of Michael, 2nd Earl of
Suffolk, and son of Michael, 1st Earl, and Katharine Wingfield.

           *   *   *   *   *   *

    9. SIR THOMAS de la POLE, of Grafton Regis, ae. 30+ in 1404, d. 21 Aug.
1420; m. Anne, dau. of Nicholas Cheney, living 21 June 1435, m. to a Sakeryle.
    10. KATHERINE de la POLE, b. c. 1416, d. Oct. 1488; m. (1) as 2nd wife,
SIR MILES STAPLETON (49-9), b. 1408, d. c. 1 Oct. 1466, of Ingham and Bedale;
m. (2) Sir Richard Harcourt, d. 1 Oct. 1486. (Swyncombe and Ewelme (1858), 310-
311).
    11. ELIZABETH STAPLETON, b. 1441/2, d. 18 Feb. 1504/5; m. (1) bef. 7
Mar. 1463/4, Sir William Calthrope, b. 30 Jan. 1409/10, d. 15 Nov. 1494, of Burnham Thorpe; m. twice more. (CP V, 397).
    12. ANNE CALTHROPE; m. Sir Robert Drury, Knt., d. 1538, of Hawstead,
co. Suffolk, Speaker of the House of Commons, 1498.
    13. ANNE DRURY; m. (1) GEORGE WALDEGRAVE (74-13), d. 1528, of Small-
bridge in Bures, co. Suffolk, son of Sir William Waldegrave, Knt., of Smallbridge;
m. (2) Sir Thomas Jermyn (See 37-16.). (Generations 8 to 13: CP V, 397, chart).
    14. EDWARD WALDEGRAVE, d. 1584, of Lawford Hall, Essex; m. 1556, Joan,
d. c. 10 Dec. 1590, dau. of George Ackworth.
    15. MARGARET WALDEGRAVE; m. William Clopton, gent., d. 9 Aug. 1616,
of Groton, co. Suffolk, Lord of the manor of Castelyns.
    16. THOMASINE CLOPTON, b. 1583, d. Groton, 8 Dec. 1616; m. 6 Dec. 1615,
Governor John Winthrop of Massachusetts; s.p. this marriage.
    16. WALTER CLOPTON (brother of Thomasine Winthrop), bp. Groton, co.
Suffolk, 30 June 1585, d. 1622, of Boxted, co. Suffolk, gent.; m. Boxted, 21 Apr.
1612, Margaret, d. 1666, dau. of Robert Maidstone, gent.
    17. THE REVEREND WILLIAM CLOPTON, bp. Boxted, 9 Oct. 1613, d. 1671;
m. Elizabeth, d. 1683, dau. of the Reverend Izaiah Sutcliffe.
    18. WILLIAM CLOPTON, b. 1655, d. in Virginia, 1733; m. Ann Booth, b. 1647,
d. 1716, dau. of Robert Booth, d. 1657, clerk of York co., Virginia. (Generations
13-18, see Erwin, Ancestry of William Clopton of York Co., Va., (Rutland, Vt.,
1939) and TAG 46: 117-8 & 47:87).

                                Line 6

    1. ROGER BIGOD, M.C. (3-1); m. Ida.
    2. HUGH BIGOD, M.C. (3-2); m. MAUD MARSHAL (148-2, 155-3).
    3. SIR SIMON le BIGOD, 3rd son, d. bef. 1242; m. Maud de Felbrigg, living
1275, dau. of Richard de Felbrigg of Felbrigg, co. Norfolk.
    4. SIR ROGER le BIGOD, liv. 1275, 1295; m. Cecilia, liv. 1295.
    5. SIR SIMON le BIGOD, KNT., alias Felbrigg of Felbrigg, liv. 1310, lord of
the manor of Felbrigg, 1316-1349; m. Alice, dau. of Sir George de Thorpe, Knt.,
lord of the manor of Breisworth, co. Suffolk.
    6. SIR ROGER le BIGOD, alias Felbrigg of Felbrigg, lord of the manor of Fel-
brigg, 1352-1368; m. Elizabeth de Scales, dau. of Robert de Scales and Catherine de Ufford.
    7. SIR SIMON de FELBRIGG, K.G., alias Bigod, lord of the manors of Fel-
brigg and Beeston Regis, co. Norfolk, and of Breisworth, co. Suffolk; m. (1) Margaret, niece of the Emperor Charles IV of Germany, and granddau. of John of Bohemia, Duke of Luxembourg and King of Bohemia, 1310-1346. (Note hypothesis of
Charles F.H. Evans "Margaret, Lady Felbrygge," Blackmansbury II (1965) 2-7).
    8. HELENA de FELBRIGG (heir of her brother Thomas to the manor of Breis-
worth in Suffolk); m. Sir William Tyndal of Dene, d. 1426.
    9. SIR THOMAS TYNDAL, of Dene, and Redenhall, co. Norfolk, lord of the
manor of Breisworth, d. 1448; m. Margaret, dau. of Sir William Yelverton.

10. SIR WILLIAM TYNDAL, K.B. , of Dene and Hockwold, co. Norfolk, d. c.
1488; inherited Worlington Manor, 1484, as an heir of Thomas, Lord Scales; declared
heir by inheritance through his great-grandmother Margaret to the Kingdom of Bohemia; m. Mary, dau. of Sir Osbert Mondeford of Feltwell, co. Norfolk.
    11. SIR JOHN TYNDAL, K.B. , of Hockwold, sold his Suffolk manor, 1524; m.
Amphillis, dau. of Sir Humphrey Coningsby.
    12. SIR THOMAS TYNDAL, of Hockwold and Great Maplestead, co. Suffolk,
High Sheriff of Norfolk and Suffolk, 1561; m. (2) c. 1533, Anne, dau. of Sir Henry
Fermor of East Bersham, co. Norfolk.
    13. SIR JOHN TYNDAL, KNT. , of Great Maplestead, murdered 12 Nov. 1616;
m. Anna (Egerton) Dean, d. July 1620, dau. of Thomas Egerton, Esq. , of Walle-
grange, co. Suffolk, and London.
    14. MARGARET TYNDAL, b. c. 1591, d. Boston, Massachusetts, 14 June 1647;
m. 28 Apr. 1618, as his 3rd wife, John Winthrop, Esq. , of Groton, co. Suffolk, England, b. Groton, 12 Jan. 1587, d. Boston, Massachusetts, 26 Mar. 1649, Governor
of Massachusetts, 1630-1634, 1637-1640, 1642-1644, 1646-1649.
    15. COLONEL STEPHEN WINTHROP (1619-1658); m. Judith Rainsborough.
    15. ADAM WINTHROP (1620-1652); m. Elizabeth Glover.
    15. DEANE WINTHROP (1623-1704); m. Sarah Glover.
    15. CAPTAIN SAMUEL WINTHROP (1627-1674); H.C. , 1646; m. June 1648,
Elizabeth; Deputy-Governor of Antigua, West Indies, 1667, 1669.

Line 7

    1. ROGER BIGOD, M. C. (3-1); m. Ida.
    2. MARGARET BIGOD; m. William de Hastings.
    3. SIR HENRY de HASTINGS, d. sh. bef. 9 Aug. 1250; m. bef. 7 June 1237,
Ada de Huntingdon, liv. 2 Nov. 1241, dau. of David, Earl of Huntingdon and Maud of
Chester. (CP VI, 345).
    4. HILLARIA de HASTINGS; m. as his 2nd wife, SIR WILLIAM de HARCOURT
(111-3), of Stanton-Harcourt, co. Oxford, and Naylston, co. Leicester, d. 1258.
    5. RICHARD de HARCOURT, of Stanton-Harcourt, d. 1293; m. Margaret
Beke, dau. of John Beke, d. c. 1303/4, Lord of Eresby, co. Lincoln, son of Walter
Beke, Lord of Eresby, and Eve, niece of Walter de Grey, Archbishop of York.
    6. SIR JOHN de HARCOURT, KNT. , of Stanton-Harcourt, co. Oxford, and
Bosworth, co. Leicester, d. 1330; m. ELLEN la ZOUCHE (146-5).

Line 8

    3. ISABEL BIGOD (4-3); m. (2) Sir John Fitz Geoffrey.
    4. ISABEL FITZ JOHN; m. Robert de Vipont, d. 7 June 1264, Lord of West-
moreland.
    5. ISABEL de VIPONT, d. 14 May 1292, Lady of Appleby and Broughham; m.
Roger de Clifford, drowned, 6 Nov. 1282.
    6. ROBERT de CLIFFORD, b. Easter, 1274, slain at Bannockburn, 25 June
1314, 1st Lord Clifford, Lord of Appleby, co. Westmoreland, Sheriff of Westmoreland, 1291; m. 13 Nov. 1295, MAUD de CLARE (144-5), d. 1 Feb. 1324/5, q.v. (CP
III, 290).
    7. IDOINE de CLIFFORD, d. 24 Aug. 1365; m. HENRY de PERCY, K.G.
(152-5), 2nd Lord Percy, d. Warkworth, end of Feb. 1351/2. (Clay, 161; CP X, 459).
    8. MAUD PERCY, d. bef. 18 Feb. 1378/9; m. as his 1st wife, JOHN de NE-
VILLE, K.G. (45-6), d. Newcastle, 17 Oct. 1388, Baron Neville of Raby. (CP IX,
502).
    9. SIR RALPH de NEVILLE, K.G. (45-7), b. c. 1346, d. Raby, 21 Oct. 1425,
cr. Earl of Westmoreland, 1395; m. (1) MARGARET STAFFORD (136-8), d. 9 June
1396; m. (2) Joan Beaufort. (Clay, 146; CP XII (2), 544).
    10. ALICE NEVILLE (by the 1st wife); m. (1) SIR THOMAS GREY (65-8) of
Heton and Warke, beheaded 5 Aug. 1415; m. (2) Sir Gilbert de Lancaster. (Clay, 88).

6 [Line 8A]

*   *   *   *   *   *

Note: MAUD GREY (Gen. 11) was sister, not dau., of SIR THOMAS GREY (65-8).
Line breaks at this point.

*   *   *   *   *   *

11. MAUD GREY (65-9),(dau. of THOMAS (65-8)), liv. 1451; m. c. 21 May 1399, Sir
Robert Ogle, Knt., b. 1369/73, d. 12 Aug. 1436, Warden of Roxborough Castle.
(Clay, 88).
12. ANNE OGLE; m. (1) 13 Jan. 1411/2, Sir William Heron, Knt., of Ford, b.
1400, d. 1425; m. (2) Sir John Middleton.
13. ELIZABETH HERON, b. 1422; m. 11 July 1438, Sir John Heron, Knt., her
cousin, slain at Towton Field, 29 Mar. 1461.
14. ELIZABETH HERON; m. SIR ROBERT TAILBOYS, KNT. (108-11), Lord
Kyme, M.P. 1472-1478, d. 1494/5. (CP VII, 361).
15. MAUD TAILBOYS, m. Sir Robert Tyrwhit, Knt., of Kettleby, b. 1482, d.
4 July 1548, High Sheriff of Lincolnshire.
16. KATHARINE TYRWHIT; m. Sir Richard Thimbleby of Irnham, lord of the
manor of East Bridgeford, co. Nottingham, d. 28 Sept. 1590.
17. ELIZABETH THIMBLEBY, m. (1) John St. Paul of Nettleby; m. (2) 20
July 1560, Thomas Welby of Moulton, d. Bath, 1570.
18. RICHARD WELBY, of Moulton, 2nd son, bp. 1564; m. 4 June 1595, FRAN-
CES BULKELEY (98-16), q.v.
19. OLIVE WELBY, b. c. 1604, d. c. 1691; m. c. 1629, Deacon Henry Farwell, d. c. 1670; they came to Concord, Massachusetts, from England, about 1635.

Line 8A

9. SIR RALPH de NEVILLE, K.G. (8-9); m. (1) MARGARET STAFFORD (136-8).
10. PHILIPPA NEVILLE, 3rd dau., seen 8 July 1453; m. bef. 20 July 1399,
Thomas de Dacre, Lord Dacre of Gillesland, b. 27 Oct. 1387, d. 5 Jan. 1457/8. (CP
IV, 7).
11. SIR THOMAS de DACRE, d.v.p.;m. c. 1430 ELIZABETH BOWET (49A-
9). (CP IV, 8).
12. JOAN de DACRE, Baroness Dacre, b. c. 1433, d. 8 Mar. 1485/6; m. June
1446, SIR RICHARD FIENNES (16C-9), Sheriff of Sussex and Surrey, 1452, Constable
of the Tower of London, 1473, 1st Lord Dacre of the South, d. 25 Nov. 1483. (CP
IV, 9).
13. SIR THOMAS FIENNES of Claverham Manor, Arlington, Sussex, 2nd son,
will dated 26 Jan. 1525/6, d. 8 Feb. 1525/6; m. Anne, dau. of Sir Thomas Urswick
or Urdiswick, baron of the Exchequer. (Sussex Archaeological Collections 58,
chart facing p. 64).
14. MARGARET FIENNES, seen 26 Sept. 1531; m. as his 2nd wife, WILLIAM
LUNSFORD (88A-14), of Lunsford and Wilegh, Sussex, will dated 10 Dec. 1530,
proved 3 May 1531, d. 3 May 1531, bur. at East Hoathley, Sussex, son of William
Lunsford of Lunsford and Wilegh, by Cicely, dau. of Sir John Pelham, Chamberlain
to Queen Catherine, consort of Henry V. (cf. John Comber, Sussex Genealogies
(Cambridge, 1933), III: 204-5; Col. Topo. et Gen. IV, 139-142).

Line 9

5. ISABEL de BEAUCHAMP (4-5), d. 1305; m. (2) 1286, Sir Hugh le Despenser.
6. SIR PHILIP le DESPENSER, d. 24 Sept. 1313; m. Margaret, b. 12 May
1294, d. 29 July 1349, dau. of Ralph de Gousille, lord of Camoys Manor, Essex.
(CP IV, 289).
7. SIR PHILIP le DESPENSER, b. co. Lincoln, 6 Apr. 1313, d. 22 or 23 Aug.
1349; m. Joan, d. c. 15 May 1357 (prob. dau. of John de Cobham, Lord Cobham).
(CP IV, 289, note b).
8. SIR PHILIP le DESPENSER, b. Gedney, 18 Oct. 1342, d. Goxhill, 4 Aug.

1401; m. Elizabeth, d. bef. 1401. (CP IV, 289).
   9. SIR PHILIP le DESPENSER, KNT., b. 1366, ae. 36+ at father's death, d.
20 June 1424; m. ELIZABETH TIBETOT (74-9). (CP IV, 290).

Line 10

   5. ISABEL de BEAUCHAMP (4-5), d. 1306; m. Sir Hugh le Despenser.
   6. MARGARET DESPENSER; m. 1310, John de St.Amand, b. 1278, d. c. 25
Jan. 1329/30, M.P.
   7. ISABELLA de ST. AMAND, d. Oct. 1361; m. (1) bef. 16 Dec. 1330, Richard
de Haudlo, d. 1343.
   8. ELIZABETH de HAUDLO, b. Wotton, Bucks, feast of St. Boniface, 13 Ed.
III, d. by 23 Feb. 1373; m. as 1st wife, Sir Edmund de la Pole, Knt., of age 25 Oct.
1358, d. 3 Aug. 1419. (Swyncombe and Ewelme (1858), 289-295).
   9. KATHERINE de la POLE; m. Robert James, d. 16 Feb. 1431/2.
   10. CHRISTINA JAMES, d. 26 Mar. 1435; m. Edmund Rede, of Hedington, co.
Oxford, d. 8 Oct. 1430.
   11. SIR EDMUND REDE, KNT., d. 7 June 1487; m. Katherine Grene, dau. of
Walter Grene, M.P., of Hayes, co. Middlesex.
   12. ELIZABETH REDE; m. Richard Hall, d. 11 Nov. 1508, of Swerford.
   13. EDMUND HALL, of Swerford; m. Elizabeth, living 1508.
   14. ALICE HALL, m. Lawrence Woodhull, of Thenford, co. Northampton,
will 20 Mar. 1529, pr. 10 Sept. 1551, son of FULK WOODHULL (111-12). (Adams,
Elkington Family, p. 18).

          *   *   *   *   *   *

   15. FULKE WOODHULL, d. 1575, of Oxford; m. Alice, dau. of Henry Wick-
liffe of Addington, co. Northampton. [Evidence of his parentage inadequate. Requires further research.]
   16. THOMAS WOODHULL, d. 1594, of Oxford; m. Margaret.
   17. ALICE WOODHULL, b. 1570, bur. Mollington, co. Oxford, 6 Nov. 1639;
m. Mollington, 16 May 1588, as his 2nd wife, William Elkington, b. Cropredy, co.
Oxford, bp. 22 July 1547, bur. Mollington, 15 July 1609, son of Richard Elkington
of Cropredy. [Evidence of generations 15-17, inadequate.]

          *   *   *   *   *   *

   18. JOSEPH ELKINGTON, bp. Mollington, 12 June 1608, bur. Mollington, 4
Feb. 1688; m. Ann, bur. Mollington, 23 Mar. 1674/5.
   19. GEORGE ELKINGTON, bp. Mollington, 7 Dec. 1650, d. 1713, came to New
Jersey, 1677; m. Burlington, New Jersey, 1688, Mary (Humphries) Core, b. 1641,
dau. of Walter Humphries. She was b. in Painswick, co. Gloucester, England. (A.
Adams, Elkington Family, 1945).

Line 11

   7. IDOINE de CLIFFORD (8-7), d. 1365; m. HENRY de PERCY (152-5).
   8. ISABEL de PERCY, d. by 25 May 1368; m. by Jan. 1326/7, Sir William de
Aton, Knt., Lord Aton, M.P., 1317-1320, b. c. 1299, d. by Mar. 1388/9. (CP I,
325).
   9. CATHARINE de ATON; m. SIR RALPH de EURE, KNT. (112-8).

Line 12

   3. ISABEL BIGOD (4-3); m. (1) Gilbert de Lacy of Trim.
   4. MAUD de LACY, d. 11 Apr. 1304; m. (1) Piers de Genevre, d. 1249 bef. 29
June; m. (2) Sir Geoffrey de Geneville, Lord Geneville, b. in or aft. 1226, d. Trim,
21 Oct. 1314, son of Simon de Joinville, Seneschal of Champagne; Seigneur de Vaucouleurs in France. (CP V, 632).
   5. SIR PIERS de GENEVILLE, d. sh. bef. 8 June 1292, of Trim and Ludlow
Castle; m. Jeanne de Lusignan, d. sh. bef. 18 Apr. 1323, wid. Bernard Ezy, sire

d'Albert (d. sh. bef. 24 May 1281), dau. of Hugh XII de Lusignan and Joanne de Fou-
geres. (CP V, 632).
    6. JOAN de GENEVILLE, b. 2 Feb. 1285/6, d. 19 Oct. 1356; m. bef. 6 Oct.
1306, SIR ROGER de MORTIMER (147-5), b. 25 Apr. or 3 May 1287, d. 29 Nov.
1330, Earl of March. (CP V, 634; VIII, 433).
    7. JOAN MORTIMER, d. betw. 1337 & 1351; m. 1330 bef. 13 June, SIR JAMES
AUDLEY, K.G. (143-6), 2nd Lord Audley. (CP I, 339).
    8. JOAN AUDLEY, m. Sir John Tuchet, of Markeaton, co. Derby, b. 25 July
1327, d. sh. bef. 10 Jan. 1361/2, son of Thomas Tuchet and Joan. (CP XII (2), 59).
    9. JOHN TUCHET, slain off La Rochelle, 23 June 1372; m. Maud, d. bef. 3
Nov. 1405. (CP XII (2), 59).
    10. SIR JOHN TUCHET, b. 23 Apr. 1371, d. 19 Dec. 1408, 2nd Lord Tuchet,
M.P., 1406-1408; m. Isabel, living 3 May 1409. (CP XII (2), 60).
    11. JAMES TUCHET, 4th Lord Audley, b. c. 1398, d. 23 Sept. 1459, M.P., 1421-
1455; m. (1) c. 1415, MARGARET de ROS (1-8), liv. 1423, q.v. (CP XI, 103; I, 340).

Line 13

    3. ISABEL BIGOD (4-3); m. (1) Gilbert de Lacy, of Ewyas Lacy.
    4. MARGARET de LACY, liv. 10 June 1276, Lady of Dulek; m. as 1st wife,
14 May 1244, John de Verdun, b. c. 1226, d. 21 Oct. 1274, son of Theobald le Bote-
ler and Rohese de Verdun. (CP XII (2), 246).
    5. THEOBALD de VERDON, b. c. 1248, d. Alton, co. Stafford, 24 Aug. 1309,
Lord Verdun; m. bef. 6 Nov. 1276, Margery. (CP XII (2), 249).
    6. SIR THEOBALD de VERDON, KNT., b. 8 Sept. 1278, d. Alton, 27 July
1316, 2nd Lord Verdun, M.P., 1299-1314; m. (1) Wigmore, 29 July 1302, Maud de
Mortimer, d. 17 or 18 Sept. 1312, dau. of SIR EDMUND de MORTIMER (147-4) and
Margaret de Fiennes; m. (2) nr. Boston, 4 Feb. 1315/6, Elizabeth de Clare, b.
Tewkesbury, 16 Sept. 1295, d. 4 Nov. 1360, dau. of SIR GILBERT de CLARE (28-4)
and Joan Plantagenet, dau. of EDWARD I (161-14), King of England, and Eleanor of
Castile.
    7. ELIZABETH de VERDON (by the 1st wife), b. c. 1306, d. 1 May 1360; m.
bef. 11 June 1320, Sir Bartholomew de Burghersh, d. 3 Aug. 1355, Lord Burghersh,
son of Robert, Lord Burghersh, and Maud de Badlesmere. (CP II, 426).
    8. BARTHOLOMEW de BURGHERSH, K.G., ae. 26+ at father's death, d. 5
Apr. 1369, Lord Burghersh, fought at Crecy, an original Knight of the Garter; m.
(1) bef. 24 Aug. 1354, Ciceley, liv. Aug. 1354, dau. of Richard de Weyland; m. (2)
bef. Aug. 1366, Margaret (wid. of John de Loveyne), d. 1 July 1393. (CP II, 427).
    9. ELIZABETH de BURGHERSH, ae. 27+ at father's death, b. c. 1342, d. 26
July 1409; m. bef. Dec. 1364, SIR EDWARD DESPENSER, K.G. (14-8), b. c. 24 Mar.
1335/6, d. 11 Nov. 1375, Lord of Glamorgan. (CP II, 427).
    10. MARGARET DESPENSER; m. SIR ROBERT de FERRERS (115-8), q.v.

Line 14

    5. ISABEL BEAUCHAMP (4-5), d. 1306; m. (2) Sir Hugh le Despenser.
    6. SIR HUGH le DESPENSER, hanged and quartered, 24 Nov. 1326, Lord
Despenser; m. 1306 aft. 14 June, ALIANORE de CLARE (34-5). (CP IV, 267).
    7. SIR EDWARD DESPENSER, d. 30 Sept. 1342; m. Groby, 20 Apr. 1335,
Anne de Ferrers, d. 8 Aug. 1337, dau. of WILLIAM FERRERS (100-5). (CP IV,
275).
    8. SIR EDWARD DESPENSER, K.G., b. Essendine, 24 Mar. 1335/6, d. Llan-
bethian, 11 Nov. 1375; m. bef. 24 Aug. 1354, ELIZABETH de BURGHERSH (13-9),
d. 26 July 1409. (CP IV, 274).
    9. ELIZABETH DESPENSER, d. 10 or 11 Apr. 1408; m. (1) SIR JOHN d'ARUN-
DEL (121-8), Lord Arundel.

Line 15

3. ISABEL BIGOD (4-3); m. (2) Sir John Fitz Geoffrey, Justiciar.
4. AVELINA FITZ JOHN, d. c. 20 May 1274; m. c. 1257, Walter de Burgh,
b. c. 1230, d. 28 July 1271, Earl of Ulster, son of Richard de Burgh, Justice, and
Egidith de Lacy. (CP XII (2), 171).
5. RICHARD de BURGH, b. c. 1259, d. Athassel, 29 July 1326, 2nd Earl of
Ulster; m. bef. 27 Feb. 1280/1, Margery, d. 1304. (CP XII (2), 173).
6. ELEANOR de BURGH; m. 3 Jan. 1297, Thomas de Multon, b. 21 Feb. 1276,
d. bef. 8 Feb. 1321/2, Lord Multon. (CP IX, 403).
8. ELIZABETH de MULTON, dau. Gen. 6, ae. 28 on 23 Nov. 1334; m. (1)
c. 1327, Sir Robert de Harington, Knt., d. Ireland, 1334, of Aldingham, son of Sir
John de Harington. (CP VI, 316).
9. SIR JOHN HARINGTON, Lord Harington, ae. 19+ on 2 July 1347, d. Glea-
ston Hall, 28 May 1363, M.P., 1347-1349. (CP VI, 316).
10. SIR ROBERT HARINGTON, K.B., Lord Harington, bp. Aldingham, 28 Mar.
1356, d. Aldingham, 21 May 1406; m. (1) c. 1376, Alice Greystoke, d. shortly; m.
(2) c. 1383, Isabel, d. 21 Aug. 1400, widow of Sir William Cogan of Huntsfield, d.
1382, dau. of Sir Nele Loring, K.G. (CP VI, 316).
11. ISABEL HARINGTON, of Hornby, co. Lancaster; said to have m. SIR JOHN
STANLEY (103-9), d. 1437.

Line 15A

4. AVELINA FITZ JOHN (15-4); m. Walter de Burgh, Earl of Ulster.
5. EGIDIA (or Jill) de BURGH; m. James Stewart, 5th High Steward of Scotland, b. c. 1243, d. 1309. (SP I:13-14).
6. WALTER STEWART, 6th High Steward of Scotland, b. 1292, d. 9 Apr.
1326; m. (1) Marjory Bruce, by whom Robert I, King of Scots; m. (2) Isabel Graham, sister of Sir John Graham of Abercorn. (SP I: 14-15).
7. EGIDIA (or Jill) STEWART, by 2nd wife, widow of Sir James Lindsay of
Crawford; m. (2), after Oct. 1357, Sir Hugh Eglinton of that Ilk. (SP I: 15).
8. ELIZABETH EGLINTON; m. Sir John Montgomery, d. bef. July 1401, captured Sir Henry "Hotspur" Percy at the battle of Otterburn, 1388. (SP III: 427-8).
9. SIR JOHN MONTGOMERY of Eglinton and Ardrossan, d. bef. 22 Nov.
1429; m. (1) Agnes of the Isles, d. bef. Mar. 1413/4. (SP III: 428-30).
10. ALEXANDER MONTGOMERY, b. bef. 1413, d. c. 1470, member of the
King's Council, cr. shortly bef. 3 July 1445, Lord Montgomery; m. Margaret, seen
16 Sept. 1453, dau. of Sir Thomas Boyd of Kilmarnock. (SP III: 431-2; CP IX, 134).
11. MARGARET MONTGOMERY, see 20 July 1461; m. contract 15 May 1438,
"neither being then of lawful age," Sir John Stewart, Lord Darnley, Earl of Lennox,
d. betw. 8 July and 11 Sept. 1495. (SP III: 433; SP V: 348-9; CP VII, 594).
12. ELIZABETH STEWART; m. ARCHIBALD CAMPBELL (41D-12), 2nd Earl
of Argyll, slain at Flodden, 1513. (SP V: 350).

Line 16

5. GUY de BEAUCHAMP (5-5), Earl of Warwick; m. Alice de Toeni.
6. MAUD de BEAUCHAMP, d. 25 July 1369; m. (1) GEOFFREY de SAY (16A-
5), d. 26 June 1356, 2nd Baron Say, Admiral of the Fleet.
7. IDONEA de SAY, d. c. 1384; m. prob. 1350, as 1st wife, Sir John Clinton,
b. not later than Mar. 1325/6, d. 6 Sept. 1398, 3rd Lord Clinton of Maxstoke, co.
Warwick, son of John Clinton, 2nd Lord Clinton, and Margery Corbet. (CP III, 314).
8. MARGARET de CLINTON; m. Sir Baldwin de Montfort, of Coleshill Manor
co. Warwick.
9. SIR WILLIAM de MONTFORT, of Coleshill Manor; m. Margaret.
10. ROBERT MONTFORT, ESQ., of Bescote, co. Stafford, and Monkspath,
co. Warwick.
11. KATHERINE MONTFORT; m. SIR GEORGE BOOTH (97-12), d. 1483, of
Dunham Massie, co. Chester.

10   [Line 16A

Line 16A

1. GEOFFREY de SAY II, b. prob. c. 1155, Magna Charta Surety, in Poitou
shortly bef. 26 Aug. 1230; m. (1) Alice, wid. Hugh de Periers, and h. (pos. dau.)
of John de Chesney; m. (2) aft. 1225, Margery, wid. 1st of a de la Ferte, 2nd of
Eudes de Dammartin, d. 1225, sis. & coh. of William de Briwerre.
2. WILLIAM de SAY III (by 1st wife), of age 1230, d. by 12 Feb. 1271/2;
m. (1) Sibyl, liv. Oct. 1250, said (without evidence) to be dau. of John Marshal
of Lenton; m. (2) Mary who survived him and m. (2) Robert de Ufford.
3. WILLIAM de SAY IV, prob. by 2nd wife (stated without evidence), b. 20
Nov. 1253, d. on or bef. 16 Sept. 1295; m. Elizabeth, who survived him.
4. GEOFFREY de SAY III, aged 14 in 1295, proved age on or shortly bef. 15
Feb. 1302/3, 1st Lord Say, d. by 3 Mar. 1321/2. Had three daus.: Katharine, m.
John, 3rd Lord St. John of Lageham; Juliane, m. Sir Roger de Northwode; Isabel,
m. John de Chaumpaigne; and h. Geoffrey, all by wife Idonea, liv. 1321/2, dau. of
William de Leyburn, Lord Leyburn, by Juliane, dau. & h. of Sir Henry de Sandwich.
(This Idonea was NOT a dau. & coh. of Roger de Vipont.)
5. GEOFFREY de SAY IV, aged 17 on Whitsun aft. 3 May 1321/2, proved age
on or shortly bef. 4 June 1326, d. 26 June 1359, 2nd Lord Say; m. MAUD de BEAU-
CHAMP (16-6), d. 28 July 1369. (Gens. 1-5, CP XI, 468-70; Gen. 4, add VII, 637,
note f).

Line 16B

4. GEOFFREY de SAY III (16A-4), 1st Lord Say; m. Idonia de Leyburn. (CP
VII, 637, note f; CP XI, 474-5).
5. JULIANA de SAY, d. 20 Feb. 1329; m. as 1st wife, Roger de Northwode,
2nd Lord Northwode, b. 1307/8, ae. 12 Easter 1319, d. 5 Nov. 1361. (CP IX, 756-
7; CP XI, 475, note g).
6. JOHN de NORTHWODE, 3rd Lord Northwode, d. 27 Feb. 1378/9; m. 1350,
Joan, dau. of Robert Hert of Faversham. She was living Sept. 1398. (CP IX, 757).
7. JULIANA de NORTHWODE, b. c. 1362; m. 1381, John Digge of Digge's
Court, Barnham, Kent. (Archaeologia Cantiana, II, 25; Visitation of Kent 1619-
1621 (Harleian Society Publications, vol. XLII) p. 65).
8. ELIZABETH DIGGE; m. Henry Aucher, gent., of Newenden Manor in the
parish of Losenham, Kent.
9. HENRY AUCHER, gent., of Newenden and Otterden, Kent; m. (2) Joan
(or Mary), dau. and heiress of Thomas St. Leger of Otterden.
10. HENRY AUCHER, gent., of Otterden, Kent, seen 19 Henry VI (1440); m.
Isabella (or Alicia) Boleyn.
11. JOHN AUCHER, gent., of Otterden, Kent, d. betw. 18 July and 26 Oct.
1502; m. Margaret Church.
12. JAMES AUCHER, gent., of Otterden, Kent, d. 6 Jan. 1508/9; m. Alice,
dau. of Thomas Hill of Eggarton, Kent.
13. SIR ANTHONY AUCHER of Otterden and Bishopsbourne, Kent, b. c. 1500,
slain at the siege of Calais, 9 Jan. 1558, knighted Feb. 1546/7, governor of Guisnes,
marshal of Calais; m. AFFRA CORNWALLIS (113A-13). (Gens. 8-13: Visitation of
Kent, 1574 (Harleian Society Publications, vol. LXXIV), pp. 24-5; Visitation of
Kent, 1619-1621 (Harleian Society Publications, vol. LXII), pp. 65,180; Virginia
Magazine of History and Biography, XXVIII, 287-95; Burke, Extinct and Dormant
Baronetcies, pp. 27-8).

Line 16C

5. SIR GEOFFREY de SAY IV (16A-5), 2nd Lord Say; m. MAUD de BEAU-
CHAMP (16-6).
6. JOAN de SAY, d. 29 June 1378; m. (1) William Fiennes, b. c. 1330, d. 31
Nov. 1359, son of Sir John de Fiennes, M.P., 1343, d. 5 Apr. 1351, by Maud, dau.
of John de Mounceaux.
7. SIR WILLIAM FIENNES, b. 1 Aug. 1357, d. 18 Jan. 1402/3, Sheriff of

Sussex and Surrey, 1396, 1398; m. Elizabeth, d. bef. 1407, dau. of William Batis-
ford.
    8. SIR ROGER FIENNES, bp. 14 Sept. 1384, d. c. 1451, Sheriff of Sussex
and Surrey, 1422, 1434, Treasurer of the Household to Henry VI; m. Elizabeth Hol-
and, sister of Sir John Holand of Northants.
    9. SIR RICHARD FIENNES, 1st Lord Dacre of the South, Sheriff of Sussex
and Surrey, 1452, Constable of the Tower of London, 1473, d. 25 Nov. 1483; m.
June 1446, JOAN DACRE, Lady Dacre (8A-12) of Gillisland. (Gen. 5: CP XI, 475-
7; Gen. 6-9: Sussex Archaeological Collections, LVIII, chart facing p. 64).

Line 17

    6. JOAN de GENEVILLE (12-6); m. SIR ROGER de MORTIMER (147-5).
    7. KATHARINE de MORTIMER; m. THOMAS BEAUCHAMP, K.G. (5-6),
Earl of Warwick.
    8. WILLIAM BEAUCHAMP, d. 8 May 1411, Lord Abergavenny; m. Joan Fitz
Alan, b. 1375, d. 14 Nov. 1435, dau. of SIR RICHARD FITZ ALAN, K.G. (121-6)
and ELIZABETH de BOHUN (19-7). (CP I, 24).
    9. JOAN BEAUCHAMP, d. 3 or 5 Aug. 1430; m. on or bef. 28 Aug 1413,
JAMES BUTLER (24-9), b. 1392, d. 1452, Earl of Ormond.
    10. THOMAS BUTLER, K.B., 7th Earl of Ormond, d. 3 Aug. 1515; m. (1) bef.
11 July 1445, ANNE HANKEFORD (17B-20), b. 1431, d. 13 Nov. 1485; m. (2) bef. Nov.
1496, Lora Berkeley, d. bef. 30 Dec. 1501, dau. of Sir Edward Berkeley of Bever-
ton, co. Gloucester, by Christian Holt, dau. of Richard Holt of Coldrey, Hampshire.
(CP X, 131-3).
    11. MARGARET BUTLER, dau. and coh. by 1st wife, b. c. 1465, d. betw. 30
Sept. 1539 and 20 Mar. 1539/40; m. bef. 1485, SIR WILLIAM BOLEYN, K.B. (137A-
10), d. 1505, of Blicking, Norf. (CP X, 137, note b; XII (2), 739; DNB II, 783).
    12. SIR THOMAS BOLEYN, K.G., Earl of Wiltshire, b. c. 1477, d. Hever,
Kent, 12 or 13 Mar. 1538/9; m. c. 1500, ELIZABETH HOWARD (64-11), q. v., d. 3
Apr. 1538, dau. of THOMAS HOWARD (64-10), Duke of Norfolk. (CP X, 137-9; DNB, ibid.).

Line 17A

    11. MARGARET BUTLER (17-11); m. SIR WILLIAM BOLEYN, K.B. (137A-10)
    12. MARGARET BOLEYN, aunt of Queen Anne Boleyn; m. John Sackville,
Esq., of Withyham and Chiddingley, Sussex, 40+ in 1524; M.P., 1528, 1541, 1547;
Sheriff of Sussex and Surrey, 1557; will dated 1 July 1556, bur. at Withyham, 5
Oct. 1557   (Collectanea Topographica et Genealogica, IV, 139-42; Archaeologica
Cantiana, XXXVIII, 6-7; Collins, The Peerage of England (Brydges ed.), II, 274.
DNB, XVII, 584, repeating an error in Collins, II, 276, calls Margaret "Anne.")
    13. MARY SACKVILLE, bur. at East Hoathley, Sussex, 30 June 1571; m.
JOHN LUNSFORD (88A-15) of Lunsford and Wilegh, Sussex. (Collectanea Topo-
graphica et Genealogica, ibid.; Collins, II, 276).

Line 17B

    15. JOAN OF ACRE, b. 1272, d. 23 Apr. 1307, dau. of EDWARD I, King of
England (161-14) by Eleanor of Castile; widow of GILBERT de CLARE, Earl of Gloucester and Hertford (28-4); m. (2) 1297, Sir Ralph de Monthermer, styled Earl of
Gloucester and Hertford during the life of his wife, cr. Lord Monthermer 1308, d.
5 Apr. 1325. (CP V, 708-712; CP IX, 140-142).
    16. SIR THOMAS de MONTHERMER, Lord Monthermer, b. 4 Oct. 1301,
knighted 1327, slain at the battle of Sluys, 24 June 1340; m. Margaret, d. May 1349,
probably the widow of Henry Tyeys, Lord Tyeys. (CP IX, 143).
    17. MARGARET de MONTHERMER, Lady Monthermer, b. Stokenham, 14
Oct. 1329, d. 24 Mar. 1394/5; m. bef. the end of 1343, Sir John de Montagu, cr.
Lord Montagu, 1357, Steward of the Household to King Richard II, 1381-1386/7, d.
25 Feb. or 4 Mar. 1389/90; yr. son of William de Montagu, Earl of Salisbury, by

12

[Line 17C

Catherine, dau. of William, Lord Grandison. (CP IX, 86-88, 143-144).

18. SIR JOHN de MONTAGU, K.G., Earl Marshal of England, b. 1350, knighted 1369, suc. his uncle as Earl of Salisbury, 1397, beheaded 5 Jan. 1399/1400; m. bef. 4 May 1383, Maud, d. 1424 bef. 5 Aug., dau. of Sir Adam Francis, M.P., lord mayor of London. (CP IX, 82, 89, 144; CP XI, 391-393).

19. ANNE de MONTAGU, d. 28 Nov. 1457; m. (l), as his second wife, Sir Richard Hankeford of Hewish, Devon; Kelynack, Cornwall; Eastbury, Bucks., b. c. 21 July 1397, knighted 1429, d. 8 Feb. 1430/1; m. (3), as his third wife, John Holand, Duke of Exeter. (CP V, 210-211, 505-507; CP IX, 393, note d).

20. ANNE HANKEFORD, b. 1430/1, d. 13 Nov. 1485; m. as his first wife, bef. 11 July 1445, SIR THOMAS BUTLER, K.B., Earl of Ormond (17-10). (CP X, 132).

Line 17C

Line developed by Wm. Addams Reitwiesner and published for the first time with his permission.

1. ROGER BIGOD, 2nd Earl of Norfolk, Magna Charta Surety, d. 1221 bef. 2 Aug.; m. Ida. (NCP IX, 586).

2. HUGH BIGOD, 3rd Earl of Norfolk, Magna Charta Surety, d. bef. 18 Feb. 1224/5; m. probably bef. Lent 1207, Maud Marshall, d. 27 Mar. 1248, dau. and (eventual) coheiress of WILLIAM MARSHALL (145-1), Earl of Pembroke, by his wife Isabel de Clare, Countess of Pembroke. (CP IX, 589).

3. ISABELLA BIGOD; m. (l) Gilbert de Lacy, d.v.p. bet. 12 Aug. and 25 Dec. 1230, son and heir (apparent) of Walter de Lacy, Lord of Meath, etc., by his wife Margaret de Braose; m. (2) Sir John Fitz Geoffrey, Justiciar of Ireland, d. 23 Nov. 1258, son of Geoffrey Fitz Piers, Earl of Essex, by his wife Aveline de Clare. (CP V, 433-437.)

4. MATILDA de LACY (by first husband), coheir of her grandfather, Walter de Lacy, d. 11 Apr. 1304; m. (l) bef. 15 May 1244, Pierre de Geneva, d.s.p. 1249 bef. 29 June, son of Humbert, Comte de Geneva, and Agnes di Savoie; m. (2) bef. 8 Aug. 1252, Geoffrey de Joinville, 1st Lord Genevil, Sire de Vaucouleurs, Lord of Ludlow, (Salop), and of Trim (in Ireland), b. c. 1226, d. at Trim, 21 Oct. 1314, son of Simon, Sire de Joinville, and Beatrix de Bourgogne. (The Genealogist, New Series, XXI, 1-16; CP V, 62).

5. JEANNE de JOINVILLE (by 2nd husband); m. (l) Gerald Fitz Maurice Fitz Gerald, under age in 1285, d. by 6 May 1292; m. (2) by 1294, Johann I, Graf [Count] von Ober-Salm, fl. 1275-1338, son of Heinrich IV, Graf von Ober-Salm, and Lauretta Graefin [Countess] von Bliescastel. (ES III, 134).

6. LORETTA, GRAEFIN von OBER-SALM (by 2nd husband), d. 1345; m. 1314, Heinrich II, Graf von Spanheim, d. 1322 c. 13 July, son of Johann II, Graf von Spanheim, and Catherina von Ochsenstein. (ES IV, 2).

7. JOHAN III, GRAF von SPANHEIM, d. 20 Dec. 1398; m. 30 Sept. 1331, Mechtild, Pfaltzgraefin [Countess-Palatine] bei Rhein, d. 25 Nov. 1375, dau. of Rudolf I, Pfaltzgraf [Count-Palatine] bei Rhein, and Mathilde von Nassau. (ES IV, 2).

8. MECHTILD, GRAEFIN von SPANHEIM, fl. 1346-1409; m. 1356, Rudolf, Markgraf [Margrave, Marquis, Marquess] von Baden, d. 21 Mar. 1372, son of Friedrich III, Markgraf von Baden, and Margarete von Baden. (ES I, 82).

9. BERNHARD I, MARKGRAF von BADEN, d. 5 May 1431; m. (l) Aug. 1384, divorced, s.p. bef. 1393, Margarete, Graefin von Hohenberg, d. 26 Feb. 1419, dau. of Rudolf IV, Graf von Hohenberg, and Ida Graefin von Toggenburg; m. (2) 1398, Anna, Graefin von Oettingen, d. 9 Nov. 1436, dau. of Ludwig XI, Graf von Oettingen, and Beatrix, Graefin von Helfenstein. (ES I, 82).

10. JÁKOB I, MARKGRAF von BADEN (by 2nd wife), b. 15 Mar. 1407, d. 13 Oct. 1453; m. 1426, Catherine de Louraine, d. 1 Mar. 1439, dau. of Charles I, Duc de Lorraine, and Margarete, Prinzessin von der Pfalz. (ES I, 82).

11. MARGARETE, MARKGRAEFIN von BADEN, b. 1431, d. 24 Oct. 1457; m. 1446, Albrecht Achilles, Kurfuerst [Elector] von Brandenburg, b. 24 Nov. 1414, d. 11 Mar. 1486, son of Friedrich I, Kurfuerst von Brandenburg, and Elisabeth von Bayern-Landshut. (ES I, 61. Margarete's brother Bernhard was canonized in 1469. See Wolfgang Müller, Die Ahnen des seligen Markgrafen Bernhard von Baden (1958).)

12. JOHANN CICERO, KURFUERST von BRANDENBURG, b. 2 Aug. 1455, d.

9 Jan. 1499; m. 25 Aug. 1476, Margarete, Herzogin [Duchess] von Sachsen, b. 1449, d. 13 July 1501, dau. of Wilhelm III, Herzog [Duke] von Sachsen, by Anna, Erzherzogin [Archduchess] von Oesterreich. (ES I, 62). From this marriage descend all later Electors of Brandenburg, Kings of Prussia, and Emperors of Germany.

13. ANNA, MARKGRAEFIN von BRANDENBURG, b. 27 Aug. 1487, d. 3 May 1514; m. 10 Apr. 1502, Frederik I, Konge til Danmark [King of Denmark], b. 3 Sept. 1471, d. 10 Apr. 1533, son of Christian I, Konge til Danmark, and Dorothea, Markgraefin von Brandenburg. (ES II, 72). From this marriage descend all later Kings of Denmark, Dukes of Schleswig-Holstein, Kings of Greece, and the Duke of Edinburgh. (The Grand dukes of Oldenburg and the Tsars of Russia are descended from the second marriage of Frederik I, to Sofie, Herzogin von Pommern.)

14. CHRISTIAN III, KONGE til DANMARK, b. 12 Aug. 1503, d. 1 Jan. 1559; m. 29 Oct. 1525, Dorothea, Herzogin von Sachsen-Lauenburg, b. 9 July 1511, d. 7 Sept. 1571, dau. of Magnus I, Herzog von Sachsen-Lauenburg, and Katharina, Herzogin von Braunschweig-Wolfenbuettel. (ES II, 72).

15. FREDERIK II, KONGE til DANMARK, b. 1 July 1534, d. 4 Apr. 1588; m. 20 July 1572, Sofie, Herzogin von Mecklenburg, b. 4 Sept. 1557, d. 3 Oct. 1631, dau. of Ulrich III, Herzog von Mecklenburg-Guestrow, and Elisabeth, Prinsesse af Danmark. (ES II, 72).

16. ANNE, PRINSESSE af DANMARK, b. 12 Oct. 1574, d. 2 Mar. 1618/9; m. 23 Nov. 1589, JAMES VI, King of Scots, later James I, King of England (92-17), b. 19 June 1566, d. 27 Mar. 1625, son of Henry Stuart, Duke of Albany, by his wife, Mary, Queen of Scots. (ES II, 64).

17. CHARLES I, KING of ENGLAND, b. 19 Nov. 1600, d. 30 Jan. 1649; m. 1 May 1625, Henrietta Maria, Princesse de France, b. 26 Nov. 1609, d. 21 Aug. 1669, dau. of Henri IV, Roi [King] de France, and Maria de' Medici. (ES II, 64).

18. CHARLES II, KING of ENGLAND, b. 29 May 1630, d. 6 Feb. 1685; m. 31 May 1662, Cataline, Infanta do Portugal, b. 25 Nov. 1638, d. 31 Dec. 1705, dau. of João IV, Rei do Portugal, and Luisa de Guzman. (ES II, 64). Catalina had no children, but Charles had 14 of more, all illegitimate. By Barbara Villiers, Duchess of Cleveland, b. c. 1641, d. 9 Oct. 1709, dau. of William, 2nd Viscount Grandison, and Mary Bayning (CP III, 280), Charles II had:

19. CHARLOTTE FITZROY, b. perhaps 5 Sept. 1664, d. 17 Feb. 1718; m. 6 Feb. 1677, Edward Henry Lee, 1st Earl of Lichfield, b. 4 Feb. 1663, d. 14 July 1716, son of Sir Francis Henry Lee, 4th Baronet, and Elizabeth Pope. (CP VII, 644).

20. LADY CHARLOTTE LEE, b. 13 Mar. 1678, d. 22 Jan. 1721; m. 2 Jan. 1699, Benedict Leonard Calvert, 4th Lord Baltimore, b. 21 Mar. 1679, d. 16 Apr. 1715, son of CHARLES, 3rd Lord Baltimore (63-16) by 2nd wife Jane Lowe. (NCP I, 394).

21. CHARLES CALVERT, 5th Lord Baltimore, b. 29 Sept. 1699, d. 24 Apr. 1751; m. 20 July 1730, Mary Janssen, d. 25 Mar. 1770, dau. of Sir Theodore Janssen and Williamsa Henley. (CP I, 395). By a woman of unknown identity, the 5th Lord Baltimore had an illegitimate son:

22. BENEDICT SWINGATE, later Benedict Calvert, b. c. 1724, d. 9 Jan. 1788; m. 21 Apr. 1748, Elizabeth Calvert, b. 24 Feb. 1730, d. 7 July 1798, dau. of Charles Calvert, Governor of Maryland, and Rebecca Gerard. (VMHB LXV (1957), 222-228; Maryland Historical Magazine XVI (1921), 50-59, 189-204, 313-318, 389-394).

Line 18

1. HENRY de BOHUN, Magna Charta Surety, 1215, son of Humphrey de Bohun IV and Margaret de Huntingdon, b. 1176, d. 1 June 1220, Sheriff of Kent, 1st Earl of Hereford, 1200-1220, hereditary Constable of England; m. MAUD FITZ GEOFFREY (160-4), d. 1236, Countess of Essex, dau. of Geoffrey Fitz Piers, d. 1213, Earl of Essex, and Beatrix de Say, dau. of William de Say. (CP VI, 457; V, 134).

2. HUMPHREY de BOHUN V, b. 1208, d. 24 Sept. 1275, 2nd Earl of Hereford and Essex, Constable of England; m. (l) Maud d'Eu, d. 14 Aug. 1241, dau. of Raoul I de Lusignan and Alice d'Eu. (CP VI, 459).

3. HUMPHREY de BOHUN VI, d. 27 Aug. 1265, Earl of Hereford and Essex; m. (l) Eleanor de Braiose, dau. of EVA MARSHAL (146-2). (CP VI, 462).

4. HUMPHREY de BOHUN VII, b. c. 1249, d. Pleshy, 31 Dec. 1298, Earl of Hereford and Essex, Constable of England; m. 1275, Maud, dau. of Enguerrand de

Fiennes, Seigneur de Fiennes in Guisnes. (CP VI, 463-466).

5. HUMPHREY de BOHUN VIII, b. c. 1276, slain at Boroughbridge, 16 Mar. 1321/2, Earl of Hereford and Essex, Lord High Constable of England; m. 14 Nov. 1302, Elizabeth Plantagenet, b. Aug. 1282, d. 5 May 1316, dau. of King EDWARD I (161-14) of England and Eleanor of Castile. (CP VI, 467-470).

6. SIR WILLIAM de BOHUN, K.G., b. c. 1312, d. Sept. 1360, fought at Crecy, Earl of Northampton, 16 Mar. 1336/7; m. 1335/8, ELIZABETH BADLESMERE (36-7). (CP IX, 664; VI, 472).

7. HUMPHREY de BOHUN IX, K.G., b. 25 Mar. 1342, d. 16 Jan. 1372/3, Earl of Hereford, Essex and Northampton; m. aft. 9 Sept. 1359, Joan Fitz Alan, d. 7 Apr. 1419, dau. of RICHARD FITZ ALAN (121-6), Earl of Arundel, and Eleanor Plantagenet, dau. of Henry Plantagenet, Earl of Lancaster (son of Edmund, Earl of Lancaster, son of HENRY III (161-13)), and MAUD de CHAWORTH (4-6). (CP VI, 473-474).

8. ALIANORE de BOHUN, d. 3 Oct. 1399; m. appt. bef. 24 Aug. 1376, Thomas Plantagenet, K.G., of Woodstock, b. 7 Jan. 1354/5, d. Calais, 8 or 9 Sept. 1397, Duke of Gloucester, son of King EDWARD III (161-16) of England and Philippa of Hainaut. (CP VI, 474-477; V, 719).

9. ANNE PLANTAGENET, Countess of Buckingham, ae 17+ in 1399/1400, d. 16 Oct. 1438; m. (1) Edmund, Earl of Stafford; m. (2) bef. 20 Nov. 1405, Sir William Bourchier, d. Troyes, 28 May 1420, Count of Eu. (CP VI, 474-477; V, 176).

10. SIR JOHN BOURCHIER, K.G., d. 16 or 21 May 1474, Knt., 1426, M.P., 1455-1472, Lord Berners; m. Margery Berners, d. 18 Dec. 1475, dau. of Sir Richard Berners and Philippa, dau. of Sir Edward Dalyngruge. (CP II, 153).

11. SIR HUMPHREY BOURCHIER, slain at Barnet Field, 14 Apr. 1471; m. Elizabeth Tylney, d. 4 Apr. 1497, dau. of Sir Frederick Tylney, of Boston, co. Lincs. (See 63-10.) (CP II, 153).

12. SIR JOHN BOURCHIER, K.B., d. Calais, 19 Mar. 1532/3, M.P., 1495-1529, Lord Berners, Chancellor of the Exchequer, 1516-1527, translator of Froissart's Chronicles; m. KATHERINE HOWARD (73-10). (CP II, 153-4).

13. JANE BOURCHIER, Lady Berners, d. 17 Feb. 1561/2; m. SIR EDMUND KNYVET (52-13). (CP II, 155).

14. JOHN KNYVET, ESQ., of Plumstead, co. Norfolk, liv. 1543, but who died in his mother's lifetime; m. c. 28 Feb. 1513, Agnes Harcourt, dau. of Sir John Harcourt, Knt., of Stanton-Harcourt. (CP II, 155).

15. SIR THOMAS KNYVET, KNT., b. c. 1539, d. 9 Feb. 1617/8, Lord Berners, Sheriff of Norfolk; m. Muriel Parry, d. 25 Apr. 1616, dau. of Sir Thomas Parry. (CP II, 155).

*   *   *   *   *   *

Note: ABIGAIL (Gen. 16) was sister, not dau., of SIR THOMAS (Gen. 15). See Langston, Buck and Beard, Peds. of Some of the Emperor Charlemagne's Descendants, II (1974), pp. xcviii-xcix.

*   *   *   *   *   *

16. ABIGAIL KNYVET; m. Sir Martin Sedley, b. 1531, will made 12 May 1608, pr. 5 Mar. 1608/9, d. 1608/9, of Morley, co. Norfolk.

17. MURIEL SEDLEY, b. 1583, d. 1661, ae. 78; m. Brampton Gurdon, Esq., will made 10 Oct. 1647, pr. 1649, d. 1649, of Assington Hall, co. Suffolk, Sheriff of Suffolk, 1625-1629, M.P., 1620, son of John Gurdon, Esq., and Amy Brampton.

18. MURIEL GURDON; m. June 1633, MAJOR RICHARD SALTONSTALL, ESQ. (44-16). (J.J. Muskett, 286-288).

Line 19

6. SIR WILLIAM de BOHUN, K.G., Earl of Northampton (18-6); m. c. 1338, ELIZABETH BADLESMERE (36-7), b. 1313, d. 1356.

7. ELIZABETH de BOHUN, d. 3 Apr. 1385; m. (1) contract 28 Sept. 1359, Richard Fitz Alan, b. 1346, beheaded, 21 Sept. 1397, 10th Earl of Arundel and Surrey, son of SIR RICHARD FITZ ALAN (121-6) and Eleanor Plantagenet.(See 18-7.) (CP I, 244).

8. ELIZABETH FITZ ALAN, d. 8 July 1425; m. (1) Sir William de Montagu; m. (2) July 1384, Sir Thomas de Mowbray, Knt. (63-7), Duke of Norfolk, b. 22 Mar. 1365/6, d. Venice, 22 Sept. 1399; m. (3) bef. 19 Aug. 1401, Sir Robert Goushill,

of Hoveringham, co. Nottingham; m. (4) bef. 3 July 1414, Sir Gerard Usflete. (CP IX, 604; I, 246, note d; II, 594).

    9. ELIZABETH GOUSHILL, living 1414; m. Sir Robert Wingfield of Letheringham. (For more details, see 20-9 which follows.)

    10. ELIZABETH WINGFIELD; m. Sir William Brandon, Knt., fl. 1497, Marshal of Marchelsea.

    11. ELEANOR BRANDON (aunt of Charles Brandon, Duke of Suffolk); m. John Glemham of Glemham, co. Suffolk.

    12. ANNE GLEMHAM; m. Henry Palgrave, Esq., b. c. 1470, d. 2 Oct. 1516, of Little Palgrave and Thruxton, co. Norfolk, son of John Palgrave and Margaret Yelverton.

    13. THOMAS PALGRAVE, gent., b. 1505/10, of Thruxton; m. Alice Gunton, dau. of Robert Gunton of Thruxton.

    14. THE REVEREND EDWARD PALGRAVE, bp. Thruxton, 21 Jan. 1540/1, d. Dec. 1623, Rector of Barnham Broom, 1567-1623; wife's name not known.

    15. DR. RICHARD PALGRAVE, b. c. 1585, d. Oct. 1651; m. Anna, d. Roxbury, Massachusetts, 17 Feb. 1669; physician at Wymondham, co. Norfolk, and Charlestown, Massachusetts, 1630; freeman, 18 May 1631.

    16. MARY PALGRAVE; m. c. 1637, Roger Wellington of Watertown, Mass.

    16. SARAH PALGRAVE; m. c. 1648, John Alcock (Harvard College, 1646), physician at Roxbury, Massachusetts.

    16. ELIZABETH PALGRAVE, b. c. 1643; m. c. 1651, John Edwards, Sr., of Boston, Massachusetts. (See NEHGR vol 67: 297.)

Line 20

    9. ELIZABETH GOUSHILL (19-9), living 1414; m. bef. 19 Aug. 1401, Sir Robert Wingfield, Knt., d. 1451, M.P., 1427-1439, of Letheringham.

    10. SIR JOHN WINGFIELD, K.B., d. 10 May 1481, Sheriff of Norfolk and Suffolk; of Letheringham; m. Elizabeth, dau. of Sir John Fitz Lewis, Knt., and Anne, d. 1497/1500, dau. of John Montagu of Salisbury.

    11. SIR RICHARD WINGFIELD, K.G., d. Toledo, Spain, 22 July 1525, of Kimbolton Castle, Ambassador to Spain; m. (2) Bridget, dau. of Sir John Wiltshire, Controller of Calais.

    12. THOMAS MARIA WINGFIELD, of Ipswich, M.P., for Huntingdon; m. a dau. of one Kerrye, co. York.

    13. EDWARD MARIA WINGFIELD, of Stonely Park, co. Huntingdon, b. c. 1570, an English merchant; 1st President of the Virginia Plantation, 1607; returned to England, 1608. (G.A. Moriarty, NEHGR, 103: 295; John Goodwin Herndon, Virginia Historical Magazine, 60: 305-322).

Line 21

    9. ELIZABETH GOUSHILL (19-9), living 1414; m. Sir Robert Wingfield, Knt.

    10. SIR HENRY WINGFIELD, KNT., d. bef. 6 May 1493, of Orford, co. Suffolk, Governor of Orford Castle; m. Elizabeth, bur. Westthorpe, co. Suffolk, dau. of Sir Thomas Rookes, Knt.

    11. SIR ROBERT WINGFIELD, d. Castre, co. Northampton, 4 Feb. 1575, was present at the Field of the Cloth of Gold, 1520; m. Margery, d. aft. 14 June 1574, dau. of John Quarles, of co. Norfolk. (Note: The chronology is very long between generations 9 and 11. These three generations need more research before complete acceptance.)

    12. SIR ROBERT WINGFIELD, d. 31 Mar. 1580, of Upton, M.P., for Peterborough, 1572; m. Elizabeth, bur. Tinwell, 6 Dec. 1611, dau. of Richard Cecil, and sister of William Cecil, Lord Burghley.

    13. SIR JOHN WINGFIELD, bur. Tickencote, 29 July 1626, M.P. for Grantham, 1621, 1625; m. (1) c. 1593, Elizabeth, dau. of Paul Gresham of Tickencote, co. Rutland.

    14. SIR JOHN WINGFIELD, d. 25 Dec. 1631, of Tickencote; m. c. 30 Jan. 1619, Frances, d. bef. 25 June 1662, dau. of Edward, Lord Cromwell of Oakham.

    15. JOHN WINGFIELD, York Herald, bp. Tickencote, 25 June 1623, d. 30 Dec.

1678; m. (1) Mary, dau. of George Owen, York Herald, and Rebecca, dau. of Sir Thomas Darrell.

16. THOMAS WINGFIELD, b. 1670, d. St. Peter's Parish, New Kent co., Virginia, 19 Dec. 1720; m. (1) Mary, d. 21 Jan. 1714; m. (2) Mary. (Children by the 1st wife: THOMAS WINGFIELD, b. c. 1693; m. Sarah Garland; JOHN WINGFIELD, b. c. 1695; m. Mary Hudson; ROBERT WINGFIELD, b. c. 1697; m. Ann. Child by the 2nd wife: OWEN WINGFIELD, b. 23 Sept. 1719.)

16. OWEN WINGFIELD, b. 1673; Sergeant in Frederick co. militia, Virginia. (Herndon, op. cit.).

Line 22

5. HUMPHREY de BOHUN VIII (18-5); m. Elizabeth Plantagenet.

6. MARGARET de BOHUN, d. 16 Dec. 1391; m. 1 Aug. 1325, HUGH de COURTENAY, K.G. (126-5), b. 1303, d. 1377, Earl of Devon. (CP IV, 324).

7. SIR EDWARD COURTENAY, d. 1364-1372, of Godlington; m. Emmeline, d. 1372, bef. 20 Sept., dau. of Sir John Dauney, Knt., and Sibyl de Treverbin. (CP IV, 325).

8. SIR HUGH COURTENAY, d. 15 Mar. 1425, of Haccombe, knight of the Shire of Devon, 1395; m. Philippa, dau. of Sir Warin Arcedekene and Elizabeth Talbot; m. (3) Maud, dau. of Sir John Beaumont of Sherwill. (CP IV, 335; I, 187-8).

9. MARGERY COURTENAY (by 3rd wife); m. Sir Theobald Grenville, Knt., of Stowe. (Gens. 6-7: see also Noble Family of Courtney (Cleveland) 151-155, 201, 209).

10. SIR WILLIAM GRENVILLE, of Biddeford, d. c. 1451; m. Philippa, dau. of Sir William Bonville, K.G., Lord Bonville, of Chewton-Mendip, near Wells Somerset. (For a descent of Sir William, Lord Bonville, from William Malet, see NGSQ Vol. 59, pp. 255-256; and notes, vol. 60, pp. 32-33; and Lines 149, gen. 3, and 59, gens. 1 and 2. Robert Behra, El Paso, Tex., has identified the wife of Sir William, Lord Bonville, as Margaret, dau. of Reginald, 3rd Lord Grey of Ruthyn, and Margaret de Ros. Evidences in an article to appear shortly.)

11. THOMAS GRENVILLE, of Stowe, Sheriff of Gloucestershire; m. Elizabeth Gorges, sister of Sir Theobald Gorges, Knt., of co. Devon. Thomas (No. 11) may not be the child of Gen. 10. Parentage is being questioned and currently under review.

12. SIR THOMAS GRENVILLE, K.B., of Stowe, d. 18 Mar. 1513; m. Isabella, dau. of Sir Otes Gilbert of Compton, co. Devon, and Elizabeth, dau. of Robert Hill, of Shilton, co. Devon.

13. SIR ROGER GRENVILLE, KNT., of Stowe and Biddeford; m. Margaret, dau. of Richard Whitleigh, of Efford, co. Devon.

14. AMY GRENVILLE, d. 18 Feb. 1577/8, is mentioned, with her husband, John Drake, in the will of her brother, Sir Richard Grenville; m. John Drake of Ashe, Musbury and Exmouth, Sheriff of Devonshire, d. 4 Oct. 1558 (GS), son of John Drake and Margaret Cole. (Generations 4 to 14: Am. Genealogist, 31: 170-171; Rogers, Antient Sepulchral Effigies ... of Devon, Exeter, 1877, pp. 204-207, 344-345. The GS of John and Amy mentions 2nd son Robert).

15. ROBERT DRAKE, 2nd son, of Wiscombe Park, co. Devon, bur. 30 Mar. 1600 (GS) (younger brother of Sir Bernard Drake); m. Elizabeth, dau. of Humphrey Prideaux, of Theuborough, co. Devon. (Ibid.).

16. WILLIAM DRAKE, of Wiscombe Park, bur. Southley (Southleigh), bef. 19 May 1625; m. Philippa, d. bef. 5 Oct. 1655, dau. of Sir Robert Dennys, Knt., of Holcombe-Burnell. (Ibid., 207).

17. JOHN DRAKE, b. at Wiscombe, 1585, came to New England, 1630; sett. at Windsor, Connecticut. (He is specifically mentioned in Vivian, Devonshire Visitations, p. 293, as "emigrated to New England.").

Line 23

12. SIR THOMAS GRENVILLE, K.B. (22-12); m. Isabella, dau. of Sir Otes Gilbert.

13. JANE GRENVILLE; m. (1) Sir John Arundell of Trerice; m. (2) Sir John Chamond, Knt., of Launcells, co. Cornwall, d. 13 Jan. 1544 (Inq. p. m. 1545), Sheriff of Cornwall, 1529, 1537, Steward of the Priory of Bodmin, from which he had a grant of the manor of Bodmin.

14. RICHARD CHAMOND, ESQ., b. c. 1514 (ae. 30 in 1544), executor of his father's will; presented to the Vicarage of Bodmin, 1550, High Sheriff of Cornwall, 1544, 1559, 1599 (Inq.p.m., 1599); m. Margaret, dau. of Richard Trevener. (Vivian, pp. 84, 191, 383).

15. GERTRUDE CHAMOND, d. 1621 (will made 26 Jan. 1621, pr. 26 May 1621); m. Walter Porter of Launcells (executor of his father's will, 20 May 1566), d. 17 Jan. 1582 (will made 14 Jan. 1582; Inq.p.m., 1582). (Ibid.).

16. MARY PORTER; m. as his 2nd wife, Richard Penhallow of Penhallow, co. Cornwall, living 1620.

17. CHAMOND PENHALLOW, gent. 2nd son, of Filley, co. Cornwall, bur. Fowey, 19 Feb. 1689 (admin. granted 20 Apr. 1690); m. St. Mabyn, co. Cornwall, 30 May 1661, Anne, bp. St. Mabyn, 29 Oct. 1643, dau. of John Tamlyn of Tregaddock and his wife Mary.

18. SAMUEL PENHALLOW, ESQ., b. St. Mabyn, 2 July 1665, bp. 20 July 1665, d. Portsmouth, New Hampshire, 2 Dec. 1726, pupil of the Rev. Charles Morton at Newington Green near London; came with him to Charlestown, Massachusetts, July 1686, with an appointment to learn the Indian language and to become a missionary for the Society for Propagating the Gospel among the Indians (The New England Company of 1649); sett. Portsmouth, N.H.; Justice-of-the-Peace, Councillor, Province Treasurer, Justice and Chief-Justice of the Superior Court of New Hampshire; historian of the Indian Wars; m. (1) Portsmouth, N.H., 1 July 1687, Mary Cutts, b. 29 July 1666, d. 8 Feb. 1713, dau. of Hon. John Cutts, 1st President of the Council of New Hampshire; m. (2) Portsmouth, 8 Sept. 1714, Abigail (Atkinson) (Winslow) Osborn of Boston, Mass.; left issue by each wife. (Vivian, Visitations of Cornwall (Heralds Visitations of 1530, 1573 and 1620), pp. 300-302, 84, 190-191, 383; St. Mabyn's Parish Registers; Vivian & Drake, Visitation of the County of Cornwall in the Year 1620 (by H. St. George and S. Lennard) (Harl. Soc. Publ., vol. 9), London, 1874, pp. 166-167, 40, 178; Sir John Maclean, History of the Deanery of Trigg Minor, London, 1872, II 537-538; Genealogical Dictionary of Maine and New Hampshire, 538).

Line 24

5. HUMPHREY de BOHUN VIII (18-5); m. Elizabeth Plantagenet.

6. ELEANOR de BOHUN, d. 7 Oct. 1363; m. (1) 1327, James Butler, Earl of Ormond, b. c. 1305, d. Jan. or Feb. 1337/8, son of Edmund Butler, d. London, 13 Sept. 1321, son of Theobald le Boteler and Joan Fitz John, dau. of Sir John Fitz Geoffrey and ISABEL BIGOD (4-3). (CP X, 116).

7. JAMES DUTLER, b. Kilkenny, 4 Oct. 1331, d. 18 Oct. or 6 Nov. 1382, 2nd Earl of Ormond; m. Elizabeth Darcy, d. 24 Mar. 1389/90, dau. of Sir John Darcy of Knayth. (CP X, 119).

8. JAMES BUTLER, d. 6 or 7 Sept. 1405, 3rd Earl of Ormond; m. bef. 17 June 1386, Anne Welles, liv. 1396, dau. of Sir John de Welles, Lord Welles. (CP X, 121).

9. JAMES BUTLER, b. prob. 1392, d. 23 Aug. 1452, Earl of Ormond; m. (1) on or bef. 28 Aug. 1413, JOAN de BEAUCHAMP (17-9), d. 3 or 5 Aug. 1430. (CP X, 123).

10. ELIZABETH BUTLER, b. 1420, d. 8 Sept. 1473; m. bef. 1444/8, SIR JOHN TALBOT, K.G. (141-9), b. c. 1413, d. at Battle of Northampton, 10 July 1460, 2nd Earl of Shrewsbury, Lord Treasurer of England.

11. SIR GILBERT TALBOT, K.G., 2nd son, b. 1452, d. 16 Aug. 1517, of Grafton, co. Worcester; m. (2) Audrey Cotton, dau. of Sir John Cotton.

12. SIR JOHN TALBOT, KNT., b. 1485, d. 10 Sept. 1549, of Albrighton and Grafton, Sheriff of Shropshire, 1527, 1537, 1541; m. (1) Margaret Troutbeck, b. 1492, liv. 1521, granddau. of MARGARET STANLEY (103-11).

13. ANNE TALBOT, b. 1515; m. Thomas Needham, of Shavington, b. 1510, son of Sir Robert Needham and Agnes Mainwaring.

14. ROBERT NEEDHAM, b. 1535, of Shavington; m. Frances Ashton, dau. of SIR EDWARD ASHTON (101-15), of Tixall, co. Stafford. (Gresleys of Drakelowe, p. 236).

15. DOROTHY NEEDHAM, b. 1570, d. aft. 1629; m. SIR RICHARD CHETWODE, KNT. (111-16), b. c. 1560, d. aft. 1631, q.v.

Line 25

8. ELIZABETH FITZ ALAN (19-8); m. (3) bef. 19 Aug. 1401, Sir Robert Goushill cf Hoveringham.

9. JOAN GOUSHILL; m. SIR THOMAS STANLEY, K.G. (103-10), Lord Stanley. (CP XII (l), 250).

10. ELIZABETH STANLEY; m. bef. 1432, Sir Richard Molyneux, Knt., of Sefton, Chief Forester of West Derbyshire, d. Blore Heath, 23 Sept. 1459.

11. SIR THOMAS MOLYNEUX, KNT., d. 12 July 1483; m. c. 11 July 1463, ANNE DUTTON (1-10), q.v.

Line 26

6. ELEANOR de BOHUN (24-6), d. 7 Oct. 1363; m. 1237, James Butler.

7. PETRONELLA BUTLER, d. aft. 28 May 1365; m. bef. 8 Sept. 1352, as lst wife, GILBERT TALBOT (141-6), b. c. 1322, d. Roales, Spain, 24 Apr. 1387, Lord Talbot. (CP XII (l), 614).

*   *   *   *   *   *

Note: No. 8 is not child of No. 7. Line breaks between gens. 7 and 8.

*   *   *   *   *   *

8. ELIZABETH TALBOT, d. 10 Jan. 1401/3; m. bef. 3 Feb. 1379/80, Sir Henry Grey, Lord Grey of Wilton, d. 22 Apr. 1396.

9. MARGARET de GREY, d. 1 June 1454; m. (l) JOHN DARCY (33-11), d. 9 Dec. 1411, 5th Baron Darcy of Knayth, q.v. (CP VI, 177).

Line 27

See notes at end. All generations in earlier editions to No. 17 replaced

7. ELIZABETH de BOHUN (19-7), d. 3 Apr. 1385; m. (l) c. 28 Sept. 1359, Richard Fitz Alan, son of SIR RICHARD FITZ ALAN, K.G. (134-7) by his 2nd wife, b. 1346, beheaded 21 Sept. 1397, 10th Earl of Arundel and Surrey. (CP I, 244-245; IV, 669).

8. ALICE FITZ ALAN, b. c. 1373-5; concubine of Henry Beaufort, Bishop of Lincoln, Bishop of Winchester, Cardinal of St. Eusebius, son of John of Gaunt, Duke of Lancaster, son of EDWARD III (161-16), b. c. 1375, d. Winchester, 11 Apr. 1447; m. by Mar. 1392, Sir John Charlton, 4th Lord Charlton of Powis, d.s.p. 19 Oct. 1401. Alice's dau. JANE BEAUFORT named in Cardinal Beaufort's will dtd. 20 Jan. 1446/7. (DNB; John of Gaunt, esp. pp. 389, 462; TAG 32: 10-11).

9. JANE BEAUFORT, b. prob. winter 1391/2; m. Sir Edward Stradling, Knt. of St. Donat's Castle, co. Glamorgan, b. c. 1389, ae. 22+ on 23 Nov. 1411, son of Sir William of same, by Isabel St. Barbe. On pilgrimage to Jerusalem 9 Hen. IV (1407-8) and returned, d. 1453. (TAG 32:11).

10. SIR HENRY STRADLING, KNT. s. & h. of Donat's Castle, b. c. 1423, ae. 30 in 1453, knighted at the Holy Sepulchre, Jerusalem, 1477, d. soon at Famagusta, Cyprus; m. Elizabeth, dau. of Sir William ap Thomas of Raglan Castle, who d. 1446. (TAG 32:11).

11. THOMAS STRADLING, of St. Donat's Castle, b. c. 1454/5, d. 8 Sept. 1480 "being under the age of 26"; m. Janet Mathew, d. 1485, dau. of Thomas Mathew of Radyr, co. Glamorgan. She m. (2) Sir Rhys ap Thomas, K.G. (TAG 32: 11-12).

12. SIR EDWARD STRADLING, of St. Donat's Castle, d. there 8 May 1535, will 27 Apr. 1535, pr. 9 Feb. 1535/6; m. Elizabeth, d. in childbirth, Merthyn Mawr, 20 Feb. 1513, dau. of Sir Thomas Arundel of Laherne, Cornwall, and Katharine, dau. of SIR JOHN DYNHAM, Lord Dynham (125-8) and Joan Arches. (The Stradling Correspondance, written in the reign of Queen Elizabeth, J. Montgomery Traherne, ed. 1840; G. T. Clark, Limbos Patrum Morganiae et Glamorganiae 1886, pp. 435-6; Genealogical Collections Illustrating the History of Roman Catholic Families of England part III, Arundel, 1887, pp. 226-7).

13. JANE STRADLING; m. Alexander Popham of Huntworth, Soms., son of John Popham of Huntworth, and Isabella, dau. & h. of Thomas Knoyle or Knowles. (References as in gen. 12; Burke, History of the Commoners, 1835, II 197; Landed

Gentry 1952, 2055).
   14. KATHARINE POPHAM, d. 1588; m. Sir William Pole, b. 31 July 1515, d.
15 Aug. 1587 ae. 72y. 15d. "of Inner Temple". Inscription in the Colyton Church
states: "here lieth the body of William Pole, late of Shute, Esq., deceased, who
married Kateryn, daught. of Alexander Poph'm of Huntworth, Esq., the said Wm.
was sonne of Wm. and of Agnes, daughter of John Drake of Ashe, which Wm. was
sonne of John and of Edith, daught. of Rychard Tytherleigh of Tytherleigh..."
(Rogers, Antient Sepulchral Effigies (1877) 153-154. They were the parents of Gen. 17.
   17. SIR WILLIAM POLE, KNT., of Shute, co. Devon, "the Antiquary" (son
of gen. 14), bp. 27 Aug. 1561, d. 10 Mar. 1635, in the 74th year of his age (Colyton
Parish Register); attended Exeter College; Inner Temple, 1578; Sheriff of Devon,
1602-1603; m. Mary Periham, b. 30 Apr. 1567, d. 2 May 1605, ae. 38 years (bur.
in Colyton Church), dau. of Sir William Periham, of Fulford, Knt., Lord Chief
Baron of the Exchequer.
   18. CAPTAIN WILLIAM POOLE, bp. 4 Dec. 1593; came to New England, c.
1630; schoolmaster at Dorchester; a founder of Taunton, Mass.; d. Dorchester, 24
Feb. 1674; m. Mary. They had six children of whom the eldest, JOHN, m. 28 Mar.
1672, Elizabeth Brenton, dau. of William Brenton; MARY, m. Daniel Henchman;
and BETHESDA was the wife of John Filer, 1686.
   18. MISTRESS ELIZABETH POOLE (or Pole), bp. 25 Aug. 1588, d. unm.,
21 May 1654, ae. 75 years (GS) at Taunton, Massachusetts; will filed 6 June 1656,
recorded at Plymouth, 17 May 1654 (Plymouth co. Probate, II part I 24-26); she
was a founder of Taunton. (Generations 17 to 18: TAG 31: 170-172; Rogers, op.
cit., pp. 153-155; S.H. Emery, History of Taunton, Massachusetts, 1893, pp. 66-
72, 94-97).

Note: Line 27 in earlier editions, through Agnes, dau. of John Drake and Amy Grenville (27-14 in earlier eds.) must be deleted. Mrs. J.J. Kiepura showed in TAG
vol. 32, p. 95 that Agnes was not dau. of Amy Grenville. Refs. for present line
as under gens. 12 and 13 above.

                                   Line 28

   1. RICHARD de CLARE (153-4), Magna Charta Surety, 1215, d. betw. 30 Oct.
& 28 Nov. 1217, Earl of Hertford, son of Roger de Clare, Earl of Hertford, and
Maud, dau. of James de St. Hilary; m. Amice, Countess of Gloucester, d. 1 Jan.
1224/5, dau. & h. of William fitz Robert, Earl of Gloucester, and Hawise de Beaumont. (CP VI, 501).
   2. SIR GILBERT de CLARE (153-5), Magna Charta Surety, 1215, b. say 1180,
d. Penrose, Brittany, 25 Oct. 1230, Earl of Gloucester and Hertford; m. as 1st
husb., 9 Oct. 1217, ISABEL MARSHAL (145-2). (CP V, 694).
   3. SIR RICHARD de CLARE. b. 4 Aug. 1222, d. Ashenfield, 15 July 1262,
Earl of Gloucester and Hertford; m. (2) on or bef. 25 Jan. 1237/8, MAUD de LACY
(107-4). (CP V, 696).
   4. GILBERT de CLARE, Earl of Gloucester and Hertford, d. 7 Dec. 1295; m.
(2) 1290, Joan Plantagenet, b. Acre, 1272, d. Clare, Suffolk, 23 Apr. 1307, dau.
of EDWARD I (161-14), King of England, and Eleanor of Castile. (CP V, 702).
   5. MARGARET de CLARE, b. c. 1292, d. 13 Apr. 1342; m. (2) Windsor,
28 Apr. 1317, HUGH de AUDLEY (150-6), d. 10 Nov. 1347, Earl of Gloucester.
(CP V, 715).
   6. MARGARET de AUDLEY, only dau. and heir, ae. 18-20 in 1347, d. 1349;
m. as his 2nd wife bef. 6 July 1336, SIR RALPH de STAFFORD, K.G. (136-6), b.
24 Sept. 1301, d. 31 Aug. 1372, K.G., 23 Apr. 1349, Earl of Stafford. By his first
wife, Katharine de Hastang, he had Margaret who married her cousin John de Stafford, Knt., of Bramshall, co. Stafford. (CP V, 715).

         *   *   *   *   *   *
This line breaks at this point. The Clare ancestry is lost to Jane Deighton.

         *   *   *   *   *   *
   7. MARGARET STAFFORD, dau. of Sir Ralph, Earl of Stafford by his 1st
wife; m. Sir John de Stafford, son of William, of Bramshall, Staffs. (TAG 26: 23).
   8. RALPH de STAFFORD, of Grafton, Broomsgrove, co. Worcester, d. 1
Mar. 1410; m. Maud de Hastings, bp. 2 Feb. 1358/9, dau. of John Hastings of Lea-

mington House, co. Warwick. (CP VI, 343, note f).

9. SIR HUMPHREY STAFFORD, KNT., of Grafton, co. Warwick, b. 1384, d. 20 Feb. 1419; m. Elizabeth Bindette, dau. of Sir John Bindette.

10. SIR HUMPHREY STAFFORD, KNT., of Grafton, b. 1400, liv. 1467; m. ELEANOR AYLESBURY (51-9), dau. of Sir Thomas Aylesbury, Knt.

11. ELIZABETH STAFFORD; m. 27 Jan. 1446/7, SIR RICHARD BEAUCHAMP (58-10), 2nd Lord Beauchamp of Powyck. (CP II, 47).

12. ANNE de BEAUCHAMP, b. 1462, d. 1535; m. Richard Lygon, Knt., of Arle Court, co. Gloucester.

13. SIR RICHARD LYGON, KNT., of Arle Court, d. 1557, Sheriff of Worcester, 1547; m. Margaret Grenville, dau. of Sir William Grenville of Arle Court and Cheltenham, Judge of Common Pleas.

14. HENRY LYGON, of Upton St. Leonard, co. Gloucester, d. c. 1577, will dated 30 July 1577, pr. Aug. 1577; m. ELIZABETH BERKELEY (51-14), dau. of Sir John Berkeley.

15. ELIZABETH LYGON; m. Edward Basset, of Uley, co. Gloucester, will dated 3 June 1601, pr. 5 Nov. 1602.

16. JANE BASSET, d. 23 Apr. 1631; m. Dr. John Deighton, gent., d. 16 May 1640, of St. Nicholas, Gloucester, will made 31 Jan. 1639, pr. 21 May 1640.

17. KATHERINE DEIGHTON, bp. Gloucester, 16 Jan. 1614/5, d. 29 Aug. 1671, m. (1) Samuel Hackburne; m. (2) Roxbury, Massachusetts, 14 Apr. 1644, GOVERNOR THOMAS DUDLEY (50-14); m. (3) Rev. John Allin of Dedham; children by all three husbands. (DEBORAH DUDLEY, m. Jonathan Wade; GOVERNOR JOSEPH DUDLEY, A.M., Harvard College, 1665, Governor of Mass., 1702-1715, m. 1669, Rebecca Tyng, dau. of Major-General Edward Tyng; HON. PAUL DUDLEY, m. Mary Leverett.)

17. FRANCES DEIGHTON, bp. 1 Mar. 1611, d. Taunton, Mass., Feb. 1705/6; m. Witcombe Magna, co. Gloucester, 11 Feb. 1632, Richard Williams, bp. Wootton-under-Edge, 28 Jan. 1607, d. Taunton, Mass., Aug. 1693.

17. JANE DEIGHTON, bp. 5 Apr. 1609, liv. at Boston, Mass., 1671; m. (1) St. Nicholas, 3 Jan. 1627, John Lugg, came to New England, 1638, d. aft. 1644; m. (2) c. 1650, Jonathan Negus, b. 1602, liv. 1678; children by both husbands.

Line 28A

1. RICHARD de CLARE (28-1) M.C. Surety, 1215, d. 1217, Earl of Clare, Earl of Hertford; m. Amice, Countess of Gloucester, d. 1 Jan. 1224/5, dau. & h. of William fitz Robert, Earl of Gloucester. (CP II, 314).

2. MAUDE (or Mathilde) de CLARE; m. William de Braose, son of William, Lord of Bramber, d. 1210 of starvation, by order of King John. (CP II, 302).

3. JOHN de BRAOSE, Lord of Gower, d. 1232; m. 1220, Margaret, d. 1263, dau. of Llewellyn ap Iorwerth, Prince of Wales. (CP II, 302-3).

4. SIR RICHARD de BRAOSE, Lord of Stinton (said to be a younger son, not fully documented), b. bef. 1232, d. bef. 18 June 1292; m. bef. Sept. 1265, Alice le Rus, dau. of William le Rus of Stinton, wid. of Richard Longespeye, d.s.p. shortly bef. 27 Dec. 1261. (CP II, 304).

5. MARGARET de BRAOSE, d. 1335; m. Sir Roger Coleville of Bytham, aged 26 in 1277, son of Walter, d. by 1287/8.

6. ALICE COLEVILLE; m. (1) Guy Gobaud; m. (2) SIR JOHN GERNON (123-5), b. c. 1295, d. betw. Apr. 1332 and 28 Feb. 1334.

Submitted by Richard G. Lewis of Pittsburgh, see also ms. file on Loring Dam, Gen. Soc. of Penna. (WLS).

Line 29

13. SIR RICHARD LYGON, KNT. (28-13); m. Margaret Grenville.

14. WILLIAM LYGON, of Redgrove and Madresfield, b. 1518, d. 29 Sept. 1567, Sheriff of Worcestershire, 1550, 1560; m. 1529, Eleanor Dennis, dau. of Sir William Dennis and Ann Berkeley, dau. of Maurice Berkeley.

15. CICELY LYGON, of Madresfield, co. Worcester; m. 1559, Edward Gorges, Esq. of Wroxall, b. 1537, d. 29 Aug. 1568, son of Edmund Gorges.

16. SIR FERDINANDO GORGES, KNT., colonizer of Maine, b. c. 1565, d. Ashton Court near Bristol, England, May 1647; m. (1) 24 Feb. 1589/90, Anne Bell, bur. London, 6 Aug. 1620, dau. of Edward Bell and MARGARET BARLEY (132-13); m. (2) 21 Dec. 1621, Mary Fulford.

Line 30

Line **not** sound to America. See note, gen. 16.

6. MARGARET de AUDLEY (28-6); m. SIR RALPH de STAFFORD, K.G. (136-6).

7. JOAN de STAFFORD, d. bef. 1397; m. John de Cherleton, ae. 26 Easter 1360, d. 13 July 1374, Lord Cherleton and lord of Powis, son of John Cherleton and Maud, dau. of SIR ROGER de MORTIMER (147-5) and JOAN de GENEVILLE (12-6). (CP III, 161).

8. SIR EDWARD CHERLETON, K.G., d. 14 Mar. 1420/1, Lord Cherleton and lord of Powis; m. (1) 1399, Eleanor (Holand) de Mortimer, d. Oct. 1405, (sister of, not same as ELEANOR (94-9)) 4th dau. of THOMAS de HOLAND, 2nd Earl of Kent (94-8). (CP III, 161).

9. JOYCE de CHERLETON, d. 22 Sept. 1446; m. sh. aft. 28 Feb. 1421/2, as 2nd wife, Sir John Tibetot, d. 27 Jan. 1442/3, Lord Tibetot and Powys. (Gens. 6-9: CP III, 161-162; XII (1), 746).

10. JOYCE de TIBETOT; m. as his 1st wife, SIR EDMUND SUTTON (80A-9), d. betw. 6 July 1483 & 30 Sept. 1487, of Dudley Castle and Gatcombe.

11. SIR JOHN SUTTON, of Dudley, lord of Aston-le-Walls.

12. MARGARET SUTTON; m. John Butler, son of Ralph Butler, of Sawbridge-worth, co. Hertford.

13. WILLIAM BUTLER, of Tighes, co. Sussex.

14. MARGARET BUTLER, of Tighes; m. 3 Aug. 1588, Lawrence Washington, of Sulgrave and Wicken, d. 13 Dec. 1616, son of Robert Washington, of Sulgrave, and Elizabeth Lyte. (Gens. 11-14: NEHGR vol. 94, p. 251 note, p. 258).

15. SIR JOHN WASHINGTON, KNT., of Thrapston, b. Sulgrave manor, c. 1591, d. c. 1668; m. c. 1621, Mary Curtis, d. c. 1625, dau. of Philip Curtis of Islip. His son John, living in England in 1661.

*　　　　*　　　　*　　　　*　　　　*　　　　*

16. JOHN WASHINGTON, b. c. 1624, sett. Surry Co., Virginia, aft. 1650, dead 1661; m. Mary (Flood) Blunt, dau. of Col. John Flood. (NEHGR vol. 43, 420 chart, 379-424). John, No. 16, must be son of another father; perhaps son of Richard (son of Lawrence, No. 14) b. c. 1598 at Sulgrave and apprenticed 7 July 1614 in London to Richard Brent of the Clothworkers' Company.

Line 31

8. SIR EDWARD de CHERLETON, K.G. (30-8); m. Eleanor, 4th dau. of THOMAS HOLAND (94-8).

9. JOAN de CHERLETON, d. 17 Sept. 1425; m. Sir John de Grey, K.G., b. aft. 1384, killed Anjoy, 22 Mar. 1420/1, Count of Tancarville in Normandy. (CP VI, 136).

10. HENRY de GREY, Earl of Tancarville, ae. one and 1/2+ at father's death, d. 13 Jan. 1449/50; m. as 1st husb, Antigone, only child (bastard) of Humphrey, Duke of Gloucester, b. 1391, d. 23 Feb. 1447, son of King Henry IV of England and Mary Bohun, and grandson of JOHN, Duke of Lancaster (161-17) and Blanche of Lancaster. (CP VI, 138).

11. ELIZABETH GREY; m. 1465, as his 2nd wife, Sir Roger Kynaston, Knt., d. 1495/6, of Tancarville, Constable of Harlech, of Middle, Salop.

11A. HUMPHREY KYNASTON, 2nd son, d. 1534, of Marton in Middle; m. (2) Elizabeth Kyffin, dau. Maredudd of Glasgoed in Denbighshire.

12. MARGARET KYNASTON; m. John ap Iewan ap Owain.

13. HUMPHREY WYNNE, of Duffryn, Montgomeryshire; m. Mawd, dau. of Ollver ap Thomas Pryce of Newtown, Montgomeryshire.

14. KATHERINE LLOYD; m. c. 1612, as his 1st wife, her cousin, John Lloyd, gent., of Dolobran Hall, Wales, Justice-of-the-Peace, b. 1575, d. c. 1636.

15. CHARLES LLOYD, ESQ., of Dolobran Hall, b. 1613, d. 17 Aug. 1657 (will made 17 June 1651); m. Elizabeth, dau. of Thomas Stanley, of Knockin, co. Salop.

16. GOVERNOR THOMAS LLOYD, of Dolobran, b. 17 Feb. 1640, d. in Pennsylvania, 10 Sept. 1694; Jesus Coll., Oxford; physician; Friends minister both in Wales and America; Deputy-Governor and President of the Provincial Council of Pennsylvania, 1684-1693; m. (l) 1665, Mary, d. 1680, dau. of Col. Roger Jones of Welshpool in Wales. (Thomas Allen Glenn, Merion in the Welsh Tract, pp. 340-342, for this line. For discussion of soundness of line, see TAG vol. 32, p. 136. However this line is supported by Charles F.H. Evans' letter to the Editor 13 May 1979. An article for publication is in preparation.)

Line 32

9. JOYCE de CHERLETON (30-9); m. Sir John de Tibetot, d. 1443.

10. JOAN de TIBETOT; m. Sir Edward de Ingaldesthorpe, Knt., fl. 1456.

11. ISABEL de INGALDESTHORPE; m. 25 Apr. 1456, John de Neville, K.G., Marquis Montagu, b. c. 1431, d. 20 May 1476, son of Richard de Neville, K.G., Earl of Salisbury, and ALICE de MONTAGU, Countess of Salisbury (94-10). (CP IX, 89).

12. LUCY de NEVILLE, d. Bagshott Manor, co. Surrey, 31 Mar. 1534, widow of Sir Thomas Fitzwilliam of Aldwarke, co. York; m. Sir Anthony Browne, Knt., d. 19 Nov. 1506 (will pr. 1506), Lieutenant of Calais and Standard Bearer to King Henry VII (Blore, Monumental Remains, etc., 1826, Section 30, p. l).

13. ELIZABETH BROWNE, d. betw. 20 Apr. and 23 Oct. 1565; m. bef. 1527, as his 2nd wife, Sir Henry Somerset, K.G., Earl of Worcester, d. 26 Nov. 1549, son of Charles Somerset, K.G., Earl of Worcester, and Elizabeth Herbert. (CP XII (2), 851).

*   *   *   *   *   *

Evidences to this point are adequate. Next 5 generations require further research and support.

14. ELIZABETH SOMERSET; m. Sir Roger Vaughan, Knt., of Talgarth and Portheme, son of Sir Roger Vaughan and Denise.

*   *   *   *   *   *

15. ELLEN VAUGHAN; m. as his 1st wife, Thomas Gwyn of Trecastle.

16. DAVID LLOYD (3rd son, called Lloyd); m. Maud, dau. of Watkin Gwllyn Prosser of Llanuwacully.

17. WATKIN DAVID LLOYD, of Cwnclydach; m. Joan, dau. of Philip Prosser of the Pool.

18. AGNES LLOYD, d. 1642; m. Edward Jeffrey of Baille Cwndwrgent.

*   *   *   *   *   *

Evidences for next 3 generations are better, though Burke's Dormant and Extinct Peerages is not an acceptable reference, and Jones' Brecknockshire should be used with caution. In addition, neither Burke nor Jones says that Elizabeth Somerset (No. 14) married Sir Roger Vaughan, and Jones gives an entirely different wife.

19. WATKIN JEFFREY; m. Gwenllian, dau. of Evan ap Owen of Cwmwd, d. 1684, bur. at Lloyd.

*   *   *   *   *   *

20. SIR JEFFREY JEFFREYS, KNT., d. Roehampton House, 1707, alderman of London, heir to his uncle, Edward Jeffrey; went to Virginia to look after his uncle Edward's interests there; m. London, Sarah Dawes, dau. of Nicholas Dawes. (The references given do NOT show Sir Jeffrey as son of Watkin and heir of uncle Edward, nor other relationship. Article in Virginia Magazine states this without citing any authority.)

21. EDWARD JEFFREYS, gent., d. in Virginia; came to Virginia, c. 1715, and was on record there in Stafford Co., 1716; m. 1730, a Miss Burt, who d. in King & Queen Co., Virginia (Generations 10 and 11: Wrottesley, Pedigrees from Plea Rolls, 1905, p. 422; generations 13 to 16: Burke, Dormant and Extinct Peerages, 272, 396; generations 14 to 21: Theophilus Jones, Brecknockshire, pp. 226-227, I Appendix, 16, 18, 20; generations 20 and 21: Virginia Magazine of History, XVII,

p. 137). Line NOT acceptable at this time.

Line 33

3. SIR RICHARD de CLARE (28-3); m. 1237/8, MAUD de LACY (107-4).
4. THOMAS de CLARE, 2nd son, d. Ireland, 1287/8, Governor of London,
Lord of Inchequin and Youghae; m. JULIANE FITZ MAURICE (144-4).
6. MARGARET de CLARE, dau. Gen. 4 (See Orpen, Ireland Under the Normans
IV 94-6; Altschul, The Clares 195-196, & ped. facing p. 332), d. 1333; m. (2) Bartholomew
de Badlesmere, ae. 26 in 1301, hanged 14 Apr. 1322. (CP I, 371-2 & 373 note c; X, 233).
7. MARGERY de BADLESMERE, b. 1306, d. sh. bef. 22 Oct. 1363; m. (1)
bef. 25 Nov. 1316, WILLIAM de ROS (1-5), Lord Ros of Helmsley, d. 3 Feb. 1342/3.
(CP XI, 98-99).
8. ALICE de ROS, d. bef. 4 July 1344; m. Sir Nicholas de Meinill, under age
23 Aug. 1322, d. bef. 20 Nov. 1341, 1st Lord Meinill of Whorlton. (Clay, 183, 136;
CP VIII, 632).
9. ELIZABETH de MEINILL, b. Whorlton, 15 Oct. 1331, d. 9 July 1368,
Baroness Meinill; m. (1) disp. 7 Jan. 1344/5, as 2nd wife, Sir John Darcy, Lord
Darcy of Knayth, ae. 30+ at father's death 20 May 1347, d. Notton, Yorks., 5 Mar.
1355/6; m. (2) bef. 18 Nov. 1356, SIR PIERS de MAULEY (87-8). (CP IV, 59-60;
Clay, 41, 136; CP VIII, 634, 567; IV, 58-61).
10. SIR PHILIP DARCY, b. York, 21 May 1352, d. 24 Apr. 1399, Lord Darcy;
m. Elizabeth Gray, d. 11 Aug. 1412, dau. of Sir Thomas de Gray of Heton and Margaret de Presfen. (Clay, 41; CP IV, 61-63).
11. JOHN DARCY, ae. 22+ or 23+ at father's death, d. 9 Dec. 1411, Lord
Darcy; m. MARGARET de GREY (26-9). (Clay, 42; CP IV, 63-65).
12. JOHN DARCY, b. c. 1400, d. 1455/6; m. Joan de Greystoke, dau. of John
de Greystoke, Lord Greystoke, and Elizabeth de Ferrers, dau. of SIR ROBERT de
FERRERS (102-8) and JOAN BEAUFORT, dau. of JOHN, Duke of Lancaster (161-17).
(Clay, 42; CP IV, 71, 73).
13. RICHARD DARCY, b. c. 1424, d.v.p.; m. Eleanor Scrope, dau. of Sir
John Scrope, Lord Scrope of Upsal, and Elizabeth Chaworth, dau. of Sir Thomas
Chaworth of Wiverton, co. Nottingham. (Clay, 42; CP IV, 71).
14. SIR WILLIAM DARCY, b. 1443, d. 30 May 1488; m. lic. 23 Jan. 1460/1,
Eupheme Langton, dau. of John Langton of Farnley. (Clay, 42; CP IV, 73).
15. SIR THOMAS DARCY, K.G., b. c. 1467, beheaded 30 June 1537, cr. 1st
Lord Darcy of Temple Hurst, 1509; m. (1) Dowsabel Tempest, d. 1503/20, dau.
of Sir Richard Tempest of Stainforth, and Mabel Strickland, dau. of Walter Strickland of Sizergh. (Clay, 43; CP IV, 73-74).
16. SIR ARTHUR DARCY, of Brimham, co. York, b. c. 1505, d. 3 Apr. 1561,
Lieutenant of the Tower of London; m. Mary Carew, dau. of Sir Nicholas Carew of
Beddington. (Clay, 43-45; CP IV, 74).
17. SIR EDWARD DARCY, KNT., of Dartford Place, co. Kent, b. c. 1534,
d. 28 Oct. 1612; matriculated at Trinity Coll., Cambridge, 1561; M.P., 1584, Knt.,
1603; m. Elizabeth Astley, dau. of Thomas Astley of Writtle, co. Essex. (Clay, 45).
18. ISABELLA DARCY, b. c. 1600, d. London, 1669, will made May 1668,
mentions "my daughter Mary Sherman"; m. (1) c. 1619, John Launce, b. c. 1597,
of Penair, St. Clement's, Cornwall, son of Robert Launce and Susan Tubb.
19. MARY LAUNCE, b. bef. 1625, d. Watertown, Massachusetts, 9 Nov.
1710; m. c. 1645, the Reverend John Sherman, ordained, Watertown, 1647, d. Watertown, Massachusetts, 8 Aug. 1685.

Line 34

4. SIR GILBERT de CLARE, KNT. (28-4); m. Joan Plantagenet, dau. of
KING EDWARD I (161-14).
5. ALIANORE de CLARE, b. Caerphilly, Oct. 1292, d. 30 June 1337; m. (1)
1306, aft. 14 June, SIR HUGH le DESPENSER, KNT. (14-6); m. (2) William la Zouche
de Mortimer, Lord Zouche. (CP IV, 267).
6. ISABEL DESPENSER, m. 9 Feb. 1320/1, SIR RICHARD FITZ ALAN (121-
6), div. 4 Dec. 1344. (CP I, 242).

24

7. ISABEL FITZ ALAN, d. 29 Aug. 1396; m. John Lestraunge, b. c. Easter
1322, d. 12 May 1361, M.P., 1360, 4th Lord Strange of Blackmere. (CP I, 244; XII
(1), 344; Le Strange Records, 289, 318-319).

8. ANKARET LESTRANGE, b. 1361 (ae. 22 in Aug. 1383), d. 1 June 1413; m.
(1) bef. 23 Aug. 1383, SIR RICHARD TALBOT (141-7). (CP XII (1), 345, 616; Le
Strange Records, 288, 319, 321-322).

9. MARY TALBOT, d. 13 Apr. 1433; m. Sir Thomas Greene, Knt., of Greene's
Norton, co. Northampton, d. 14 Dec. 1417, Sheriff of Northamptonshire, 1416.

10. SIR THOMAS GREENE, of Greene's Norton, b. Norton, 10 Feb. 1399/1400,
d. 18 Jan. 1461/2, Sheriff of Northamptonshire, 1454; m. (1) PHILIPPA de FERRERS
(115-9), d. 3 Nov. 1415. (Mr. John G. Hunt has questioned this generation based on
an inscription on the tomb of Sir Thomas Greene.)

11. ELIZABETH GREENE; m. c. 1440, William Raleigh, Esq., of Farnborough,
co. Warwick, d. 1460.

12. SIR EDWARD RALEIGH, KNT., of Farnborough, b. c. 1441, d. bef. 20
June 1509, Sheriff of Warwickshire and Leicestershire; m. 1467, Margaret Verney,
dau. of Sir Ralph Verney, Lord Mayor of London.

13. SIR EDWARD RALEIGH, KNT., of Farnborough, b. c. 1470, d. c. 1517;
m. ANNE CHAMBERLAYNE (53-13).

14. BRIDGET RALEIGH; m. Sir John Cope, Knt., of Canons Ashby, co. Northampton, d. 22 Jan. 1557/8, Sheriff of Northamptonshire, 1545, M.P., 1547.

15. ELIZABETH COPE; m. John Dryden, Esq., of Canons Ashby, d. 3 Sept.
1584. (Meredith B. Colket, Jr., Marbury Ancestry, 1936).

16. BRIDGET DRYDEN, b. c. 1563, d. bef. 2 Apr. 1645; m. c. 1587, the
Reverend Francis Marbury, bp. 27 Oct. 1555, d. c. 1611, son of William Marbury
and Agnes Lenton.

17. KATHERINE MARBURY, b. c. 1610, d. Newport, Rhode Island, 2 May
1687; m. Berkhampstead, co. Hertford, 7 June 1632, Richard Scott, d. Providence,
Rhode Island, bef. Mar. 1681.

17. ANNE MARBURY, bp. Alford, 20 July 1591, killed by the Indians, 1643;
m. London, 9 Aug. 1612, William Hutchinson, bp. Alford, co. Lincoln, 14 Aug.
1586, d. Boston, Massachusetts, 1642, son of Edward Hutchinson. (R.I. Historical
Society Collections, 1939, vol. XXXII, 87-96; Lincolnshire Pedigrees, pp. 638-
639; Colket, Marbury Ancestry, 1936).

Line 35

6. ISABEL DESPENSER (34-6); m. 1320/1, SIR RICHARD FITZ ALAN (121-6).

7. SIR EDMUND FITZ ALAN, KNT., 2nd son, liv. 1377; m. bef. July 1349,
Sibyl de Montagu (Montacute), dau. of William de Montagu, d. 30 Jan. 1343/4, Earl
of Salisbury.

8. ALICE FITZ ALAN; m. Sir Leonard Carew, b. 1342, d. 1370, son of Sir
John Carew and Eleanor de Mohun.

9. SIR THOMAS CAREW, d. 25 Jan. 1431; m. c. 1390, Elizabeth Bonville, d.
betw. 8 Feb. & 26 July 1451, dau. of Sir William Bonville, Knt., d. 14 Feb. 1408.
(See note (22-10). Identification is by Robert Behra, El Paso, Texas.)

10. SIR NICHOLAS CAREW, d. 1446, of Molesford; m. Joan Courtenay, dau.
of SIR HUGH COURTENAY (22-8) and Philippa.

11. SIR THOMAS CAREW, of Ashwater; m. Joan Carmino.

12. SIR NICHOLAS CAREW, of Ottery-Mohun, d. 6 Dec. 1470; m. Margaret,
d. 13 Dec. 1470, dau. of Sir John Dinham.

13. SIR EDMUND CAREW, KNT., of Mohuns-Ottery, d. 24 June 1513; m.
Katherine, dau. of Sir William Huddlesfield, Knt.

14. KATHERINE CAREW; m. SIR PHILIP CHAMPERNOUN (126-11), b. 2 Aug.1545.

15. SIR ARTHUR CHAMPERNOUN, KNT., of Dartington, d. bef. 19 Apr. 1578;
m. Mary Norris, dau. of Sir Henry Norris of Rycote.

16. GAWINE CHAMPERNOUN, ESQ., of Dartington, d. bef. 3 Apr. 1592; m.
Gabrielle Roberta.

17. ARTHUR CHAMPERNOUN, ESQ., of Dartington, liv. 1620; m. Dunsford,
17 June 1598, Bridget Fulford, dau. of Sir Thomas Fulford, Knt. (Her sister, Mary
Fulford, m. SIR FERDINANDO GORGES (29-16), q.v.)

18. CAPTAIN FRANCIS CHAMPERNOUN, of York, Maine, 1665; will made
11 Nov. 1686, proved 28 Dec. 1687.

Line 36

6. MARGARET de CLARE (33-6); m. (2) Bartholomew de Badlesmere.
7. ELIZABETH de BADLESMERE, d. 8 June 1355; m. (l) 27 June 1316, Edmund Mortimer, Lord Mortimer, b. 1305/6, d. sh. bef. 21 Jan. 1331/2; m. (2) 1335-8, SIR WILLIAM de BOHUN (18-6), b. c. 1312, d. Sept. 1360, Earl of Northampton. (CP IX, 284, 664).
8. SIR ROGER MORTIMER, K.G., b. Ludlow, 11 Nov. 1328, d. 26 Feb. 1359/60, 2nd Earl of March; m. Philippa de Montagu, d. 5 Jan. 1381/2, dau. of William de Montagu, Earl of Salisbury, and Katharine Grandison (CP VIII, 442).
9. EDMUND MORTIMER, Earl of March, b. 1 Feb. 1351/2, d. 21 Dec. 1381; m. 1368, PHILIPPA PLANTAGENET (161-18), dau. of LIONEL of Antwerp, Duke of Clarence (161-18).
10. ELIZABETH, b. 12 Feb. 1370/1, d. 20 Apr. 1417; m. (l) bef. 10 Dec. 1379, SIR HENRY PERCY, K.G. (44-7), "Harry Hotspur," killed at Shrewsbury, 14 Aug. 1403; m. (2) Thomas, Lord Camoys. (Clay, 162; DNB; CP IX, 713).
11. ELIZABETH de PERCY, d. 26 Oct. 1437; m. (l) betw. Aug. 1403 & Nov. 1412, JOHN de CLIFFORD (113-9), b. c. 1388, d. Meaux, France, 13 Mar. 1421/2, M.P., 1411-1421, 7th Lord Clifford, Sheriff of Westmoreland; m. (2) Ralf Nevill, 2nd Earl of Westmoreland. (Clay, 23-24; CP III, 293).
12. THOMAS de CLIFFORD, b. 25 Mar. 1414, slain St. Albans, 22 May 1445; m. aft. Mar. 1424, Joan Dacres (See (113-10).) (Clay, 24).
13. MATILDA CLIFFORD; m. (l) Sir John Harrington; m. (2) as his 2nd wife, SIR EDMUND SUTTON, KNT. (80A-9) (See (30-10)), son of Sir John Sutton, K.G., 1st Lord Dudley, and ELIZABETH BERKELEY (80A-8). (Twamley, Hist. of Dudley Castle, p. 19, chart fac. p. 11; Jackson, Peds. of Cumberland and Westmoreland, II, pp. 137-140, 145, 148, chart fac. 150). (Clay calls him "Sir Edmund Dudley," p. 24.)
14. THOMAS SUTTON, d. 1530; m. Grace Trekeld, dau. of Lancelot Trekeld, Esq., of Yeanwith. (Jackson, loc. cit. and chart fac. p. 136).
15. RICHARD SUTTON, of Yeanwith, took the name of Dudley; m. Dorothy Sanford, dau. of Edward Sanford of Asham. (Idem.).
16. ELIZABETH DUDLEY; m. John Tichborne, of Cowden, Kent, son of Sir John Tichborne, Knt., Sheriff of Hampshire, 1488, 1496, and Margaret Martin, dau. of Richard Martin, of Edenbridge, co. Kent.
17. JOHN TICHBORNE, 2nd, of Cowden; m. Margaret Waller.
18. JOHN TICHBORNE, 3rd, of Cowden; m. Dorothy Challoner, dau. of Francis Challoner, of Lindfield, co. Sussex.
19. ROBERT TICHBORNE, of Farrington within, London; m. Joan Banckes, dau. of Thomas Banckes, merchant and alderman of London.

      *   *   *   *   *   *

There is no proof that Elizabeth, dau. of Robert Tichborne, m. Pardon Tillinghast. She was unmarried in 1630, while her alleged son was born in 1622.

      *   *   *   *   *   *

20. ELIZABETH TICHBORNE; m. Pardon Tillinghast, 2nd, of Alfriston, co. Sussex, son of Pardon Tillinghast.
21. THE REVEREND PARDON TILLINGHAST, b. Seven Cliffs, co. Sussex, 1622, d. 29 Jan. 1718; sett. Providence, Rhode Island, 1643.

Line 37

11. ELIZABETH de PERCY (36-11); m. 1404, JOHN de CLIFFORD (113-9).
12. MARY de CLIFFORD; m. Sir Philip Wentworth, son of Sir Roger Wentworth, Knt., of North Elmsall, and MARGERY DESPENSER (74-10). (CP IV, 292).
13. SIR HENRY WENTWORTH, KNT., Lord le Despencer, d. betw. 17 Aug. 1499 & 27 Feb. 1500/1, of Nettlestead; m. (l) 20 Feb. 1484, Anne, dau. of Sir John de Saye, Knt., and Elizabeth Cheyne, dau. of Lawrence Cheyne, of Ditton, co. Cambridge. (CP IV, 292-293).
14. SIR RICHARD WENTWORTH, Lord le Despencer, liv. 11 Nov. 1529, b. c. 1485, d. 17 Oct. 1528; m. Anne, dau. of Sir James Tyrelle, Knt., of Gippinge, co. Suffolk, by Anne, dau. of Sir John Arundelle, of Lanherne, co. Cornwall. (CP IV, 294).

15. DOROTHY WENTWORTH; m. Sir Lionel Talmache, son of Sir Lionel
Talmache, Esq., of Helmingham Hall, co. Suffolk.
16. MARY TALMACHE, bur. Depden, co. Suffolk, 6 Aug. 1606; m. John
Jermyn, Esq., of Rushbrook, bur. Depden, 25 Nov. 1606, elder son of Sir Thomas
Jermyn and ANNE (5-13), d. 1572, dau. of Sir Robert Drury of Hawstead. (See (74-
13).)
17. THOMAS JERMYN, ESQ., bp. Depden, co. Suffolk, 1561, d. c. 1617 (adm.
on his estate gr. 5 July 1617 to Sarah, his widow); m. (2) Sarah, d. Depden, 1641,
dau. of John Stephens of Althorn, co. Essex. (Harl. Soc. ms 1110, folio 113; Blois
and Jermyn mss).
18. JANE JERMYN; m. Depden, 1600, Thomas Wright, Esq., of Kilverston,
co. Norfolk, d. c. 1653 (will pr.), son of Thomas Wright and Agnes Fisher of Whittingham Magna, co. Norfolk.
19. JERMYN WRIGHT, of Wangford, co. Suffolk; m. Anne, dau. of Richard
Blatchford, Esq., of Bexwell, co. Norfolk. (Generations 18 and 19: Rushbrook
Parish Registers, 1567-1850, 1903, pp. 122-124).
20. SIR ROBERT WRIGHT, KNT., Chief Justice; entered his pedigree in
Suffolk Visitations, 1664; m. (2) Susan, dau. of the Rt. Rev. Matthew Wren, b. 1586,
d. 24 Apr. 1667, Bishop of Ely.
21. THE HON. ROBERT WRIGHT, d. 1757, Chief Justice of South Carolina,
1730-1739; m. the widow Isabella Pitts, d. 21 Nov. 1752, ae. 77 yrs. Their son,
SIR JAMES WRIGHT, d. 1786, was Governor of Georgia. (Generations 13 to 21: J.
J. Muskett, Suffolk Manorial Families, II 254-256; Visitations of Suffolk, 1561,
70-71, 74, 77, 190; Stephen Wren, History of the Wren Family, London, 1750;
Page, History of Suffolk).

Line 38

13. SIR HENRY WENTWORTH, KNT. (37-13); m. 20 Feb. 1484, Anne Saye.
14. MARGERY WENTWORTH, d. 1550; m. Sir John Seymour, b. 1476, d. 21
Dec. 1536, ae. 60 yrs., of Wolf Hall, Savernake, Wiltshire. (Their dau. Jane
Seymour (1509-1537), m. King Henry VIII, and they were the parents of King Edward
VI. DNB).
15. SIR HENRY SEYMOUR, K.B., 2nd son, of Marvel, Hampshire; m. Barbara, dau. of Thomas Morgan, Esq.
16. JANE SEYMOUR; m. Sir John Rodney, b. 1555, d. 6 Aug. 1612, of Stoke-
Rodney and Pilton, co. Somerset.
17. WILLIAM RODNEY, b. 1610, d. Hantsfield, co. Somerset, 12 June 1699;
m. Alice, dau. of Sir Thomas Caesar, b. 1561, d. 1610, baron of the Exchequer,
and his wife Susan, dau. of Sir William Ryder, Lord Mayor of London. (DNB).
17A. WILLIAM RODNEY; m. Rachel, liv. May 1708, named in son William's
will.
18. WILLIAM RODNEY, ESQ., bp. Bristol, 14 Mar. 1660, d. 8 Apr. 1708, ae.
56 yrs., came to Pennsylvania bef. 1681, and in 1704 became 1st Speaker of the
Delaware legislature; m. (1) Philadelphia, Pa., 1688, Mary Hollyman, d. 1692;
m. (2) Sarah Jones. (Generations 15 and 16: Visitations of Somerset, 1623, p. 94;
McCracken, Welcome Claimants (Welcome Soc. 1970), 439-460).

Line 39

13. MATILDA CLIFFORD (36-13); m. SIR EDMUND SUTTON, KNT. (80A-9).
14. DOROTHY SUTTON; m. Richard Wrottesley, of Wrottesley, High Sheriff
of Staffordshire, 1492, 1502, 1516.
15. ELEANOR WROTTESLEY; m. Richard Lee, Esq., of Langley, Salop.
16. DOROTHY LEE; m. (settlement, 27 July 1566), Thomas Mackworth, of
Betton Grange, liv. 10 Jan. 1585, son of John Mackworth and Elizabeth Hosier.
17. RICHARD MACKWORTH, of Betton Grange; m. Dorothy Cranage, dau.
of Laurence Cranage, gent.
18. AGNES MACKWORTH (sister of Colonel Humphrey Mackworth, of Betton
Grange, Governor of Shrewsbury); m. (1) Richard Watts, d. 1635; m. (2) bef. 1640,
Colonel William Crowne, gent., b. c. 1617, d. Boston, Massachusetts; appointed

Rouge-Dragon, 1638; Lieutenant-Colonel, 1650; was present at the coronation of
King Charles II, 1661. Their son, Henry Crowne, left issue. (NEHGR, 108: 176-
177).

Line 40

4. SIR GILBERT de CLARE, Earl of Gloucester and Hertford (28-4, 34-4);
m. 1290, Joan Plantagenet, dau. of King EDWARD I (161-14).
5. ELIZABETH de CLARE, ae. 19 or 20 in 1314, d. 4 Nov. 1360; m. bef. 3
May 1317, Roger Damory, Lord Damory, d. 13 or 14 Mar. 1321/2, of Bletchington,
co. Oxford, M.P., 1317-1321. (CP IV, 42-45).
6. ELIZABETH DAMORY, Lady Damory, only dau. and heir, b. sh. bef.
23 May 1318, living 1360, d. bef. 1363; m. Sir John Bardolf, Lord Bardolf, b. 13
Jan. 1313/4, d. Assisi, Italy, 29 July 1363, M.P., 1336-1363. (CP I, 418-419; IV,
45-46).
7. WILLIAM BARDOLF, Lord Bardolf, b. 21 Oct. 1349, d. 29 Jan. 1385/6,
M.P., 1375-1385; m. Agnes Poynings, d. 12 June 1403, dau. of Michael, Lord
Poynings, and Joan, dau. of Sir Richard Rokesley. (CP I, 414-419).
8. CICELY BARDOLF, d. 29 Sept. 1432; m. SIR BRIAN STAPLETON, KNT.
(49-8), q.v. (CP I, 414).

Line 41

2. SIR GILBERT de CLARE, M.C. (28-2); m. ISABEL MARSHAL (145-2).
3. ISABEL de CLARE, b. 2 Nov. 1226, d. aft. 10 July 1264; m. as his 1st
wife, May 1240, Sir Robert de Brus, b. 1210, d. Lochmaben Castle, 31 Mar. 1295,
Lord of Anandale, son of Robert de Brus, d. 1251, and Isabella, dau. of David of
Huntingdon and Maud of Chester. (CP II, 258-260; III, 55-56).
4. SIR ROBERT de BRUS, b. July 1243, d. bef. 14 June 1304, Earl of Carrick, Lord of Anandale; m. (1) N. by whom had Isabel, m. Thomas Randolph,
Chamberlain of Scotland; m. (2) Turnberry, 1271, as her 1st husb., Margaret,
Countess of Carrick, d. 1292, dau. of Nigel, Earl of Carrick, and Margaret, dau.
of Walter, 3rd High Steward of Scotland. (CP II, 360; III, 55-56; IX, 167, note c).
5. ROBERT de BRUCE I, Earl of Carrick, b. Writtle, co. Essex, 11 July
1274, d. Cadross, Sootland, 7 June 1329, King of Scots, 27 Mar. 1306-1329; a national hero of Scotland; m. (1) c. 1295, Isabel, d. 1297, dau. of Donald, Earl of Mar,
by his first wife, Helen, dau. of Llewellyn ap Iorwerth, Prince of Wales. (CP I,
310-311; II, 360; III, 55-56; VIII, 403, note g).
6. MARJORY de BRUCE, d. 2 Mar. 1316; m. 1315, Walter Stewart, b. 1292,
d. 9 Apr. 1326 (bur. at Paisley, Scotland), High Steward of Scotland, son of James
Stewart (d. 1309) and Cecilia, dau. of Patrick, Earl of Dunbar. (CP I, 310-311;
DNB LIV 294-295).
7. ROBERT II STEWART, b. 2 Mar. 1315/6, d. Dundonald Castle, 19 Apr.
1390, Earl of Atholl, 1341, Earl of Strathern, 1358, King of Scotland, 22 Feb. 1370/1-
1390; m. (1) 22 Nov. 1347 (Papal dispensation), Elizabeth, dau. of Sir Adam Mure, of
Rowallan, co. Ayr, and Joan Cunningham. (CP I, 310-311; III, 58; XII (1), 389).
8. ROBERT III STEWART (called John at birth), b. 1347, d. 4 Apr. 1406,
Earl of Carrick, 22 June 1368, King of Scotland, 1390-1406; m. in or bef. 1367, Annabella, d. 1401, dau. of Sir John Drummond and Mary Pontifex, of Stobhall. (CP I, 154-
155; III, 58).
9. MARY STEWART, liv. 1458; m. (1) 24 May 1397 (marriage contract),
George Douglas, 1st Earl of Angus, 1389-1402, d. of the plague in England, 1402.
(CP I, 154-155; VI, 421).
10. MARY DOUGLAS; m. Sir David Hay of Locherworth and Yester, d. betw.
3 Apr. and 2 Sept. 1478. (CP VI, 421).
11. JOHN HAY, cr. Lord Hay of Yester, 29 Jan. 1487/8, d. bef. 23 Oct. 1508;
m. (2) 17 Dec. 1468 (marriage contract), Elizabeth, d. betw. 16 Dec. 1528 and 7
Dec. 1529, dau. of George Cunningham of Belton. (CP VI, 421-422, and note e).
12. JOHN HAY, 2nd Lord of Yester, killed at Flodden Field, 9 Sept. 1513; m.
Elizabeth Crichton, liv. 6 July 1524. (CP VI, 423).
13. CHRISTIAN HAY; m. 6 July 1524 (marriage contract), WILLIAM STEWART

(91-13), of Traquair, co. Peebles, liv. 1538, d. bef. 1548. (CP VI, 423, note j)

14. JAMES STEWART, of Traquair, d. 9 Mar. 1607; m. Katherine Ker, d. 28 Feb. 1606.

15. SIR ROBERT STEWART, of Schillinglaw, tutor to his nephew, the first Earl of Traquair, buried Feb. 1623; m. Alice, dau. of Samuel Cockburn of Temple.

16. CHRISTIAN STEWART; m. John Cranstoun of Bold, son of James Cranstoun of Bold in Traquair, and Jane Dewar. (NEHGR, 79: 63). Witness to a charter made at Edinburgh, 12 May 1608. (Reg. Great Seal, VI No. 2131; VII No. 25); named as "of Bold" in a charter in 1638. (NEHGR, 79: 64-65).

17. THE REVEREND JAMES CRANSTOUN, A.M., of St. Mary Overy, Southwark; one of the chaplains to King Charles I of England. (NEHGR, 79: 65-66).

18. GOVERNOR JOHN CRANSTON, b. c. 1626, brought to New England by Captain Jeremy Clarke in 1638, aged 12 years; settled at Newport, Rhode Island; Governor of Rhode Island, 8 Nov. 1678-1680; d. Newport, Rhode Island, 12 Mar. 1680; m. 3 June 1658, MARY CLARKE (100-17), dau. of Captain Jeremy Clarke. (NEHGR, 79: 57). (This line is used with the kind permission of Commander Peter G. Van der Poel. The research in English manuscript and printed material was carried out successfully by Anthony R. Wagner, Esquire, C.V.O., then Richmond Herald, College of Arms, London.)

Line 41A

9. MARY STEWART (41-9); m. George Douglas, 1st Earl of Angus.

10. ELIZABETH DOUGLAS; m. betw. 6 & 16 Oct. 1423, Sir Alexander Forbes, 1st Lord Forbes, b. c. 1380, d. 1448. (SP I, 174; SP IV, 47-9).

11. ANNABELLA FORBES; m. bef. 1445, Patrick Gray, Master of Gray, d.v.p. bef. 1 Sept. 1464, son of Andrew Gray, 1st Lord Gray, and Elizabeth, dau. of Sir John Wemyss of Rires and Isabel Erskine. (SP IV, 50, 273-5).

12. ELIZABETH GRAY; m. c. 1460, David Rollock or Rollo of Ballachie, d. bef. 1510, Lord Auditor of Causes, 1481-2, burgess and bailie of Dundee. (SP IV, 275; SP VII, 183).

13. ELIZABETH ROLLOCK or Rollo, d. in or bef. 1509; m. bef. 12 Mar. 1490/1, Sir Thomas Maule, laird of Panmure, slain at Flodden, 1513. (SP VII, 10, 184).

14. SIR ROBERT MAULE, laird of Panmure (111A-13); m. (2) ISABEL ARBUTHNOTT (91A-14), dau. of James Arbuthnott of that Ilk. (SP VIII, 10-12).

Line 41B

4. SIR ROBERT de BRUS, Lord of Anandale (41-4); m. Margaret, Countess of Carrick.

5. CHRISTIAN BRUCE, d. 1357; m. (1) Gratney, Earl of Mar, d. bef. 1305, son of Donald, Earl of Mar, by Helen or Elen, illegitimate dau. of Llewellyn ap Iorwerth, Prince of Wales, widow of Malcolm, Earl of Fife. (SP V, 577-9).

6. ELLEN of MAR, seen 1342; m. betw. 1320 & 1323, Sir John Menteith, Lord of Arran, d. c. 1344. (SP V, 579-80).

7. CHRISTIAN MENTEITH, d. c. 1387; m. (1) Sir Edward Keith of Synton, d. 1350; m. (2) 1352, as his 2nd wife, Sir Robert Erskine of Erskine, d. 1385, High Chamberlain of Scotland. He purchased the lands of Dun in 1348. (SP V, 580, 592-6).

8. JANET KEITH, d. 1413; m. (1) Sir David Barclay of Brechin, seen 1364, bro. of JEAN BARCLAY (108A-7); m. (2) bef. 13 Apr. 1370, Sir Thomas Erskine (son of her mother's 2nd husband by his 1st wife, Beatrice, dau. of Alexander Lindsay of Crawford), d. 1403, knighted betw. 1365 & 1370, keeper of Edinburgh Castle, Sheriff of Edinburgh. On 8 Nov. 1376 he had a royal charter of the barony of Dun on his father's resignation. (SP V, 580-1, 595-600; Alexander J. Warden, Angus of Forfarshire (Dundee, 1880), III, 171).

9. SIR JOHN ERSKINE, 2nd son, laird of Dun, seen 18 Mar. 1400 and 9 Nov. 1409, had on 25 Oct. 1392 a charter of the barony of Dun from Robert III on his father's resignation; m. N. (SP V, 600; The Scottish Antiquary VI (1892), 51; Warden, op. cit., III, 172).

10. ALEXANDER ERSKINE, laird of Dun, seen 1451; m. N. (The Scottish

Antiquary VI, 51).
11. JOHN ERSKINE, laird of Dun, d. 17 May 1504, had a charter of the barony of Dun on his father's resignation, 28 Jan. 1449; m. ELIZABETH GRAHAM of Fintry (43C-11). (The Scottish Antiquary VI, 51; John Guthrie Smith, Strathendrick (Glasgow, 1896), p. 155).

Line 41C

7. ROBERT II STEWART (41-7), King of Scots; m. (2) Euphemia, dau. of Hugh, Earl of Ross.
8. EDIGIA (or Jill) STEWART; m. 1387, Sir William Douglas, Lord of Nithsdale, d. c. 1392, illegitimate son of Sir Archibald Douglas, "the Grim," 3rd Earl of Douglas, who was the illegitimate son of Sir James Douglas, Lord of Galloway. Known to the Scots as "good Sir James," and to the English as "the Black Douglas," he was, with Wallace and Bruce, one of the three great heroes of Scottish independence. (CP IV, 431-3; SP I, 16; SP III, 142-6, 163-4).
9. EGIDIA (or Jill) DOUGLAS, seen 1438; m. bef. 17 Nov. 1407, Henry Sinclair, 2nd Earl of Orkney, b. c. 1375, d. 1 Feb. 1420/1, son of Henry Sinclair, Lord of Roslin, Earl of Orkney, and Jean, dau. of Sir Walter Haliburton of Dirleton. (CP X, 93-6; SP III, 164; SP VI, 570).
10. WILLIAM SINCLAIR, d. 1480, Lord Sinclair, 3rd Earl of Orkney (which earldom he resigned into the hands of King James III, 1470), cr. 28 Aug. 1455 Earl of Caithnes, Admiral of Scotland and High Chancellor; m. (1) ELIZABETH DOUGLAS (165-10), d. c. 1451, dau. of Archibald Douglas, 4th Earl of Douglas and Margaret, dau. of ROBERT III STEWART (41-8), King of Scots; m. (2) bef. 15 Nov. 1456, Marjory, dau. of Alexander Sutherland of Dunbeath. (CP II, 477-8; CP X, 96-7; SP VI, 571).
11. ELEANOR SINCLAIR, dau. by the 2nd wife, d. 21 Mar. 1518; m. bef. 19 Apr. 1475, as his 2nd wife, SIR JOHN STEWART of Balveny, Earl of Atholl (91A-11), b. c. 1440, d. 15 Sept. 1512. (CP I, 312-3; SP I, 441-2).

Line 41D

7. ROBERT II STEWART (41-7), King of Scots; m. (1) Elizabeth Mure.
8. ROBERT STEWART, Earl of Fife, Earl of Menteith, Duke of Albany, Great Chamberlain, Regent of Scotland, b. 1339, d. 2 Sept. 1420; m. (1) c. 1360, Margaret, d. betw. 20 July 1372 and 4 May 1380, suo juris Countess of Menteith. (CP VIII, 667-8; SP I, 146-9).
9. MARJORY STEWART, d. bef. Aug. 1432; m. Sir Duncan Campbell of Lochaw, co. Argyll, Justiciar of Argyll, cr. 1445, Lord Campbell, d. 1453. (CP II, 512-3; SP I, 149, 330-1).
10. ARCHIBALD CAMPBELL, Master of Campbell, seen 1414 and 24 Apr. 1431, d.v.p., bef. Mar. 1440; m. (1) Elizabeth, dau. of John Somerville, 3rd Lord Somerville. (CP III, 513; SP I, 332).
11. COLIN CAMPBELL, 2nd Lord Campbell, d. 19 May 1493, Justiciar of Scotland, cr. 1457; m. bef. 9 Apr. 1465, ISOBEL (or Elizabeth) (42A-11), eldest dau. of JOHN STEWART (42A-10), 2nd Lord Lorn. (CP I, 198-9; SP I, 334-5).
12. ARCHIBALD CAMPBELL, 2nd Earl of Argyll, named in 1500 Lieut.-Gen. of the Isles, slain at Flodden, 1513; m. ELIZABETH (15A-12), dau. of John Stewart, Lord Darnley, Earl of Lennox, and MARGARET (15A-11), dau. of ALEXANDER MONTGOMERY (15A-10), 1st Lord Montgomery. (CP I, 198-9; SP I, 334-5).
13. JANET CAMPBELL, d. c. 2 Feb. 1545-6; m. JOHN STEWART, 2nd Earl of Atholl (91A-12), d. 1521, son of SIR JOHN STEWART (91A-11), Earl of Atholl, by his 2nd wife, ELEANOR SINCLAIR (41C-11). (CP I, 313; CP IV, 434; SP I, 336, 441-3).

Line 41E

9. MARY STEWART (41-9), dau. of ROBERT III (41-8) King of Scots; m. George Douglas, 1st Earl of Angus.

30   [Line 41E

10. SIR WILLIAM DOUGLAS, 2nd Earl of Angus, d. Oct. 1437, Ambassador
to England, 1430, commanded the Scots in their victory over the English at the
battle of Piperdean, 10 Sept. 1436; m. (dispensation, 1425) Margaret, seen 22 Apr.
1484, dau. of Sir William Hay of Yester and Jean, dau. of Hew Gifford of Yester.
(CP I, 155; SP I, 174-5).

11. GEORGE DOUGLAS, d. 12 Mar. 1463, 4th Earl of Angus, suc. his bro.,
the 3rd earl, bef. 9 Sept. 1446, Warden of the Marches, Ambassador to England,
1451; m. as her first husband, Isabel, d. bef. Feb. 1502/3, only dau. of Sir John
Sibbald of Balgony, Master of the Household to King James II. (CP I, 156; SP I,
176-7).

12. ARCHIBALD DOUGLAS, "Bell the Cat," b. c. 1454, d. betw. 29 Nov.
1513 and 31 Jan. 1513/4, 5th Earl of Douglas, popularly called "The Great Earl,"
High Chancellor of Scotland, 1493-98; m. (1) 4 Mar. 1467/8, Elizabeth, d. bef. 21
Feb. 1497, only dau. of Robert Boyd, 1st Lord Boyd, Great Chamberlain of Scotland, and Mariot, dau. of Sir Robert Maxwell of Calderwood. (CP I, 156-7; SP I,
178-9).

13. GEORGE DOUGLAS, Master of Angus, b. c. 1469, d.v.p. at Flodden, 9
Sept. 1513; m. bef. Mar. 1487/8, Elizabeth, seen 21 Aug. 1514, dau. of John Drummond, 1st Lord Drummond, and ELIZABETH LINDSAY (43D-12). (CP I, 157).

14. ALISON DOUGLAS; m. (2) Sir David Home, 5th Laird of Wedderburn,
slain in battle with the English, July 1524, avenged the murder of his chief, Alexander, 3rd Lord Home, by assassinating Anthony de la Bastie, Sept. 1517. (The surname Home is pronounced, and frequently spelled, Hume.) (Alexander Ross and
Francis J. Grant (eds.) Alexander Nisbet's Heraldic Plates (Edinburgh, 1892), p.
50).

15. SIR DAVID HOME, 7th Laird of Wedderburn, suc. his bro., who was
slain at the battle of Pinkie, 10 Sept. 1547, d. July 1574; m. as her 2nd husband,
Mariot, d. 24 Feb. 1589, dau. of Andrew Johnston of Elphinston. (Ross and Grant,
ibid.).

16. SIR GEORGE HOME, 8th Laird of Wedderburn, d. 24 Nov. 1616, M.P.
for Berwickshire, 1590, 1592-4, 1604-5, Warden of the Marches, 1578. Comptroller of Scotland, 1597; m. Jean, dau. of John Haldane of Gleneagles. (Ross and
Grant, ibid.).

17. COL. SIR DAVID HOME, BT., 9th Laird of Wedderburn, served heir to
his father 10 Apr. 1617, slain at the battle of Dunbar, 3 Sept. 1650, M.P. for Berwickshire, 1621, 1639-41, 1645-6, 1649-50; m. (contract 6 Mar. 1607), MARGARET
HOME (91C-16), dau. of SIR JOHN HOME (91C-15), 4th Laird of Cowdenknows, and
his 1st wife, Marie, dau. of John Sinclair, Master of Caithness. (Ross and Grant,
ibid.; SP IV, 476; G.E. Cokayne, Complete Baronetage II, 442).

18. LIEUT.-COL. GEORGE HOME, younger of Wedderburn, slain with his
father at the battle of Dunbar, 3 Sept. 1650;m. contract 14 Aug. 1635, KATHERINE (111A-
16), bp. 16 Feb. 1615, dau. of Sir Alexander Morrison of Prestongrange and ELEANOR
MAULE (111A-15). (Ross and Grant, loc. cit. and p. 136; G E. Cokayne, loc.
cit.).

19. CAPT. SIR GEORGE HOME, BT., 10th Laird of Wedderburn, b. 1641,
d. bef. 1715, M.A., St. Andrews University, M.P. for Berwickshire, 1685, succeeded to his grandfather's baronetcy, 3 Sept. 1650; m. Isabel, dau. of Francis Liddell
of Ravensworth, co. Durham. (Ross and Grant, op. cit., 50; Cokayne, loc. cit.).

20. SIR GEORGE HOME, BT., 11th Laird of Wedderburn, d. 1720, Lieut.,
Grenadier Company, Royal Scots Fusileers, 1702, served with the Jacobite army in
the rising of 1715, captured at Preston, 14 Nov. 1715; convicted of high treason, his
baronetcy was forfeited and estates confiscated. (His younger bro. Francis Home
of Quixwood, advocate, was also captured at Preston.   Deported to Virginia,
where he died 1717, he became factor for his cousin, GOV. ALEXANDER SPOTS-
WOOD (43A-19).); m. (contract 3 Oct. 1695), Margaret, d. 13 Apr. 1765, eldest
dau. of Sir Patrick Home of Lumsden. (Ross and Grant, loc. cit; Cokayne, op.
cit., 442, note f; Sir Robert Douglas, The Peerage of Scotland (London, 1813), II,
175; Virginia Magazine of History and Biography, XXXVIII: 102-7, 336).

21. GEORGE HOME, 2nd son, b. at Wedderburn Castle, 30 May 1698, bp.
in the parish church of Duns, 4 Jan. 1698/9, d. Culpepper co., Virginia, betw. 2
Apr. and 19 June 1760; a Jacobite soldier, he was captured with his father at the
battle of Preston, 14 Nov. 1715; emigrated to Virginia, 1721; Surveyor, Spotsylvania
Co., 1728, Lieut., Spotsylvania Co. Militia, 1729. With George Washington as his
assistant, he surveyed Frederick Co., Virginia; m. 16 Dec. 1727, Elizabeth, dau.
of George Proctor of St. George's Parish, Spotsylvania Co., Va., by whom he left

issue. (Ross and Grant, loc. cit.; VMHB XXXVIII: 100, 108, 124, 130, 195-234, 293-305, 315-18, 345-6).

Line 41F

10. WILLIAM SINCLAIR (41C-10), 3rd Earl of Orkney, 1st Earl of Caithness; m. (2) Marjory Sutherland.

11. WILLIAM SINCLAIR, 2nd Earl of Caithness, slain at Flodden, 9 Sept. 1513; m. Margaret, dau. of Sir Gilbert Keith of Inverugy. (SP II, 337).

12. JOHN SINCLAIR, 3rd Earl of Caithness, slain at Somersdale, 18 May 1529; m. Elizabeth, dau. of William Sutherland of Duffus. (SP II, 337-8).

13. GEORGE SINCLAIR, 4th Earl of Caithness, d. at Edinburgh, 9 Sept. 1582; m. ELIZABETH GRAHAM (41G-14), dau. of WILLIAM GRAHAM (41G-13), 2nd Earl of Montrose. (SP II, 340-1).

14. JOHN SINCLAIR, Master of Caithness, eldest son, b. 1543, imprisoned by his father at Girnigo Castle under the most miserable conditions, he d.v.p. Sept. 1575, of "famine and vermine"; m. betw. 10 Dec. 1565 and 16 Jan. 1566/7, as her 2nd husband, JANE HEPBURN (91D-14), only dau. of PATRICK HEPBURN (91D-13), 3rd Earl of Bothwell, and Agnes Sinclair. (SP II, 160-1, 338-41; IX, 51).

15. MARIE SINCLAIR, seen 20 Feb. 1582, d. bef. 29 Oct. 1608, sister of George Sinclair, 5th Earl of Caithness; m. as his 1st wife, SIR JOHN HOME 4th Laird of Cowdenknows ('91C-15). (SP II, 342; IV, 474-5).

Line 41G

10. WILLIAM DOUGLAS, 2nd Earl of Angus (41E-10); m. Margaret Hay

11. HELEN DOUGLAS, seen 20 Nov. 1486; m. (l) bef. 1460, WILLIAM GRAHAM (43E-11), 2nd Lord Graham, M.P., d. 1472. (CP VI, 52-3; SP VI, 222-3; IX, 12).

12. WILLIAM GRAHAM, 3rd Lord Graham, b. c. 1463, slain at Flodden, 9 Sept. 1513, a familiar friend of James IV, he was cr. in 1503 Earl of Montrose; m. (l) 25 Nov. 1479, ANNABELL DRUMMOND (43D-13), dau. of John Drummond, 1st Lord Drummond. (SP VI, 223-5).

13. WILLIAM GRAHAM, 2nd Earl of Montrose, d. 24 May 1571, a Regent of Scotland, 1536, Privy Councillor to Mary, Queen of Scots, 1561; m. Dec. 1515, Janet, dau. of William Keith, 3rd Earl Marischal, by Elizabeth, dau. of George Gordon, 2nd Earl of Huntley. (SP VI, 226-9).

14. ELIZABETH GRAHAM, will recorded 4 Apr. 1576; m. bef. 1543, GOERGE SINCLAIR, 4th Earl of Caithness (41F-13). (SP II, 340).

Line 41H

7. ROBERT II STEWART (41-7), King of Scots; m. (l) Elizabeth Mure.

8. ELIZABETH STEWART; m. bef. 7 Nov. 1372, Sir Thomas Hay of Erroll, d. July 1406, Constable of Scotland, a hostage in England for the ransom of King David II in 1354. (CP XI, 187).

9. ELIZABETH HAY, seen Feb. 1397/8; m. bef. 1380, Sir George Leslie of Rothes, b. c. 1350, d. Feb. 1411/2, Sheriff of Fife, 1409. (CP XI, 186-7; SP III, 562; VII, 273).

10. SIR NORMAN LESLIE of Rothes, b. c. 1380, d. betw. 19 May 1439 and 3 Feb. 1439/40, a hostage for the ransom of King James I, 1425-7; m. (dispensation 2 Sept. 1416), Christian, dau. of Sir John Seton of Seton. (CP XI, 187).

11. GEORGE LESLIE of Rothes, b. bef. but legitimated by his parents' marriage, d. betw. 31 Aug. 1489 and 24 May 1490, cr. 1445 Lord Leslie, cr. 1457 Earl of Rothes; m. (2) Christian, dau. of Walter Haliburton of Dirleton, by his 2nd wife, Isobel, dau. of ROBERT STEWART, Duke of Albany (41D-8).

12. CHRISTIAN LESLIE, seen 22 Feb. 1492/3, d. bef. 16 Mar. 1500/1; m. (dispensation 29 Apr. 1458), WILLIAM SINCLAIR (165-11), 2nd Lord Sinclair, d. sh. aft. 14 July 1487. (CP XI, 737-8).

Line 42

5. ROBERT BRUCE I (41-5), b. 11 July 1274, d. 7 June 1329, Earl of Carrick, King of Scots, 1306-1329; m. (2) Elizabeth de Burgh, d. 26 Oct. 1327, dau. of Richard de Burgh, Earl of Ulster, son of Walter de Burgh and AVALINA FITZ JOHN (15-4), and his wife Margaret (or Margery) de Burgh, dau. of SIR JOHN de BURGH (55-3) and CECILY de BALIOL (140-3). (CP II, 360).

6. MATILDA de BRUCE, d. 20 July 1353; m. Thomas Isaac (or Ysac).

7. JOANNA Isaac; m. John de Ergardia, Lord of Lorn.

8. ISOBEL de ERGARDIA, d. 21 Dec. 1439; m. Sir John Stewart, d. 26 Apr. 1421, Lord of Innermeath and Lorn.

9. CHRISTIAN STEWART; m. James de Dundas, d. bef. Nov. 1451.

10. (DAU.) de DUNDAS; m. Sir Alexander Livingston, executed 1431, Lord of Callender.

11. SIR JAMES LIVINGSTON, of Callender, d. c. 26 Apr. 1467; m. Marian of Berwick, d. betw. 4 June and 19 Oct. 1478, widow of William Olyphant, and dau. of Thomas of Berwick.

12. SIR ALEXANDER LIVINGSTON, Lord of Callender, d. bef. 1 Nov. 1472; wife unknown.

13. SIR JAMES LIVINGSTON, of Callender, d. c. 1505; m. (1) c. 1470, Beatrice (or Elizabeth) Fleming, b. c. 1451, d. c. 1491, dau. of Robert Fleming, 1st Lord Flemingsby, by his 1st wife, Janet Douglas.

14. SIR WILLIAM LIVINGSTON, of Callender, d. bef. 25 Apr. 1518; m. bef. 5 Apr. 1501, Agnes Hepburn, dau. of Alexander Hepburn, the Younger, of Whitsome.

         *   *   *   *   *   *

Note: SP V, 435, note 3 doubts this connection.

15. JAMES LIVINGSTON, slain at the battle of Pinkie, near Edinburgh, 10 Sept. 1547; m. c. 1544, wife, name unknown.

17. REVEREND ALEXANDER LIVINGSTON, Rector of Monyabroch, d. c. 1598; m. c. 1570, Barbara Livingston, "of the House of Kilsyth," dau. of Alexander Livingston of Inches, by his 1st wife, Barbara Forrester.

17. REVEREND WILLIAM LIVINGSTON, Rector of Monyabroch, b. c. 1576, d. Lanark, 1641; m. Falkirk, 6 Jan. 1601, Agnes Livingston, dau. of Alexander Livingston of Falkirk, by Marian Bryson of Falkirk.

18. REVEREND JOHN LIVINGSTON, of Ancrum, b. Kilsyth, 21 June 1603, d. Rotterdam, Holland, Aug. 1672; m. Edinburgh, 13 June 1635, Janet Fleming, b. 1613, d. Rotterdam, Feb. 1690/1, dau. of Bartholomew Fleming by Marian Hamilton. (See van Rensselaer, The Livingston Family in America, 1949, p. 6.)

19. COLONEL ROBERT LIVINGSTON, 13th son, b. 13 Dec. 1654, d. 1728; m. Albany, New York, 1674, Alida (Schuyler) van Rensselaer; became lord of the Manor of Livingston, in New York Province, 1686; Speaker of the N.Y. legislature, 1718-1725, Colonel in the Provincial militia.

19. JAMES LIVINGSTON (brother of Col. Robert above), b. Stranraer, Scotland, 22 Sept. 1646, d. 1700; m. (1) name of wife unknown.

20. ROBERT LIVINGSTON (son of James); m. 1697, Margaretta Schuyler, d. 1725, dau. of Colonel Peter Schuyler. (Edwin Brockholst Livingston, Livingston of Callender; E.B. Livingston, The Livingstons of Livingston Manor, 1910, p. 6, chart, p. 74; Florence van Rensselaer, The Livingston Family in America, N.Y., 1949).

Line 42A

8. ISOBEL de ERGARDIA (42-8); m. Sir John Stewart of Innermeath and Lorn.

9. ROBERT STEWART, a hostage for the ransom of James I in 1424, cr. bef. 5 Sept. 1439, Lord Lorn, d. bef. 1449; m. (dispensation 27 Sept. 1397) Joan, dau. of ROBERT STEWART, Duke of Albany (41D-8), prob. by his 1st wife, Margaret Graham, Countess of Menteith. (CP VIII, 138; SP V, 2-3).

10. JOHN STEWART, Lord Lorn, M.P., 1445, 1449, seen 20 June 1452, d.s.p.m. 20 Dec. 1463; m. N. (CP VIII, 138-9; SP V, 3).

11. ELIZABETH (or Isobel) STEWART, d. 26 May 1510; m. bef. 9 Apr. 1465, COLIN CAMPBELL (41D-11), Earl of Argyll, Lord High Chancellor of Scotland. (SP I, 332; V, 3-4).

Line 43

7. ROBERT II STEWART (41-7), King of Scots; m. (1) Elizabeth Mure; m. (2) Eupheme, dau. of Hugh, Earl of Ross, and widow of John Randolph, Earl of Moray. (Generations 7 and 8: Dunbar, Scottish Kings, 159-160: CP III, 507-509).

8. ELIZABETH STEWART (by the 2nd wife); m. (dispensation, 22 Feb. 1374/5), Sir David Lindsay, Earl of Crawford, 1381-1400, b. c. 1360, d. Feb. 1406/7, ae. 41 yrs., Admiral of Scotland, bef. Oct. 1403. (Generations 8 to 16: CP III, 507-509; Lindsay, W.M.C., Lives of the Lindsays, I, 98-99, 120-133, 132, 381-382, 385, 394, 396; SP I, 16; II, 570; III, 15-20, cf. 19 notes 13 to 16, 507-515).

9. SIR ALEXANDER LINDSAY, KNT., Earl of Crawford, b. c. 1387, d. 1438, aft. 31 Mar., Ambassador to England, 1429-1430; m. bef. 1410, Marjory, prob. a dau. of the Earl of Dunbar. (CP III, 509).

10. SIR DAVID LINDSAY, KNT., 3rd Earl of Crawford, Sheriff of Aberdeen, d. 17 Jan. 1445/6; m. (papal dispensation, 4 Mar. 1422/3), Marjory, living 1460, dau. of Alexander Ogilvie, of Auchterhouse. (CP III, 509-511, chart p. 511).

11. SIR WALTER LINDSAY, of Beaufort and Edzell, d. 1475; m. Isabella Livingstone of Saltcoats. She m. (2) William, Lord Ruthven. (CP III chart p. 511, 515).

12. SIR DAVID LINDSAY, of Beaufort and Edzell, M.P., 1487, d. 1528; m. (1) Katherine, dau. of Thomas Fotheringham of Powrie. (Ibid.).

13. SIR WALTER LINDSAY, killed at Flodden Field, 9 Sept. 1513; m. N. (43C-12) dau. of John Erskine of Dun. (Ibid.)

14. ALEXANDER LINDSAY, 2nd son, of Edzell, d. 1558; m. a dau. of Barkley of Mathers.

15. RT. REV. DAVID LINDSAY, b. 1532, of Pittorlie, Dec. 1576, d. 14 Aug. 1613, ae.81 yrs.; minister at Leith and Bishop of Ross, 1600-1613; member of the Privy Council (m. King James IV of Scotland to Anne of Denmark; baptized Prince Henry; attended the coronation of King James I of England; and baptized King Charles I); m. (1) Janet, dau. of George Ramsey of Clattie. (SP III, 19 and notes 13 to 16)

16. SIR JEROME LINDSAY, d. 1642, Lord of Annatland and the Mount, Commissary of Edinburgh, 10 Nov. 1642; m. (1) Margaret Colville, d. 10 May 1603, dau. of John Colville and Janet Russell.

17. THE REVEREND DAVID LINDSAY, bp. South Leith, 2 Jan. 1602/3, d. Cherry Neck Point, Virginia, 3 Apr. 1667 (GS) (will dated 2 Apr. 1667), matriculated, St. Andrews, 1618, grad. 1621, ord. and came to Virginia, c. 1640; m. (1) wife, name unknown, d. bef. 1652; m. (2) Susannah (no issue by the 2nd marr.). (M.I. Lindsay, Lindsays of America, 26-35; Wm. & Mary Quarterly, 1st series, XVI (1907), p. 16).

Line 43A

15. RT. REV. DAVID LINDSAY (43-15), b. 1532, d. 14 Aug. 1613, Bishop of Ross, 1600-1613; m. (1) Janet, dau. of George Ramsay of Clattie. (SP III, 19; Hew Scott, Fasti Ecclesiae Scoticanae (Edinburgh, 1915-1928), I, 160-1).

16. RACHEL LINDSAY; m. 1599, Rt. Rev. John Spotswood or Spottiswood of Dairsey, b. 1565, d. 26 Nov. 1639, bur. in Westminster Abbey; M.A. Glasgow University, 1581; Privy Councillor, 1605; Archbishop of St. Andrews, 1615-1637; crowned King Charles I at Holyrood, 1633; chancellor of Scotland, 1635. (Scott, op. cit., I, 175-6; SP III, 20; DNB XVIII, 802-823).

17. SIR ROBERT SPOTSWOOD or Spottiswood of Dunipage, Sterlingshire, 2nd son, b. 1596, executed 16 Jan. 1646; M.A., Glasgow University, 1613; Privy Councillor, 1622; Lord President of the College of Justice, 1638; Secretary of State for Scotland, 1643; m. 6 June 1629, BETHIA (111A-16), d. 17 Nov. 1639, dau. of Sir Alexander Morrison of Prestongrange, Haddington, by ELEANOR (111A-15), dau. of WILLIAM MAULE (111A-14) (41A-14) of Glaster and Edinburgh. (Andrew Ross and Francis J. Grant (eds.) Alexander Nisbet's Heraldic Plates (Edinburgh, 1892), p. 136; DNB XVIII, 824-5; Spotswood Papers (mss.), Colonial Williamsburg, Williamsburg, Virginia).

18. ROBERT SPOTSWOOD, b. Edinburgh, 17 Sept. 1637, d. 1688, 4th son; to Tangiers with the Earl of Middleton, 1669; author of a work in Latin, "A Catalogue of Plants Growing Within the Fortification of Tangier" (1673), published in Philosophical Transactions, XIX (London, 1698) 239-49, commission as surgeon to the

British garrison at Tangiers signed at Whitehall, 1 Mar. 1677; m. Catherine Mercer, d. in Ireland betw. 24 Dec. 1709 and 14 Mar. 1710, widow of William Elliott of Wells, by whom she was the mother of Roger Elliott, ensign of the Tangier Regiment of Foot, later major general and Governor of Gibraltar. (Sir Robert Spottishwood, Practicks of the Laws of Scotland (Edinburgh, 1706), p. xl; Charles Dalton, English Army Lists and Commission Registers, 1661-1714 (London, 1892), I: 229; James Maidment (ed.) The Spottiswoode Miscellany (Edinburgh, 1844), I: 187-8; Sir Robert Douglas, The Baronage of Scotland (Edinburgh, 1798), pp. 448-9; Spotswood Papers (mss.); VMHB XIII: 95-9).

19. MAJ. GEN. ALEXANDER SPOTSWOOD, b. Tangiers, 1676, d. Annapolis, Maryland, 7 June 1740; lieutenant quartermaster-general under Lord Cadogan during the War of the Spanish Succession; wounded at Blenheim; appointed Lt. Governor of Virginia 23 June 1710 and served until 1722; appointed postmaster general for the American colonies, 1730; commissioned major general of British colonial troops, 1740; m. London, 1724, Anne Butler Brayne, dau. of Richard and Anne Brayne of St. Margaret's, Westminster. (Douglas, op. cit., pp. 448-9; DNB XVIII: 817-8; DAB XVII: 467-9; VMHB LX: 211-240; Spotswood Papers (mss.)).

Line 43B

13. SIR WALTER LINDSAY (43-13); m. N. (43C-12), dau. of John Erskine.

14. DAVID LINDSAY, 9th Earl of Crawford, M.P., 1542-43, P.C., 1546, d. 20 Sept. 1558; m. (2) 1549, Catherine, d. 1578, dau. of ARCHIBALD CAMPBELL (41D-12), 2nd Earl of Argyll, by ELIZABETH (15A-12), dau. of John Stewart,, 1st Earl of Lennox. (CP I, 119; CP III, 515; SP III, 28-9).

15. SIR DAVID LINDSAY of Edzell, Senator of the College of Justice, d. Dec. 1610; m. (1) 1570, Helen, d. Dec. 1579, dau. of David Lindsay, 10th Earl of Crawford, by Margaret, illegit. dau. of His Eminence, David Cardinal Bethune (or Beaton), Archbishop of St. Andrews and Papal Legate, by Marion, dau. of James Ogilvie, 1st Lord Ogilvie of Airlie. (CP III, 515, note c; CP XII (1), 140; SP III, 29-30; Walter Macfarlane, Genealogical Collections Concerning Families in Scotland (Edinburgh, 1900), I: 9; DNB II, 17-18).

16. MARGARET LINDSAY, d. 9 July 1614; m. (contract 8 Oct. 1595) David Carnegie, b. 1575, d. 1657/8, cr. Lord Carnegie of Kinnaird, 1616, cr. Earl of Southesk, 1633. (CP XII (1), 140; Macfarlane, I: 9).

17. CATHERINE CARNEGIE, seen 1 Nov. 1655; m. (contract 14 Sept. 1620), Sir John Stuart, b. c. 1600, M.P., 1621, knighted bef. 29 Jan. 1621/2, P.C., 1627, cr. Lord Stuart of Traquair, 1628, cr. Earl of Traquair, 1633; Lord High Treasurer of Scotland; d. 27 Mar. 1659; grandson of JAMES STEWART of Traquair (41-14); son of John Stewart, d.v.p., by Margaret, dau. of Andrew Stewart of Ochiltree. (CP XII (2), 6-9).

18. JOHN STUART, 2nd Earl of Traquair, b. aft. 8 Mar. 1623/4, d. Apr. 1666; m. (2) Anne, dau. of George Seton, 3rd Earl of Winton, by Elizabeth, dau. of John Maxwell, 6th Lord Herries of Terregles. (CP XII (2), 9-10).

19. CHARLES STUART, 4th Earl of Traquair, b. 1659, d. 1741; m. 9 Jan. 1693/4, Mary, dau. of Robert Maxwell, 4th Earl of Nithsdale, by Lucy, dau. of William Douglas, 1st Marquess of Douglas, and MARGARET HAMILTON (92A-16). (CP XII (2), 11).

20. JOHN STUART, 6th Earl of Traquair, b. 3 Feb. 1698/9, d. 28 Mar. 1799; one of the seven founders of the Association of Scottish Jacobites; m. 1740, Christian, dau. of Sir Philip Anstruther of Anstrutherfield, by Elizabeth, dau. of James Hamilton. (CP XII (2), 13).

21. CHRISTINA STUART, b. 1741, d. Williamsburg, Virginia, 1807; m. Edinburgh, 29 Apr. 1770, Cyrus Griffin, b. Richmond Co., Va., 16 July 1748, d. Yorktown, Va., 14 Dec. 1810; studied law at Edinburgh University, admitted to the Middle Temple, London, 31 May 1771; President of the Continental Congress, 1788. (DAB VII, 619; VMHB, I: 25-6; XXIII, 58-9; George Crawfurd, A General Description of the Shire of Renfrew Including an Account of the Noble and Ancient Families... Published in 1710...and Continued to the Present Period by George Robertson (Paisley, 1818), p. 467; John Insley Coddington, "Ancestors and Descendants of Lady Christina Stuart (1741-1807) Wife of the Hon. Cyrus Griffin of Virginia," NGSQ, 52: 25-36).

Line 43C

9. MARY STEWART (41-9), liv. 1458; m. (3) bef. 1416 (as his 2nd wife), Sir William Graham of Kincardine, taken prisoner at the battle of Homildon Hill, 14 Sept. 1402, auditor in Exchequer, 1405-1418, d. 1424. (SP I, 18; VI, 217).

10. SIR ROBERT GRAHAM, 1st laird of Fintry, Provost of Dundee, 1465, d. bef. 7 Jan. 1492/3; m. (1) Janet, dau. of Sir Richard Lovell of Ballumbie; m. (2) Matilda, dau. of Sir James Scrimgeour of Dudhope. (SP VI, 218-9; John Guthrie Smith, Strathendrick (Glasgow, 1896), pp. 154-6).

11. ELIZABETH GRAHAM, d. 15 Mar. 1508, dau. of Sir Robert Graham, prob. by his 1st wife; m. JOHN ERSKINE (41B-11), laird of Dun, d. 17 May 1504. (Smith, loc. cit.; cf. Northern Notes and Queries, IV (1890) 117-8, which, however, confuses Elizabeth with her sister Marjory, who m. Andrew Haliburton of Pitcur).

12. N. ERSKINE; m. SIR WALTER LINDSAY (43-13), slain at Flodden, 1513. (SP III, 19; CP III, 515; Northern Notes and Queries, IV (1890) 118).

Line 43D

10. SIR DAVID LINDSAY (43-10), 3rd Earl of Crawford; m. Marjory Ogilvie.

11. SIR ALEXANDER LINDSAY,"The Tiger," 4th Earl of Crawford, d. Sept. 1453, Sheriff of Aberdeenshire 1445-1452, Ambassador to England, 1451, Guardian of the Marches, 1453; m. as her 1st husb., MARGARET DUNBAR (108B-9), d. betw. July 1498 and Jan. 1499/1500, dau. of SIR DAVID DUNBAR of Cockburn (108B-8). (CP III, 510; SP III, 21).

12. ELIZABETH LINDSAY, seen 22 Sept. 1509; m. John Drummond, lord of Stobhall, b. c. 1438, d. 1519, son of Sir Malcolm Drummond of Stobhall by Mariot, dau. of Sir David Murray of Tullibardine; M.P. 1471, Seneschal of Stratherene, 1473, cr. 29 Jan. 1487/8, Lord Drummond. (CP IV, 469).

13. ANNABELL DRUMMOND, 4th dau., seen 1492, d. bef. 17 Mar. 1504/5; m. 25 Nov. 1479, as his 1st wife, WILLIAM GRAHAM (41G-12), 1st Earl of Montrose, b. 1463 or 1464, slain at Flodden, 9 Sept. 1513. (CP IV, 469, note e; IX, 146; SP VI, 225).

Line 43E

8. ELIZABETH STEWART (43-8), dau. of ROBERT II, King of Scots (43-7) (41-7); m. Sir David Lindsay, 1st Earl of Crawford.

9. ELIZABETH LINDSAY; m. soon aft. 20 Dec. 1400, Sir Robert Erskine of Erskine, d. betw. 7 Sept. 1451 and 6 Nov. 1452, cr. 1438 Lord Erskine, assumed 1438 the title Earl of Mar. (CP V, 104).

10. CHRISTIAN ERSKINE, seen 1479, 2nd dau.; m. Patrick Graham, d. 1466, a hostage in England 1427-32 for the ransom of King James I, cr. 28 June 1445, Lord Graham. (CP VI, 52-3).

11. WILLIAM GRAHAM, 2nd Lord Graham, b. 1742; m. bef. 1460, HELEN (41G-11), seen 20 Nov. 1468, dau. of SIR WILLIAM DOUGLAS (41E-10), 2nd Earl of Angus, by Margaret Hay. (CP VI, 53; SP VI, 222-3; IX, 12).

Line 44

1. JOHN FITZ ROBERT (156-3), Magna Charta Surety, 1215, lord of Wark-worth, co. Northampton, d. 1240; m. (2) Ada de Baliol, d. Stokesley, 29 July 1251, dau. of Hugh de Baliol of Barnard Castle and Cicely de Fontaines. Ada was sister of John de Baliol who m. Devorgilla of Galloway. (Clay, 5, 21).

2. ROGER FITZ JOHN, d. Normandy, about Whitsun 1249, lord of Warkworth and of Clavering; m. Isabel. (Clay, 21).

3. ROBERT FITZ ROGER, b. 1247, d. 1310, Lord fitz Roger of Clavering, M.P., 1295-1309; m. 1265, Margery de la Zouche. (Clay, 21; CP III, 274).

4. EUPHEMIA de CLAVERING; m. as 1st wife, Randolph de Neville, b. 18

Oct. 1262, d. shortly aft. 18 Apr. 1331, 1st Lord Neville of Raby. (CP IX, 497).

5. RALPH de NEVILLE, Lord Nevill of Raby, ae 40+ at father's death, b.c. 1291, d. 5 Aug. 1367; m. lic. 14 Jan. 1326/7, ALICE de AUDLEY (150-6), d. 13 Jan. 1373/4. (CP IX, 499).

6. MARGARET de NEVILLE, d. May 1372; m. (1) William de Ros, Lord Ros, of Helmsley, b. Frieston, Lincs., 19 May 1329, d. bef. 3 Dec. 1352, s.p.; m. (2) 12 July 1358, Henry de Percy, K.G., cr. 1377, Earl of Northumberland, b. 10 Nov. 1341, slain 19 Feb. 1407/8, son of HENRY de PERCY (152-6) and Mary Plantagenet, dau. of Henry de Lancaster and MAUD de CHAWORTH (4-6). (CP IX, 708).

7. SIR HENRY de PERCY, K.G., "Harry Hotspur", b. 20 May 1364, d.v.p., slain at Shrewsbury, 21 July 1403; m. bef. 10 Dec. 1379, ELIZABETH MORTIMER (36-10). (CP IX, 713).

8. SIR HENRY de PERCY, K.G., b.3 Feb. 1392/3, slain at St. Albans, 22 May 1455, Earl of Northumberland, 1403, K.B., 1400, Warden of the Marches of Scotland; m. sh. aft. Oct. 1414 ELEANOR de NEVILLE (45-8) (CP IX, 715).

9. SIR HENRY de PERCY, KNT., b. 25 July 1421, slain at Towton Field, 29 Mar. 1461, Earl of Northumberland; m. on or about 25 June 1435, Eleanor Poynings, d. Feb. 1483/4, dau. of Richard Poynings, Lord Poynings.

10. MARGARET de PERCY; m. Sir William Gascoigne, Knt., d. 1486, of Gawthorpe, co. York, son of Sir William Gascoigne of Gawthorpe and JANE de NEVILLE (102-11), q.v. (CP IX, 717, note d).

11. DOROTHY GASCOIGNE, d. 4 Mar. 1486; m. Sir Ninian Markenfield, Knt., of Markenfield Hall, Ripon, co. York, Commander at Flodden Field, 1513.

12. ALICE MARKENFIELD; m. c. 1 Dec. 1524, Sir Robert Mauleverer, bur. Bardsay, 31 Jan. 1540/1.

13. DOROTHY MAULEVERER; m. Bardsay, 21 Jan. 1542/3, John Kaye, Esq., of Woodsome, co. York, 1585.

14. ROBERT KAYE, ESQ., of Woodsome, liv. 1612, J.P.; m. Anne Flower, dau. of John Flower of Whitewell, co. Rutland.

15. GRACE KAYE; m. Sir Richard Saltonstall, of Huntwick, b. 1586, d. c. 1658, one of the patentees of Massachusetts and Connecticut; sett. Watertown, Massachusetts, 1630, J.P.

16. MAJOR RICHARD SALTONSTALL, ESQ., b. 1610, d. 1694; sett. Watertown, Massachusetts, 1630, Ipswich, 1634; m. June 1633, MURIEL GURDON (18-18), q.v.

Line 45

Note: Generations 12-14 are different from those shown in previous editions.

5. RALPH de NEVILLE (44-5); m. ALICE de AUDLEY (150-6).

6. JOHN de NEVILLE, K.G., Lord Neville of Raby, b. c. 1331, d. Newcastle, 17 Oct. 1388, K.G., 1369; m. (1) MAUD PERCY (8-8), d. 18 Feb. 1378/9. (CP IX, 502).

7. SIR RALPH de NEVILLE, K.G., b. c. 1346, d. Raby, 21 Oct. 1425, (see 8-9) cr. 1st Earl of Westmoreland, 1397; m. (1) MARGARET STAFFORD (136-8), d. 9 June 1396; m. (2) bef. 29 Nov. 1396, Joan Beaufort, d. Howden, 13 Nov. 1440, wid. of Robert Ferrers, dau. of JOHN (161-17), son of KING EDWARD III (161-16) of England and Philippa of Hainaut. (CP XII (2), 544).

8. ELEANOR de NEVILLE (by 2nd wife); m. Berwick, sh. aft. Oct. 1414, SIR HENRY de PERCY, K.G. (44-8), Earl of Northumberland. (CP IX, 715).

9. KATHERINE de PERCY, b. 28 May 1423; m. bef. Jan. 1458/9, Edmund Grey, Lord Grey of Ruthin, Earl of Kent, b. 26 Oct. 1416, d. 22 May 1490. (CP VII, 164).

10. ANNE GREY; m. Sir John Grey of Wilton, d. 3 Apr. 1499, son of Reynold de Grey of Wilton, and Tacyn Beaufort, natural dau. of JOHN BEAUFORT (161-18), Duke of Somerset. (CP VI, 180).

11. EDMUND GREY, b. c. 1469, ae 30+ at father's death, d. 5 May 1511, Lord Grey of Wilton; m. bef. May 1505, Florence Hastings, dau. of Sir Ralph and Anne Hastings.

12. TACY GREY, b. c. 1490, bur. at Elmore, co. Gloucester, 15 Nov. 1558; m. c. 1510, John Gyse, Esq., b. c. 1485, d. 20 Dec. 1556, bur. at Elmore, son of Sir John Gyse of Aspley Gyse and Agnes Berkeley of Stoke Giffard. (Sir Robert

Atkyns, ... State of Gloucestershire..., 1712, p. 325; Burke, Peerage and Baronetage, 1949, p. 899).
   13. WILLIAM GUISE, b. c. 1514, d. 7 Sept. 1574, bur. at Elmore; m. bef.
1540, Mary Rotsy, bur. at Elmore, 24 Nov. 1558, dau. of John Rotsy of Kings Norton, co. Worcester, by Margaret, dau. of John Walsh of Sheldesby Walsh, co. Worcester.
   14. JOHN GYSE, b. c. 1540, d. 24 Jan. 1587/8, bur. at Elmore; m. at Elmore,
22 Jan. 1564, Jane Paunceforte, bur. at Elmore, 27 June 1587, dau. of Richard
Paunceforte of Hasfield, co. Gloucester.
   15. ELIZABETH GUISE, bp. Elmore, 1 Aug. 1576; m. Kenn, co. Somerset,
7 July 1604, Robert Haviland, Esq., of Hawkesbury Barnes, co. Gloucester, bp. at
St. Werbergh's Church, Bristol, 11 Feb. 1577, bur. at Bristol, 19 July 1648, son of
Matthew Haviland of Bristol and Mary, dau. of Robert Kytchin of Bristol. Matthew
Haviland, Esq., of Hawkesbury Barnes, son of Robert Haviland and Elizabeth Guise,
by will proved at Canterbury, 4 Feb. 1671, mentions his "sister Jane, late wife of
William Torrey, Gent., of New Ingland." (Chronicle of the de Havilands, pp. 74,
77-78; Haviland Genealogy, p. 399. For generations 12 to 15, see Sir John MacLean,
"Elmore and the Family of Guise," in Transactions of the Bristol and Gloucestershire
Archaeological Society, vol. 3 (1878-1879), pp. 49-78, particularly 69-71; for generation 15, also see The Visitation of Gloucestershire, 1623, in Harl. Soc. Publ., vol. XXI).
   16. JANE HAVILAND, bp. 2 Aug. 1612; m. 27 Apr. 1629, Captain William
Torrey, bp. 21 Dec. 1618, d. Weymouth, Massachusetts, 10 June 1690, son of Philip
Torrey and Alice Richards; Deputy, and member of the Ancient and Honorable Ar-
tillery Company of Boston.
   17. WILLIAM TORREY, b. England, 1638, d. Weymouth, Mass., 11 Jan.
1717/8; m. c. 1669, Deborah Greene, b. Warwick, Rhode Island, 10 Aug. 1649, d.
Weymouth, 8 Feb. 1728/9, dau. of Deputy-Governor John Greene and Ann Almy.
They had a son: DEACON HAVILAND TORREY, b. 1684, who left issue. (NEHGR,
108: 117. In this reference by error two generations were interpolated between
Edmund Grey (No. 11) and Tacy Grey (No. 12) his daughter.)

                                   Line 46

   7. SIR RALPH de NEVILLE (45-7), Earl of Westmoreland; m. (1) MARGA-
RET STAFFORD (136-8).
   8. MARGARET NEVILLE, d. 1463; m. (1) bef. 31 Dec. 1413, RICHARD le
SCROPE (149A-9), 3rd Lord Scrope, b. 31 May 1394, d. 29 Aug. 1420. (CP XI, 542;
Va. Hist. Mag., vol. VI, pp. 408-410, chart; Clay, 199).
   9. SIR HENRY le SCROPE, b. Bolton, 4 June 1418, d. 14 Jan. 1458/9, Lord
Scrope of Bolton; m. in or sh. bef. 1435, Elizabeth, liv. 20 Oct. 1498, dau. of John,
4th Lord Scrope of Masham, and Elizabeth Chaworth. (CP XI, 543).
   10. MARGARET le SCROPE; m. John Bernard, b. c. 1437, d. c. 1485/6, of
Abingdon. (Va. Hist. Mag., VI, 408-410; Higgins, Bernards of Abingdon, I, 20-74).
   11. JOHN BERNARD, b. 1469, d. 1508, of Abingdon; m. Margaret, dau. of
John Daundelyn. (Ibid.).
   12. JOHN BERNARD, b. 1491, d. 1549; m. Cecily Muscote. (Ibid.).
   13. FRANCIS BERNARD, b. c. 1528; m. Alice Hazelwood. (Va. Hist. Mag.,
loc. cit.; Bernards of Abingdon, I, 34-40).
   14. FRANCIS BERNARD, of Kinsthorpe, b. 1558, d. 1630; m. Mary Woolhouse.
(Va. Hist. Mag., VI, 409).
   15. COLONEL WILLIAM BERNARD, b. Northamptonshire, England, 1598,
d. in Virginia, 1665; came to Virginia, 1625, lived in Nansemond and Isle of Wight
Counties; member of the Council, 1647-1648, 1655-1660; m. by 1655, Lucy (Higginson)
Burwell, when she is named in the York Co. records as his wife. (Clayton Torrence,
Winstons of Virginia, p. 215).

                                   Line 47

   7. SIR RALPH de NEVILLE (45-7), Earl of Westmoreland; m. (2) Joan Beaufort, dau. of JOHN (171-17), Duke of Lancaster and Katharine (Roet) Swynford.
   8. SIR EDWARD de NEVILLE, K.G., d. 18 Oct. 1476, Lord Burgavenny; m.

(1) bef. 18 Oct. 1424, Elizabeth de Beauchamp, b. 16 Sept. 1415, d. 18 June 1448, only dau. of Richard de Beauchamp, K.B. (son of WILLIAM de BEAUCHAMP, K.G. (17-8) and Joan Fitz Alan, q.v.) and Isabel Despenser (dau. of Thomas le Despenser and Constance, dau. of EDMUND (161-17), Duke of York). (CP I, 27-30).

9. GEORGE NEVILLE, Lord Burgavenny (by 1st wife), b. Raby Castle, d. 20 Sept. 1492, M.P., 1482-1492; m. (1) Margaret, d. 28 Sept. 1485, dau. of Sir Hugh Fenne. (CP I, 30-31).

10. GEORGE NEVILLE, K.G., ae 16+ at mother's death, d. 1535, Lord Burgavenny; m. (3) June 1519, Mary Stafford, dau. of Edward de Stafford, K.G., 3rd Duke of Buckingham, and Eleanor de Percy, dau. of Henry de Percy, 4th Earl of Northumberland, by 1st wife Maud Herbert. He s. & h. HENRY de PERCY (44-9). (CP I, 31-3).

11. URSULA NEVILLE; m. Sir Warham St. Leger, Knt., of Ulcombe, Sheriff of Kent, 1560.

12. SIR ANTHONY ST. LEGER, of Ulcombe, d. 1603; m. c. 1578, Mary, dau. of Sir Thomas Scott.

13. SIR WARHAM ST. LEGER, of Ulcombe, d. c. 1631; m. Mary, d. 1662, dau. of Sir Rowland Heyward, Knt., Lord Mayor of London.

14. URSULA ST. LEGER, d. c. 1672; m. c. 1627, Rev. Daniel Horsmanden, D.D., Rector of Ulcombe, 1622-1645, d. c. 1655; came to Virginia, sett. Charles City Co., where he was a Burgess and a member of the Governor's Council.

15. COLONEL WARHAM HORSMANDEN, of Purleigh, co. Essex; came to Virginia, c. 1649; member of the Governor's Council, 1658; returned to England where he died. Wife unidentified.

16. MARIA HORSMANDEN, d. 9 Nov. 1699; m. (2) c. 1673, Colonel William Byrd I, of London, England, and of Virginia, b. c. 1652, d. in Virginia, 4 Dec. 1704. Their son: COLONEL WILLIAM BYRD II, of "Westover," Charles City Co., Va., was b. there 10 Mar. 1674, and d. there 26 Aug. 1744.

14. KATHARINE ST. LEGER, d. c. 1658, prob. in Va.; m. Wycombe, Kent, 10 July 1628, Thomas Culpeper of the Middle Temple, b. c. 1602, son of John (1565-1635) of Feckingham, Worcs., a Member of the Virginia Company 1609-1625, and Ursula (1566-1612), dau. of Ralph Woodcock, alderman of London. Thomas Culpeper was a 1/7 proprietor of the Northern Neck under the charter of 1649; prob. came with Sir Dudley Wyatt, d. Va., c. 1652.

15. ANNE CULPEPER, bp. Hollingbourne, Kent, 16 Sept. 1630, bur. York, 1695; m. in Va., c. 1652, Christopher Danby of Thorpe Perrow, Yorks. A dau. m. Joseph Goodrich of Rappahannock, Va.

15. ALEXANDER CULPEPER, b. c. 1631, will dtd. 29 Nov. 1691, pr. 5 Jan. 1694/5, Surveyor General of Va., 1671-1694; d. unm.

15. JOHN CULPEPER, bp. Hollingbourne, 4 Apr. 1633, d. aft. 1680, of Albemarle, N.C. (Possibly father of Henry Culpeper, d. Norfolk co., Va., 1699.)

15. FRANCES CULPEPER, bp. Hollingbourne, 27 May 1634, d. c. 1690/1 in Va.; m. (1) 1652, Samuel Stephens (d. 1670) of Warwick Co., Va., sometime Gov. of N.C. (Albemarle); m. (2) 1670 SIR WILLIAM BERKELEY (69-14), d. 1677, Gov. of Va. 1642-1654, 1661-1676); m. (3) 1680, Philip Ludwell, d. 1723, sometime Gov. of N.C. (Gens. 14-15: Va. Mag. Hist. and Biog. vol. 33, pp. 113+ chart op., 343-58).

14. MARY ST. LEGER, bp. 1612; m. Lenham Parish, lic. 27 Nov. 1632, as his 2nd wife, William Codd, b. 1604, will dtd. 16 Dec. 1652, pr. 25 July 1653, of Pellicans in Watringbury, Kent.

15. COL. ST. LEGER CODD, b. 1635, will dtd. 7 Nov. 1702, pr. (in Md.) 9 Feb. 1707/8 and (in Lancs. Co., Va.) 8 Apr. 1708; in Northumberland Co., Va. by 1671; burgess from that co. 1680, 1682; member Md. legislature from Cecil Co. 1694, 1702; m. (1) prob. a dau. of Richard Perrott, Lancs. Co., Va.; m. (2) Anne Bennett, dau. of Col. Richard Bennett, Gov. of Va. 1652-5, and wid. of Theodore Bland. (Gens. 14-15: Va. Mag. Hist. and Biog. vol. 10, pp. 374-5; vol. 23, pp. 382-3; vol. 33, p. 145; d'Angerville, Living Descendants of the Blood Royal (not a good reference) vol. 5, p. 306, with sources cited therein).

Line 48

11. URSULA NEVILLE (47-11); m. Sir Warham St. Leger, Knt.

12. ANNE ST. LEGER; m. Thomas Digges, of Digges Court, co. Kent, an

English mathematician, A.B., Cambridge, 1551, M.P., 1572, mustermaster-general of the armies in the Low Countries, 1586-1594, d. 24 Aug. 1595, son of Leonard Digges of Wotten Court, co. Kent, d. c. 1571, and Bridget Wilford, dau. of Thomas Wilford of Hartridge in Cranbrook, co. Kent, and Elizabeth, dau. of Walter Culpeper; Leonard Digges was son of James Digges, Knt., of Digges Court in the Parish of Barham. Leonard was also a mathematician and studied at Oxford. (Berry, Visitation of Kent, 1619, p. 65; Century Dictionary, Proper Names, 326; DNB, see Sir Warham St. Leger and Thomas Digges).

13. SIR DUDLEY DIGGES, of Chilham Castle, co. Kent, b. 1583, d. 18 Mar. 1638/9; Christ Ch. Coll., Oxford, 1601; Ambassador to Russia, 1618, Master of the Rolls, 1630; member of the Virginia Company; m. Mary, dau. of Sir Thomas Kempe, Knt.

14. GOVERNOR EDWARD DIGGES, sett. Virginia, c. 1650, member of the Council, 1654-1675, Governor of Virginia, 1655; m. Elizabeth, dau. of Col. John Page.

15. COLONEL WILLIAM DIGGES, b. Chilham Castle; J.P., 1671; came to Virginia, and was Sheriff of York co., 1679; removed in 1680 to St. Mary's co., Md.; Dep.-Gov. of Maryland; m. Elizabeth (Sewall) Wharton. (Va. Mag. Hist., 29:232; Records of the Parish of Cranbrook, Kent; Hasted, Kent, VII 98-99; Berry, Genealogies of Kent, 134-135; Berry, Visitation of Kent, 1619, p. 65; Visitations of Essex, 1558, I 128).

Line 49

3. ROBERT FITZ ROGER (44-3); m. 1265, Margery de la Zouche.

4. JOHN FITZ ROBERT, afterwards de Clavering (which name he assumed), of Costessey, Norfolk, b. c. 1266, ae 44+ in 1299, d.s.p.m. Aynhoe, bef. 23 Jan. 1331/2; summoned to Parliament during the life of his father as Lord Clavering; m. 1278, Hawise, d. bef. 14 Apr. 1345, dau. of Robert de Tibetot, a crusader. (CP III, 275; XII (2), 89-93).

5. EVE de CLAVERING, Baroness Clavering, b. c. 1302, ae 40+ at mother's death, d. c. 1369, bur. at Langley Abbey, Norfolk; m. (2) bef. 2 Dec. 1308, Sir Thomas de Ufford, b. bef. 1286, said to have been slain at Bannockburn, 24 June 1314, bur. at Langley Abbey, Norfolk. (CP III, 275-6; IX, 498, note a; XII (2), 154).

6. EDMUND de UFFORD, Lord Clavering, 2nd but only surviving son, d. betw. 1 Sept. and 3 Oct. 1374 (yr. bro. of John de Ufford, Lord Ufford, d.s.p.m. 1361); m. Sibilla, dau. of Sir Simon de Pierpont. (CP XII (2), 154-156, note f; Sussex Archaeological Collections, XI: 87).

7. ELA de UFFORD, bur. Ingham Priory, 1425; m. Sir Miles de Stapleton, b. c. 1357, d. 10 Apr. 1419, of Ingham and Bedale.

8. SIR BRIAN STAPLETON, KNT., b. 1379, d. 7 Aug. 1438, of Ingham and Bedale; m. CECILY BARDOLF (40-8), d. 29 Sept. 1432, q.v. (CP I, 414).

9. SIR MILES STAPLETON, d. 1466; m. KATHERINE de la POLE (5-10). (Generations 7 to 9: CP V, 397).

Line 49A

6. EDMUND de UFFORD (49-6); m. Sibilla de Pierpont.

7. ROBERT de UFFORD, Lord Clavering, seen 1389, d.s.p.m. bef. 1393, m. ELEANOR de FELTON (137A-7). (CP V, 294; VII, 561; Sussex Archaeological Collections, XI:87).

8. JOAN de UFFORD, 2nd dau., bur. at Langley Abbey, Norfolk; m. Sir William Bowet of Horsford, Norfolk, taken prisoner at the battle of Beauje, 22 Mar. 1421. (Sussex Archaeological Collections, XI: 88; LVIII: chart facing p. 64).

9. ELIZABETH BOWET, dau. and heiress; m. c. 1430, SIR THOMAS de DACRE (8A-11). (CP IV, 7-9; Sussex Archaeological Collections, loc. cit.).

Line 50

1. ROBERT FITZ WALTER, Leader of the Magna Charta Barons, 1215, of Woodham, d. 9 Dec. 1235, Lord of Dunmow Castle; m. Rohese.
2. SIR WALTER FITZ ROBERT, d. bef. 10 Apr. 1258, of Woodham-Walter, Burnham, Roydon, Dunmow, Henham, Wimbish, and Tey, co. Essex; m. IDA de LONGESPEE (142-2).
3. ELA FITZ WALTER; m. William de Odyngsells, of Maxstoke, co. Warwick, d. 1294, son of William and Joan Odyngsells. (CP VI, 144).
4. MARGARET de ODYNGSELLS; m. (1) Sir John de Grey of Rotherfield, d. 17 Oct. 1311, M.P., 1297; m. (2) by 1319, Robert de Moreby. (CP VI, 144-6).
5. SIR JOHN de GREY, K.G., of Rotherfield, b. 9 Oct. 1300, d. 1 Sept. 1359, 1st Lord Grey of Rotherfield, K.G., 23 Apr. 1349; m. (1) by 1 Mar. 1311/12, Catharine, dau. and h. of Sir Bryan fitz Alan; m. (2) Avice, dau. of Sir John Marmion, Lord Marmion. (CP VI, 145-6).
6. MAUD de GREY (by 2nd wife); m. (2) c. 1374, SIR THOMAS de HARCOURT, KNT. (146-7).
7. SIR THOMAS de HARCOURT, KNT., of Stanton-Harcourt, d. 1420; m. Jane Franceys, dau. of Sir Robert Franceys of Formark, co. Derby.
8. SIR RICHARD HARCOURT, KNT., d. 1 Oct. 1468, of Wytham, Berkshire; m. (1) c. 1445, Edith Seint Clere, d. bef. 8 Nov. 1472, dau. of Thomas St. Claire of Wethersfield.
9. ALICE HARCOURT; m. William Bessiles, of Bessiles-Leigh, Berkshire, d. 1515.
10. ELIZABETH BESSILES; m. Richard Fettiplace, of East Shelford, Berkshire, d. 1511.
11. ANNE FETTIPLACE, b. Shelford Parva, 16 July 1496, d. 3 Aug. 1567; m. Edward Purefoy, of Shalston, Bucks, b. 13 Jan. 1494, d. 1558.
12. MARY PUREFOY, of Yardley-Hastings, co. Northampton; m. Thomas Thorne, gent., of Yardley-Hastings, d. 1589.
13. SUSANNA THORNE, bp. Yardley-Hastings, 5 Mar. 1559/60, liv. 29 Oct. 1588; m. CAPTAIN ROGER DUDLEY (149B-15), d. 1585.
14. GOVERNOR THOMAS DUDLEY, bp. Yardley-Hastings, 12 Oct. 1576, bur. Roxbury, Massachusetts, 31 July 1653, aged 76 years; Governor and Deputy-Governor of Massachusetts, 1630-1653; m. (1) Hardingstone, near Northampton, 25 Apr. 1603, Dorothy York, bur. Roxbury, 27 Dec. 1643, dau. of Edmund Yorke of Cotton End, co. Northampton; m. (2) Roxbury, 14 Apr. 1644, KATHERINE (DEIGHTON) HACKBURNE (28-17), q.v. (Children by the first wife: REV. SAMUEL DUDLEY, bp. 30 Nov. 1608; minister at Exeter, New Hampshire; ANNE DUDLEY, b. c. 1612, poet; m. 1628, Governor Simon Bradstreet of Massachusetts; MERCY DUDLEY, b. 1621; m. 1639, the Rev. John Woodbridge of Andover and Newbury, Mass.; PATIENCE DUDLEY, m. 1632, Maj.-Gen. Daniel Denison of Roxbury; SARAH DUDLEY, bp. 1620; m. (1) Maj. Benjamin Keayne; m. (2) 1649, Thomas Pacey. For other children see 28-17). (v. Redlich and Adams, op. cit., pp. 255-256).

Line 51

1. WILLIAM de HUNTINGFIELD, Magna Charta Surety, 1215, of Frampton, d. bef. 25 Jan. 1220/1, Keeper of Dover Castle, 1203, Warden of the Cinque Ports, Sheriff of Norfolk and Suffolk, 1210-1212, 1215, son of Roger de Huntingfield and Alice de Senlis; m. by 1194, Isabel, d. 1209, dau. of William Fitz Roger of Gressinghall, Norfolk, and widow of Osmond de Stuteville. (CP VI, 671).
2. SIR ROGER de HUNTINGFIELD, of Huntingfield, co. Suffolk, and Frampton, d. on or bef. 10 July 1257; m. (2) 1236, Joan de Hobrugg, d. on or bef. 7 Sept. 1297, dau. of William de Hobrugg. (CP VI, 671).
3. SIR WILLIAM de HUNTINGFIELD, of Huntingfield, b. 24 Aug. 1237, d. bef. 2 Nov. 1290; m. (1) Emma de Grey, d. 1264, dau. of Sir John de Grey of Shirland, co. Derby, and Emma de Glanville. (CP VI, 664).
4. SIR ROGER de HUNTINGFIELD, of Huntingfield and Frampton, d. bef. 5 Dec. 1302; m. c. 1277, Joyce d'Engaine, d. aft. 6 Mar. 1302/3, dau. of Sir John d'Engaine of Colne Engaine and Laxton, and Joan de Greinville, dau. of Gilbert

de Greinville of Halton. (CP VI, 666).

5. JOAN de HUNTINGFIELD; m. Sir Richard Basset, 1st Lord Basset of
Weldon, Great Weldon, co. Northampton, b. c. 1273, d. betw. 24 June and 18 Aug.
1314; taken prisoner at Bannockburn. (CP II, 10).

5A. RALPH BASSET of Great Weldon, b. Huntingfield, 27 Aug. 1300, d. sh.
bef. 4 May 1341; m. Joan, liv. 1346, wid. of Robert de Fourneux. (CP II, 10-11).

6. JOAN BASSET; m. Thomas de Aylesbury of Aylesbury, d. c. 1350. (CP
II, 13).

7. SIR JOHN AYLESBURY, of Milton Keynes, co. Buckingham, d. 1410; m.
Isabel, said to be dau. of Eubulo (1373-1411), a clerk, son of Roger, 5th Lord Strange
of Knockyn. (CP II, 13).

8. SIR THOMAS AYLESBURY, of Milton Keynes, b. c. 1369, d. 9 Sept. 1418;
m. Katherine Pabenham, b. 1372, d. 17 June 1436, dau. of Sir Lawrence de Pabenham and Elizabeth d'Engaine.

9. ELEANOR AYLESBURY; m. SIR HUMPHREY STAFFORD, KNT. (28-10),
of Grafton, b. 1400, liv. 1467.

10. SIR HUMPHREY STAFFORD, KNT., of Grafton, executed at Tyburn, 8
July 1486; m. Catherine Fray, dau. of Sir John Fray, Chief Baron of the Exchequer.

11. ANNE STAFFORD; m. Sir William Berkeley, K.B., of Stoke-Gifford,
Sheriff of Gloucester, 1485.

12. RICHARD BERKELEY, of Stoke-Gifford; m. Elizabeth Conningsby, dau.
of Sir Humphrey Conningsby, Knt.

13. SIR JOHN BERKELEY, of Stoke-Gifford; m. Isabel Dennis, dau. of Sir
William Dennis, Knt., of Dunham, co. Gloucs., and ANNE BERKELEY (66-10).

14. ELIZABETH BERKELEY; m. HENRY LYGON (28-14), q.v.

Line 52

6. RALPH BASSET (51-5A), b. 27 Oct. 1300, d. sh. bef. 4 May 1341; m. Joan.
(CP II, 10-11).

7. ALIANORE BASSET; m. Sir John Knyvet, of Winwick, co. Northampton,
Chief Justice of the King's Bench, Lord Chancellor of England, d. 1381. (CP II, 13).

8. JOHN KNYVET, ESQ., d. 1418; m. Joan, dau. of John de Botetourt, son
of Otho. (CP II, 13).

9. SIR JOHN KNYVET; m. Elizabeth Clifton, dau. of Constantine Clifton and
Elizabeth Scales, dau. of Robert, Lord Scales.

10. SIR JOHN KNYVET; m. Alice Lynnes, dau. of William Lynnes.

11. SIR WILLIAM KNYVET; m. Alice de Grey, dau. of John de Grey (brother
of Reynold de Grey, Lord Grey of Ruthin).

12. SIR EDMUND KNYVET, d. in a sea fight, time of King Henry VIII; m.
Eleanor Tyrelle, dau. of Sir William Tyrelle, Knt.

13. SIR EDMUND KNYVET, b. 1490, d. 31 Apr. 1539, of Ashwellthorpe; m.
JANE BOURCHIER, Lady Berners (18-13), q.v.

Line 53

9. SIR JOHN KNYVET (52-9), Sheriff of Northamptonshire, 1427, d. 1446;
m. Elizabeth Clifton.

10. MARGARET KNYVET, b. c. 1412, d. 1458; m. Richard Chamberlayne,
of Tilsworth, co. Bedford, b. c. 1392, d. 1439.

11. WILLIAM CHAMBERLAYNE, gent., b. c. 1436, d. bef. 1471; m. Joan,
liv. in 1477.

12. RICHARD CHAMBERLAYNE, of Sherbourne Castle, co. Oxford, d. 28
Aug. 1497; m. Sibyl, d. 1525, dau. of Richard Fowler of Sherbourne, Chancellor
of the Duchy of Lancaster.

13. ANNE CHAMBERLAYNE; m. SIR EDWARD RALEIGH, KNT. (34-13), q.v.

Line 54

1. JOHN de LACY, Magna Charta Surety, 1215, b. c. 1192, d. 22 July 1240, Earl of Lincoln, 1232, Constable of Chester, son of Roger de Lacy and Maud de Clare; m. (2) bef. 21 June 1221, MARGARET de QUINCY (107-3). (CP VII, 676).

Line 55

1. WILLIAM de LANVALLEI (159-4), Magna Charta Surety, 1215, d. 1217, of Great Bromley, co. Essex; m. a dau. of ALAN BASSET, one of the nobles Named in the Magna Charta, 1215.
2. HAWISE de LANVALLEI, d. 1249; m. John de Burgh, b. 1210, d. 1275.
3. SIR JOHN de BURGH, d. 1279; m. CECILY de BALIOL (140-3), d. bef. 1273.
4. HAWISE de BURGH, b. 1256, d. aft. 1282; m. Sir Robert de Grelle, of Manchester, b. 1252, d. 15 Feb. 1282, son of Robert de Grelle.
5. JOAN de GRELLE, d. 20 or 21 Mar. 1352/3; m. soon aft. 19 Nov. 1294, John de la Warre, 2nd Lord de la Warre, of Manchester, d. 9 May 1347, son of Sir Roger de la Warre, 1st Lord de la Warre, and Clarice de Tregoz. (CP IV, 141).
6. CATHERINE de la WARRE, d. 9 Aug. 1361; m. (2) in or bef. 1328, Sir Warin le Latimer, Lord Latimer, b. c. 1300, d. 13 Aug. 1349, son of Thomas, Lord Latimer, and Lora de Hastings, dau. of Henry de Hastings. (CP VII, 453).
7. ELIZABETH LATIMER; m. Thomas Griffin.
8. RICHARD GRIFFIN, d. 1411; m. Anna Chamberlayne, dau. of Richard Chamberlayne.
9. NICHOLAS GRIFFIN, d. 12 Oct. 1436; m. Margaret Pilkington, dau. of Sir John Pilkington.
10. NICHOLAS GRIFFIN, b. Brixworth, 5 June 1426, d. 6 June 1482, Lord Latimer, Sheriff of Northamptonshire, 1473; m. (1) Catherine Curzon, dau. of Richard Curzon. (CP VII, 457).
11. CATHERINE GRIFFIN; m. Sir John Digby, of Eye Kettleby, co. Leicester, knighted at Bosworth Field, d. c. 1533, son of Everard Digby and Jacquette Ellis, dau. of Sir John Ellis.
12. WILLIAM DIGBY, ESQ., of Kettleby and Luffenham, co. Leicester, d. bef. 1 Aug. 1529; m. (1) Rose Prestwich, dau. of William Prestwich and his wife, a dau. of Sir Thomas Poultney.
13. SIMON DIGBY, of Beadell, co. Rutland; m. Anne Grey, dau. of Reginald Grey of York.
14. EVERARD DIGBY; m. Katherine, dau. of a Stockbridge de Newkirk.
15. ELIZABETH DIGBY, living in London, 1651; m. Hackney, 25 Oct. 1614, Enoch Lynde, shipping merchant in the Netherlands, c. 1637.
16. SIMON LYNDE, b. June 1624, d. 22 Nov. 1687; m. Boston, Massachusetts, 22 Feb. 1652/3, Hannah Newgate (or Newdigate).
17. NATHANIEL LYNDE; m. SUSAN WILLOUGHBY (83-18), q.v.

Line 56

5. JOAN de GRELLE (55-5); m. John de la Warre, d. 9 May 1347.
6. JOHN de la WARRE, d. sh. bef. 24 June 1331; m. Margaret Holand, d. 20 or 22 Aug. 1349, dau. of Sir Robert Holand of West Derby, Lancashire. (CP IV, 144).
7. ROGER de la WARRE, b. 30 Nov. 1326, d. Gascony, 27 Aug. 1370, Lord de la Warre; m. (3) bef. 23 July 1358, ALIANORE MOWBRAY (4-8), q.v. (CP IV, 144).

Line 57

1. SIR WILLIAM MALET, Magna Charta Surety, 1215, d. 1217, of Curry Malet,

Sheriff of Somerset and Devon; m. Aliva Basset, dau. of THOMAS BASSET, who was named in the Magna Charta, 1215.

2. HAWISE MALET; m. (1) Sir Hugh Poyntz (see also 60-2); m. (2) bef. 11 Feb. 1220/1, Sir Robert de Muscegros, of Charlton, d. 29 Jan. 1253/4.

3. SIR JOHN MUSCEGROS, of Charlton, b. 10 Aug. 1232, d. 8 May 1275; m. Cecily, d. sh. bef. 10 Aug. 1301, dau. of Sir William Avenal. (CP V, 308 e).

4. SIR ROBERT de MUSCEGROS, b. c. 1252, d. 27 Dec. 1280; m. Agnes, liv. 9 May 1281, not dau. of Sir William de Ferrers, Earl of Derby, and Margaret de Quincy. (See CP V, 308 c.)

5. HAWISE de MUSCEGROS, b. 21 Dec. 1276, d. aft. 24 June 1340; m. (2) betw. 2 Feb. 1297/8 and 13 Sept. 1300, SIR JOHN de FERRERS (102-5), Lord Ferrers of Chartley, d. 1312; m. (3) Sir John de Bures, d. Bodington, 21 or 22 Dec. 1350. (CP V, 305).

6. CATHERINE de BURES, d. bef. 1315, liv. Oct. 1355; m. bef. 21 May 1329, Sir Giles de Beauchamp, of Beauchamp's Court, d. Oct. 1361. (Generations 1 to 6: CP V, 320-321 chart). Note: CP II, 44 says Roger (No. 7) said to be son of Giles, son of Walter of Powick and Alcester. Dugdale says Roger, grandson of Walter, but does not identify father.

7. ROGER de BEAUCHAMP, d. 3 Jan. 1379/80, 1st Lord Beauchamp of Bletsoe, M.P., 1364-1380; m. (1) bef. 1336/7, Sibyl de Patshull, liv. 26 Oct. 1351.

8. ROGER de BEAUCHAMP, d. bef. his father, wife unidentified.

9. ROGER de BEAUCHAMP, KNT., ae. 17+ at grandfather's death, proof of age 1374, d. 3 May 1406, of Bletsoe and Lydiard Tregoz; m. Joan Clopton. (CP II, 45).

10. SIR JOHN de BEAUCHAMP, KNT., of Bletsoe, d. c. 1412; m. (1) c. Jan. 1405/6, Margaret Holand, dau. of Sir John Holand; m. (2) Esther Stourton, dau. of Sir John Stourton, she m. (2) Sir Robert Shottesbrooke and d. 13 June 1441. (CP II, 45).

11. MARGARET de BEAUCHAMP (by 2nd wife), b. c. 1412, d. 1482; m. (1) Sir Oliver de St. John, Knt., d. 1437, of Penmark, co. Gloucester; m. (2) John Beaufort, Duke of Somerset. (CP II, 45, note c).

12. EDITH ST. JOHN; m. as his 1st wife, Sir Geoffrey Pole, Knt., of Medmenham and Ellesborough, co. Buckingham, will pr. 21 Mar. 1474/5.

13. SIR RICHARD POLE, K.G., d. bef. 18 Dec. 1505; m. 1491/4, Margaret Plantagenet, Countess of Salisbury, b. Aug. 1473, executed 28 May 1541, dau. of George Plantagenet, Duke of Clarence (son of RICHARD, Duke of York (161-19)), and his wife, Isabel Neville. (CP XI, 399).

14. SIR HENRY POLE, Lord Montagu, b. c. 1492, executed 9 Jan. 1538/9 (brother of Reginald, Cardinal Pole); m. Jane Neville, d. bef. 26 Oct. 1538, dau. of Sir George Neville, Lord Abergavenny. (CP IX, 94).

15. CATHERINE POLE, d. 23 Sept. 1576; m. 1532, Sir Francis Hastings, K.G., 2nd Earl of Huntingdon, b. c. 1514, d. 23 June 1560, ae. 47 yrs. (CP VI, 655).

16. CATHERINE HASTINGS, b. 11 Aug. 1542, d. bef. 20 Oct. 1586; m. as 1st wife, betw. 10 Dec. 1555 and 30 Apr. 1557, Sir Henry Fiennes, K.B. (or Clinton), 2nd Earl of Lincoln, M.P., 1571-1583, d. 29 Sept. 1616, son of Sir Edward Fiennes, Earl of Clinton, Saye and Lincoln. (Clay p. 102; CP VII, 693).

17. THOMAS FIENNES (or Clinton), 3rd Earl of Lincoln, A.M., Oxford, 1588, b. 1568, d. 15 Jan. 1618/9; m. sh. aft. 21 Sept. 1584, Elizabeth Knyvet of Charlton, Wiltshire, d. long aft. 1619, dau. of Sir Henry Knyvett. (CP VII, 695).

18. SUSAN FIENNES; m. (2) as his 3rd wife, Col. John Humphrey, of Chaldon, Dorset, b. 1595, d. 1661, Deputy-Governor of Massachusetts; came with his wife to New England, July 1634; founder of Lynn; Maj.-General, 1641; returned to Sandwich, England, 26 Oct. 1641. (See 80-17). (CP VII, 696 & note c; TAG 15: 124).

18. ARBELLA FIENNES, d.s.p. Salem, Massachusetts, Aug. 1630; m. Isaac Johnson, Esq., d. Boston, 30 Sept. 1630. Governor Winthrop's flagship, the "Arbella", was named for Lady Arbella Fiennes.

Note: Ref. on Beauchamp - see Baker, Northamptonshire II, 218-219.

Line 58

6. CATHERINE de BURES (57-6); m. Sir Giles de Beauchamp.

7. SIR JOHN de BEAUCHAMP, d. 1378-1401; m. Elizabeth, d. 1411 (perhaps dau. of Sir John St. John).

8. SIR WILLIAM de BEAUCHAMP, of Powyck and Alcester, d. bef. 1431,
Sheriff of the shires of Worcester and Gloucester; m. bef. Mar. 1414/5, Catherine
Usflete, dau. and coh. of Sir Gerard de Usflete.
9. SIR JOHN de BEAUCHAMP, K.G., d. betw. 9 and 19 Apr. 1475, cr. Lord
Beauchamp of Powyck, 2 May 1447, Justice of South Wales, Lord Treasurer of
England, 1450-1452; m. 1434, Margaret Ferrers, d. 29 Jan. 1487, sister of Richard
Ferrers. (CP II, 46).
10. SIR RICHARD de BEAUCHAMP, K.B., b. 1435, ae. 40+ at father's death,
d. 19 Jan. 1502/3, 2nd Lord Beauchamp of Powyck; m. 27 Jan. 1446/7, ELIZA-
BETH STAFFORD (28-11), dau. of SIR HUMPHREY STAFFORD, KNT., of Grafton
(28-10). (CP II, 47).

Line 59

1. SIR WILLIAM MALET (57-1); m. Aliva, dau. of THOMAS BASSET.
2. MABEL MALET; m. Hugh de Vivonia.
3. HELOISE de VIVONIA; m. Walter de Wahul, b. c. 1227, d. 1269, son of
Saier de Wahul.
4. JOHN de WAHULL, KNT., d. 1296, of Wodhull and Longford; m. Agnes,
dau. of Henry de Pinkney by Alicia, dau. of John de Lindesay. (CP XII (2), 294).
5. THOMAS de WODHULL, KNT., d. 1304; m. Hawise.
6. JOHN de WODHULL, KNT., d. 1337; m. Isabel.
7. NICHOLAS WODHULL, d. 24 Oct. 1410, of Odell and Pateshull, co. Bedford; m. Margaret, dau. of John Foxcote.
8. THOMAS WODHULL, b. 1389, d. Mar. 1421; m. Elizabeth, dau. of Sir
John Chetwode of Warkworth, co. Northampton.
9. THOMAS WODHULL, b. 1411, d. 8 Aug. 1441, of Warkworth; m. ISABEL
TRUSSELL (111-10).

Line 60

2. HAWISE MALET (57-2), living 4 May 1287; m. (1) bef. 23 Mar. 1216/7,
Sir Hugh Poyntz, d. 4 Apr. 1220, son of Nicholas Poyntz, d. bef. 2 Nov. 1223, and
Julian, dau. of Hugh Bardolf; with his father, Hugh Poyntz joined the Barons in their
struggle against King John, and was captured at Worcester, 17 July 1216, and imprisoned; Hawise m. (2) bef. 11 Feb. 1220/1, Robert de Muscegros, of Charlton, d.
29 Jan. 1253/4. (CP V chart, 320-321; X, 671-672).
3. SIR NICHOLAS POYNTZ, b. c. 1220, d. bef. 7 Oct. 1273; m. Elizabeth,
prob. dau. of Timothy Dyall, Esq. (CP X, 673).
4. HUGH POYNTZ, KNT., b. 25 Aug. 1252, fought in Wales, 1277-1294, 1st
Lord Poyntz, 1295, d. bef. 4 Jan. 1307/8; lord of Curry Malet, as were his father
and grandfather. His wife may have been a Paveley - prob. not. (CP X, 673-674).
5. SIR NICHOLAS de POYNTZ, KNT., 2nd Lord Poyntz, b. c. 1278, d.
bef. 12 July 1311, M.P., 1308-1311; m. (1) as a boy, bef. 20 Jan. 1287/8, Elizabeth,
dau. of EUDO la ZOUCHE, of Harringworth (74-4) and MILICENT CANTELOU
(146-4), d. aft. 1297; m. (2) bef. 9 Feb. 1308/9 Maud, dau. of John de Acton. (CP
X, 674).
6. NICHOLAS POYNTZ, 2nd son, (by 1st wife) of Hoo, co. Kent, 1311 (younger
brother of Sir Hugh de Poyntz, Knt., d. bef. 2 May 1337, M.P., 1317-1336). (CP X,
675-676; Maclean, Family of Poyntz).
7. NICHOLAS POYNTZ, ESQ., of North Okenden, co. Essex, d. 1372; m.
wife's name unknown. (Generations 6 to 12: See Sir John Maclean, Memoir of the
Family of Poyntz, p. 47. Though generally accepted at this time by most genealogists,
the users of this reference are cautioned that not all its statements are entirely
satisfactory).
8. PONTIUS POYNTZ, ESQ., of North Okenden, fl. 1393; m. Eleanor, dau.
of ——— Baldwin, of North Okenden, living 1393. (Generations 5 to 13: Visitations
of Essex, I 268-269).
9. SIR JOHN POYNTZ, KNT., d. 1447 (will dated 12 Mar. 1446/7), of North
Okenden; m. a dau. of William Perth, of Aveley, co. Essex.
10. WILLIAM POYNTZ, ESQ., d. 1494, of North Okenden; m. Elizabeth, d.

21 Aug. 1493, dau. of Sir Edmund Shaw, Sheriff, 1474, Lord Mayor of London, 1484, and sister of Sir Edmund Shaw.

11. THOMAS POYNTZ, ESQ., d. London, 5 May 1562, of North Okenden; m. Ann, dau. of John Calva, a German. (Poynter Harl. mss. 1432, 53b).

12. SUSANNA POYNTZ, will made 16 Nov. 1612, d. 1613, bur. at South Okenden; m. Sir Richard Saltonstall, Knt., b. c. 1517, will made 1597, d. 17 Mar. 1600/1, aged 80 years, Lord Mayor of London, 1597/8 (uncle of Sir Richard Saltonstall, one of the founders of the Massachusetts Bay Colony. See 44-15). (Harl. Soc. Publ., 1878, vol. 13, Visitations of Essex, I pp. 268-269; Saltonstall Pedigree).

13. ELIZABETH SALTONSTALL; m. 18 Feb. 1583/4, Richard Wyche, gent., of London, b. 1554, d. 20 Nov. 1621, and is bur. in the Church of St. Dunstans in the East, son of Richard Wyche and Margaret Haughton. (Visitations of Chester, 1613, p. 270; Century Dictionary, Proper Names, 889; Mass. Hist. Soc. Publ.: Winthrop Papers, I (1929), p. 417 note; William & Mary Quarterly, XIV 255).

14. THE REVEREND HENRY WYCHE, d. Sept. 1678, Rector of Sutton, co. Surrey, 1636; m. Ellen, dau. of Ralph Bennett, of Old Place Yard, Westminster. (Ibid.).

15. HENRY WYCHE, b. in England, d. Virginia (will pr. 1714), came to Virginia, 1678; sett. South side of the James River, Surry Co., Virginia.

*   *   *   *   *   *

13. JUDITH SALTONSTALL (dau. of SUSANNA POYNTZ (47-12) and Richard Saltonstall); m. (1) Edward Rich of Horndon, b. c. 1570; m. (2) Sir Arthur Forest, Huntingdonshire.

14. EDWARD RICH of Southwark, b. c. 1598; m. Susan Percy, Wilts.

15. SIR PETER RICH of Southwark and Lambeth, Surrey, b. c. 1631, d. 26 Aug. 1692, ae. 60+; of London ae. 43 m. 1674; m. Anne, dau. of Richard Evans of London.

16. EDWARD RICH, b. c. 1671 (ae. 3 in 1674), wife unidentified.

17. ANNE RICH, b. c. 1696, d. Ware Psh., Gloucester Co., Va., 10 June 1727 in 32nd year (GS); m. Col. Francis Willis. (TAG vol. 21, pp. 237-8).

Line 61

11. MARGARET de BEAUCHAMP (57-11); m. Sir Oliver de St. John, Knt.

*   *   *   *   *   *

12. SIR JOHN de ST. JOHN, K.B., of Penmark, fl. 1488; m. Alice Bradshaw, dau. of Sir Thomas Bradshagh of Haigh, co. Lancaster. (CP II, 206). This gen. questionable. See Gen. Mag. V, 358-9.

*   *   *   *   *   *

13. SIR JOHN de ST. JOHN, K.B., of Bletsoe, co. Bedford, fl. 1508; m. Sibyl, dau. of Morgan ap Jenkins ap Philip. (CP II, 206).

14. SIR JOHN ST. JOHN, KNT. of Bletsoe, M.P. for Bedfordshire, 1547-1552; m. Margaret, dau. of Sir William Waldegrave, by whom he had legitimate issue. The eldest legitimate son cr. Lord St. John of Bletsoe. (CP XI, 333). By Anne Nevell, dau. of Thomas Nevell, of Cotterstock, co. Northampton, 2nd son of William Nevell, of Holte, co. Leicester, he also had a bastard dau. Cressett (Cressitt, Cressyd or Crestyde), who m. John Boteler and left issue. (Visitations of Bedfordshire, pp. 10, 53; Harl. mss. 1531; Visitations of Essex, 1558, I 49; 1612, I 169-170, 192; 1634, I 365).

15. CRESSETT ST. JOHN (bastard dau.); m. as his 1st wife, John Boteler, Esq., d. 1612/3, of Sharnbrook, co. Bedford, and Thobie, co. Essex, son of George Boteler, gent., of Tofte in Sharnbrook, and his wife, Mary Throckmorton, dau. of Richard Throckmorton, Esq., of Higham Park, co. Northampton. John Boteler made his will 1 Sept. 1612, which was proved at London, 20 Jan. 1612/3. He had m. (2) Mary, dau. of James Gedge, but had no issue by her. (Ibid.; his eldest son and heir was Sir Oliver Boteler, Knt., of Sharnbrooke, co. Bedford, who m. Ann Barham of Kent; see also Clayton Torrence in Va. Hist. Mag., vol. 56, pp. 430-460, cf. 459-460).

16. JOHN BOTELER, of Little Burch Hall and Newlands Hall, Roxwell, co. Essex, younger son; m. Roxwell, 27 Dec. 1599, Jane Elliott, bp. 22 June 1576, dau. of Edward Elliott, of Newlands Hall, co. Essex, and Jane, dau. of James

Gedge, gent., of Shenfield, co. Essex. They had six children of whom four were
daughters: Jane, Sarah, ELIZABETH, and Cresset. (Ibid.).
    17. CAPTAIN JOHN BOTELER, bp. Roxwell, co. Essex, 7 Dec. 1600; sett.
Kent Island, Maryland, 26 May 1640, when he is called "Cleyborne's brother-in-
law"; will made 1 Apr. 1640, probated 1 July 1642.
    17. THOMAS BUTLER (brother of Capt. John Boteler); m. London, 16 Jan.
1625/6, Joan Mountstephen, widow of Nicholas Mountstephen. Thomas also resided
for a time in Maryland.
    17. ELIZABETH BOTELER (sister of Captain John Boteler), b. c. 1610/2,
d. in Virginia aft. 1668/9; m. bef. Apr. 1638, The Hon. Colonel William Claiborne,
gent., bp. Crayford, co. Kent, 10 Aug. 1600, d. c. 1677/8, son of Thomas Cleyborne and Sarah (Smyth) James, of King's Lynn, Stepney, London and Crayford.
Col. William was adm. to Pembroke Coll., 31 May 1616, ae. 16; arriv. in Va., Oct.
1621, as Surveyor for the Virginia Company of London; was Secretary of the Colony
of Virginia, 1625-1637, 1652-1660, Governor's Councillor, 1625-1660; Treasurer
for life, 1642; Deputy-Governor of Va., sometime betw. 1652-1655; sett. Kent Island,
Md., 1631, as factor for Clobery & Co., London; Captain and Colonel in militia
activities against the Indians; later, 1664, chosen Chief Commander against the
Indians. His line cannot at present be traced back of his grandfather, Thomas
Cleyborne, of the well known family of that name in Westmoreland. Children:
CAPT. WILLIAM CLAIBORNE, JR., d. 1682, of New Kent Co., Va.; m. Elizabeth
Wilkes; LT.-COL. THOMAS CLAIBORNE, b. 17 Aug. 1647, d. 7 Oct. 1683, sett.
New Kent Co.; m. Sarah Fenn; LEONARD CLAIBORNE, d. Jamaica, 1694; JOHN
CLAIBORNE, of New Kent Co.; and JANE CLAIBORNE, m. bef. May 1661, Col.
Thomas Brereton of Northampton Co., Va. (Va. Hist. Mag., 1948, vol. 56, pp.
335-336, 340-360).

Line 62

See Rivigny, Plantagenet Roll of the Blood Royal; Clarence Vol., tables II, LVII,
LXIII, and pp. 53, 518-533.

    14. SIR HENRY POLE (57-14), b. c. 1492, executed 9 Jan. 1538/9, Lord Mon-
tagu; m. Jane Neville.
    15. WINIFRED POLE, d. 22 Feb. 1601/2; m. (1) Sir Thomas Hastings; m.
(2) Thomas Barrington, Knt., of Barrington Hall, Braddocks and Hatfield, co.
Essex.
    16. SIR FRANCIS BARRINGTON, b. c. 1570, d. 3 July 1628, 1st Baronet,
M.P., Knight for the Shire of Essex, 1623, 1629; m. Joan, living 1587, dau. of Sir
Henry Cromwell, of Hichinbrook, aunt of Oliver Cromwell.
    17. JOAN BARRINGTON, b. 1621, d. 1653; m. Sir Richard Everard, 1st Baro-
net, of Langleys, Much-Walton, co. Essex, son of Hugh Everard and Mary Bond.
(Cokayne, Complete Baronetage II, 67-68).
    18. SIR RICHARD EVERARD, 2nd Baronet, d. 1694; Sheriff of Essex; m.
Elizabeth, dau. of Sir Henry Gibbs, of Falkland, Scotland. (Cokayne, loc. cit.).
    19. SIR HUGH EVERARD, 3rd Baronet, d. 1705; m. Mary, dau. of Dr. John
Brown of Salisbury. (Cokayne, loc. cit.).
    20. SIR RICHARD EVERARD, 4th Baronet, b. 1683, d. London, 17 Feb.1732/3,
of Broomfield Hall, co. Essex, Captain General and Governor of North Carolina,
1725-1731; m. Susanna Kidder, d. 12 Sept. 1739, dau. of the Rt. Rev. Richard Kidder, Bishop of Bath and Wells. (Cokayne, loc. cit.).

Note: dau. Susanna (gen. 20) given in earlier editions should be omitted.

Line 63

    1. WILLIAM de MOWBRAY (158-6), Magna Charta Surety, 1215, of Thirsk
and Slingsby, crusader, 1193, Baron of Axholme, d. Axholme, by Mar. 1223/4;
m. Avice (or Agnes), "dau. of the Earl of Arundel." (Clay, 139; CP IX, 373-4).
    2. ROGER de MOWBRAY, of Thirsk and Slingsby, minor 2 Oct. 1230 when
succeeded bro. Nele, d. about Nov. 1266; m. Maud, d. bef. Apr. 1273, dau. of

William de Beauchamp, Lord Beauchamp of Bedford; she m. (2) Roger le Strange. (Clay, 139; CP IX, 375-6).

3. ROGER de MOWBRAY, KNT., minor 1266, d. bef. 21 Nov. 1297, 1st Lord Mowbray of Thirsk and Hovingham, M.P., 1295-1297; m. 1270, ROESE de CLARE (107-5), liv. 1316, q.v. (Clay, 139-140; CP IX, 376-7).

4. JOHN de MOWBRAY, KNT., 2nd Lord Mowbray of Thirsk, b. 4 Sept. 1286, M.P., 1307-1321, warden of the marches near Carlisle and of the town and castle of Scarborough, 1317, executed after the battle of Boroughbridge, at York, 23 Mar. 1321/2; m. Swansea, 1298, Aline, d. bef. 20 July 1331, dau. of William de Braiose, Lord of Bramber and Gower in Wales; she m. (2) Sir Richard de Peshale, liv. Nov. 1342. (CP IX, 377-380).

5. JOHN de MOWBRAY, b. Hovingham, co. York, 29 Nov. 1310, d. York, 4 Oct. 1361, 3rd Lord Mowbray of Thirsk, M.P., 1327-1360; m. (1) c. 28 Feb. 1326/7, JOAN PLANTAGENET (4-7), d. 7 July 1349; m. (2) Elizabeth, d. Aug. or Sept. 1375, dau. of JOHN de VERE (120-5), 7th Earl of Oxford, and wid. of Hugh de Courtenay, s. & h. of Hugh, 2nd Earl of Devon. She m. (3) bef. 18 Jan. 1368/9, Sir William de Cosynton. (Gens. 1-5: CP IX, 373-383).

6. JOHN de MOWBRAY, b. Epworth, 25 June 1340, d. Thrace, 1368, 4th Lord Mowbray, crusader; m. c. 1349 Elizabeth, Lady Segrave, b. 25 Oct. 1338, dead 1368, dau. of John, Lord Segrave, by Margaret, dau. of Thomas de Brotherton, Earl of Norfolk, son of EDWARD I (161-14). (CP IX, 383-4, 596-601).

7. SIR THOMAS de MOWBRAY, K.G., b. 22 Mar. 1365/6, d. Venice, 22 Sept. 1399, Lord Mowbray, Segrave, and Stourton, Earl of Nottingham, 1383, Earl Marshal of England, 1384, Duke of Norfolk, 1397; m. (1) Elizabeth, Baroness Strange of Blackmere, d.s.p. 1383; m. (2) July 1384, ELIZABETH FITZ ALAN (19-8), q.v. (CP IX, 601-604).

8. MARGARET de MOWBRAY; m. c. 1420, Sir Robert Howard, K.G., b. c. 1383, d. 1436, of Stoke-by-Nayland, co. Suffolk, son of Sir John Howard. (CP IX, 610, chart after p. 612).

9. SIR JOHN HOWARD, K.G., slain at Bosworth Field, 22 Aug. 1485, Duke of Norfolk, 1483, Earl Marshal; m. (1) 1440, Catherine Moleyns, d. 3 Nov. 1465, dau. of Sir William Moleyns of Stoke Poges, co. Buckingham; m. (2) bef. 22 Jan. 1467, Margaret, dau. of Sir John Chedworth, and wid. of (1) Nicholas Wyfold and (2) John Norreys. She d. 1494. (CP IX, 610-612).

10. SIR THOMAS HOWARD, son by the first wife, b. 1443, d. 21 May 1524, Earl of Surrey, Earl Marshal and Duke of Norfolk; m. (1) 30 Apr. 1472, Elizabeth, d. 4 Apr. 1497, dau. of Sir Frederick Tylney of Ashwellthorpe, wid. of SIR HUMPHREY BOURCHIER (18-11); m. (2) Agnes, dau. of Hugh Tylney, bur. 31 May 1545. (CP IX, 612-615).

11. EDMUND HOWARD, Marshal of the Horse in the battle of Flodden Field, 1513; m. (1) Joyce, dau. of Sir Richard Culpeper.

12. MARGARET HOWARD (sister of Queen Katherine); m. Sir Thomas Arundell, Knt., of Wardour Castle, beheaded 26 Feb. 1552.

13. SIR MATTHEW ARUNDELL, of Wardour Castle, d. Dec. 1598; m. Margaret Willoughby, dau. of Sir Henry Willoughby, Knt., of Wollaton. (CP I, 263).

14. SIR THOMAS ARUNDELL, b. c. 1560, d. 7 Nov. 1639, Lord Arundell of Wardour; m. (2) 1 July 1608, Anne, d. 28 June 1649, dau. of Miles Philipson of Crook, Westmoreland. (CP I, 393, 263-4).

15. ANNE ARUNDELL, d. 23 July 1649; m. settlement 20 Mar. 1627/8, Cecil Calvert, bp. 2 Mar. 1605/6, d. Dec. 1675, 2nd Lord Baltimore. (CP I, 393-4).

16. CHARLES CALVERT, b. 27 Aug. 1637, d. 21 Feb. 1714/5, 3rd Lord Baltimore, Lord Proprietor of Maryland, Governor of Maryland, 1661-1684, Major-General, 1704; m. (1) c. 1660 a sis. of Sir John Darnall, dau. of Ralph, d. in childbed in Md. (CP I, 394); m. (2) c. 1667, Jane Lowe, d. on or bef. 19 Jan. 1700/1, dau. of Vincent Lowe, of Denby, co. Derby, wid. of Henry Sewell, Sect'y of the Province of Md.; m. (3) Mary (Baakes) Thorpe, a wid., bur. in England, 12 Mar. 1710/11; m. (4) Margaret, dau. of Thomas Charleton, of Hexham, Northumberland. She m. (3) Lawrence Eliot and d. 20 July 1731. (Generations 13 to 16: CP I, 263, 393-394; ms. "Lowes of Denby," in Maryland Historical Society; "Sewell Family," Maryland Historical Mag. vol. IV, 290-295; CP II, 394; see also "Lowe of Denby, co. Derby, England and Maryland," NGSQ, (1963) 51: 32-43). Charles Calvert had by (2) his event. heir, BENEDICT LEONARD CALVERT (17C-20).

48   [Line 64

Line 64

10. SIR THOMAS HOWARD, Duke of Norfolk (63-10); m. (1) Elizabeth (Tylney)
Bourchier.
11. ELIZABETH HOWARD, d. 3 Apr. 1538; m. c. 1500, SIR THOMAS BO-
LEYN, K.G. (17-12), b. c. 1477, d. 12 or 13 Mar. 1538/9, Earl of Wiltshire and
Ormond. (CP X, 137-139).
12. MARY BOLEYN, sister of Queen Anne; m. WILLIAM CARY (80-13), q.v.

Line 65

6. JOHN de MOWBRAY (63-6), 4th Lord Mowbray; m. Elizabeth de Segrave.
7. CATHERINE de MOWBRAY; m. Sir Thomas Grey of Heaton, d. c. 30 Nov. 1400.
8. SIR THOMAS GREY, of Heaton, beheaded 5 Aug. 1415; m. ALICE NEVILLE
(8-10), q.v. She m. (2) Sir Gilbert de Lancaster. (NEHGR vol. 105, p. 155).

    *   *   *   *   *   *
Note: MAUD GREY (Gen. 9) was sister, not dau. of SIR THOMAS GREY (65-8).

    *   *   *   *   *   *
9. MAUD GREY (8-11), (dau. gen. 7) liv. 22 Aug. 1451; m. c. 21 May 1399, Sir
Robert Ogle, Knt., of Ogle, b. 1369/73, d. 12 Aug. 1436, Warden of Roxborough Castle.
(CP VI, 488: X, 28-29).
10. MARGARET OGLE; m. Sir Robert Harbotel, d. 14 Mar. 1443.
11. BERTRAM HARBOTEL, d. 1466; m. 1439, Joan, dau. of Thomas Lord Lumley.
12. AGNES HARBOTEL; m. Sir Roger Fenwick, Sheriff, 1492. (New Co. Hist.
of Northumb., vol. XIV, chart 353; Hodgson, Northumberland, vol. II, Part II, p. 113).
12A. RALPH FENWICK of Stanton, j.u.; m. Margery Mitford, heiress of
Stanton. (Hodgson, Northumberland, vol. II, Part II, p. 113).
13. SIR JOHN FENWICK; m. Mary, dau. of Sir Ralph Grey of Chilham, son
of Thomas Grey and Margery Greystoke.
14. RALPH FENWICK; m. Barbara Ogle, dau. of John Ogle, b. Ogle Castle.
(New County Hist. of Northumberland, vol. XIV, p. 328).
15. RICHARD FENWICK, b. Heaton; m. Margaret, dau. of William Mills of
Gray's Inn. (Ibid., XII, 352-353).
16. WILLIAM FENWICK, b. 22 Sept. 1581, d. 12 June 1647; m. 27 July 1605,
Elizabeth, bp. 19 Feb. 1577/8, dau. of Sir Cotton Gargreve. (Ibid., XII, 352-353;
Pennsylvania Magazine of History and Biography, vol. 49, p. 151; vol. 50, p. 267;
Yorks P.R.S. v.105, pp. 24, 65).
17. JOHN FENWICK, yr. son, b. Stanton, co. Northumberland, 1618, d.
Salem, New Jersey, 1683/4; m. Elizabeth, dau. of Sir Walter Covert, of Boxley,
and Maidstone, Kent, a cousin of Sir Walter of Hougham, Sussex, who d. bef. 29
Mar. 1654. (Penna. Mag. of Hist. & Biog., loc. cit.; John Fenwick's will in N.J.
Archives, vol. I, Abstracts of Wills).
17. EDWARD FENWICK of Stanton, eldest s. & h., b. 29 Nov. 1606, d. 14
Aug. 1689, had 11 chn.; m. by 9 July 1636, Sarah, d. 17 Apr. 1691, dau. of Francis
Nevill of Chete.
18. ROBERT FENWICK, 5th son, b. 8 June 1646, d. Morpeth, 23 June 1693;
m. Anne Culcheth of Edington, d. 3 Feb. 1732.
19. JOHN FENWICK, 6th son, emigrated to South Carolina where he lived with 4 or
5 chn. including a son Edward. (General ref. for Fenwick, see Hodgson, Northumberland, vol. II, Part II, pp. 113-114; Penna. Mag. of Hist. & Biog., vol. 49, pp. 158-159).

Note: Barbara who m. John Ogle of Ogle Castle may have been a dau. of No. 12A
above, Ralph Fenwick and Margery Mitford, and mother of Phillis Ogle, Line 81: 14.

Line 66

7. THOMAS de MOWBRAY, Duke of Norfolk (63-7), d. 1399; m. (2) ELIZA-
BETH FITZ ALAN (19-8).
8. ISABEL de MOWBRAY, d. 27 Sept. 1452; m. (2) 1423/4, James de Berke-

ley, Lord Berkeley, b. c. 1394, d. Nov. 1463, M.P., 1421-1461. (CP II, 132).

9. MAURICE de BERKELEY, b. c. 1435, ae. 56 in 1492, d. Sept. 1506, ae. 70 years, 2nd son, Lord Berkeley; m. 1465, Isabel Mead, d. Coventry, aft. May 1514, ae. 70, dau. of Philip Mead, Mayor of Bristol.

10. ANNE BERKELEY; m. Sir William Dennis, of Dunham, co. Gloucester.

11. ELEANOR DENNIS, living 1579; m. 1529, William Lygon, of Madresfield, d. 29 Sept. 1567, Justice of the Hundred of Cheltenham, son of SIR RICHARD LYGON, KNT. (28-13) and Margaret Grenville. (Generations 7 to 11; CP II, 132, 135; Visitations of Gloucester, Harl. Soc. Pub., vol. 29, pp. 37, 39, 75; The Ligon Family, 205; William & Mary Quarterly, 2nd Series, vol. XVI, 294).

12. THOMAS LYGON, 2nd son; m. his cousin, Frances Dennis, dau. of Hugh Dennis; her will was dated 17 Oct. 1622 and proved at Coventry, 1 June 1625. She bur. Coventry, 30 Jan. 1624/5.

13. THOMAS LIGON, farmer, of Stoke-by-Coventry, and Calouden, Warwickshire, b. c. 1577 (Chancery depositions, Eliz. I - Chas. I, gp. 3, bundle E-20, suit 23 - "aged 44 or thereabouts" in 1621); m. at Sowe (perhaps as 2nd wife), 18 Aug. 1623, Elizabeth Pratt (bp. Stoke-Biggin, 10 Oct. 1602, dau. of Dennis Pratt). He bur. Sowe, 20 Dec. 1626, admin. wid. Elizabeth, 16 Feb. 1626/7. She bur. same, 19 Aug. 1631.

14. THOMAS LIGON, bp. Sowe, Warwickshire, 11 Jan. 1623/4. He appears "almost certainly" to be the immigrant Lt. Col. Thomas Ligon of Virginia, surveyor and burgess of Henrico Co., will 10 Jan. 1675, admin. 16 Mar. 1675/6; m. c. 1650, Mary Harris, b. c. 1625, will pro. 1 Feb. 1703/4. Richard Ligon, historian of Barbadoes (at death 1662, one of his next of kin was a Thomas Ligon who made no claim on the estate and appears to have been the Virginian) appears to have been a younger brother of No. 13. (Gens. 12-14: The Va. Gen. 22 (1978): 253-5; 23 (1979): 80). Research is continuing. Gary Boyd Roberts, Boston, Mass.

Line 67

Note: Line 67 has been questioned as insufficiently supported by contemporary evidence. At this time it can only be considered as possible and not proven. See Va. Mag. of Hist. and Biog., Oct. 1948, pp. 488-492, Martha Hiden's review of The Ligon Family.

11. ELEANOR DENNIS (66-11); m. 1529, William Lygon, d. 1567.

12. ELIZABETH LYGON; m William Norwood, d. 1602.

13. RICHARD NORWOOD; m. Elizabeth, dau. of Nicholas Studart.

  *   *   *   *   *   *

14. WILLIAM NORWOOD, sett. Surry Co., Virginia, 1656; sold land in Isle of Wight Co., Va., c. 1657. (Boddie, 17th Century Isle of Wight County, Virginia, p. 581).

Boddie is NOT an acceptable reference for identification of the parents of a colonist. There is no acceptable evidence of genetic links between gen. 13 and 14 or between gen. 14 and 15. Without citing authority, Va. Mag. of Hist. & Biog., vol. 33 (1925), p. 4 note A, states William is "another authenticated member" of this family.

  *   *   *   *   *   *

15. JOHN NORWOOD, ordered in 1649, by the co. court of Lower Norfolk "to conform ... to the Established Church"; moved to Anne Arundel Co., Maryland, and later to North Carolina. (Boddie, op. cit., pp. 59, 79; Ligon Family, p. 860; Va. Mag. of Hist. and Biog. (1925) v. 33).

Line 68

12. ELIZABETH LYGON (67-12); m. William Norwood, d. 1632.

13. HENRY NORWOOD, d. 1616; m. Elizabeth, dau. of Sir John Rodney.

14. HENRY NORWOOD, came to Virginia, 1647; Treasurer of the Colony, 1661-1673; d. in England, 1689, wife unidentified.

50   [Line 69

15. CHARLES NORWOOD, Clerk of the Virginia Assembly, 1654-1656; d. in
England. (Ligon Family, 860; Va. Mag. of Hist. & Biog. vol. 33 (1925), pp. 1-10).

Line 69

11. ELEANOR DENNIS (66-11); m. 1529, William Lygon, d. 1567.
12. MARGARET LYGON, d. 1617; m. Sir Henry Berkeley, Knt., d. 1601.
13. SIR MAURICE BERKELEY, b. 1617; m. Elizabeth, dau. of Sir William
Killigrew. (Ligon Family, 860).
14. SIR WILLIAM BERKELEY, d. London, England, 1677; Governor of Virginia, 1642-1654, 1661-1676; m. 1670 FRANCES CULPEPER (47-15). (Ibid. ; Cent.
Dict., Proper Names, p. 149).

Line 70

11. ELEANOR DENNIS (66-11); m. 1529, William Lygon, d. 1567.
12. KATHERINE LYGON; m. Thomas Foliot, of Pirton, co. Worcester, d.
1617. (Nash, Worcestershire, 1781, II 258).
13. SIR JOHN FOLIOT, KNT., of Naunton, co. Worcester; m. Elizabeth,
dau. of the Rt. Rev. John Aylmer, Bishop of London, 1577-1594, b. at Tivetshall
St. Mary, co. Norfolk, 1521, d. Fulham, near London, 3 June 1594. (Ligon Family,
101-102; Cent. Dict., Proper Names, 102).
14. THE REVEREND EDWARD FOLIOT, B.C.L. (also spelled Folliott), b.
1610, d. York Parish, York Co., Virginia, 1690 (will pr. 1690); matric. Hart Hall,
Oxford, 13 Apr. 1632, ae. 22, B.C.L., 24 Nov. 1632; Rector, Foots Cray, co. Kent,
1634; Alderton, co. Northampton, 1634-1640; came to Virginia, 1652; sett. York
Parish, 1652-1690; sett. Cople Parish, Westmoreland Co., Virginia, c. 1673; sett.
York-Hampton Parish, Virginia. He left issue in Virginia. (Ligon Family, 101-
102; Weis, Colonial Clergy of Virginia, North Carolina and South Carolina, 1955,
p. 18, q.v.).

Line 71

8. MARGARET de MOWBRAY (63-8); m. Sir Robert Howard, K.G.
9. CATHERINE HOWARD, liv. 29 June 1478; m. (spec. disp., 5 Oct. 1448),
as his 2nd wife, SIR EDWARD de NEVILLE, K.G., Lord Bergavenny (47-8), d. 18
Oct. 1476. (CP I, 30).
10. CATHERINE de NEVILLE; m. Robert Tanfield, Esq., of Gayton, co.
Northampton, fl. 1505 (son of Robert Tanfield of Gayton by Elizabeth, dau. of Edward Brook, Lord Cobham, and Elizabeth, dau. of James Tuchet, Lord Audley,
K.G.).
11. WILLIAM TANFIELD, ESQ., of Gayton, d. 1529; m. Isabel, dau. of
William Staveley, of Bignell, co. Buckingham.
12. FRANCIS TANFIELD, of Gayton, d. 1588; m. Bridget, dau. of Thomas
Cave, of Stanford. (Generations 8 to 15: V.C.H. Northampton; Northamptonshire
Families; Visitations of Essex, I 294-295).
13. ANNE TANFIELD; m. Clement Vincent, of Harpole, co. Northampton,
son of George Vincent of Peekleton. (Generations 10 to 13: Bridges, History of
Northamptonshire, pp. 275-276).
14. ELIZABETH VINCENT; m. Richard Lane, of Curtenhall, co. Northampton, son of Francis Lane of Bromley Hall, co. Stafford.
15. DOROTHY LANE; m. (2) William Randolph, of Little Houghton, co. Northampton, b. 1572, d. 1660, son of Robert Randolph, of Hams, co. Sussex, gent.,
and Rose, dau. of Thomas Roberts, of Hawkhurst, co. Kent.
16. RICHARD RANDOLPH, b. 21 Feb. 1621, d. Dublin, Ireland, 1671, of
Morton Hall, co. Warwick; m. Elizabeth Ryland, dau. of John Ryland.
17. COLONEL WILLIAM RANDOLPH, b. 1651, d. 11 Apr. 1711, came to Virginia c. 1660, settled at "Turkey Island," Clerk of Henrico Co.; Attorney-General
of Virginia, 1670-1671; Burgess and Speaker; President of the Council; Captain, 1680;

Lieut. Col., 1699; m. Mary Isham, dau. of Capt. Henry Isham of Bermuda Hundred. (William & Mary Quarterly, 1st Series, vol. VII, p. 122; Soc. Col. Wars, 1922, p. 390, Supp. 1941, p. 209; Generations 13 to 17: Ancestral Records and Portraits, II, pp. 750-751; Brainard, A Survey of Ishams in England & America (1938) for generations 15-17).

Line 72

9. CATHERINE HOWARD (71-9); m. 1448, EDWARD de NEVILLE, Lord Bergavenny (47-8).

10. MARGARET NEVILLE, d. 30 Sept. 1506; m. as his 2nd wife, John Brooke, under age 10 Dec. 1467, d. 9 Mar. 1511/2, 7th Lord Cobham, son of Edward Brooke and Elizabeth Tuchet, dau. of James, Lord Audley. (CP III, 346-347).

11. THOMAS BROOKE, d. 19 July 1529, 8th Lord Cobham; m. (1) Dorothy, dau. of Sir Henry Heydon, of Baconsthorpe, co. Norfolk, and his wife Anne Boleyn, dau. of Sir Geoffrey Boleyn and Anne Hoo. (CP III, 347).

12. ELIZABETH BROOKE; m. (1) Sir Thomas Wyatt, of Allington Castle, co. Kent, b. Kent, 1503, d. Sherborne, co. Dorset, 10 Oct. 1542, poet to King Henry VIII, son and h. of Sir Henry Wyatt and executor of his will; m. (2) Edward Warner. (Va. Hist. Mag. XXXI, 237 (will of Sir Henry Wyatt); Arthur Oswald, County Houses in Kent, 7 ff.).

13. SIR THOMAS WYATT, b. c. 1522; beheaded 11 Apr. 1554; m. 1537, Jane, dau. of Sir William Haute (or Hawte) and his wife, Mary, dau. of Sir Richard Guilford and Anne Pimpe. (For Hawte ancestry see Walter G. Davis, Ancestry of Mary Isaac, pp. 97-193; for Guilford, pp. 69-96. Thomas Hawte was leader of a badly organized rebellion against Queen Mary. For this generation see Mary Isaac, pp. 191-192.)

14. GEORGE WYATT, b. 1550, d. 1625, of Allington Castle and Boxley Abbey, co. Kent; m. 8 Oct. 1582, Jane Finch, living 29 Apr. 1639, when admin. estate son Hawte, dau. of Sir Thomas Finch, of Eastwell, co. Kent. (Stanard, Some Immigrants to Virginia, 1916, pp. 92-93; Va. Hist. Mag., II 177-180, XVI 204-205; William & Mary Quarterly, 1st Series, X 59-60, XII 34-35, 111-116; Mary Isaac, p. 192).

15. THE REVERED HAWTE WYATT, b. 1596, d. 31 July 1638, bur. 1 Aug.; came to Virginia in the "George," 1621, with his brother, Sir Francis Wyatt; minister at Jamestown, 1621-1625; m. (1) 1619, Barbara Elizabeth Mitford, d. 31 Oct. 1626; m. (2) Ann Cox; he returned to England and d. at Boxley, where an inscription on his tomb states that he had "Issue living in Virginia." (Harl. Soc. Publ., vol. 58, p. 12; J.C. Hotten, Lists, etc., p. 173; Va. Hist. Mag., II 177-180, XVI 204-205; William & Mary Quarterly, 1st Series, X 59-60, XII 34-35, 111-116; Stanard, Some Immigrants to Va., 1916, pp. 92-93; Weis, Colonial Clergy of Virginia, North Carolina and South Carolina, 1955, q.v.; Mary Isaac, p. 192).

15. SIR FRANCIS WYATT (brother of the Rev. Hawte Wyatt), came with his brother to Virginia, 1621, d. 1644; Governor of Virginia, 1621-1626, 1638-1641; author of A Briefe Declaration of the Plantation of Virginia during the First Twelve Yeares, 1624. (Va. Hist. Mag., X 265; Colonial Records of Virginia, 67; Mary Isaac, p. 192).

Line 73

9. SIR JOHN HOWARD, K.G. (63-9); m. (2) Margaret (Chedworth) (Wyfold) Norreys.

10. KATHERINE HOWARD, d. 12 Mar. 1535/6; m. SIR JOHN BOURCHIER, K.B. (18-12). (CP II, 153-155, see esp. 154, note c).

    *   *   *   *   *   *

Note: Sir John had only one child, JANE (18-13) by Katharine. By a concubine, Elizabeth Bacon he had other, illegitimate, issue.

    *   *   *   *   *   *

11. SIR JAMES BOURCHIER; m. (2) Mary, dau. of Sir Humphrey Banister.

12. SIR RALPH BOURCHIER; m. (1) Elizabeth, dau. of Francis Hall, of Grantham.

13. SIR JOHN BOURCHIER, KNT., 2nd son adm., Gray's Inn, 23 Nov. 1584, knighted, 2 July 1609; m. Elizabeth.

14. MARY BOURCHIER, only dau., b. England, c. 1598; m. England, Jabez Whitaker, b. 1595, d. 1626, son of the Rev. William Whitaker by his 2nd wife; came to Virginia bef. 1620; Captain; Burgess, 1623-1624; member of the Council, 1626; Lieut.-Colonel in the Virginia militia. (Soc. Col. Wars, Supp., 1941, p. 283; Allen, Our Children's Ancestors, 47, 49, 64; P.C.C. Administration Act. Book, 5 Apr. 1626: commission granted to Mary Bourchier, alias Whitaker, wife of Jabez Whitaker, dau. of Sir John Bourchier (late parishioner of Lambeth, co. Surrey, deceased), to administer the goods of said deceased - Elizabeth Bourchier, relic of said having renounced. Records of Virginia Colony, vol. I, p. 370).

Line 74

1. SAIER de QUINCY, Magna Charta Surety, 1215, b. 1155, d. Damietta, 3 Nov. 1219, 1st Earl of Winchester, 1207-1219, crusader, 1219; m. bef. 1173, Margaret de Beaumont, d. bef. 12 Feb. 1234/5, dau. of Robert, 3rd Earl of Leicester. (CP XII (2), 748).

2. ROGER de QUINCY, d. 25 Apr. 1264, 2nd Earl of Winchester, Constable of Scotland; m. (1) HELEN of GALLOWAY (139-2). (CP XII (2), 751).

3. ELENA de QUINCY, d. sh. bef. 20 Aug. 1296; m. bef. 1242 Sir Alan la Zouche, d. 12 Aug. 1270, Lord Zouche of Ashby la Zouche, co. Leicester, Constable of the Tower of London, and a descendant of the Counts of Porhoet in Brittany. (CP XII (2), 932).

     *   *   *   *   *   *
Note: Line breaks at this point. Alan, No. 3, and Eudo, No. 4, were brothers, not father and son.

     *   *   *   *   *   *
4. EUDO la ZOUCHE, of Haryngworth, d. betw. 28 Apr. and 25 June 1279; m. MILICENT de CANTELOU (146-4). (CP XII (2) 937+).

5. SIR WILLIAM la ZOUCHE, KNT., Lorde Zouche of Haryngworth, b. 1276, d. Mar. 1351/2, M.P., 1308-1348; m. bef. 15 Feb. 1295/6, Maud, dead 1346, dau. of John Lovel, Lord Lovel.

6. MILICENT la ZOUCHE, d. 22 June 1379; m. bef. 26 Mar. 1326, SIR WILLIAM DEINCOURT (149A-6) of Blankney, co. Lincoln, 2nd Lord Deincourt, d. 2 June 1364. (Gens. 5, 6: CP XII (2), 938; IV, 120-122). They were parents of No. 8.

Note: William, No. 7 in past editions, was brother, not father, of Margaret, No. 8.

8. MARGARET DEINCOURT, d. 2 Apr. 1380; m. (1) SIR ROBERT de TYBETOT (2-7), Lord Tybetot, of Nettlestead, co. Suffolk, d. 13 Apr. 1372. (CP IV, 118; XII (2), 97).

9. ELIZABETH de TIBETOT, b. 1371, d. bef. her husband; m. (2) SIR PHILIP le DESPENSER, KNT. (9-9), of Goxhill, Camoys Manor, Lord le Despenser, b. 1365/6, ae. 36+ on 4 Aug. 1401, d. 20 June 1424. (CP IV, 290).

10. MARGERY DESPENSER, ae. 24+ or 26+ at father's death, d. 20 Apr. 1478; m. (2) bef. 25 June 1423, Sir Roger Wentworth, Knt., d. c. 24 Oct. 1452, of North Elmsall, co. York, and Nettlestead, co. Suffolk. (CP IV, 291).

11. SIR HENRY WENTWORTH, d. 22 Mar. 1482/3, of Nettlestead and Codham Hall, Wethersfield, co. Essex; m. (1) Elizabeth Howard, dau. of Henry Howard, Esq.

12. MARGERY WENTWORTH, bur. Bures, co. Suffolk, 7 May 1540; m. bef. 1483, Sir William Waldegrave, K.B., bur. Bures, 30 Jan. 1527/8.

13. GEORGE WALDEGRAVE, ESQ., b. 1483, d. 1528, of Smallbridge; m. ANNE DRURY (5-13).

14. PHILLIS WALDEGRAVE (sister of Sir William Waldegrave); m. Thomas Higham, son of Sir John Higham, of Higham, co. Suffolk.

15. BRIDGET HIGHAM, liv. 1595; m. (1) Thomas Burrough, Esq., bp. Wickhambrook, co. Suffolk, d. 19 June 1597, son of William Burrough, gent., will made 12 May 1595, pr. 26 June 1597; arms granted, 1596.

16. REV. GEORGE BURROUGH, LL.B., bp. Wickhambrook, 26 Oct. 1597,
bur. Pettaugh, 24 Feb. 1653, LL.B., Trinity Hall, 1600, Rector of Pettaugh and
Gosbeck; m. Frances, dau. of Nicholas Sparrow of Wickhambrook, sister of Nicholas Sparrow of Gosbeck.
17. NATHANIEL BURROUGH, of Limehouse, co. Middlesex, living, 1663,
will dated 1681, pr. 23 Mar. 1682; m. a sister (prob. Rebecca) of John Style of Stepney, co. Middlesex, will made 26 Oct. 1658. On 19 July 1657, Mrs. Rebecca Burrows adm. 1st Church of Roxbury, Mass. 29. 9 mo. 1674, Mrs. Burrows recom-
mended and dismissed, going to England. (NEHGR, 33, p. 239 and note).
18. THE REVEREND GEORGE BURROUGHS, A.B., b. c. 1650, executed for
witchcraft, Salem, 19 Aug. 1692, ae. 42; Harvard College, A.B., 1670; minister at
Portland, Maine, 1674-1676, 1683-1690; ordained, Danvers, Massachusetts, 25
Nov. 1690. (Weis, Colonial Clergy of New England, 1936, p. 47; Generations 4 to
10: CP IV, 122, 290; 10 to 18: Muskett, Suffolk Manorial Families, I 311-314;
NEHGR, 108: 174-175).

Line 75

13. GEORGE WALDEGRAVE (74-13), of Smallbridge; m. ANNE DRURY (5-13),
dau. of Sir Robert Drury of Hawstead, Knt.; she m. (2) Sir Thomas Jermyn, Knt.
(See 37-16). (Visitations of Essex, 1558, I 120).
14. SIR WILLIAM WALDEGRAVE, KNT., d. 2 May 1554, of Smallbridge, co.
Suffolk, and of Waltham-Stow, co. Essex; m. Julian, dau. of Sir John Rainesford,
Knt. (Ibid., I 121).
15. DOROTHY WALDEGRAVE; m. Arthur Harris, Esq., of Woodham Mortimer and Creeksea, co. Essex, son of Sir William Harris of Creeksea. (Ibid., I
121; Muskett, I 45, 47; Morant, Essex, I 363).
16. DOROTHY HARRIS, will made 1626; m. Robert Kempe, Esq., b. 1565,
d. 1612, ae. 47 yrs.; will pr. 1613, buried in Gissing Church, Gissing, co. Norfolk,
son of Richard Kempe, will made 12 Mar. 1599, of Wasbrooke, co. Suffolk, and
Gissing, by his wife, Alice Cockram, of Hampstead, co. Middlesex. (Visitations
of Norfolk, 175-176, 297-298).
17. RICHARD KEMPE, of Gissing, made his will, 1649, pr. at London, 6 Dec.
1656, Secretary of Virginia, 1634; m. Elizabeth Lunsford, who probated her husband's will; left issue. (Muskett, II 230, 237; Visitations of Norfolk, 176).
17. EDMUND KEMPE (brother of Richard), came to Virginia, 1644, as attor-
ney for his brother, Sir Robert Kempe, 1st Baronet. Edmund left issue in Virginia.
(Ibid.; Musket, II 236-237; Gens. 16 & 17, see Hitchin-Kemp, A General History
of the Komp Families of Great Britain and her Colonies (1902)).

Line 76

10. MARGERY DESPENSER (74-10); m. (2) Sir Roger Wentworth, Knt.
11. AGNES WENTWORTH, 3rd dau., d. 1450; m. Sir Robert Constable, Knt.,
d. 1488, of Flambrough, co. York. (Visitations of Essex, 1612, I 314).
12. SIR MARMADUKE CONSTABLE, KNT., of Flambrough, M.P., b. 1443,
d. 1518; m. Joyce, dau. of Sir Humphrey Stafford, of Grafton.
13. SIR ROBERT CONSTABLE, KNT., of Flambrough; m. Jane, dau. of Sir
William Ingelby of Ripton, co. York.
14. CATHERINE CONSTABLE, d. York, 1585; m. 1512, Sir Roger Cholmley,
Knt., of Roxby, co. York, d. London, 28 Apr. 1531.
15. SIR RICHARD CHOLMLEY, KNT., b. 1516, bur. Thornton-le-Dale, 17
May 1579, ae. 63 years, of Roxby, co. York; m. (2) Catherine Clifford, bur. at
Whitby, 1598, dau. of Sir Henry Clifford, K.G., 1st Earl of Cumberland, by his
wife, Margaret Percy, dau. of Sir Henry Percy, K.G., b. 1478, d. 1527, 5th Earl
of Northumberland, by his wife, Katherine Spencer, dau. of Sir Robert Spencer,
Knt., by his 2nd wife (m. in or bef. 1470), ELEANOR BEAUFORT (80-11).
16. SIR HENRY CHOLMLEY, KNT., bur. St.John's Ch., York, 13 Jan.
1615/6, of Grandmount, Whitby and Roxby, co. York; m. Margaret, bur. St.John's,
15 Apr. 1628, dau. of Sir William Babthorpe, Knt.
17. MARY CHOLMLEY, of Whitby, b. 1593, d. 8 Jan. 1649/50, ae. 56, bur.

at Bolton-Percy; m. St. Helen's, York, 4 Feb. 1626/7, the Hon. and Rev. Henry
Fairfax, A.M., b. Denton, co. York, 14 Jan. 1588, d. 6 Apr. 1665, of Oglethorpe,
rector of Bolton-Percy, co. York, 1646-1660, son of Sir Thomas Fairfax, of Cameron, 1st Lord Fairfax.
    18. HENRY FAIRFAX, bp. Ashton-under-Lyne, 20 Oct. 1631, d. 9 Apr. 1688,
of Oglethorpe, 4th Lord Fairfax of Cameron, 1671, M.P. for the co. of York, 1678;
m. Frances, d. 14 Feb. 1683/4, dau. of Sir Robert Barwick of Toulston, co. York.
(CP V, 231).
    19. HENRY FAIRFAX, b. Bolton-Percy, 20 Apr. 1659, d. 1708, of Denton
and Toulston, High Sheriff of Yorkshire, 1691; m. Anne, dau. of Richard Harrison.
    20. WILLIAM FAIRFAX, bp. Newton-Kyme, 30 Oct. 1691, d. 3 Sept. 1757,
of "Belvoir," Virginia, President of the Council of Virginia; m. (1) 1717, Sarah,
d. in Massachusetts, 18 Jan. 1731, dau. of Major Thomas Walker; m. (2) Deborah,
dau. of Francis Clark, of Salem, Massachusetts. (Joseph Foster, Pedigrees of
the County Families of North and East Riding of Yorkshire, 3 vols., see the Fairfax pedigree; Ruvigny, Plantagenet Roll of the Blood Royal Exeter vol. (1907) pp.
68, 657-660).

Line 77

    11. AGNES WENTWORTH (76-11); m. Sir Robert Constable, Knt., d. 1488.
    12. SIR WILLIAM CONSTABLE, KNT., 5th son, d. 1528, of Caythorpe and
Wassand, co. York; m. Joan Fullthorpe, will pr. 18 Dec. 1540, dau. of Thomas
Fullthorpe, d. 1468, of Rudstan, co. York.
    13. MARMADUKE CONSTABLE, ESQ., of Wassand in Holderness, co. York,
d. 1558; m. Elizabeth Stokes, d. 1560, bur. at Goxhill, dau. of Robert Stokes, of
Goxhill and Bycherton, co. York, by Bridget (Carleton?), d. 1556, widow of Sir
William Gascoigne. (Visitations of Yorkshire, 298).
    14. MARMADUKE CONSTABLE, of Wassand, bur. Goxhill, 11 July 1568, will
proved same month; m. Catherine, will dated 1628, bur. 9 June 1634, ae. 90 yrs.,
dau. of John Holme, of Paull Holme, co. York.
    15. WILLIAM CONSTABLE, gent., of Drax Abbey, co. York, 1613, d. 1618;
name of wife not known.
    16. THE REV. MARMADUKE CONSTABLE, A.M., b. 1593/4, d. Everingham,
co. York, 18 Aug. 1638; A.B., Queens Coll., Camb., 1614/5, A.M., 1618, Rector
of Newton-by-Tofte, co. Lincoln, 1618, and of Everingham, co. York, 1618-1638;
m. Everingham, 17 May 1632, Katherine Elithorpe, prob. b. at Holme-on-Spalding-
Moor, co. York, d. Wallingford, Connecticut, 27 Jan. 1687/8; she m. (2) c. 1641/2,
Deacon Richard Miles of Milford and New Haven, Conn. (by whom she had 3 children).
    17. GEORGE CONSTABLE, bp. 23 Dec. 1635, took oath of fidelity at New
Haven, Conn., 7 Apr. 1657, but returned to England. He had two elder brothers;
WILLIAM, bp. 3 June 1633, and MARMADUKE, bp. 28 Aug. 1634, of whom one is
supposed to have d.y., and the other to have returned to England. (Joseph Foster,
Pedigrees, etc., of Yorkshire, London, 1874 (families alphabetically arranged,
see Constable); John I. Coddington, "The Elithorpe Family," The American Genealogist, Jan. 1955, vol. 31, pp. 24-29).

Line 78

    13. SIR WILLIAM CALVERLEY, KNT. (87-13), d. 1488; m. 1441, Agnes Tem-
pest.
    14. ELIZABETH CALVERLEY; m. Thomas Wentworth, of North Elmsall, son
of Sir John Wentworth, of North Elmsall, co. York, and Jane, dau. of Richard
Beaumont. (Generations 13 to 18: Lincolnshire Pedigrees, pp. 1062-1063; Wentworth Genealogy, I 55-63; Marbury Ancestry, p. 25; William Flower, Visitations
of Yorkshire, 1563-1564).
    15. THOMAS WENTWORTH, of North Elmsall, in the Parish of Kirkby, co.
York, will dated 1522/3; m. Jane, dau. of Oliver Mirfield, of Howley, co. York,
by Isabel Eland. (Michael Stead, Records of the Parish of Batley, p. 274). Thomas
Wentworth of Elmsall and Sir William Mirfield were appointed administrators of

the estate of Isabel (Eland) (Mirfield) Ayshton, 22 Nov. 1488 (Stead, p. 300). This confirms the marriage of Thomas (d. 1523) and Jane, only sister and heir of Sir William who d.s.p. After his death the Mirfield estates went to the heirs of Thomas and Jane. Sir Thomas Wentworth is given by Stead (p. 134, Records of Batley) as the husband of Jane, dau. of Oliver Mirfield, which is undoubtedly correct.

16. OLIVER WENTWORTH, gent., of Goxhill, co. Lincoln, will dated 7 Dec. 1558, pr. 28 Jan. 1558/9; m. Jane, who proved her husband's will. (Wentworth Genealogy, I 55).

   *   *   *   *   *   *

The parentage of William, No. 17, has not been determined.

17. WILLIAM WENTWORTH, of Waltham, Kirton in Lindsey, and Goxhill, co. Lincoln, d. 22 May 1574, will dated 16 May 1574, pr. 24 May 1574; m. (2) Anne, surviving in 1574.

18. CHRISTOPHER WENTWORTH, of Barrow and Alford, co. Lincoln, b. 1556 (ae. 18 in 1574 at Waltham), supervisor to Francis Wentworth, 1611, will dated 8 Dec. 1628, pr. at Alford, 15 May 1633; m. St. Peter-at-Gowts, Lincoln, co. Lincoln, 19 Aug. 1583, KATHERINE MARBURY (78A-15). (Meredith B. Colket, Jr., Marbury Ancestry, p. 25; Wentworth Genealogy, 60-63).

19. ANNE WENTWORTH, bp. Irby-on-Humber, 28 Oct. 1585, living 1628; m. the Rev. John Lawson. (Lincolnshire Pedigrees, pp. 1062-1063).

20. CHRISTOPHER LAWSON, b. c. 1616, sett. Exeter, N.H., 1639; m. Elizabeth Fitton. (Gen. Dict. of Me. and N.H., p. 419).

19. PRISCILLA WENTWORTH, bp. Waltham, 14 June 1594 (sister of Anne Wentworth above); m. Waltham, 1 Sept. 1619 (mar. lic. 28 Aug. 1619, ae. 24), William Helme, b. 1581 (ae. 38 in 1619).

20. CHRISTOPHER HELME, of Exeter, N.H., 1639.

19. WILLIAM WENTWORTH, bp. 8 June 1584, of Risby, co. Lincoln, eldest son in 1628; m. Alford, co. Lincoln, 28 Nov. 1614, Susanna (Carter) Fleming, prob. dau. of Edward Carter, and widow of Uther Fleming (bur. Alford, 22 Jan. 1613/4). (Marbury Ancestry, p. 25; Wentworth Genealogy, I 63-65; Lincolnshire Pedigrees, 1062-1063).

20. ELDER WILLIAM WENTWORTH, of Exeter, New Hampshire, 1639, bp. Alford, co. Lincoln, 15 Mar. 1615/6, d. 15 Mar. 1696/7, ordained Ruling Elder at Dover, N.H., 10 Mar. 1655/6, preached at Dover and Salmon Falls, N.H., and at South Berwick, Maine, 1665-1690, and at Exeter, N.H., 1690-1693. (Colket, Marbury Ancestry, p. 25; Noyes, Libby, and Davis, Genealogical Dictionary of Maine and New Hampshire, I 324; Weis, Colonial Clergy of New England, 1936, p. 219; Richard LeBaron Bowen, NEHGR, (1944) 98:10-25; Lincolnshire Pedigrees, 1062-1063; Dr. John Wentworth, Wentworth Genealogy, Boston, 1878, I 66-70).

Since the above line breaks down at generation 17, the descendants of Elder William Wentworth will be interested in the following alternative MC line, leading back to deVere.

Line 78A

5. SIR JOHN GERNON, KNT. (123-5), aged 37 in 1327 at father's death, d. 1333/4, of Lexton Hundred, East Thorpe and Great Birch; m. (1) Isabella Bygot, d. ae. 13 in 1311; m. (2) 1313, Alice, dau. of Sir Roger de Colville of Bytham, co. Lincoln, and wife Margaret de Braiose, dau. of Richard, yr. son of John de Braiose and his wife Margaret, dau. of Llewellyn ap Iorworth, Prince of Wales. Alice was wid. of Guy Gobaud by 14 Apr. 1313. Sir John m. (3) Margaret, dau. of Sir John Wigton.

6. MARGARET GERNON (by 2nd wife), occ. 1330-1352; m. Sir Geoffrey de Gresley of Drakelow, occ. 1309, dead 1331/2. (Refs. for all Gresley generations see Staffs. Hist. Cols. ns I 223-5, 240).

7. SIR JOHN de GRESLEY of Drakelow, b. c. 1328, d. c. 1395; m. (1) Alice de Swynnerton, d. c. 1350, dau. of Sir Thomas de Swynnerton and his wife Mathilda de Holand; m. (2) Joan, wid. of Sir Thomas de Wastneys, d. 1393.

8. SIR NICHOLAS de GRESLEY, b. c. 1345-50, d. c. 1374-89; m. Thomasine

de Wastneys.

    9. SIR THOMAS de GRESLEY, b. c. 1365-7, d. c. 1445; m. Margaret Walsh, occ. 1392-1421.

    10. MARGARET de GRESLEY; m. as 1st wife, Sir Thomas Blount, Treas. of Normandy, d. 1456. (CP IX, 333-4; Colket, Marbury Ancestry, 46-7).

    11. SIR THOMAS BLOUNT, b. c. 1420, d. c. 1468; m. c. 1453, Agnes Hawley, bur. 14 Oct. 1462. (Colket).

    12. ANN BLOUNT, b. c. 1453-62; m. William Marbury, b. c. 1448-53, d. c. 1506-13. (Colket).

    13. ROBERT MARBURY, b. c. 1490, d. 1545; m. Katharine, d. 17 Aug. 1525. (Colket).

    14. WILLIAM MARBURY, b. c. 1524; m. Agnes Lenton, d. 1581. (Colket).

    15. KATHARINE MARBURY; m. 1583, CHRISTOPHER WENTWORTH (78-18) of Barrow, Lincs., d. 1633. (Colket).

Line 79

    5. SIR WILLIAM la ZOUCHE (74-5), b. 18 or 21 Dec. 1276, d. 11 or 12 Mar. 1351/2; m. bef. 15 Feb. 1295/6, Maud, dau. of John Lovel, Lord Lovel. (CP XII (2), 938 et seq. for all refs. gens. 5-13).

    6. EUDO la ZOUCHE of Haryngworth, b. 1297/8, d. 24 Apr. 1326; m. bef. June 1322, Joan, ae. 22 or 23 in 1322, dead Jan. 1359/60, dau. of William Inge, Chief Justice, 1316-17.

    7. WILLIAM la ZOUCHE, 1st Lord Zouche of Haryngworth, b. 1321, d. 23 Apr. 1382, M.P., 1348-51; m. bef. 16 July 1334, Elizabeth, will 16 May 1380, dau. of WILLIAM de ROS, 2nd Lord Ros of Helmsley (1-5).

    8. WILLIAM la ZOUCHE, Lord Zouche of Haryngworth, b. c. 1342, d. 13 May 1396, M.P. 1382/3; m. (1) by 27 Oct. 1351, Agnes, prob. dau. of Sir Henry Green, d. betw. 2 Dec. 1391 and 28 Apr. 1393; m. (2) Elizabeth, dau. of Edward, 1st Lord Despenser. She d. 10 or 11 Apr. 1408.

    9. WILLIAM la ZOUCHE, K.G., Lord Zouche of Haryngworth (by 1st wife), b. c. 1373, d. 3 Nov. 1415, M.P., 1415; m. bef. 1402, Elizabeth, said to be dau. of Sir William Crosse.

    10. WILLIAM la ZOUCHE, Lord Zouche of Haryngworth, b. c. 1401, M.P., 1425/6, d. 25 Dec. 1462; m. (1) bef. 8 Mar. 1423/4, ALICE SEYMOUR, Lady St. Maur and Lovel (99-10), seen 1430/1; m. (2) by 2 Apr. 1450 Elizabeth de St. John.

    10A. WILLIAM la ZOUCHE, Lord Zouche, b. c. 1432, ae. 30+ at father's death, d. 15 Jan. 1467/8; M.P., 1455/6; m. (1) Katharine, dau. of Sir Rowland Lenthall, by Lucy, aunt and, in her issue, coh. of Henry Grey, 7th Lord Grey of Codnor, dau. of Richard, 4th Lord Grey; m. (2) Katharine Plumpton.

    11. JOHN la ZOUCHE (by 1st wife), Lord Zouche of Haryngworth, b. 1459, d. c. Mar. 1525/6, M.P., 1482/3; m. bef. 26 Feb. 1486/7, JOAN DINHAM (125-9), d. aft. 1507.

    12. JOHN la ZOUCHE, Lord Zouche of Haryngworth, b. c. 1486, d. 10 Aug. 1550, M.P., 1529; m. (1) Dorothy, d. by 8 Oct. 1527, dau. of Sir William Capell, Lord Mayor of London; m. (2) Susan (Welby) Davenport.

    13. RICHARD la ZOUCHE, by (1), Lord Zouche, b. c. 1510, d. 22 July 1552; twice m.

    14. DOROTHY (by unidentified mistress), bastard dau.; m. in or aft. 1553, Sir Arthur Grey, K.G., Lord Grey of Wilton, Gov. of Ireland, b. 1536, d. 14 Oct. 1593. (CP VI, 186-7). Before the line was corrected, he appeared in generation 13, line 45. There is no line in the current edition running through Sir Arthur, Lord Grey. (Gens. 5-13: CP XII (2), 397-449).

Line 80

    4. EUDO la ZOUCHE (74-4), d. betw. 28 Apr. and 25 June 1279; m. MILICENT de CANTELOU (146-4).

    5. EVA la ZOUCHE, d. 5 Dec. 1314; m. 1289, SIR MAURICE de BERKELEY (88-5), b. Apr. 1281, d. 31 May 1326, Lord Berkeley of Berkeley Castle. (CP II, 128).

    6. THOMAS de BERKELEY, ae. 30+ at father's death, d. 27 Oct. 1361, Lord Berkeley, Marshal in France, 1340, Captain of the Scottish Marches, 1342; m. (1)

1320, Margaret de Mortimer, d. 5 May 1337, dau. of SIR ROGER de MORTIMER, Earl of March (147-5) and JOAN de GENEVILLE (12-6); m. (2) 30 May 1347, Katherine, d. 13 Mar. 1385, widow of Sir Piers le Veel, dau. and heir of Sir John Clivedon, of Charfield, Gloucester, by Emma his wife. (CP II, 129).

7. MAURICE de BERKELEY (by 1st wife), b. 1330, d. 8 June 1368, Lord Berkeley, M.P., 1362-1368; m. Aug. 1338, Elizabeth Despenser, d. 13 July 1389, dau. of SIR HUGH le DESPENSER (14-6) and ALIANORE de CLARE (34-5). (CP II, 130).

8. THOMAS de BERKELEY, b. Berkeley Castle, 5 Jan. 1352/3, d. 13 July 1417, Lord Berkeley, M.P., 1381-1415; m. Nov. 1367, Margaret de Lisle, b. 1360, d. betw. May and Sept. 1392, dau. of Warin de Lisle, Lord Lisle. (CP II, 130; VIII, 53).

9. ELIZABETH de BERKELEY, Lady Lisle and Teye, ae. 30 in 1417, d. 28 Dec. 1422; m. RICHARD de BEAUCHAMP, K.G. (147-8), Earl of Warwick and Albemarle.

10. ELEANOR BEAUCHAMP, b. 1407, d. 6 Mar. 1466/7; m. (1) Thomas, Lord Ros; m. (2) c. 1436, EDMUND BEAUFORT (90-10), Duke of Somerset; m. (3) Walter Rokesley, Esq.

11. ELEANOR BEAUFORT, d. 16 Aug. 1501; m. (1) James Butler, b. c. 1420, beheaded 1 May 1461, Earl of Ormond and Wiltshire; m. (2) in or bef. 1470, Sir Robert Spencer, Knt., of Spencercombe, co. Devon, b. c. 1435, living 1502. (CP X, 126).

12. MARGARET SPENCER, b. c. 1472; m. c. 1490, Thomas Cary of Chilton Foliot, Wiltshire, b. c. 1460.

13. WILLIAM CARY, b. c. 1495, d. 22 June 1529, Gentleman of the Privy Chamber and Esquire of the Body to King Henry VIII; m. 31 Jan. 1520/1, MARY BOLEYN (64-12), d. 19 July 1543 (sister of Queen Anne).

14. MARY CARY, d. 15 Jan. 1568/9, Chief Lady of the Bedchamber to Queen Elizabeth; m. c. 1539, Sir Francis Knolleys, K.G., b. c. 1514, d. 19 July 1596, of Rotherfield Greys, co. Oxford.

15. ANNE KNOLLYS, living 30 Aug. 1608; m. 19 Nov. 1571, SIR THOMAS WEST (4-15), 2nd Lord Delaware. (CP IV, 159-60).

16. ELIZABETH WEST, b. 11 Sept. 1573, d. 12 Jan. 1632/3; m. as his 2nd wife, Wherwell, Hants, 12 Feb. 1593/4, Herbert Pelham I, of Fordingham, co. Dorset, and Hellingly, co. Sussex (father, by his 1st wife, of Herbert Pelham II (1580-1624) who m. Penelope West (see below) sister of Elizabeth West above). He b. c. 1564, d. 12 Apr. 1620.

17. ELIZABETH PELHAM, b. Hellingly, 27 Apr. 1604, d. 1 Nov. 1628; m. Salisbury, 4 Sept. 1621, Col. John Humphrey, gent., of Chaldon (ae. 25 years in 1621), who m. (3) 1630/4, SUSAN FIENNES (57-18), q.v. (NEHGR, 33: 288).

18. ANNE HUMPHREY, only surviving child, bp. Fordingham, 17 Dec. 1625; m. (1) William Palmes; m. (2) Rev. John Miles of Swansea, Mass.

19. THE REVEREND SAMUEL MYLES, A.M. (H.C., 1684), Rector of King's Chapel, Boston, Massachusetts, 1689-1728.

16. PENELOPE WEST (sister of Elizabeth above), b. 9 Sept. 1582, d. c. 1619; m. c. 1599, Herbert Pelham II, b. c. 1580, d. Boston, England, 20 July 1624, of Hastings, Sussex, and Boston, co. Lincoln.

17. HERBERT PELHAM III, ESQ., b. c. 1600, buried, Bures, Suffolk, 1 July 1673, came to New England, 1639/40; first Treasurer of Harvard College, 1643; m. (1) Jemima Waldegrave, dau. of Thomas and granddau. of Thomas Waldegrave; m. (2) 1638, ELIZABETH (BOSVILE) HARLAKENDEN (95-19), dau. of COL. GODFREY BASSEVILLE (or BOSVILE) (95-18) of Gunthwaite, co. York, and widow of ROGER HARLAKENDEN (89-18), of Cambridge, Massachusetts.

18. PENELOPE PELHAM, bp. Bures, 1633 (child of the 1st wife), b. 1631, d. 1703; m. Governor Josiah Winslow, b. 1628, d. 1680, Governor of Plymouth Colony.

18. CAPTAIN EDWARD PELHAM, GENT. (son by the 2nd wife), of Newport, Rhode Island, b. c. 1650, d. 20 Sept. 1730; m. 18 Apr. 1682, Freelove Arnold, dau. of Governor Benedict Arnold of Rhode Island.

17. PENELOPE PELHAM (sister of Herbert Pelham III), b. c. 1619, d. 28 May 1702; m. 9 Nov. 1641, Richard Bellingham, b. 1592, d. 1672, M.P., 1628-1629; Governor of Massachusetts, 1641, 1654, 1665-1672 (no issue by this marriage). (See Line 4 for other West descendants.)

Line 80A

6. THOMAS de BERKELEY, Lord Berkeley (80-6); m. (2) Katherine Clivedon.
7. SIR JOHN BERKELEY of Beverstone, Gloucester, b. 1352, d. 1428, M.P.,
Sheriff of Gloucester; m. (1) Elizabeth, dau. and heir of Sir John Betteshorne.
(John Smyth, The Berkeley Manuscripts (ed. by Sir John Maclean), 3 vols., Gloucester, 1883-5, I: 349-51, III: 100).
8. ELIZABETH BERKELEY, d. sh. bef. 8 Dec. 1478; m. (2) aft. 14 Mar.
1420/1, Sir John Sutton, K.G. (See (36-13) and (30-10)), b. 25 Dec. 1400, d. 30 Sept.
1487, 1st Lord Dudley, Lord Lieutenant of Ireland, 1428-30, Constable of the Tower
of London, 1470-83. (CP IV, 479-80).
9. SIR EDMUND SUTTON; m. JOYCE de TIBETOT (30-10).

Line 81

12. MARGARET SPENCER (80-12), b. c. 1472; m. c. 1490, Thomas Cary.
13. MARY CARY; m. Sir John Delaval of Seaton Delaval, b. 16 Apr. 1498,
d. Dec. 1562, son of John and Ann (Gray) Delaval.
14. EDWARD DELAVAL, of Tynemouth, d. bef. 1562; m. Phillis Ogle, d.
1606, dau. of John Ogle. (See note, Line 65).
15. BARBARA DELAVAL; m. John Watson, d. New Castle on Tyne, 1612, son
of the Hon. John Watson of Bedlington.
16. MARY WATSON; m. Christopher Wetherill, bur. at Stockton, 25 May
1622, son of Gyles Wetherill, of Stockton-on-Tees, co. Durham.
17. THOMAS WETHERILL, bur. at New Castle, 26 Dec. 1672; m. New Castle,
16 July 1633, Isabel Maugham, d. bef. Sept. 1658.
18. CHRISTOPHER WETHERILL, b. c. 1648, of Burlington, New Jersey,
1683. (Generations 12 to 18: See Walter Lee Sheppard, Jr.,"The Wetherill-Watson
Ancestry, " in NEHGR, 104: 270-282).

Line 82

5. EVA la ZOUCHE (80-5); m. 1289, SIR MAURICE de BERKELEY (88-5).
6. ISABEL BERKELEY, d. 25 July 1362; m. (1) June 1328, ROBERT de
CLIFFORD (144-6), Lord Clifford, b. 5 Nov. 1305, d. 20 May 1344. (CP III, 291).
7. SIR ROGER de CLIFFORD, b. 10 July 1333, d. 13 July 1389, Lord Clifford,
Sheriff of Cumberland, Governor of Carlisle Castle, 1377; m. Maud de Beauchamp,
d. Jan. or Feb. 1402/3, dau. of THOMAS de BEAUCHAMP, Earl of Warwick (5-6),
and KATHERINE de MORTIMER (147-6), q.v. (CP III, 292).
8. KATHERINE CLIFFORD, d. 23 Apr. 1413; m. Ralph de Greystoke, b. 18
Oct. 1353, d. 6 Apr. 1418, Lord Greystoke. (CP VI, 190-196).
9. MAUD de GREYSTOKE; m. Eudo de Welles, d. bef. 26 Aug. 1421, grandson of JOHN de MOWBRAY (63-6), see TAG 37: 114-5; 38: 180. (CP XII (2), 443).
10. SIR LIONEL de WELLES, K.G., b. 1406, d. Towton, 29 Mar. 1461, Lord
Welles, Governor of Ireland, 1438-1442; m. (1) Methley, 15 Aug. 1417, Joan de
Waterton, d. betw. 14 Oct. 1434 and 14 Apr. 1447, dau. of Robert de Waterton of
co. York. (CP XII (2), 443).
11. MARGARET de WELLES, d. 13 July 1480; m. (1) Sir Thomas Dymoke,
Knt., of Scrivelsby, co. Lincoln, son of Sir Philip Dymoke, b. c. 1428, beheaded
12 Mar. 1470.
12. SIR LIONEL DYMOKE, KNT., d. 17 Aug. 1519; m. Joan, dau. of Richard
Griffith. (See also 84-12.)
13. ANNE DYMOKE; m. John Goodrick, of Kirby, co. Lincoln. (See Early
Chancery Proceedings, Bundle 444/43).
14. LIONEL GOODRICK; m. prob. Winifred, dau. of Henry Sapcott.
15. ANN GOODRICK; m. Benjamin Bolles, of Osberton, co. Nottingham.
16. THOMAS BOLLES, of Osberton, 1614; m. Elizabeth Perkins, dau. of
Thomas Perkins, of Fishlake, co. York.
17. JOSEPH BOWLES (or Bolles), bp. at Worksop, 19 Feb. 1609; d. 1678;
settled at Winter Harbor, Maine, 1640; later at Wells, Maine; m. Mary, prob. a

sister or dau. of Morgan Howell.

Line 83

10. SIR LIONEL de WELLES, K.G. (82-10); m. Joan de Waterton.
11. CICELY de WELLES; m. Sir Robert Willoughby of Parham, d. 30 May 1465, son of Sir Thomas Willoughby of Eresby and Joan, dau. of Sir Richard Fitz Alan, Knt. (d. 3 June 1419, and Alice, his wife, d. 30 Aug. 1436, widow of Roger Burley), son of SIR JOHN d'ARUNDEL, KNT. (121-7) and his wife, ELEANOR MALTRAVERS (88-8). (E. & E. Salisbury, Family Histories and Genealogies, 1892, I Part II, p. 603; CP XII (2), 449, note j).
12. SIR CHRISTOPHER WILLOUGHBY, Lord Willoughby, K.B., b. 1453, will dtd. 1 Nov. 1498, pr. 13 July 1499; m. bef. 28 Mar. 1482, Margaret, d. 1515/6, dau. of Sir William Jenney, Knt., of Knotteshall, co. Suffolk.
13. SIR THOMAS WILLOUGHBY, Chief Justice of the Common Pleas (will dated 20 July 1544, proved 5 Nov. 1545); m. Bridget, dau. of Sir Robert Read, Knt., of Blore Place, co. Kent, Chief Justice of the Common Pleas.
14. CHRISTOPHER WILLOUGHBY, of St. George the Martyr, Southwark, co. Surrey (will proved 11 Jan. 1586); m. Margery, sister of Thomas Tottishurst, executor of Christopher Willoughby's will.
15. CHRISTOPHER WILLOUGHBY, of Chiddingstone, co. Kent, d. bef. 1633; m. Martha.
16. COLONEL WILLIAM WILLOUGHBY, of London and Portsmouth, Commissioner of the Royal Navy, b. c. 1588; m. Elizabeth. (For their wills, see Salisbury, op. cit., pp. 517-523).
17. DEPUTY-GOVERNOR FRANCIS WILLOUGHBY, d. Charlestown, Massachusetts, 3 Apr. 1671 (will made 4 June 1670, proved 10 Apr. 1671, see Salisbury, op. cit., pp. 543-547), of London, M.P., Commissioner of the Royal Navy; came to New England, 1638; selectman, deputy, magistrate, 1650-1654; Deputy-Governor of Massachusetts, 1665-1667, 1668-1670; m. (1) Mary; m. (2) Sarah Taylor; m. (3) c. Aug. 1658/9, Margaret (Locke) Taylor.
18. SUSANNA WILLOUGHBY, b. Charlestown, 10 Aug. 1664; d. Saybrook, Connecticut, 21 Feb. 1709/10; m. 1683, NATHANIEL LYNDE (55-17), b. 22 Nov. 1659, d. Saybrook, Conn., 5 Oct. 1729, son of the HON. SIMON LYNDE (55-16) and his wife, Hannah (Newdigate) Lynde. (Salisbury, op. cit., pp. 507-604, and chart).

Line 84

12. SIR LIONEL DYMOKE, KNT. (82-12), 2nd son of Mareham-on-the-Hill, Sheriff of Lincolnshire, 1516, d. 7 Aug. 1519; m. Joan, dau. of Richard Griffith, Esq., of Stockford. (Visitation of Lincolnshire, 1562/4; Genealogist IV (1880), p. 19; Frank Allaben, Ancestry of Leander Howard Crall, N.Y., 1908, 161, 195-198, 204-206. This pedigree was furnished by T.M.I. Watkins, Portcullis, College of Arms, London, 28 June 1896).
13. ALICE DYMOKE; m. as his 2nd wife, Sir William Skipwith, Knt., b. 1488 (ae. 30 in 1518), d. 7 July 1547, of South Ormsby, co. Lincoln, High Sheriff of Lincolnshire, 1527. (Harl. Soc. Publ., 53: 1204; Allaben, op. cit., 183).
14. JOHN SKIPWITH, ESQ., of Walmsgate, 2nd son, d. 1585, admin. gr. to his widow, 5 Nov. 1585; m. Eleanor, dau. of John Kingston, of Great Grimsby, d. 4 June 1599 (will dated 2 Jan. 1593/4, codicil, 4 June 1599, pr. 31 Dec. 1599).
15. MARY SKIPWITH, will made 12 Mar. 1626/7, pr. 2 Oct. 1627; m. John Newcomen, of Saltfleetby, bur. there 1 May 1621, will made 29 Jan. 1616/7, pr. 15 May 1621.
16. ELEANOR NEWCOMEN, bp. Saltfleetby, 10 Nov. 1576, living Oct. 1627 (as executrix of her mother's estate), bur. Saltfleetby, 19 Nov. 1634; m. Saltfleetby, 20 Apr. 1597, William Asfordby of Saltfleetby, All Saints, and Newark-on-Trent, bur. Saltfleetby, by May 1623.
17. JOHN ASFORDBY, son and heir, liv. 11 Nov. 1657; m. 14 Oct. 1634, Alice Wolley, bp. Cumberworth, 14 Dec. 1610, bur. 16 June 1638, dau. of William Wolley and Anne Lemyng of Cumberworth.

18. HON. WILLIAM ASFORDBY, bp. Saltfleetby, 29 Mar. 1638, will made 6
Nov. 1697, pr. 24 Feb. 1697/8, of Stayne-in-the-Marsh, co. Lincoln, and Kingston
and Marbletown (Ulster Co.), N.Y., came to N.Y., bef. 1674, member of the first
N.Y. Assembly and Sheriff of Ulster Co.; m. c. 1666, Martha, d. 20 Apr. 1711, dau.
of William Burton, of Burgh-in-the-Marsh, co. Lincoln, England; she was living
in England, 18 Mar. 1668, and was sole heir and executrix of her husband's estate
in Ulster Co., N.Y., 1698.

Line 85

13. ALICE DYMOKE (84-13); m. Sir William Skipwith, Knt.
14. HENRY SKIPWITH, d. 1588, of Cotes and "Prestwould," co. Leicester,
M.P., for Leicestershire, 1585; m. Jane, dau. of Francis Hall, of Grantham.
15. SIR WILLIAM SKIPWITH, KNT., d. 1610; m. Margaret, dau. of Roger
Cave, of Stanford.
16. SIR HENRY SKIPWITH, KNT., living 1653; m. Amy, dau. and coh. of
Sir Thomas Kempe.
17. SIR GREY SKIPWITH, KNT., d. 1680, sett. in Virginia, ca. 1660, established "Prestwould," in Virginia; m. Elizabeth.
18. SIR WILLIAM SKIPWITH, KNT.; m. Sarah Peyton, dau. of John Peyton,
of Gloucester Co., Va. (Lincolnshire Pedigrees, III 889-890).

Line 86

11. MARGARET de WELLES (82-11); m. Sir Thomas Dymoke, Knt.
12. SIR ROBERT DYMOKE, KNT., of Scrivelsby, co. Lincoln; m. (2) Jane,
dau. of John Sparrow.
13. SIR EDWARD DYMOKE, of Scrivelsby; m. ANNE TAILBOYS (108-13).
14. FRANCES DYMOKE; m. Sir Thomas Windebank, Knt., of Haynes Hill,
Hurst Parish, Berkshire.
15. MILDRED WINDEBANK; m. c. 1600, Robert Reade, of Linkenholt Manor.
16. COLONEL GEORGE READE, b. c. 1608, came to Virginia, c. 1637; d.
c. 1671; Acting Governor of Virginia, 1638-1639, Burgess, 1649, 1655/6, ff., member of the Governor's Council, 1657-1671; m. Elizabeth, dau. of Captain Nicholas
Martiau, of York Co., Virginia, Burgess, and Justice, and his wife, Jane Berkeley.
17. MILDRED READE; m. Colonel Augustine Warner, Jr., of Warner Hall,
Gloucester Co., Va., member and Speaker of the Virginia House of Burgesses,
b. 3 July 1642 or 1643, d. June 1681, son of Captain Augustine Warner.
18. MILDRED WARNER; m. Captain Lawrence Washington, b. c. 1659, d.
1697/8, son of Colonel John Washington, by his wife, Anne Pope, dau. of Lieutenant-
Colonel Nathaniel Pope, of Charles Co., Maryland.
19. CAPTAIN AUGUSTINE WASHINGTON, of Stafford Co., Virginia, b. c.
1694, d. 12 Apr. 1743; m. 6 Mar. 1730/1, Mary Ball, b. 1707/8, d. 25 Aug. 1789,
dau. of Colonel Joseph Ball, of Epping Forest, Lancaster Co., Virginia.
20. GENERAL GEORGE WASHINGTON, 1st President of the United States,
b. at Wakefield, Westmoreland Co., Virginia, 22 Feb. 1731/2, d. at Mount Vernon,
Virginia, 14 Dec 1799.
20. ELIZABETH WASHINGTON (sister of George), b. 20 June 1733, d. 31
Mar. 1797; m. 7 May 1750, Colonel Fielding Lewis. (TAG 51: 167-171; 54: 215-216).

Line 87

6. ISABEL BERKELEY (82-6); m. 1328, ROBERT de CLIFFORD (144-6).
(CP III, 290-1).

      *   *   *   *   *   *

Note: Clay (133-4) says No. 7 child of Gen. 6, but on p. 22 does not show Margaret
with children of Gen. 6. CP says only Sir Piers (Gen. 7) m. Margaret said to be
dau. of Robert Lord Clifford, but does not say which, and no evidence cited. Line

not proven at this point.

      *   *   *   *   *   *

    7. MARGARET de CLIFFORD, d. 8 Aug. 1382; m. in or bef. 1322, Piers de Mauley, Lord Mauley of Mulgrave Castle, b. c. 1300, d. 18 Jan. 1354/5. (CP VIII, 565-7, and note c, p. 567).

    8. SIR PIERS de MAULEY, Lord Mauley of Mulgrave Castle, b. 1330, ae. 24+ at father's death, d. 20 Mar. 1382/3; m. bef. 18 Nov. 1356, ELIZABETH de MEINILL (33-9). (CP VIII, 567-8).

    9. PIERS de MAULEY, Lord Mauley of Mulgrave Castle, d. betw. Jan. 1377/8 and Mar. 1382/3; m. c. 1371, Margery de Sutton, d. 10 Oct. 1391, dau. of Sir Thomas de Sutton. (CP VIII, 568-9).

    10. CONSTANCE de MAULEY, will dated 1 Jan. 1449/50; m. (1) William Fairfax, d.s.p.; m. (2) Sir John Bigod of Settrington, d. c. 1425, son of Sir John Bigod, Knt., of Settrington, d. 1389, grandson of SIR ROGER BIGOD, KNT. (3-5), d. 1362, of Settrington, co. York, q.v.

    11. JOANNA BIGOD; m. Sir William de Calverley, als. Scot, Knt., of Calverley, co. York, son of Walter Calverley and Margery de Dineley.

         *   *   *   *   *   *

The line breaks here. Walter was not son of Joan Bigod but by other wife.

         *   *   *   *   *   *

    12. WALTER CALVERLEY, or Scot, fl. 1429, d. 1466; m. Elizabeth, dau. of Sir Thomas Markenfield.

    13. SIR WILLIAM CALVERLEY, or Scot, Knt., d. 1488; m. 1441, Agnes Tempest, dau. of Sir John Tempest, Knt., of Bracewell, Sheriff of Yorkshire, 1440, 1459, and Alice Sherburne, dau. of Sir Robert Sherburne of Stonyhurst, 1443.

    14. JOAN CALVERLEY; m. 1467, Christopher Lister, of Medhope, co. York, son of Laurence Lister who m. a dau. of Richard Banester of Brokden.

    15. WILLIAM LISTER, of Medhope, Esq., bur. at Gisburn, 1537/9; m. Elizabeth Banester, dau. of Thurstan Banester of Swinden.

    16. CHRISTOPHER LISTER, of Medhope, 1521, d. 1548; m. Eleanor Clayton, dau. of John Clayton, Esq., of Clayton, Lancashire.

    17. SIR WILLIAM LISTER, d. 1582, of Thornton and Medhope, will probated 1582, mentions dau. and son-in-law Thomas Southworth, son of Sir John Southworth; m. Bridget Pigot, dau. of Bartholomew Pigot of Aston Rowen, co. Oxford, and widow of Thomas Banister of Brokden.

    18. ROSAMOND LISTER; m. THOMAS SOUTHWORTH (96-16)

Line 88

    2. ROGER de QUINCY, Earl of Winchester (74-2), d. 1264; m. HELEN of GALLOWAY (139-2).

    3. MARGARET de QUINCY, d. sh. bef. 12 Mar. 1280/1; m. in or bef. 1238, as his 2nd wife, William de Ferrers, bur. 31 May 1254, Earl of Derby. (CP IV, 196).

    4. JOAN FERRERS, d. 19 Mar. 1309/10; m. 1267, Sir Thomas de Berkeley, b. 1245, d. 23 July 1321, son of Maurice de Berkeley, b. 1218, d. 1281, and Isabel, dau. of Richard Fitz Roy, bastard son of King JOHN (161-12) of England. (CP II, 127).

    5. SIR MAURICE de BERKELEY, b. Apr. 1281, d. 31 May 1326, Lord Berkeley of Berkeley Castle; m. (1) 1289, neither being over eight years of age, EVA la ZOUCHE (80-5). (CP II, 128).

    6. MILICENT de BERKELEY (also called Ela), d. aft. 1322; m. c. 1313 as 1st wife, John Maltravers, b. c. 1290, d. 16 Feb. 1363/4, Lord Maltravers, Knt., 22 May 1306, son of Sir John de Maltravers (or Mautravers) and Eleanor de Gorges. (CP VIII, 581).

    7. SIR JOHN MALTRAVERS, d. 22 Jan. 1348/9; m. Gwenllian, d. 1375.

    8. ELEANOR MALTRAVERS, Lady Maltravers, b. c. 1345, ae. 19 in 1364, d. 10 Jan. 1405/6; m. (1) 17 Feb. 1358/9, SIR JOHN d'ARUNDEL (121-7). (CP I, 259; VIII, 586).

    9. JOAN FITZ ALAN, of Arundel, d. 1407; m. (1) Sir William de Brien; m. (2) c. 1401, Sir William de Echyngham of Echyngham, co. Suffolk, d. 1412.

62   [Line 88A

10. SIR THOMAS de ECHYNGHAM, of Echyngham, d. 1444; m. (2) Margaret,
dau. of Sir Thomas Knyvet of co. Norfolk.
11. SIR THOMAS de ECHYNGHAM, of Echyngham, d. 1482; m. Margaret
West, dau. of SIR REYNOLD de WEST (4-10), q.v.
12. MARGARET de ECHYNGHAM, d. 1481; m. (1) Sir William Blount, d. of
wounds 14 Apr. 1471, Knight of the Shire of Derby, 1467, son of Sir Walter Blount,
K.G., Lord Mountjoy, Treasurer of England, and Ellen, dau. of Sir John Byron
of Clayton. (CP IX, 336).
13. ELIZABETH BLOUNT, d. bef. husb.; m. SIR ANDREWS WINDSOR, K.B.
(127-11), d. 30 Mar. 1543, Baron of Stanwell, co. Middlesex, M.P.; attended the
"Field of the Cloth of Gold," 1520. (CP XII (2), 792).
14. EDITH WINDSOR; m. George Ludlow, Esq., will proved 4 Feb. 1580/1,
of Hill Deverell, Wiltshire, Sheriff of Wiltshire, 1567, son of William Ludlow and
Jane Moore.
15. THOMAS LUDLOW, of Maiden Bradley, Dinton, and Baycliffe, Wiltshire,
bur. at Dinton, 25 Nov. 1607, will proved June 1608; m. Jane Pyle, dau. of Thomas
Pyle.
16. DEPUTY-GOVERNOR ROGER LUDLOW, bp. Dinton, 7 Mar. 1590, d.
Dublin, Ireland, 1666; Baliol Coll., 1610; came to New England, 1630, Deputy-Governor of Massachusetts, 1634, and of Connecticut, 1639, 1642 and 1648; m. Mary
Cogan.
17. SARAH LUDLOW, b. Fairfield, Connecticut, 1639; m. 1656, the Reverend
Nathaniel Brewster of Brookhaven, Long Island, New York.

16. GABRIEL LUDLOW, ESQ. (brother of Roger), lawyer, c. 1637, d. c.
1639; m. Phyllis.
17. SARAH LUDLOW, d. Lancaster Co., Virginia, c. 1668; m. Colonel John
Carter, of Corotoman, Lancaster Co., Virginia; member of the Governor's Council.
18. COLONEL ROBERT CARTER, of Corotoman, b. c. 1663, d. 1732, Speaker, Councillor, and Acting Governor of Virginia; m. c. 1688, Judith, dau. of Colonel John Armistead.
19. ANNE CARTER; m. 1722, Benjamin Harrison, of Berkeley, Charles City
co., Virginia, member of the House of Burgesses, d. 1744/5. (See new volume
of Carter ancestry by Noel Currer-Briggs.)

16. THOMAS LUDLOW (brother of Roger and Gabriel), bp. Baverstock,
Wilts., 3 Mar. 1593, d. Warminster, Wilts., 1646; m. 1624, Jane, bp. Warminster, 15 Apr. 1604, d. 19 Dec. 1683, dau. of John Bennett of Steeple Ashton and
Smallbrook.
17. GABRIEL LUDLOW, bp. Warminster, Wilts., 27 Aug. 1634, of Frome,
Somerset; m. Martha.
18. GABRIEL LUDLOW, b. Castle Cary, Soms., 2 Nov. 1663, bp. 1 Dec.
1663, d. 1736; to New York, 1694, clerk of New York House of Assembly, 1699-1733,
merchant; m. 5 Apr. 1697, Sarah, dau. of Rev. Joseph Hanmer, formerly of Iscoyd,
Flint, chaplain to His Majesty's Forces, New York, and Martha Eddowes, formerly
of Whitchurch, Salop, whose m. banns pub. Whitchurch, 27 Mar. 1659. (Gens. 16-
18: H. F. Seversmith, Colonial Fams. of Long Island, vol. 5 (The Ancestry of Roger
Ludlow) 1958, p. 2097; NYGBR, 50 (1919): 34-38).

Line 88A

10. SIR THOMAS de ECHYNGHAM (88-10), d. 15 Oct. 1444, will dated 20 Aug.
and proved at Lambeth, 28 Oct. 1444; m. (1) Agnes, dau. of John de Shoyswell, of
Shoyswell, Sussex; m. (2) Margaret, dau. of Sir Thomas Knyvet, co. Norfolk. It
is not known which wife was the mother of his dau. Elizabeth. (Spencer Hall, Echyngham of Echyngham (London, 1850), pp. 13-14).
11. ELIZABETH de ECHYNGHAM; m. (2) Sir John Lunsford of Lunsford and
Wilegh, co. Sussex, seen 1428. (Hall, p. 14; Collectanea Topographica et Genealogica, III: 306, IV: 140; see also TAG 46: 117-118, 47: 87).
12. WILLIAM LUNSFORD of Lunsford and Wilegh, seen 1438; m. as her 1st
husband, Thomasina, d. 16 Jan. 1498, dau. and heiress of John Barrington. (Topo.
and Geneal., IV: 141).
13. WILLIAM LUNSFORD of Lunsford and Wilegh, ae. 50+ in 1498; m. Cicely,

dau. of Sir John Pelham, chamberlain to Queen Catherine, consort of Henry V, by Joan de Courcy. (John Comber, Sussex Genealogies (Cambridge, 1933), III: 204-5; Topo. and Geneal., IV: 141).

14. WILLIAM LUNSFORD of Lunsford and Wilegh, d. 3 May 1531, will dated 10 Dec. 1530, proved 3 Sept. 1531; m. (2) MARGARET FIENNES (8A-14), seen 26 Sept. 1531, dau. of SIR THOMAS FIENNES of Claverham (8A-13). (Topo. and Geneal., IV: 141; Sussex Archaeological Collections, LVIII, chart facing p. 64).

15. JOHN LUNSFORD of Lunsford and Wilegh, b. c. 1510, will dated 19 Oct. 1581, proved 29 Jan. 1581/2, bur. at East Hoathley, Sussex, Nov. 1581; m. MARY (17A-13), bur. at East Hoathley, 30 June 1571, dau. of John Sackville of Withyham and Chiddingley, Sussex, by MARGARET BOLEYN (17A-12). (Topo. and Geneal., IV: 140-1).

16. SIR JOHN LUNSFORD of Lunsford and Wilegh, b. c. 1551, bur. at East Hoathley, 5 May 1618, Sheriff of Sussex and Surrey, 1611; m. (1) Barbara, dau. of John Lewknor, gent., of Buckingham, Sussex; m. (2) Horsham, 2 Sept. 1577, Anne, bp. Horsham, 2 Mar. 1557, bur. East Horthly, 10 Sept. 1612, dau. of John Apsley of Thaneham. (Topo. and Geneal., IV: 141).

17. THOMAS LUNSFORD of Lunsford and Wilegh, gent. (by 2nd wife), b. c. 1586, d. at Greenwich, where he was bur. 4 Nov. 1637; m. Katherine, bur. at East Hoathley, 19 May 1642, dau. of Sir Thomas Fludd of Milgate, Kent, and sister of Robert Fludd, M.D. Christ Church, Oxon., Fellow of the College of Physicians, the eminent Rosicrucian. (Topo. and Geneal., IV: 141; DNB VII: 348-50).

18. SIR THOMAS LUNSFORD of Lunsford and Wilegh and Virginia, b. c. 1610, d. Williamsburg, Virginia, 1653; appointed Lieutenant of the Tower of London by Charles I, 22 Dec. 1641, knighted 28 Dec. 1641, Gov. of Sherborne Castle, 1642, gov. of Monmouth, 1644, captured at Hereford, Dec. 1645 by the Cromwellians and imprisoned in the Tower. License to go to Virginia granted 7 Aug. 1649; member of the Council and Lieutenant-General of Virginia troops, 1651; m. (1) a Hudson, bur. at East Hoathley, 28 Nov. 1638; m. (2) 1640, Katherine Neville, d. in Virginia, 1649, dau. of Sir Henry Neville of Billingbear, Berks.; m. (3) Elizabeth Wormeley, prob. dau. of Henry Wormeley of Riccal, Yorks. Sir Thomas Lunsford's issue by his 2nd wife returned to England as wards of their grandmother, Dame Elizabeth Neville. By his 3rd wife, he had a dau. Katherine, who m. her cousin, Ralph Wormeley of Middlesex Co., Va., and had issue. (Top. and Gen., IV: 142, note d; DNB XII: 281-3; Virginia Magazine of History and Biography, XVII: 30-33).

Line 89

Generations 4-8 same as Line 57.

9. ROGER de BEAUCHAMP (57-9), d. 1406; m. Joan Clopton.

10. MARGARET BEAUCHAMP; m. Robert Mauteby, of Mauteby, co. Norfolk.

11. JOHN MAUTEBY, of Mauteby; m. Margaret, dau. of John Berney, of Reedham. (James Gardiner, The Paston Letters, 1422-1509, Introduction and Supplement, 1901, p. ccxxxvi).

12. MARGARET MAUTEBY, d. 4 Nov. 1484; m. John Paston, Esq., of Paston, co. Norfolk, fl. 1421, Sheriff of Norfolk and Suffolk, 1451-1452, d. 21/22 May 1466 (Inq. p. m., Oct. 1466). (Ibid., 11, 44, 105 xlvi cccliii, ccxxxiv footnote 9, cclxv; Blomfield, Norfolk, XI 228).

13. SIR JOHN PASTON, the younger of two brothers named John b. c. 1442, d. 1503 (the older brother d. unm., Nov. 1479), held the manors of Marlingfield, Oxnead, Paston, Crowmer, and Caister, Sheriff of Norfolk, knighted at the battle of Stoke, 16 June 1487; m. fall of 1477, Margery, dau. of Sir Thomas Brews, of Hinton Hall, co. Norfolk. (Gardiner, op. cit., cclxxiii, cccxliii, cccxlv, cccli, 157; Norfolk Archaeology, IV; see Sanford: "Genealogy of the Paston Family," brought down to 1674).

14. DOROTHY PASTON, d. 1533; m. as his 1st wife, Thomas Hardres (not Christopher, as in earlier editions), d.s.p.

    *   *   *   *   *   *

Line terminates here. See TAG 14: 209-214. Dr. Arthur Adams, before he died, wrote a letter to this editor, dated 28 Oct. 1959, in which he stated, "There were no children by the Paston marriage."

Christopher Hardres, of Hardres, co. Kent, d. 1536, was father of:

15. THOMAS HARDRES, ESQ., of Hardres, d. 1556; m. Mary, dau. of Edward
Oxinden, of Wingham.
16. ELIZABETH HARDRES; m. (1) George Harlakenden, Esq., bur. at Wood-
church, co. Kent, 15 Oct. 1565; will pr. 10 Dec. 1565 at Canterbury; m. (2) Wood-
church, 28 Jan. 1566/7, Roger Harlakenden, Esq., of Kenardington, co. Kent, and
Earl's Colne, co. Essex, b. c. July 1541, bur. Earl's Colne, 21 Jan. 1602/3, ae.
61 yrs. 5 months (Inq. p.m., 16 May 1603), 3rd son of Thomas Harlakenden, Esq.,
of Warehorn, co. Kent, and Mary Londenoys, sister and heir of Robert Londenoys,
Esq., of Bread, co. Sussex. (Top. & Gen., I (1846) 233-234).

But the mother of Roger Harlakenden was not Mary Londenoys, but Margaret Huberd. See NEHGR, 120: 243-247.

17. THOMAS HARLAKENDEN, gent., 3rd son of Roger and Elizabeth, d.
Earl's Colne, 27 Mar. 1648; m. (1) Dorothy Cheyne, b. 1570, d. 1620, dau. of John
Cheyne, Esq., of Drayton Beauchamp, co. Buckingham, called "the Lady Cheyne"
by her son-in-law, Deputy-Governor Samuel Symonds, in his will. (Top. & Gen.,
I 234; Morant, Essex).
18. DOROTHY HARLAKENDEN, bp. Earl's Colne, 12 Dec. 1596, d. bef. 3
Aug. 1636; m. as his 1st wife, 2 Apr. 1617, Deputy-Governor Samuel Symonds, Esq.,
b. Yeldham, Essex, 1595, d. Boston, Massachusetts, 12 Oct. 1678; came to New
England, 1637, sett. Ipswich, Mass.; deputy, 1638-1643, magistrate, 1643-1649,
Deputy-Governor of Massachusetts, 1673-1678; left a distinguished posterity. (Ibid.)

17. RICHARD HARLAKENDEN, ESQ., heir of Roger and Elizabeth (Hardres)
Harlakenden, b. 22 July 1568, d. 22 Aug. 1631, bur. Earl's Colne (Inq. p.m., 1631),
of Staple's Inn and Earl's Colne Priory, 1592; m. St. Dunstan's in Warehorne, co.
Kent, 11 Feb. 1592/3, MARGARET (89A-14), bur. Earl's Colne, 4 June 1632 (Inq. p.m.,
6 June 1632), dau. of EDWARD HUBERT (or Huberd), Esq. (89A-13), of Stanstead-
Montfichet, co. Essex, one of the six clerks in Chancery. (Top. & Gen., I 234-235).
18. COLONEL ROGER HARLAKENDEN, ESQ., of Earl's Colne, bp. 1 Oct.
1611, d. Cambridge, Massachusetts, 17 Nov. 1638; m. (2) 4 June 1635, ELIZABETH
BOSVILE (95-19), q.v. for further details.
18. MABEL HARLAKENDEN (dau. of Richard and sister of Lt. Col. Roger), bp.
Earl's Colne Priory, co. Essex, 27 Dec. 1614, d. July 1655; m. c. 1626, Colonel
John Haynes, b. England, c. 1594, d. Hartford, Connecticut, 1 Mar. 1653/4, Governor of Massachusetts, 1635-1636, Colonel, 1636, 1st Governor of Connecticut, 1639,
and Governor or Deputy-Governor thereafter until his death. (Ibid., 235; Adams,
Soc. of Col. Wars in the State of Conn., 1941, pp. 3, 1179, etc.).
19. RUTH HAYNES, b. Hartford, Conn., 1639, d. there c. 1688; m. c. 1654,
Samuel Wyllys, A.B. (H.C., 1643), bp. Fenny Compton, co. Warwick, 19 Feb.
1631/2, d. Hartford, Conn., 30 May 1709, son of Governor George Wyllys and Mary
(Smith) Bisby. (Generations 9 to 14: Rye, Visitation of Norfolk, 1563 (Harl. Soc.
Publ., vol. 32), see "Paston"; generations 14 to 16: Keith W. Murray, "Extracts
from a Seventeenth Century Notebook," in Genealogist, New Series, 32: 124; Jenkins,
"On the Gates of Boulogne, at Hardres Court," in Archaeologia Cantiana, IV (1861),
Chart opp. p. 56; Burke, Extinct & Dormant Baronetcies (1844), p. 242; generations
16 to 18: G.S. Steinman, "Pedigree of Harlakenden, of Kent and Essex," in Topogra-
pher and Genealogist, I (1846), 233-234; Metcalfe, Visitations of Essex ... 1582,
I 210-212). This line was suggested by Professor Charles J. Jacobs of the University of Bridgeport.

Line 89A

This line developed by Sir Anthony Richard Wagner, KCVO, Garter.

9. JOHN CHAUNCEY (3-9) of Gilston and Sawbridgeworth, Herts., aged 27+
on 5 Aug. 1479, d. 8 June 1510, bur. Yardley, Herts.; m. Alice, dau. of Thomas
Boyse, living 4 Nov. 1519 (NEHGR, 120: 244).
10. WILLIAM CHAUNCEY of Sawbridgeworth, seen in brother's will 1520; m.
a Garland, liv. 1557. (Ibid.).

11. HENRY CHAUNCEY of Sawbridgeworth, seen in will of uncle, 1520, d. 1558; m. Joan, sister of Robert Tenderyng of Sawbridgeworth, whose will 20 July 1562, pro. 20 Mar. 1653. Her will 7 Nov. 1562, no probate date. (NEHGR, 120: 244-5).

12. ELIZABETH CHAUNCEY, d. betw. 5 Dec. 1577 & 6 Nov. 1579; m. well bef. 1562, Richard Huberd of Birchanger, Essex, churchwarden "lately deceased," 5 Dec. 1577. (NEHGR, 120: 245).

13. EDWARD HUBERD of Stanstead-Montfitchet, Essex, will 16 Mar. 1601, pr. 14 May 1602; m. (1) well bef. 1590, Jane, dau. of John Southall, citizen & clothmaker, London, b. Albrighton, Salop., will 4 Oct. 1590, pro. 31 May 1592; m. (2) Eleanor, ment. in husband's will. (NEHGR, 120: 245-6).

14. MARGARET HUBERD (uncertain by which wife), under 21 in 1592, bur. Earl's Colne, Essex, 4 June 1634; m. St. Dunstan-in-the-West, 11 Feb. 1592/3, RICHARD HARLAKENDEN (89-17) of Earl's Colne, bur. 24 Aug. 1631, will 29 June 1631, pro. 19 Oct. 1631. (NEHGR, loc. cit.)

Line 90

3. ELENA de QUINCY (74-3), d. 1296; m. Sir Alan la Zouche.

4. SIR ROGER la ZOUCHE, b. 1240-2, d. sh. bef. 15 Oct. 1285, Lord Zouche of Ashby and Brockley; m. bef. 1267, ELA LONGESPEE (144-3) (CP XII (2), 934).

5. ALAN la ZOUCHE, b. North Molton, 9 Oct. 1267, d. sh. bef. 25 Mar. 1313/4, Lord Zouche of Ashby, 1299-1314, Governor of Rockingham Castle and Steward of Rockingham Forest; prob. m. Eleanor, dau. of Nicholas Segrave. (CP XII (2), 935).

6. MAUD la ZOUCHE, ae. 24 in 1314, b. c. 1290, d. 31 May 1349; m. c. 1311, Sir Robert de Holand, of Upholland, co. Lancaster, b. prob. c. 1270, executed in Boreham Wood, 7 Oct. 1328, Lord Holand, M.P., 1314-1321, son of Sir Robert de Holand and Elizabeth de Samlesbury. (CP VI, 528-530).

7. SIR THOMAS de HOLAND, K.G., Earl of Kent, d. Normandy, 26 or 28 Dec. 1369; m. in or bef. 1339, JOAN PLANTAGENET (114-6), Countess of Kent, the "Fair Maid of Kent," d. Wallingford Castle, 8 Aug. 1385.

8. SIR THOMAS de HOLAND, K.G., of Woodstock, ae. 9+ or 10+ at father's death, d. 25 Apr. 1397, 2nd Earl of Kent; m. sh. aft. 10 Apr. 1364, Alice Fitz Alan, d. 17 Mar. 1415/16, dau. of SIR RICHARD FITZ ALAN (121-6) and Eleanor Plantagenet. (CP VI, 533; VII, 154-156).

9. MARGARET de HOLAND, d. 30 Dec. 1429, m. (1) bef. 28 Sept. 1397, John Beaufort, K.G., Earl and Marquis of Somerset, b. c. 1371, d. 16 Mar. 1409/10, son of JOHN of Gaunt (161-17) Duke of Lancaster. (CP XII (1), 39).

10. EDMUND BEAUFORT, Duke of Somerset, b. c. 1406, slain at the Battle of St. Albans, 22 May 1455; m. c. 1436, ELEANOR (BEAUCHAMP) ROS (80-10). (CP XII (1), 49).

11. HENRY BEAUFORT, b. c. Apr. 1436, beheaded at Hexham, 15 May 1464, Duke of Somerset, Constable of Dover Castle and Warden of the Cinque Ports, 1459, attainted, 1461. (CP XII (1), 54-57 and note b p. 57).

12. CHARLES SOMERSET, bastard son by Joan Hill, b. c. 1460, d. 15 Apr. 1526, cr. Earl of Worcester, 1 Feb. 1513/4; m. (2) Elizabeth, dau. of THOMAS WEST, Lord de la Warre (4-12). (CP XII (1), 57 note b; XII (2), 846).

13. MARY SOMERSET (by 1st wife, Elizabeth Mortimer); m. Sir William Grey, K.G., Lord Grey of Wilton.

Line 91

9. MARGARET de HOLAND (90-9); m. John Beaufort, Marquis of Somerset.

10. JOAN BEAUFORT, d. 15 July 1445; m. (1) 2 Feb. 1423/4, James I, King of Scotland, b. Dec. 1394, d. 20/21 Feb. 1437; m. (2) bef. 21 Sept. 1439, Sir James Stewart, "The Black Knight of Lorn," 3rd son of Sir John Stewart, Lord of Innermeath and Lorn, by ISOBEL de ERGADIA (42-8). (CP I, 312; VIII, 138, note b; SP I, 18-19; DNB X, 677-8).

11. SIR JAMES STEWART (2nd son by the 2nd marriage), d. betw. Jan. 1497 and Jan. 1499/1500, cr. Earl of Buchan, 1469, High Chamberlain of Scotland, 1471-

1473, 1478-1484, Ambassador to France, 1473. (CP II, 378-379, and note a, p. 379).

12.. JAMES STEWART (natural son by Margaret Murray, widow of William
Murray; legitimated under the Great Seal, 20 Feb. 1488/9); ancestor of the Earls
of Traquair; granted Traquair by his father, 18 May 1491; killed at Flodden Field,
9 Sept. 1513; m. Catherine, younger dau. of Philip Rutherfurd of Rutherfurd. (CP
II, 379 note a).

13. WILLIAM STEWART, of Traquair, liv. 1538, d. bef. 1548; m. 6 July 1524,
CHRISTIAN HAY (41-13), q.v. (CP VI, 423 note j).

Line 91A

10. JOAN BEAUFORT (91-10), dowager Queen of Scots; m. Sir James Stewart,
"The Black Knight of Lorn."

11. SIR JOHN STEWART of Balveny, eldest son, b. c. 1440, d. 15 Sept. 1512;
cr. Earl of Atholl, c. 1457; Ambassador to England, 1484; m. (2) ELEANOR (41C-11),
d. 21 Mar. 1518, dau. of WILLIAM SINCLAIR, 3rd Earl of Orkney and 1st Earl of
Caithness, by his 2nd wife, Marjory, dau. of Alexander Sutherland of Denbeath.
(CP I, 312-3: VIII, 138, note b; SP I, 441-2; DNB XVIII, 1201-2).

12. JOHN STEWART, 2nd Earl of Atholl, d. 1521; m. JANET (41D-13), d. c.
2 Feb. 1545/6, 3rd dau. of ARCHIBALD CAMPBELL (41D-12), Earl of Argyll, by
Elizabeth, dau. of John Stewart, Lord Darnley, Earl of Lennox. (CP I, 198-9,
313; VII, 594-6; SP I, 335-6, 442).

13. JEAN STEWART; m. (contract 31 Aug. 1507) James Arbuthnott of Arbuthnott, who had a Crown charter of the barony of Arbuthnott on 29 Jan. 1506/7, d.
bef. 13 Mar. 1521, son of Robert Arbuthnott of Arbuthnott by his 2nd wife, Mariot,
dau. of Sir James Scrymgeour, constable of Dundee. (SP I, 228, 443).

14. ISABEL ARBUTHNOTT, d. 1558; m. in or aft. 1540 (as his 2nd wife) SIR
ROBERT MAULE, laird of Panmure (41A-14) (111A-13), b. c. 1497, d. 3 May 1560,
Sheriff of Angus. (SP I, 288-9; VII, 10-12; Walter Macfarlane, Genealogical Collec-
tions (Edinburgh, 1900), II: 146-8).

Line 91B

12. JOHN STEWART (91A-12), 2nd Earl of Atholl; m. JANET (41D-13), dau.
of ARCHIBALD CAMPBELL, Earl of Argyll (41D-12).

13. JOHN STEWART, 3rd Earl of Atholl, only son, b. 6 Oct. 1507, d. 1542,
enfeoffed 3 May 1522; celebrated for his hospitality, he entertained James V and the
Papal Nuncio with great éclat in 1529; m. (1) Grizel, seen 1537, granddau. and se-
nior heir of line of Sir John Rattray of that Ilk. (SP I, 442-3; IX, 28).

14. CHRISTIAN STEWART, b. c. 1521; m. c. 1534, John Bethune, 7th Laird
of Bethune-Balfour, b. c. 1491, d. 1544; nephew of James Bethune (or Beaton),
Archbishop of St. Andrews and Chancellor of Scotland, and of Sir David Bethune of
Creich, Treasurer of Scotland; elder bro. of David Cardinal Bethune (or Beaton),
Lord Privy Seal, 1533, Archbishop of St. Andrews, Papal Legate, assassinated,
1548. (SP I, 444; IX, 211, 857).

15. JOHN BETHUNE, 8th Laird of Bethune-Balfour, b. c. 1535, Keeper of
the Castle of St. Andrews, had custody of and buried the body of David Cardinal
Bethune in the family vault at Kilrenny; m. c. 1548, Agnes, d. 14 Feb. 1582, dau.
of David Anstruther. (Walter Macfarlane, Genealogical Collections (Edinburgh,
1900), I: 11-21; Walter Wood, The East Neuk of Fife (Edinburgh, 1887), p. 376;
Matthew F. Conolly, Eminent Men of Fife (Edinburgh, 1866), p. 50).

16. MARGARET BETHUNE, b. c. 1548; m. c. 1561, the Rev. John Row, b.
nr. Dunblane, c. 1526, d. 16 Oct. 1580; M.A., St. Andrews University, 1550, sent
to Rome as Procurator of the Archbishop of St. Andrews in that year; granted a
Licentiate in Canon Law by Pope Paul IV, 20 July 1556; awarded the degree of LL.D.
by the University of Padua on the nomination of his patron, Guido Ascanio Cardinal
Sforza; returned to Scotland as Papal Nuncio to report on the growth of Protestan-
tism, 1558; influenced by John Knox, he joined the Reformers in 1560; first Reformed
Minister of Kennoway and Perth, Moderator of the Kirk of Scotland General Assembly, 1567, 1576, and 1578. (DNB XVII, 327-9; Hew Scott, Fasti Ecclesiae Scoticanae, (Edinburgh, 8 vols., 1915-1950), IV: 229, hereinafter cited as FES).

17. REV. JOHN ROW, JR., 5th son, b. at Perth, Dec. 1568, bp. 6 Jan.
1568/9, d. 26 June 1646; M.A., Edinburgh University, 1 Aug. 1590; tutor to the sons
of John Bethune, 9th Laird of Bethune-Balfour and to William, Earl of Morton; Minister of Carnock, Fifeshire, 1592-1646; author of The History of the Kirk of Scotland; m. 4 Jan. 1595, Grizel, b. 15 Feb. 1575/6, dau. of the Rev. David Ferguson,
first Reformed Minister of Dunfermline, by Isobel Durham. (DNB VI, 1205-6;
XVII, 329-30; FES IV, 229; V, 7-8; Henry Patton, Parish Register of Dunfermline,
1561-1700 (Edinburgh, 1911), p. 49).

18. REV. JOHN ROW III, b. 1598, d. at Kinnelar, Aberdeenshire, Oct. 1672;
M.A., St. Andrews University, 1617, tutor to George Hay, afterwards 2nd Earl of
Kinnoull; Rector of Perth Academy, 1632-41, ordained 14 Dec. 1641, Principal of
King's College, Aberdeen University 1652-1661; m. Elspet Gillespie. (DNB XVII,
330-1; FES VI, 14; VII, 366; VIII, 330-1).

19. LILIAS ROW, b. 1636, d. 31 Oct. 1713; m. 1652, Rev. John Mercer, b.
1624, d. 7 Aug. 1676; educated at Marischal College, Aberdeen University, 1642-4;
Minister of Kinellar, Aberdeenshire, 1650-1676, son of Lancelot Mercer by Agnes
Bean. (FES VI, 59; VIII, 539).

20. THOMAS MERCER, M.A., of Todlaw, Lanarkshire, and Smiddyburn, b.
28 Jan. 1658; m. (2) Isobel, dau. of Robert Smith of Smiddyburn. (FES VI, 59).

21. REV. WILLIAM MERCER, 3rd son, b. 22 Mar. 1696, d. 28 Aug. 1767;
M.A., Marischal College, Aberdeen University, 1712; chaplain to Sir Henry Innes
of that Ilk, 1717, Minister of Pitsligo, 1720-1748; m. 18 June 1723, Ann, d. 19 Jan.
1768, dau. of Andrew Munro, sheriff-clerk at Elgin (not the dau. of Sir Robert
Munro of Foulis, as stated in John T. Goolrick, The Life of General Hugh Mercer,
at p. 104). (FES VI, 235; VIII, 585).

22. GEN. HUGH MERCER, b. Pitsligo, Aberdeenshire, Scotland, 16 Jan.
1726, mortally wounded at the battle of Princeton, New Jersey, 3 Jan. 1777, d. 12
Jan. 1777, bur. Christ Church, Philadelphia; educated at Marischal College, Aber-
deen University, 1740-44; surgeon's mate in the army of Prince Charles Edward
Stuart at Culloden; immigrated to Pennsylvania, 1747, Lieut. Col., 3rd Battalion,
Penn. Militia, 1758, commandant at Fort Pitt; removed to Fredericksburg, Virginia,
Jan. 1761, where he practiced medicine; Colonel, 3rd Virginia Regiment, 11 Jan.
1776; commissioned Brigadier-General by the Continental Congress on the nomina-
tion of George Washington, 5 June 1776; m. Fredericksburg, Va., bef. 1 Oct. 1764,
Isabel, dau. of John Gordon and Margaret Tennant. (DNB XIII, 264-5; DAB XII,
541-2; FES VI, 235).

Line 91C

11. SIR JAMES STEWART, Earl of Buchan (91-11).

12. ELIZABETH STEWART, illegitimate dau. by Margaret Murray; m. bef.
11 Mar. 1507, Mungo Home, 1st Laird of Cowdenknows, d. 1513, son of John Home
of Ersiltoun, Ambassador to England, 1491, by Elizabeth, dau. of Sir Adam Hepburn of Hailes. (SP IV, 468-9).

13. SIR JOHN HOME, 2nd Laird of Cowdenknows, d. bef. Nov. 1573; m. bef.
24 Mar. 1563, Margaret, dau. of Sir Alexander Ker of Cessford by Agnes, dau. of
Sir Patrick Crichton. (The surname Home is pronounced, and frequently spelled,
Hume.) (SP IV, 469-70).

14. SIR JAMES HOME, 3rd Laird of Cowdenknows, d. on or bef. 22 Apr.
1592, Warden of the East March, Capt. of Edinburgh Castle; m. (contract 13 Aug.
1562) Katherine, d. bef. 6 Apr. 1592, dau. of John Home of Blackader. (SP IV,
472-3).

15. SIR JOHN HOME, 4th Laird of Cowdenknows, d. bef. 1629, appointed by
Parliament 3 July 1604 to confer with English commissioners on the proposed union
of the Kingdoms of Scotland and England; m. (1) MARIE (41F-15), d. bef. 29 Oct.
1608, dau. of JOHN SINCLAIR (41F-14), Master of Caithness, by JANE (91D-14),
only dau. of PATRICK HEPBURN (91D-13), 3rd Earl of Bothwell. (SP II, 341-2;
IV, 474-5).

16. MARGARET HOME; m. (2) (contract 6 Mar. 1607), COL. SIR DAVID
HOME, BT., 7th Laird of Wedderburn (41E-17), slain at the battle of Dunbar, 3
Sept. 1650. (SP IV, 476; G. E. Cokayne, Complete Baronetage, II: 442).

Line 91D

11. SIR JAMES STEWART, Earl of Buchan (91-11).
12. AGNES STEWART, illegitimate dau. by Margaret Murray, legitimated
under the Great Seal, 31 Oct. 1552, d. Feb. 1557; m. (l) soon after 28 Aug. 1511,
Adam Hepburn, b. c. 1492, d. 9 Sept. 1513, 2nd Earl of Bothwell, High Admiral
of Scotland. (CP II, 238; SP II, 156-7).
13. PATRICK HEPBURN, b. 1512, d. Sept. 1556, 3rd Earl of Bothwell, ban-
ished for treasonous correspondence with Henry VIII of England; m. (l) 1533 or 1534,
Agnes Sinclair, dau. of HENRY SINCLAIR (165-12), 3rd Lord Sinclair, by Margaret,
dau. of Adam Hepburn, Master of Hailes. (CP II, 238-9; SP II, 157-9; VII, 571;
IX, 41).
14. JANE HEPBURN, sister-in-law of Mary, Queen of Scots; m. (2) betw.
10 Dec. 1565 and 16 Jan. 1566/7, JOHN SINCLAIR (41F-14), Master of Caithness,
d.v.p. Sept. 1575. (SP II, 160-1, 338-41; IX, 51).

Line 92

10. JOAN BEAUFORT (91-10); m. (l) James I, King of Scotland.
11. JAMES II, b. 16 Oct. 1430, d. at the siege of Roxburgh Castle, 3 Aug.
1460, King of Scots; m. 3 July 1449, Marie, d. 1 Dec. 1463, dau. of Arnold, Duke
of Guelders.
12. JAMES III, b. 10 July 1451, murdered 11 June 1486, King of Scots; m. 13
July 1469, Margaret, b. 23 June 1456, d. 14 July 1486, dau. of Christian I, King of
Denmark.
13. JAMES IV, b. 17 Mar. 1472/3, d. Flodden Field, 9 Sept. 1513; had by concubine, Margaret Drummond, dau. of John, Lord Drummond:
14. MARGARET STEWART, b. c. 1497; m. (l) Nov. 1512, John Gordon, Master
of Huntly, d. 5 Dec. 1517, son of Alexander Gordon, Earl of Huntly.
15. ALEXANDER GORDON, Bishop of Galloway, 1558, Privy Councillor, 1565,
d. 11 Nov. 1575.
16. JOHN GORDON, D.D., Bishop of Galloway and Dean of Salisbury, Laird
of Glenluce, d. c. 1619; m. (2) c. 1594, Genevieve, dau. of Gideon Petau, Lord of
Maule.
17. LOUISA GORDON; m. London, 16 Feb. 1613, Sir Robert Gordon, Sheriff
of Inverness, 1629, b. 14 May 1580, d. Mar. 1656, son of Alexander Gordon, Earl
of Sutherland, and Jane, dau. of George Gordon, Earl of Huntly.
18. KATHARINE GORDON, b. 11 Jan. 1621, d. c. 1663; m. 26 Jan. 1647/8,
Colonel David Barclay, Laird of Urie, co. Kincardine, b. c. 1610, d. 12 Oct. 1686.
19. ROBERT BARCLAY, Laird of Urie, a Friend, Governor of East New
Jersey, b. 23 Dec. 1648, d. 3 Oct. 1690; m. 16 Feb. 1669, Christiana, dau. of
Gilbert Mollison of Aberdeen, Scotland. (Their granddau., Christiana Forbes,
m. 1732, William Penn III, grandson of William Penn, Founder of Pennsylvania,
also a member of the Society of Friends). (v. Redlich and Adams, op. cit., pp. 244-
245; see also "John Barclay of Perth Amboy" Proceedings of the N.J. Hist. Soc.
July & Oct. 1940).

*   *   *   *   *   *

13. JAMES IV of Scotland, b. 17 Mar. 1472/3, killed at Flodden Field, 9 Sept.
1513; m. 8 Aug. 1503, PRINCESS MARGARET TUDOR (161-22), eldest dau. of HENRY
VII (161-21), King of England, b. 29 Nov. 1489, d. 18 Oct. 1541; she m. (2) 6 Aug.
1514, Archibald Douglas, 6th Earl of Angus, div. 1527/8; she m. (3) bef. Apr. 1528,
Henry Stewart, Lord Methven. (By a concubine, Margaret Drummond, dau. of
John, Lord Drummond, he had Margaret, m. Alexander Gordon.)
14. JAMES V of Scotland, b. 10 Apr. 1512, d. 14 Dec. 1542; m. (l) 1 Jan.
1536/7, Madeline de Valois, d.s.p. 7 July 1537, dau. of Francis I, King of France;
m. (2) June 1538, Marie, d. 10 June 1560, wid. of Louis d'Orleans, Duke de Longue-
ville, dau. of Claude de Guise Lorraine, Duke d'Aumale.
15. MARY, Queen of Scots, only child, b. 7 or 8 Dec. 1542, beheaded 8 Feb.
1586/7; m. (l) 24 Apr. 1558 Francis le Dauphin, afterwards Francis II, King of
France, d.s.p. 5 Dec. 1560; m. (2) 29 July 1565, her cousin Henry Stuart, Lord
Darnley, Duke of Albany (see 161-22), killed 10 Feb. 1566/7; m. (3) as his 2nd wife,

James Hepburn, d. 14 Apr. 1578, Earl of Bothwell, Duke of Orkney.

17. JAMES VI of Scotland, only child, by 2nd husb., b. 19 June 1566, crowned King of Scotland, 29 July 1567, ascended throne of England as JAMES I (founder of House of Stuart) on death of Queen Elizabeth, 24 Mar. 1603, d. 27 Mar. 1625; m. 24 Nov. 1589, ANNE (17C-16) Princess of Denmark, d. 2 Mar. 1618/19, dau. of FREDERICK II, King of Denmark (17C-15).

Line 92A

11. JAMES II, King of Scots (92-11); m. Marie, dau. of Arnold, Duke of Gueldres.

12. MARY STEWART, b. sh. bef. 16 May 1452, d. c. May 1488; m. (2) bef. Apr. 1474, as his 2nd wife, Sir James Hamilton, b. c. 1415, d. 6 Nov. 1479, lord of Cadzow, co. Lanark; P.C. 1440; cr. 28 June or 3 July 1445, Lord Hamilton. (CP VI, 255-6; SP I, 20; IV, 349-53).

13. JAMES HAMILTON, Lord Hamilton, b. c. 1475, d. bef. July 1529; P.C. 1503; cr. 11 Aug. 1503, Earl of Arran; m. (2) betw. 11 and 23 Nov. 1516, Janet, d. c. 1522, dau. of Sir David Bethune (or Beaton) of Creich, Treasurer of Scotland (cf. 91B-14). (CP I, 221; SP IV, 355-60).

14. SIR JAMES HAMILTON, 2nd Earl of Arran, d. 22 Jan. 1574/5; Regent of Scotland, 1542; cr. 8 Feb. 1548/9 Duke of Chatellerault by Henry II, King of France; m. sh. bef. 23 Sept. 1532, Margaret, seen 24 May 1579, dau. of James Douglas, 3rd Earl of Morton, by Catherine, illegit. dau. of King JAMES IV (92-13) by Margaret Boyd. (CP I, 221-2; SP I, 22; IV, 366-8).

15. CLAUDE HAMILTON, 5th son, bp. (prob.) 9 June 1546 in Edinburgh Castle, d. bef. 3 May 1621; commendator of the Abbey of Paisley, co. Renfrew, 5 Dec. 1553; cr. 29 July 1587 Lord Paisley; m. 1 Aug. 1574, Margaret, d. bef. 10 Feb. 1615/6, dau. of George Seton, 5th Lord Seton, by Isabel, dau. of Sir William Hamilton of Sanquhar. (CP X, 291-2; SP I, 37-9; IV, 369).

16. MARGARET HAMILTON, d. 11 Sept. 1623, ae. 38; m. 1601, as his 1st wife, William Douglas (43B-19), b. 1589, d. 19 Feb. 1659/60, 11th Earl of Angus, cr. 14 June 1633 Marquess of Douglas, son of William Douglas, 10th Earl of Angus by Elizabeth, dau. of Laurence Oliphant, 4th Lord Oliphant. (CP IV, 437; SP I, 45, 202-4).

17. JEAN DOUGLAS, 2nd dau., d. 1669; m. 1632, Sir John Hamilton of Bargeny, co. Ayr, d. Apr. 1658; cr. 16 Nov. 1641 Lord Bargeny; son of Sir John Hamilton of Lettrick (illegit. son of John Hamilton, 1st Marquess of Hamilton) by Jean, dau. of Alexander Campbell, Bishop of Brechin. (CP I, 421-2; SP I, 205; II, 28).

18. ANNE HAMILTON, d. 12 Mar. 1678; m. Sir Patrick Houstoun of that Ilk, of co. Renfrew and Leny, co. Midlothian, d. 1696, son of Sir Ludovick Houstoun, M.P., by Margaret, dau. of Patrick Maxwell; M.P., 1661, 1678, 1681-2; cr. a Baronet 29 Feb. 1668; had a Crown charter of the Barony of Houstoun, 23 Feb. 1671. (SP II, 28; G.E. Cokayne, The Complete Baronetage, IV: 268).

19. PATRICK HOUSTOUN, 2nd son, d. bef. 1717, merchant of Glasgow; m. Isabel, dau. and heiress of George Johnstone of Glasgow. (Complete Baronetage, IV: 268).

20. SIR PATRICK HOUSTOUN, 5th Baronet, b. c. 1698, d. 5 Feb. 1762 at Savannah, Georgia; matric. Glasgow University 1713; comptroller of customs at Glasgow, 1723, Chamberlain of Kinneil, 1730; immigrated to America, 1734; delegate to the Provincial Assembly of Georgia 1751-4, President of the Royal Council of Georgia 1754-62; suc. to the baronetcy (but not to any of the family estates in Scotland) on the death s.p. of his cousin Sir John Houstoun of Houstoun, Bt.; m. 1740 Priscilla Dunbar, d. Savannah, Ga., 26 Feb. 1775, ae. 64. He and his wife had issue, one dau. and five sons: SIR PATRICK HOUSTOUN, 6th Baronet; SIR GEORGE HOUSTOUN, 7th Baronet; JOHN HOUSTOUN, Governor of Georgia; DR. JAMES HOUSTOUN, delegate to the Georgia General Assembly and surgeon in the Continental Army; and WILLIAM HOUSTOUN, delegate from Georgia to the First Continental Congress and to the Constitutional Convention of the United States. (Complete Baronetage, IV: 268; DAB IX, 268; E.D. Johnston, The Houstouns of Georgia (Athens, Ga., 1950) passim).

Line 92B

14. JAMES V, King of Scotland (92-14), b. Linlithgow, 10 Apr. 1512, d. Falkland Castle, 14 Dec. 1542, had by Catharine or Elizabeth, dau. of Sir John Carmi-
chael, of Crawford (she afterwards m. Sir John Somerville), a son, legitimated by
Papal decree 1534. (SP II, 168; NEHGR, 122: 270-1 & note 53, p. 274).
15. LORD JOHN STEWART, Prior of Coldingham, b. c. 1532, d. Inverness,
Oct. or Nov. 1563; m. Crichton Castle, 4 Jan. 1561/2, Jean, who m. (2) John Sinclair, and (3) Archibald Douglas; dau. of PATRICK HEPBURN, 3rd Earl of Bothwell (91D-13), and Agnes Sinclair.
16. FRANCIS STEWART, 1st Earl of Bothwell, b. c. 1563, d. bef. 30 July
1614; m. bef. 1 July 1592, Margaret Douglas, d. 1640, wid. of Sir Walter Scot of
Buccleuth, and dau. of David Douglas, 7th Earl of Angus, and Margaret Hamilton.
17. JOHN STEWART of Coldingham; m. Margaret (Gens. 15-17: CP II, 240-1;
SP II, 160-1, 168-171).
18. MARGARET; m. Sir John Home of Renton, Lord Justice Clerk, d. 1671.
19. SIR PATRICK HOME of Lumsden, 1st Bt., 2nd son, b. c. 1650, d. Feb.
1723, created Scots Bt. 31 Dec. 1697; m. Jean, bp. 19 Apr. 1688, d. 23 Jan. 1756,
dau. of William Dalmahoy of Raveling and Helen Martin. (Cokayne, Complete
Baronetage, IV: 375 (1904)).
20. MARGARET HOME, d. 13 Apr. 1765; m. by contract 3 Oct. 1695, SIR
GEORGE HOME, 3rd Bt. (41E-20).

Line 93

10. JOAN BEAUFORT (91-10); m. (1) James I, King of Scots. (CP I, 312).
11. JOAN STEWART, 3rd dau.; m. 1458/9, James Douglas, d. 1493, Lord
Dalkeith, Earl of Morton.
12. JANET DOUGLAS; m. 1480/1, Sir Patrick Hepburn, of Dunsyre, Earl of
Bothwell, Admiral of Scotland, d. 18 Oct. 1508, son of Adam Hepburn, of Hailes,
and Helen, dau. of Alexander, Lord Home.
13. JANET HEPBURN, d. aft. 10 May 1558; m. bef. Dec. 1506, George, Lord
Seton, killed at Flodden Field, 9 Sept. 1513.
14. GEORGE SETON, Lord Seton; m. (1) Elizabeth Hay, dau. of JOHN HAY
(41-11), Lord Hay of Yester, co. Haddington, 1487/8. (CP VI, 421-422).
15. BEATRIX SETON; m. Sir George Ogilvie, of Dunlugas and Boyne, co.
Banff.
16. JANET OGILVIE; m. William Forbes, Laird of Tolquohon.
17. THOMAS FORBES, Laird of Watertown, Aberdeenshire.
18. GRIZEL FORBES; m. John Douglas, of Tilquhille.
19. JOHN DOUGLAS, of Tilquhille; m. Agnes, dau. of the Rev. James Horn,
of Westhall, minister of Elgin, and Isabel Ramsey of Balmain.
20. EUPHEMIA DOUGLAS, d. 21 Dec. 1766; m. c. 1733, Charles Irvine, of
Cults, near Aberdeen, Scotland, d. 28 Mar. 1779.
21. JOHN IRVINE, M.D., b. 15 Sept. 1742, came to Georgia c. 1765, d. Savannah, Ga., 15 Oct. 1808; m. (1) Sunbury, Ga., 5 Sept. 1765, Ann Elizabeth Bailie,
dau. of Col. Kenneth Bailie.

Line 94

8. SIR THOMAS de HOLAND, K.G., 2nd Earl of Kent (90-8), m. 1364, Alice Fitz
Alan, d. 17 Mar. 1415/6, dau. of SIR RICHARD FITZ ALAN (121-6) and Eleanor
Plantagenet.
9. ELEANOR de HOLAND, 4th dau. (sister (not same Eleanor) of the Eleanor
who married Edward Cherlton (30-8)) living 1413; m. as 1st wife, on or bef. 23 May
1399, Thomas de Montagu, K.G., under age 1401, d. 3 Nov. 1428, Earl of Salisbury.
(CP XI, 393).
10. ALICE de MONTAGU, Countess of Salisbury, d. bef. Feb. 1462/3; m. in
or bef. Feb. 1420/1, Sir Richard de Neville, K.G., beheaded at Pontefract, 31 Dec.
1460, Earl of Salisbury, j.u., son of SIR RALPH de NEVILLE (45-7), Earl of West-

moreland, and Joan Beaufort. (CP XI, 395).

11. ALICE de NEVILLE, living 22 Nov. 1503; m. Henry Fitz Hugh, ae. 23+ in 1452 d. 8 June 1472 Lord Fitz Hugh. (CP V, 428).

12. ELIZABETH FITZ HUGH, d. bef. 10 July 1501; m. (1) as his 2nd wife, SIR WILLIAM PARR, K.G. (118-10), of Kendal, b. c. 1434, d. sh. bef. 26 Feb. 1483/4, grand-parents of Queen Katharine Parr; m. (2) Nicholas Vaux, Lord Vaux of Harrowden, b. c. 1460, d. 14 May 1523. (CP XII (2), 216).

13. KATHARINE VAUX; m. Sir George Throckmorton, Knt., of Coughton, co. Warwick, d. 6 Aug. 1552, son of Robert Throckmorton and Elizabeth Baynham.

14. CLEMENT THROCKMORTON, of Haseley, co. Warwick, d. 14 Dec. 1573, M.P., 1541, 1562, 1572; m. Katherine Neville, dau. of Sir Edward Neville, Knt., of Aldington, and Eleanor, dau. of Lord Windsor.

15. KATHERINE THROCKMORTON; m. as his 3rd wife, Thomas Harby of Adston, co. Northampton, son of William Harby of Ashby.

16. KATHERINE HARBY; m. Dr. Daniel Oxenbridge, of Daventry, co. Northampton, son of the Reverend John Oxenbridge. (CP IV, 635, 637).

17. THE REVEREND JOHN OXENBRIDGE, A.M., b. Daventry, 30 Jan. 1608/9; A.B., A.M., Oxford U.; installed, Boston, Massachusetts, First Church in Boston, 10 Apr. 1670, d. Boston, Mass., 28 Dec. 1674; m. (2) Frances Woodward, of Uxbridge, England.

18. THEODORA OXENBRIDGE, b. 1658, d. Milton, Massachusetts, 18 Nov. 1697; m. 21 Nov. 1677, the Reverend Peter Thacher, A.M. (H.C., 1671). Oxenbridge Thachers in the classes of 1698, 1738, 1796 and 1901 at Harvard College are among their descendants. For an interesting discussion of other descendants, see John I. Coddington, in TAG, vol. 31 (1955), pp. 60-62. (NEHGR, 108: 178; Weis, Colonial Clergy of New England, 1936, pp. 155, 210).

Line 94A

15. KATHARINE THROCKMORTON (94-15); m. as his 3rd wife, Thomas Harby.

16. EMMA HARBY, d. 24 June 1622; m. Robert Charlton, Esq., of Whitton, Salop., and London, 2nd son of Robert Charlton, Gent., of Tern, Salop. (The Visitation of Northamptonshire, 1681 (Harleian Society Publications, vol. LXXXVII), p. 84; John Bernard Burke, Extinct and Dormant Baronetcies (London, 1844), pp. 241-2).

17. KATHERINE CHARLTON, d. 29 Mar. 1668; sister of Sir Job Charlton, Bt., speaker of the House of Commons; m. 26 Dec. 1644, Richard Coke, Esq., of Trusley, Derby, b. 7 Dec. 1617, d. 12 Mar. 1664. (G.E. Cokayne, Complete Baronetage, IV: 141; John Talbot Coke, Coke of Trusley in the County of Derby (London, 1880), p. 23).

18. RICHARD COKE of Dalbury, Derby, 7th son, bp. at Trusley, 16 Feb. 1664, d. Dalbury, Oct. 1730; m. Elizabeth, d. Nov. 1730, dau. of Thomas Robie of Donnington, Leicester. (Coke, op. cit., pp. 24, 38).

19. JOHN COKE, b. Dalbury, Derby, 6 Apr. 1704, 3rd son, settled at Williamsburg, Virginia, 1724, will proved York Co., Va., 16 Nov. 1767; m. bef. 1738, Sarah, bp. 27 Apr. 1718, Abingdon Parish, Gloucester Co., Va., seen 21 May 1744, dau. of George Hoge or Hogg of Gloucester Co. (Coke, op. cit., pp. 38-40; William and Mary Quarterly (1st series), VII: 127-8).

Line 95

12. WALTER CALVERLEY (87-12), fl. 1429, d. 1466; m. (mar. covenant), 1 Mar. 1415, Elizabeth, dau. of Sir Thomas Markenfield, Knt.

13. MARGARET CALVERLEY; m. (mar. cov.), 1442/3, Thomas Clapham, of Beamsley, co. York, son of Thomas Clapham and Elizabeth Moore.

14. ANNE CLAPHAM, widow of Richard Redman of Hareworth, co. York; m. (2) John Bosvile, Esq., of Gunthwaite, co. York, liv. 1516, son of Richard, Bosvile, d. 1501, and Jane Neville, of Gunthwaite.

15. JOHN BOSVILE, d. 12 Feb. 1544, of Gunthwaite; m. Muriel, dau. of Charles Barnaby, of Barnaby Hall, co. York, by Dionis, dau. of Sir Robert Hilliard, Knt.

72 [Line 96

16. SIR RALPH BOSVILE, of Gunthwaite, 2nd son, sett. Bradbourne, co.
Kent, bur. at Sevenoaks, 8 Aug. 1580; m. (1) Anne, dau. of Sir Richard Clement,
and wid. of Sir Thomas Castillon or Castleton, co. Surrey; m. (2) Benedicta, dau.
of Anthony Skinner of London.
17. CAPTAIN RALPH BOSVILE, 3rd son (by 2nd wife) of Gunthwaite, d. in
Ireland; m. Sproatsborough, co. York, 10 Apr. 1592, Mary, dau. of Christopher
Copley, Esq., of Wadsworth.
18. COLONEL GODFREY BOSVILE, ESQ., of Gunthwaite, co. York, and
Wroxall, co. Warwick, bp. Sproatsborough, 12 Apr. 1596, colonel and justice-of-
the-peace, d. 1658; m. Margaret, dau. of Sir Edward Greville, of Harold Park, co.
Essex, by Jane his wife, dau. of John, Lord Grey, brother of the Duke of Suffolk.
A portrait of Colonel Godfrey Bosvile and of his dau. Elizabeth Bosvile existed in
1842, when they were sold by the executor of a descendant.
19. ELIZABETH BOSVILE, d. Bures, co. Suffolk, c. 25 Apr. 1659 (NEHGR,
33:292); m. in England, 4 June 1635, LIEUT. COLONEL ROGER HARLAKENDEN,
ESQ. (89-18), q.v. of Earl's Colne, co. Essex; they came with the Rev. Thomas
Shepard, to Cambridge, Massachusetts, 1635. Squire Harlakenden, b. c. 1611, d.
Cambridge, Mass., 17 Nov. 1638, leaving two daughters by his wife Elizabeth;
ELIZABETH, b. Dec. 1636, and MARGARET, b. Sept. 1638. Elizabeth (Bosvile)
Harlakenden, m. (2) at Cambridge, c. 1638/9, as his 2nd wife, HERBERT PELHAM,
ESQ. (80-17), q.v. By his 2nd marriage, Mr. Pelham had at least five children:
MARY, b. 12 Nov. 1640; FRANCES, b. 9 Nov. 1643; HERBERT, b. 3 Oct. 1645,
bur. Cambridge, 2 Jan. 1645/6; CAPTAIN EDWARD PELHAM (80-18), who sett.
in Newport, R.I., q.v.; and HENRY, perhaps b. in England. (William Flower,
Visitation of Yorkshire, 1563-1564, pp. 47, 55, 29, 12-13, 30; Joseph Foster, Pedigrees of the County Families of Yorkshire, North and East Riding, see pedigrees
of Calverley, Clapham, Bosvile, Neville of Leversedge. In the Bosvile pedigree,
Foster mentions the fact that Elizabeth Bosvile married Herbert Pelham. Rev.
Lucius Robinson Paige, D.D., History of Cambridge, Mass., pp. 574, 625-626, cf.
626, where data is given about the sale of the portraits. Corrections from 1st edition by F. L. Weis, letter to editor 9 Apr. 1958.)

Line 96

6. MAUD la ZOUCHE (90-6); m. c. 1311, Sir Robert de Holand.
7. MAUD HOLAND; m. Sir Thomas de Swynnerton, d. Dec. 1361, Lord
Swynnerton, son of Sir Roger de Swynnerton and Matilda. (The will and inquisition
post mortem of Sir Thomas are lacking.) (CP XII (1), 587).

Proof that Thomas de Swynnerton's wife was Maud Holand is lacking. See CP
XII (1), 588 note c, and NGSQ vol. 60, pp. 25, 26.

8. SIR ROBERT de SWYNNERTON, KNT., d. c. 1385, of Swynnerton; m.
Elizabeth Beke, dau. of Sir Nicholas Beke, Knt., by Papal dispensation. Relationship not clear.
9. MAUD de SWYNNERTON, only dau.; m. (3) Sir John Savage, of Clifton,
Knt., d. 1 Aug. 1450. (See line 98A. Hist. Coll. Staffs. VII (2), 44-52).
10. MARGARET SAVAGE; m. 1418, Sir John Dutton of Dutton, d. 1445, son of
Sir Piers de Dutton.
11. SIR THOMAS DUTTON, d. 23 Sept. 1459, of Dutton; m. ANNE TUCHET
(1-9).
12. ISABEL DUTTON; m. Sir Christopher Southworth, Knt., b. 1443, d. 1487,
Lord of Samlesbury, knighted, 1482, son of Richard de Southworth of Samlesbury
and Elizabeth Molyneux.
13. SIR JOHN de SOUTHWORTH, KNT., b. 1478, d. 1517/8, Lord of Samlesbury, Sheriff of Lancashire, knighted, 1503/4; m. Helen de Langton, dau. of Sir
Richard de Langton and Isabel Gerard.
14. SIR THOMAS SOUTHWORTH, KNT., of Samlesbury, b. 1497, d. 13 Jan.
1546, fought at Flodden Field, 1513, High Sheriff of Lancashire, 1542, enlarged
Samlesbury Hall; m. (2) c. 9 Aug. 1518, Margery Boteler, granddau. of Sir John
Boteler and MARGARET STANLEY (103-11).
15. SIR JOHN SOUTHWORTH, KNT., b. 1526, d. 3 Nov. 1595, of Samlesbury,
knighted, 1547, High Sheriff of Lancashire, 1562, M.P., 1566, he was land poor;

Sir John and his son Thomas were in London, 1590, when the latter's son, Edward, was born there; m. 23 July 1547, Mary (Asheton) Gouland, of Offerton, co. Derby, dau. of Sir Richard Asheton, Knt., of Middleton, Lancashire.

16. THOMAS SOUTHWORTH, eldest son and heir, b. c. 1548, d. 30 Nov. 1616; m. 1563/71, ROSAMOND LISTER (87-18), q.v.

17. EDWARD SOUTHWORTH, youngest son, named in the will of his grand-father, Sir William Lister; was b. London, 1590, d. London, 1620/22.

*   *   *   *   *   *

17. EDWARD SOUTHWORTH (perhaps identical with the above, but not proven, though his descendants used the Southworth of Samlesbury arms in contra-distinction to the regular Southworth arms); m. Leyden Holland, 28 May 1613, Alice Carpenter, b. c. 1590, d. Plymouth, Massachusetts, 26 Mar. 1690, dau. of Alexander Carpenter, of Wrington, co. Somerset; came to Plymouth, Massachusetts, 1623; she m. (2) Plymouth, 14 Aug. 1623, Governor William Bradford of Plymouth Colony, who brought up Thomas and Constant Southworth in his own family.

18. ENSIGN CONSTANT SOUTHWORTH, b. Leyden, Holland, 1614; d. Duxbury, Mass., 10 Mar. 1678/9; m. Duxbury, 2 Nov. 1637, Elizabeth, dau. of William Collier.

18. CAPTAIN THOMAS SOUTHWORTH, b. Leyden, 1616; m. Sept. 1641, Elizabeth Raynor; sett. Plymouth Colony.

Line 97

10. MARGARET SAVAGE (96-10); m. 1418, Sir John Dutton of Dutton.

11. MAUD de DUTTON; m. Sir William Booth, Knt., of Dunham-Massie, co. Chester, Sheriff of Chester, fl. 1476.

12. SIR GEORGE BOOTH, KNT., of Dunham-Massie, d. 1483; m. KATHERINE MONTFORT (16-11), dau. of ROBERT MONTFORT, ESQ., of Bescote, co. Stafford (16-10).

13. SIR WILLIAM BOOTH, KNT., of Dunham-Massie, d. 9 Nov. 1519; m. (2) Ellen Montgomery, dau. of Sir John Montgomery, of Throwley.

14. JANE BOOTH; m. (1) Hugh Dutton; m. (2) Sir Thomas Holford, Esq., of Holford, co. Chester.

15. DOROTHY HOLFORD; m. John Bruen, of Stapleford, Cheshire, d. 1587, son of John Bruen, Esq.

16. JOHN BRUEN, ESQ., of Stapleford, b. c. 1560, d. 18 Jan. 1625/6; m. (2) aft. 1596, Anne Fox, dau. of John Fox, of Rodes, Lancashire.

17. OBADIAH BRUEN, bp. Tarvin, 25 Dec. 1606, d. Newark, New Jersey, bef. 1690; sett. Marshfield, Massachusetts, 1640, Gloucester, Massachusetts, 1642, New London, Connecticut, 1651; m. Sarah, d. c. 25 Mar. 1684.

18. MARY BRUEN, bp. Stapleford, 14 June 1622, d. Milford, Conn., 2 Sept. 1670; m. John Baldwin, of Milford, Connecticut, d. 1681.

Line 98

5. ALAN la ZOUCHE (90-5), b. 1267, d. 1313/4; m. Eleanor Segrave.

6. ELENA la ZOUCHE, b. 1288, liv. Oct. 1334; m. (1) Apr. 1314, Nicholas de St. Maur (Seymour), d. 8 Nov. 1316, M.P., 1314/5, Knight of the Shire of Gloucester, Lord St. Maur; m. (2) c. 1317, Alan de Charlton, d. 2 Dec. 1360, of Apley, Shropshire. (CP XI, 356-358).

7. ALAN de CHARLTON, b. c. 1318/9, d. 3 May 1349; m. Margery Fitz Aer, b. 4 Apr. 1314, d. 1349.

8. THOMAS de CHARLTON, of Appleby, co. Salop, b. 1345, d. 6 Oct. 1387.

9. ANNA de CHARLTON, b. bef. 1380, d. by 1399; m. William de Knightley.

10. THOMAS de KNIGHTLEY de CHARLTON, b. c. 30 Mar. 1394, d. 4 Jan. 1460; m. Elizabeth Francis, dau. of Sir Robert Francis of Foremark. (TAG 35:62-3).

11. ROBERT CHARLTON, b. bef. 1430, d. 1471; m. Mary Corbet, dau. of Robert Corbet of Morton, Shropshire.

12. RICHARD CHARLTON, b. 1450, d. 1522; m. Anne Mainwaring, dau. of William Mainwaring of Ightfield, Shropshire.

13. ANNE CHARLTON, b. 1480; m. 1500, RANDLE GROSVENOR (98A-12), b. say 1480, d. 1559/60, of Bellaport, Shropshire, son of Randle. A royal line for Randle Grosvenor is cited in AR. See 98A for the line and a discussion of it. Randall Grosvenor was a descendant of MAUD (HOLAND) de SWYNNERTON (96-7).

14. ELIZABETH GROSVENOR, b. 1515; m. Thomas Bulkeley, b. 1515, d. 1591, of Woore, Shropshire.

15. THE REVEREND EDWARD BULKELEY, D.D., b. c. 1540, bur. 5 Jan. 1620/1; m. Olive Irby, b. c. 1547, bur. 10 Mar. 1614/5.

16. THE REVEREND PETER BULKELEY, D.D., b. Odell, co. Bedford, 31 Jan. 1582/3, d. Concord, Massachusetts, 9 Mar. 1658/9; St. John's Coll., Cambridge, 1604/5, A.B., A.M., B.D., Rector of Odell, succeeding his father, 1610-1635; ordained, Cambridge, Massachusetts, Apr. 1637 (for settlement at Concord); sett. Concord, Massachusetts, 1636-1659; m. (1) Goldington, co. Bedford, 12 Apr. 1613, Jane Allen, d. Odell, 8 Dec. 1626; m. (2) Apr. 1635, GRACE CHETWODE (111-17), q.v.

16. SARAH BULKELEY (sister of Peter), b. 1580, d. 1611; m. 1597, Sir Oliver St. John, of Keysoe, b. c. 1575, d. Keysoe, 23 Mar. 1625/6.

17. ELIZABETH ST. JOHN, bp. Bletsoe, 12 Jan. 1604/5, d. Lynn, Massachusetts, 3 Mar. 1676/7; m. Boston, England, 6 Aug. 1629, the Rev. Samuel Whiting, A.M., b. Boston, England, 20 Nov. 1597, d. Lynn, Mass., 11 Dec. 1679, minister at Lynn, Mass., 1636-1679, son of the Hon. John Whiting, Mayor of Boston, England.

18. THE REVEREND SAMUEL WHITING, JR., A.M. (H.C., 1661), minister at Billerica, Massachusetts, 1658-1713.

18. THE REVEREND JOSEPH WHITING, A.M. (H.C., 1661), minister at Lynn, Mass., 1680-1682, minister at Southampton, Long Island, New York, 1682-1723.

16. MARTHA BULKELEY (sister of Peter; m. Abraham Mellows.

16. FRANCES BULKELEY (sister of Peter); m. RICHARD WELBY (8-18).

17. OLIVE WELBY; m. Dea. Henry Farwell, of Concord and Chelmsford.

16. ELIZABETH BULKELEY (sister of Peter); m. (1) Richard Whittingham; m. (2) Atherton Haugh, gent.

17. CAPTAIN JOHN WHITTINGHAM; m. Martha Hubbard; ancestors of the Rev. Samuel Mather, D.D., of Boston, where he was sett. 1732-1785.

17. THE REVEREND SAMUEL HAUGH, minister at Reading, Mass., 1648-1662.

16. DORCAS BULKELEY (sister of Peter); m. Anthony Ingoldsby.

17. OLIVE INGOLDSBY, bp. 1602; m. the Rev. Thomas James, A.M., bp. Boston, co. Lincoln, 5 Oct. 1595, A.B., Emmanuel Coll., Cambridge, 1614/5, A.M.; ordained at Charlestown, Mass., 2 Nov. 1632-1636; sett. New Haven, Conn., 1636-1642; d. Needham-Market, England, Feb. 1682/3, ae. 90 years.

18. THE REVEREND THOMAS JAMES, b. c. 1620, d. 1696; minister at Southampton, Long Island, New York, 1650-1696; m. Ruth Jones. (Jacobus, Bulkeley Gen.).

Line 98A

9. MAUD de SWYNNERTON (96-9), b. c. 1370; m. (1) Humphrey de Peshale; m. (2) Wm. de Ipstones; m. (3) by 1409, Sir John Savage of Clifton, Knt., d. 1 Aug. 1450.

10. SIR JOHN SAVAGE of CLIFTON, b. c. 1410, d. 29 June 1463; m. Elizabeth or Eleanor, dau. of Sir William de Brereton. (Hist. Cols. Staffs. NS xii 144; Ormerod, Cheshire (Helsby edition) III 88/9; Gens. 10A & 10B: Ormerod, op. cit., III 80; Gens. 10B, 11, 12: Jacobus, Bulkeley Gen., pp. 8-9).

10A. MARGARET SAVAGE; m. (1) John Maxfield; m. (2) Randle le Mainwaring, 3rd son of Randle of Over Peover, purch. Carincham, Cheshire, sett. 23 Hen. IV; ob. 13 Edw. IV.

10B. RANDLE MAINWARING of Carincham, IPM 3 Hen. VII, naming Randle aged 18 eldest s. & h.; m. Margaret, dau. of Hugh Davenport, Esq. of Henbury.

11. MARGARET MAINWARING, dau. of Randle Mainwaring of Carincham; m. Randle Grosvenor of Bellaport, Salop, b. say 1450-5, d. 1 Mar. 1521/2 IPM 8 July 1522.

12. RANDLE GROSVENOR of Bellaport, b. say 1480, d. 1559/60, will pro. 3 May 1560 names "son-in-law Thos. Bulkeley;" m. 1500 ANNE CHARLTON (98-13)

of Apley, Salop.

Line 99

6. ELENA la ZOUCHE (98-6); m. (1) Apr. 1314, Nicholas de St. Maur, Lord St. Maur.
7. NICHOLAS de ST. MAUR, KNT. (Seymour), d. 8 Aug. 1361, Lord St. Maur, J.P., 1351, M.P., 1351-1360; m. Muriel Lovel, d. bef. 1361, Lady Lovel. (CP XI, 359; VIII, 205).
8. RICHARD SEYMOUR, KNT., d. 15 May 1401, Lord St. Maur and Lovel, M.P., 1380-1400; m. aft. 1374, Ela de St. Lo, d. betw. 28 Nov. 1409 & 13 Feb. 1409/10, dau. of Sir John de St. Lo. (CP XI, 360).
9. RICHARD SEYMOUR, d. Jan. 1408/9, Lord St. Maur and Lovel, J.P., 1405, M.P., 1402-1407; m. Mary (Peyvre) Broughton, d. bef. 26 July 1409, dau. of Thomas Peyvre of Toddington, and Margaret, dau. of Sir Nele Loring, K.G.
10. ALICE SEYMOUR, Lady St. Maur and Lovel, b. 24 July 1409, seen 1430/1; m. bef. 8 Mar. 1423/4, WILLIAM de la ZOUCHE (79-10), d. 1462, Lord Zouche of Haryngworth. (CP XI, 356-362).

Line 100

3. MARGARET de QUINCY (88-3); m. in or bef. 1238, William de Ferrers, Earl of Derby.
4. SIR WILLIAM de FERRERS, of Groby, b. c. 1240, d. sh. bef. 20 Dec. 1281, Earl of Derby; m. (1) Anne (possibly dau. of Hugh le Despenser). (CP V, 340).
5. SIR WILLIAM de FERRERS, of Groby, b. Yoxale, co. Stafford, 30 Jan. 1271/2, d. 20 Mar. 1324/5, 1st Lord Ferrers; m. Ellen, liv. 9 Feb. 1316/7 (possibly dau. of Sir John de Savage). (CP V, 343).
6. HENRY FERRERS, ae. 22+ at father's death, d. Groby, co. Leicester, 15 Sept. 1343, 2nd Lord Ferrers of Groby; m. bef. 20 Feb. 1330/1, Isabel de Verdon, b. Amesbury, Wiltshire, 21 Mar. 1316/7, d. 25 July 1349, dau. of Sir Theobald de Verdon and Elizabeth de Clare, and granddau. of SIR GILBERT de CLARE, KNT. (28-4), q.v., and Joan Plantagenet, dau. of King EDWARD I (161-14) and Eleanor of Castile.
7. WILLIAM FERRERS, KNT., b. Newbold Verdon, co. Leicester, 28 Feb. 1332/3, d. Stebbing, 8 Jan. 1370/1, 3rd Lord Ferrers of Groby, knighted 6 May 1351; m. (1) bef. 25 Apr. 1344, Margaret de Ufford, dau. of Robert de Ufford, Earl of Suffolk, and Margaret de Norwich.
8. HENRY FERRERS, b. 16 Feb. 1355/6, d. 3 Feb. 1387/8, 4th Lord Ferrers of Groby; m. bef. 27 Apr. 1371, Joan, d. 30 May 1394, prob. dau. of Sir Thomas de Hoo and Isabel St. Leger.
9. WILLIAM FERRERS, bp. Luton, co. Bedford, 25 Apr. 1372, d. 18 May 1445, 5th Lord Ferrers of Groby; m. (1) aft. 10 Oct. 1388, Philippa, liv. 4 July 1405, dau. of SIR ROGER de CLIFFORD (82-7) and Maud de Beauchamp; m. (2) Margaret, dau. of John de Montagu, Earl of Salisbury. (CP V, 354-5).
10. THOMAS FERRERS, ESQ. (by 1st wife), d. 6 Jan. 1458/9; m. Elizabeth Freville, dau. of Sir Baldwin Freville, of Tamworth Castle, co. Warwick, and his wife, Joyce de Botetourte, a descendant of King EDWARD I (161-14). (CP V, 357, note a).
11. SIR HENRY FERRERS, KNT., of Hambleton, co. Rutland, d. 28 Dec 1500; m. Margaret Heckstall, dau. of Sir William Heckstall. (CP V, 357, note a).
12. ELIZABETH FERRERS; m. c. 1508, James Clerke, gent., of Forde Hall, d. 20 Sept. 1553, son of John Clerke, of Ford, co. Kent.
13. GEORGE CLERKE, gent., b. 1510, d. 8 Mar. 1558; m. c. 1533, Elizabeth Wilsford, dau. of Thomas Wilsford of Hartridge.
14. JAMES CLERKE, gent. b. c. 1540, d. 1614, of East Farleigh, co. Kent, will made 13 July 1614; m. c. 1566, Mary Saxby, dau. of Sir Edward Saxby, Baron of the Exchequer.
15. WILLIAM CLERKE, gent., of East Farleigh and London; m. London, 10 Feb. 1598/9, Mary Weston, dau. of Sir Jerome Weston.
16. CAPTAIN JEREMY CLARKE, bp. East Farleigh, 1 Dec. 1605, d. Newport,

76

Rhode Island, Nov. 1651; m. 1637, Frances (Latham) Dungan, dau. of Lewis Latham.
17. THE HONORABLE WESTON CLARKE, b. Newport, R.I., 5 Apr. 1648,
d. aft. 1728; Attorney-General and Treasurer of Rhode Island, 1681-1685; m. Newport, 25 Dec. 1668, Mary Easton, granddau. of Governor Nicholas Easton and of
Governor John Coggeshall of Rhode Island.
17. MARY CLARKE; m. 3 June 1658, GOVERNOR JOHN CRANSTON (41-18) of
Rhode Island, b. c. 1626, d. Newport, R.I., 12 Mar. 1680, son of the Rev. James
Cranstoun, A.M., chaplain to King Charles I.
18. GOVERNOR SAMUEL CRANSTON, b. Newport, R.I., 1658, Governor of
Rhode Island, 1698-1717; m. 1680, Mary Hart, a granddau. of the Rev. Roger Williams, of Providence, Rhode Island.

17. THE REVEREND JAMES CLARKE (son of Captain Jeremy Clarke), b.
Newport, R.I., 1649, ordained, Newport, 1701; settled at Newport, 1700-1736; d.
Newport, R.I., 1 Dec. 1736, ae. 87 years.

Line 101

9. WILLIAM de FERRERS (100-9); m. aft. 10 Oct. 1388, Philippa de Clifford.
10. MARGARET de FERRERS, d. 16 Jan. 1451/2; m. (1) as his 2nd wife, 1427,
Richard Grey, ae. 3+ in 1396, d. 13/20 Aug. 1442, Lord Grey of Wilton, son of
Henry de Grey, Lord Grey of Wilton. (CP VI, 177-179).
11. ALICE GREY; m. Sir John Burley, of Castle Broncroft, Salop; Speaker
of the House of Commons, 1436-1443. (Visitations of Shropshire, 1623, p. 255;
Shropshire Arch. Soc., 4th Series, vol. 6, p. 228; Wedgewood, History of Parliament, p. 134; generations 11 to 15: Burke, Dormant & Extinct Peerages, 1883, 341-
342, 14). (Burke is not a good reference.)
12. JOAN BURLEY; m. (2) Sir Thomas Lyttleton, K.B., d. 23 Aug. 1481,
Steward of the King's Household, son of Thomas Wescote, Esq. and Elizabeth de
Lyttleton. (Generations 11-12: Charles Oman, Castles, 1926, pp. 146-147).
13. SIR WILLIAM LYTTLETON, of Frankley; m. Ellen, widow of Thomas
Fielding, and dau. of William Walshe, Esq., of Wanslip, co. Leicester.
14. JOAN LYTTLETON; m. Sir John Aston, K.B., d. 1523/4, of Heywood,
co. Stafford, and Tixall (or Tixwell), son of Sir John de Aston, d. 1583/4, and
Elizabeth Delves.
15. SIR EDWARD ASTON, of Tixall, d. c. 1568; m. (2) Joan, d. 15 Sept.
1562, dau. of Sir Thomas Bowles, of Penho, co. Carnarvon. (Generations 15 to 18:
Visitations of London, 1633/4, p. 29; William Salt Soc. (1914), p. 133, Pire-Hill
Hundred).
16. LEONARD ASTON, of Langdon, co. Stafford, gent., b. at Tixwell, 2nd
son; m. Elizabeth Barton. (Generations 14 to 17: F. Madan, The Gresleys of Drakelow, p. 236).
17. WALTER ASTON, gent., of Langdon; m. Joyce Nason, of Rougham, co.
Warwick.
18. COLONEL WALTER ASTON, b. Langdon, c. 1607, d. 6 Apr. 1656, bur.
at Westover, Virginia; was in the West Indies, 1633/4, and in Virginia, 1634; member of the House of Burgesses, 1642-1643. (Va. Hist. Mag., XII 111, 282, 401).
19. MARY ASTON, m. c. 1647, Col. Richard Cocke, b. 1600, d. 1665/6.

Line 102

3. MARGARET de QUINCY (88-3); m. in or bef. 1238, William de Ferrers.
4. ROBERT de FERRERS, b. c. 1239, d. 1279, Earl of Derby; m. (2) 26 June
1269, Alianore, d. 20 Feb. 1313/4, dau. of SIR HUMPHREY de BOHUN VI (18-3) and
Eleanor de Braiose, dau. of William de Braiose and EVA MARSHAL (146-2). (CP
IV, 198).
5. SIR JOHN FERRERS, b. Cardiff, 20 Jan. 1271, d. Gascony, Aug. 1312, of
Southoe and Keyston, 1st Lord Ferrers of Charley; m. betw. 2 Feb. 1297/8 & 13
Sept. 1300, HAWISE de MUSCEGROS (57-5). (CP V, 305).
6. SIR ROBERT de FERRERS, Lord Ferrers of Chartley, b. 25 Mar. 1309,
d. 28 Aug. 1350; m. (1) betw. 21 Nov. 1324 & 20 Oct. 1330, Margaret, liv. Aug. 1331;

m. (2) Joan de la Mote, Lady of Willisham, d. London, 29 June 1375. (CP V, 310-312, table betw. 320 & 321).

7. SIR ROBERT de FERRERS, of Willisham (by 2nd wife), b. c. 1350, d. 24 or 31 Dec. 1380; m. betw. 1369 & 1379, ELIZABETH BOTILLER (135-8), of Wem, d. June 1411, Lady Boteler, ae. 24+ on 14 Aug. 1369. (CP V, 311; II, 232).

8. SIR ROBERT de FERRERS, of Willisham, b. 1373, ae. 8+ in 1381, d. bef. 29 Nov. 1396; m. as her 1st husb., Joan Beaufort, d. Howden, 13 Nov. 1440, dau. of JOHN of Gaunt (161-17) of England. (CP V, table, cit.; II, 232-3).

9. MARY de FERRERS, Lady of Oversley, b. bef. 1394, d. 25 Jan. 1457/8; m. SIR RALPH NEVILLE (136-9), d. 26 Feb. 1457/8.

10. JOHN NEVILLE, ESQ., d. 17 Mar. 1481/2, of Althorpe, co. Lincoln, M.P., 1444, Sheriff of Lincolnshire, 1439-1440, 1452-1453; m. (1) Elizabeth Newmarch, dau. of Robert Newmarch of Wormsley.

11. JANE NEVILLE, of Oversley and Wormsley; m. c. 1458/60, Sir William Gascoigne of Gawthorpe, co. York, d. 1463/4. (See 44-10).

12. MARGARET GASCOIGNE; m. Sir Christopher Ward, d. 31 Dec. 1521, of Givendale, co. York.

13. ANNE WARD; m. 1500/1, SIR RALPH NEVILLE (112-13), of Thornton Bridge.

14. KATHERINE NEVILLE, b. c. 1500; m. (1) 1515, SIR WALTER STRICKLAND (119-12), of Sizergh, co. Westmoreland, d. 9 Jan. 1527/8.

15. WALTER STRICKLAND, ESQ., of Sizergh, b. 5 Apr. 1516, d. 8 Apr. 1569; will dated 25 Jan. 1568/9, left 200 pounds sterling to his dau. Ellen.

16. ELLEN STRICKLAND (natural dau.), liv. 1622; m. 1582, John Carleton, of Beeford, co. York, b. c. 1550/5, bur. 27 Jan. 1622/3, son of Thomas Carleton and Jenett Wilson.

17. WALTER CARLETON, bp. Beeford, 28 Dec. 1582, d. Horsea, 4 Oct. 1623; m. 1607, Jane Gibbon, liv. 1639.

18. EDWARD CARLETON, bp. Beeford, 20 Oct. 1610; sett. Rowley, Massachusetts, 1639; m. York, England, 6 Nov. 1636, Ellen Newton, bp. Hedon, 24 Feb. 1614, dau. of Launcelot Newton and Mary Lee. Ref: "Ancestry of Edward Carleton and Ellen Newton His Wife," W. L. Sheppard, Jr., (microfilm copyright 1978) 860+ pp., charts and text, available from author.

Line 103

5. SIR JOHN FERRERS (102-5); m. HAWISE de MUSCEGROS (57 6).

6. ALIANORE FERRERS; m. bef. 21 May 1329, Sir Thomas Lathom of Lathom and Knowsley, co. Chester, b. 1300, d. 17 Sept. 1370, son of Sir Thomas Lathom and Katherine, dau. of Thomas de Knowsley.

7. SIR THOMAS de LATHOM, KNT., d. bef. Mar. 1381/2; m. Joan Venables of Kinderton (CP XII (1), 249).

8. ISABEL de LATHOM, d. 26 Oct. 1414; m. c. 1385, Sir John Stanley, K.G., b. 1350, d. Ardee, Ireland, 6 Jan. 1413/4, Lord Lieutenant of Ireland, 1399-1401, Governor of the city and co. of Chester, 1403, K.G., 1405, King's Lieutenant for the Isle of Man, 1405, Constable of Windsor Castle, 1409-1414, son of Sir William Stanley, and Alice, prob. dau. of Hamon Mascy, of Timperley. (Generations 8 to 10: CP XII (1), 247-251).

9. SIR JOHN de STANLEY, KNT., d. 27 Nov. 1437, Steward of Macclesfield, 1413/4, Lord of Man, 1414/5, Knight of the Shire of Lancaster, 1415, Justice of Chester, 1426-1427; said to have m. ISABEL HARINGTON (15-11), dau. of Sir John Haryngton of Hornby Castle. (CP, loc. cit.).

10. SIR THOMAS STANLEY, K.G., Lord Stanley of Lathom, b. bef. 1405, d. 11 Feb. 1458/9, Lord Lieutenant of Ireland, 1430/1, Chamberlain of North Wales, Forester of Macclesfield, 1439, Justice of the co. of Chester, Flintshire and North Wales, 1448, and of Lancaster; Warden of Calais, 1451, M.P., 1455/6, K.G., 1457; m. JOAN GOUSHILL (25-9), who survived him, dau. of Sir Robert Goushill of Hoveringham, by Elizabeth, dau. of Sir Richard Fitz Alan of Arundel. (CP, loc. cit.).

11. MARGARET STANLEY; m. (1) 1459, Sir William Troutbeck, Knt., b. c. 1432, d. Blore Heath, 23 Sept. 1459; m. (2) 1460, Sir John Boteler, Knt., Baron of Warrington, d. 26 Feb. 1463; m. (3) Lord Grey of Codnor. (CP I, 205).

12. JOAN TROUTBECK, b. 1459; m. (2) Sir William Griffith of Penrhyn, co. Carnarvon, Chamberlain of North Wales. (Dwnn II, 167-168).

13. SIR WILLIAM GRIFFITH, of Penrhyn, liv. 1520; m. Jane, dau. of Thomas Stradling of St. Donat's, co. Glamorgan. (Dwnn II, 154-159).

14. DOROTHY GRIFFITH; m. William Williams, Esq., of Cochwillam, co. Carnarvon (son of William Williams and Lowry, dau. of Henry Salusbury, Esq., of Llanrhaiadr). (Ibid., 166).

15. JANE WILLIAMS; m. WILLIAM COYTMORE (104-15), of Coytmore, co. Carnarvon. (Genealogist's Magazine, VIII 204).

16. ROWLAND COYTMORE, grantee of the 2nd Charter of Virginia, 23 May 1607, widower at Wapping, d. 1626, will proved at Canterbury, 24 Nov. 1626; m. (1) Stepney, co. Middlesex, 13 Jan. 1590/1, Christian Haynes; m. (2) Whitechapel, 28 Mar. 1594/5, Dorothy Harris; m. (3) Harwich, co. Essex, 23 Dec. 1610, Katherine (Miles) Gray, d. Charlestown, Massachusetts, 28 Nov. 1659, widow of Thomas Gray, bp. Harwich, 18 Aug. 1572, bur. there, 7 May 1607, whom she had married in 1592.

17. ELIZABETH COYTMORE (by the 3rd wife), b. c. 1617; m. as his 2nd wife, Captain William Tyng, Treasurer of the Massachusetts Bay Colony, 1640-1644, d. Braintree, Massachusetts, 18 Jan. 1652/3. (NEHGR, 108: 172-174; TAG, 32: 16-17).

Line 104

12. JOAN TROUTBECK (103-12); m. (2) Sir William Griffith of Penrhyn, co. Carnarvon, Chamberlain of North Wales. (Generations 12 to 15: Thomas Allen Glen, Griffith of Garn and Plasnewydd, 1934, chart opp. p. 208, pp. 273, 277; John E. Griffith, Pedigrees of Anglesey and Carnarvonshire Families, 1914, pp. 168, 184-185, 277).

13. ALICE GRIFFITH; m. Piers Coytmore (or Coetmor) of Coytmore.

14. WILLIAM COYTMORE, of Coytmore; m. Ellen Puleston.

15. WILLIAM COYTMORE, of Coytmore, co. Carnarvon; m. JANE WILLIAMS (103-15). (Generations 15 to 19: Genealogist's Magazine, VIII 204-205).

16. ALICE COYTMORE (7th dau.); m. 1610, Hugh Wynne, of Efenechtyd, parish of Llandisilio-in-Yale, co. Denbigh.

17. WILLIAM WYNNE, of Wynne Hall, Ruabon, co. Denbigh, eldest son, b. 4 June 1615, d. 6 Oct. 1692, bur. Wrexham, co. Denbigh.

18. SARAH WYNNE, d. at Wynne Hall, bur. Wrexham, Wales, 14 Aug. 1724; m. 24 Mar. 1693/4, the Reverend Archibald Hamilton, b. 1658, d. 30 Apr. 1709, parson of Corstorphine, co Edinburgh, Scotland.

19. SARAH HAMILTON, b. 29 Sept. 1695, bp. 3 Oct. 1695; bur. Wales, 27 Oct. 1775; m. (2) 14 Feb. 1722/3, the Reverend John Kenrick, b. 1683/4, d. Wrexham, 28 Jan. 1744/5, minister of the Chester Street Presbyterian Chapel, Wrexham, 1707-1744.

20. JOHN KENRICK, of Wynne Hall, b. Wrexham, 31 Aug. 1725, d. Wynne Hall, 15 July 1803, ae. 78; m. (lic.), 18 Dec. 1750, Mary Quarrell, b. Llanfyllan, co. Montgomery, c. 1718; d. Wynne Hall, 10 Oct. 1801, ae. 83, dau. of Timothy Quarrell of Llanfyllan. (NEHGR, 90: 83-84, 92-94).

21. SARAH KENRICK, b. Wynne Hall, 1755, d. "Stapeley", Foxchase, Philadelphia, Pa., 30 July 1815; m. Ruabon, co. Denbigh, 25 Feb. 1777, Ralph Eddowes, b. Whitchurch, co. Salop, 28 Aug. 1751, d. Philadelphia, Pa., 29/30 Mar. 1833, ae. 81.   (TAG, 24: 216-220, cf. 219-220). We are indebted to Mr. John I. Coddington for this line.

Line 105

13. SIR WILLIAM GRIFFITH (103-13); m. (2) 1522, Jane Puleston.

14. SIBYL GRIFFITH; m. 1563, Owen ap Hugh, d. 1613.

15. JANE OWEN; m. Hugh Gwynn of Pennarth.

16. SIBYL GWYNN; m. John Powell (i.e. ap Howell), d. 1636.

17. ELIZABETH POWELL; m. 1625, Humphrey ap Hugh, d. 1664.

18. OWEN HUMPHREY, b. 1625, d. bef. 1699; m. (2) Margaret Vaughan.

19. JOSHUA OWEN, b. Wales, d. Burlington Co., New Jersey, 4 Mar. 1727; m. 1696/7, Martha Shinn, a member of the Burlington monthly meeting of Friends. (Generations 14 to 19: Glenn, Merion in the Welsh Tract, pp. 210, 240, 241, 246, 247, 249. Line requires better documentation).

20. MARGARET OWEN, b. 1701, d. May 1753, of Radnor monthly meeting; m. Burlington, N.J. (m.m.), 21 Aug. 1722, Benjamin Crispin, b. Sept. 1699, d. Dec. 1753, son of Silas Crispin and Mary Stockton.

Line 106

10. SIR THOMAS STANLEY, K.G. (103-10); m. JOAN GOUSHILL (25-9).
11. KATHERINE STANLEY; m. Sir John Savage of Clifton, d. 22 Nov. 1495, ae. 73 yrs., son of SIR JOHN SAVAGE of Clifton (98A-10), d. 29 June 1463, ae. 53 yrs., son of Sir John Savage of Clifton, Knt., d. 1 Aug. 1450 (fought at Agincourt, 1415, knt., 1416), by MAUD de SWYNNERTON (96-9), q.v.
12. KATHERINE SAVAGE; m. (lic. 4 Nov. 1479), Thomas Legh, Esq., of Adlington, co. Chester, b. 1452, d. Adlington, 8 Aug. 1519, son of Robert de Legh and Ellen, dau. of Sir Robert Booth of Dunham Massey.
13. GEORGE LEGH, ESQ., of Adlington, b. 1497, d. Fleet Prison, 12 June 1529; m. c. 1523, Joan, dau. of Peter Larke of London; she m. (2) George Paulet.
14. THOMAS LEGH, ESQ., of Adlington, b. 1527, d. Eaton, co. Chester, 17 May 1548; m. Mary, d. 26 Mar. 1599, dau. of Richard Grosvenor, Esq. of Eaton.
15. THOMAS LEGH, ESQ., of Adlington, b. 1547, d. 25 Jan. 1601/2; rebuilt Adlington Hall, 1581, High Sheriff of Cheshire, 1599; m. Cheadle, 29 June 1563, Sibyl, bur. 19 Feb. 1609/10, dau. of Sir Urian Brereton, Knt., of Handford.
16. SIR URIAN LEGH, KNT., of Adlington, bp. Cheadle, 1566, knt., 26 June 1596, High Sheriff of Chester, 1613, d. 2 June 1627; m. c. 9 Sept. 1586, Margaret, dau. of Sir Edmund Trafford, Knt., of Trafford, co. Lancaster.
17. LUCY LEGH, bp. Manchester, 12 July 1596, bur. 5 Mar. 1643/4; m. Colonel Alexander Rigby, Esq., of Middleton, Lancashire, b. 1594, d. 18 Aug. 1650, son of Alexander Rigby and Anne Asshaw of Wigan. Col. Rigby was Deputy-President of Lygonia (Maine), 1643-1644.
18. EDWARD RIGBY succeeded to his father's rights in Maine; his brother ALEXANDER RIGBY, was bp. at Petersbury, 26 Aug. 1620; there were four children by Lucy (Legh) Rigby.

Line 107

1. SAIER de QUINCY, M.C. (74-1); m. Margaret de Beaumont.

      *   *   *   *   *   *

But see Sidney Painter, "The House of Quency, 1134-1264" in Medieval et Humanistica XI 3-9 also his Feudalism and Liberty pp. 230-239. Robert, No. 2, was yr. brother of Saier, No. 1.

      *   *   *   *   *   *

2. ROBERT de QUINCY, d. London, 1217, crusader; m. Hawise of Chester, b. 1180, d. betw. 6 June 1241 & 3 Mar. 1242/3, Countess of Lincoln. (CP VII, 675).
3. MARGARET de QUINCY, d. bef. 30 Mar. 1266 (Clay, p. 116, says 1279); m. (1) bef. 21 June 1221, JOHN de LACY (54-1), Magna Charta Surety, 1215, Earl of Lincoln. (CP VII, 676).
4. MAUD de LACY, d. bef. 10 Mar. 1288/9; m. on or bef. 25 Jan. 1237/8, SIR RICHARD de CLARE (28-3). (CP V, 696).
5. ROESE de CLARE, living 1316; m. ROGER de MOWBRAY (63-3), q.v. (CP IX, 376).

Line 108

2. ROGER de QUINCY (74-2); m. HELEN of GALLOWAY (139-2).
3. ELIZABETH de QUINCY, d. bef. Nov. 1328; m. Alexander Comyn, Earl of Buchan, Constable of Scotland, Justiciar, d. 1290, son of William Comyn and Margaret, Countess of Buchan. (Clay, 223-224; CP II, 374).
4. ELIZABETH COMYN, d. sh. bef. 17 Feb. 1328/9; m. Gilbert de Umfreville, Lord Umfreville, Earl of Angus, b. c. 1244, d. sh. bef. 13 Oct. 1307, M.P.,

1296-1307, son of Gilbert de Umfreville and Maud, dau. of Malcolm, Earl of Angus, by Mary, dau. of Sir Humphrey Berkeley. (CP I, 147).

5. ROBERT de UMFREVILLE, ae. 30+ at father's death, d. 2 Apr. 1325, Earl of Angus, M.P., 1308-1325; m. (1) 1303, Lucy de Kyme, dau. of Philip, Lord Kyme and Joan le Bigod; m. (2) Alianor, d. 31 Mar. 1368. (CP I, 149).

6. ELIZABETH de UMFREVILLE (by the 1st wife); m. Gilbert de Borough-don of Boroughdon, Sheriff of Northumberland, 1323-1324, 1339-1341. (CP VII, 358).

7. ELEANOR de BOROUGHDON, Baroness Kyme; m. Henry Tailboys, d. 23 Feb. 1368/9, son of William and Margaret Tailboys. (CP VII, 358).

8. SIR WALTER TAILBOYS, Lord Kyme, Sheriff of Lincoln, b. c. 1351, d. 20 or 21 Sept. 1417; m. Margaret. (CP VII, 358).

9. WALTER TAILBOYS, Lord Kyme, Sheriff of Lincolnshire, 1423, b. 1391, d. 13 Apr. 1444; m. (1) N.; m. (2) in or bef. 1432, Alice, d. by 24 Apr. 1448, widow of Sir Henry Cheney, Knt., and dau. of Sir Humphrey Stafford. (CP VII, 358).

10. SIR WILLIAM TAILBOYS, KNT. (by the 1st wife), Lord Kyme, b. c. 1415, beheaded c. 26 May 1464; m. Elizabeth Bonville, d. 14 Feb. 1490/1, dau. of William, Lord Bonville. (see 22-10) (CP VII, 359).

11. SIR ROBERT TAILBOYS, KNT., Lord Kyme, b. c. 1451, d. 30 Jan. 1494/5; m. ELIZABETH HERON (8-14). (CP VII, 361).

12. SIR GEORGE TAILBOYS, b. 1477, d. 21 Sept. 1538, Lord Kyme; m. (2) bef. Apr. 1493, Elizabeth, d. 1559, dau. of Sir William Gascoigne. (CP VII, 361).

13. ANNE TAILBOYS; m. (1) SIR EDWARD DYMOKE (86-13), d. c. 1566, of Scrivelsby.

Line 108A

3. ELIZABETH de QUINCY (108-3); m. Alexander Comyn, Earl of Buchan, Constable of Scotland.

4. ELENA COMYN, 4th dau., seen 1302; m. Sir William de Brechin, a regent of Scotland 1255, M.P., 1283/4, d. bef. 10 Dec. 1292. He was the son, by Juliana his wife, of Henry de Brechin, Lord of Brechin, d. bef. Aug. 1238, illegitimate son of David, Earl of Huntingdon. (CP II, 374-5; SP I, 4; SP II, 215-8, 254-6; William Anderson, The Scottish Nation (Edinburgh, 1863), I: 378-9).

5. SIR DAVID de BRECHIN, lord of Brechin, seen 1292, said to have been a crusader, executed for treason against Robert I, 1320; m. (1) in or aft. 1298, Margaret, dau. and heiress of Sir Alexander Bonkyl of that Ilk, widow of Sir John Stewart of Bonkyl. (SP II, 218-21; Andrew Jervise, The Land of the Lindsays (Edinburgh, 1882, pp. 139-41; Anderson, op. cit., I: 387).

6. MARGARET de BRECHIN; m. c. 1315, Sir David Barclay of Cairny-Barclay and Brechin, Sheriff of Fife, 1328, arranged the funeral of Robert I, 1329, slain at Aberdeen, 25 Jan. 1350. He was granted Brechin by Robert I following the execution of his father-in-law, Sir David de Brechin. (SP II, 222-3; Anderson, op. cit., I: 240).

7. JEAN BARCLAY; m. as his 1st wife, Sir David Fleming of Biggar and Cumbernauld, slain at the battle of Otterburn, 1388. (SP II, 223; SP VIII, 527-9; Anderson, op. cit., I: 241).

8. MARION FLEMING, seen 30 Sept. 1389; m. WILLIAM MAULE of Panmure (111A-7), d. bef. 12 Aug. 1407, who claimed the barony of Brechin in right of his wife. (SP II, 223; SP VIII, 529).

Line 108B

3. ELIZABETH de QUINCY (108-3); m. Alexander Comyn, Earl of Buchan, Constable of Scotland.

4. MARJORY COMYN, eldest dau., seen 29 Apr. 1296; m. in or sh. bef. 1282, Patrick de Dunbar, 7th Earl of Dunbar or March, b. 1242, d. 10 Oct. 1308, a competitor for the Crown of Scotland, 1291. (CP IV, 507; SP II, 254-6; III, 263).

5. SIR ALEXANDER DUNBAR, 2nd son, seen 1286 and 26 June 1331; m. N. (SP III, 259-60).

6. SIR PATRICK DUNBAR, fought at the battles of Durham, 1346, and Poitiers, 19 Sept. 1356, d. in Crete on his way to the Holy Land, 1356/7; m. Isabel,

seen 20 July 1361, dau. of Thomas Randolph, 1st Earl of Moray, son of Thomas Randolph, Chamberlain of Scotland, by Isabel de Brus, dau. of SIR ROBERT de BRUS (41-4), b. 1243, d. bef. 14 June 1304, Lord of Anandale, by his 1st wife, N. (CP IV, 508; IX, 167-8, 167 note c; SP III, 260).

7. GEORGE DUNBAR, 9th Earl of Dunbar or March, b. c. 1336, d. bef. 31 Mar. 1423, Warden of the Marches, 1372; m. Christian, seen 7 Mar. 1401/2, dau. of Alan de Seton (formerly Wintoun), by Margaret, dau. and heiress of Sir Alexander Seton of Seton. (CP IV, 508-9).

8. SIR DAVID DUNBAR of Cockburn and Auchtermonzie, b. c. 1376, yr. bro. of George Dunbar, last Earl of Dunbar or March; m. N. (CP III, 510).

9. MARGARET DUNBAR, d. betw. July 1498 & Jan. 1499/1500; m. (1) SIR ALEXANDER LINDSAY, "The Tiger," 4th Earl of Crawford, d. 1453 (43D-11), Sheriff of Aberdeenshire, 1446-1452, Ambassador to England, 1451. (CP III, 510; IV, 469; SP II, 250-6).

Line 109

5. ROBERT de UMFREVILLE (108-5); m. (2) Alianor.

6. THOMAS de UMFREVILLE, of Harbottle Castle, co. York, d. 21 May 1387; m. Joan, dau. of Adam de Roddam. (CP I, 151). (Joan may not have been m. to Thomas.)

7. SIR THOMAS de UMFREVILLE, eldest son by Joan, ae. 26 at father's death, of Harbottle Castle, d. 12 Feb. or 8 Mar. 1390/1; m. Agnes, d. 25 Oct. 1420, prob. dau. of Sir Thomas de Grey of Heton. (CP I, 151).

8. MARGARET de UMFREVILLE, d. 23 June 1444; m. (1) William Lodington of Gunby, co. Lincoln; m. (2) 1423, Sir John Constable, Knt., d. 1449/52, of Halsham in Holderness.

9. SIR JOHN CONSTABLE, KNT., of Halsham, d. aft. 20 Dec. 1472; m. Lora Fitz Hugh, dau. of Sir William Fitz Hugh and Margery Willoughby.

10. JOAN CONSTABLE; m. Sir William Mallory, Knt., of Stewdley. (Generations 5 to 10: Clay, 28-29).

11. SIR JOHN MALLORY, KNT., of Stewdley; m. Margaret, dau. of Edward Thwaytes, of Laund.

12. SIR WILLIAM MALLORY, KNT., of Stewdley; m. Jane, dau. of Sir John Conyers, Knt., of Norton, High Sheriff of Yorkshire, 1507-1508, 1514.

13. SIR WILLIAM MALLORY, KNT., of Stewdley; m. Ursula, dau. of George Gale, Esq., Lord Mayor of York, 1534 and 1546.

14. THE REVEREND THOMAS MALLORY, Dean of Chester, d. Chester, 3 Apr. 1644; m. Elizabeth, dau. of the Rt. Rev. Richard Vaughan, Bishop of Chester.

15. MARTHA MALLORY; m. Captain John Batte, of Okewell Hall, co. York, son of Robert Batte, Master of University College, Oxford.

16. CAPTAIN HENRY BATTE, of Okewell Hall, came to Virginia, c. 1646, Burgess, 1685-1686, 1692, Justice of Charles City Co., Va., 1693; m. Mary, dau. of Henry Lound, of Henrico Co., Va.

17. MARY BATTE; m. John Poythress, Burgess for Charles City Co., Va., 1723; d. Charles City Co., Va. 1723/4.

17. ELIZABETH BATTE; m. William Lygon II. (See Line 66.)

Line 110

7. SIR THOMAS de UMFREVILLE (109-7); m. Agnes (prob. Grey of Heton).

8. ELIZABETH de UMFREVILLE, b. 1381, d. 23 Nov. 1424; m. Sir William Elmeden of Elmeden. (CP I, 152).

9. JOAN de ELMEDEN (one of four daughters -- CP I, 152), m. Thomas Forster, Esq., of Buckton in the parish of Holy Island, co. Durham. (Clay, Extinct & Dormant Peerages of the Northern Counties, 223 ff; Hodgson, Hist. of Northumberland, II pp. 6, 36).

10. THOMAS FORSTER, of Etherstone (Edderston); m. Elizabeth de Etherstone, sister and heir of Roger, de Etherstone.

11. THOMAS FORSTER, of Etherstone; m. a dau. of Fetherstonhaugh of Stanhope Hall.

12. SIR ROGER FORSTER; m. Joan Hussey of Sussex co.
13. THOMAS FORSTER, 2nd son, fl. 1574, d. 11 Oct. 1599, of Hunsden, co.
Hertford; m. Margaret Browning of Chelmsford, co. Essex.
14. SIR THOMAS FORSTER, KNT., b. 1548, d. 1612, Justice of the Court
of Common Pleas, knighted, 1604; m. 1575, Susan Foster, d. 3 Apr. 1625, dau. of
Thomas Foster, of Iden, co. Sussex.
15. SUSAN FORSTER, bur. 18 Sept. 1612 (Whitechurch Register); m. Thomas
Brooke, d. 13 Sept. 1612 (will made 11 Sept. 1612, proved 30 Nov. 1612), of Whitechurch, co. Northampton, son of Richard Brooke and Elizabeth Twyne. (Generations 10 to 15: Raine, Hist. of Durham, pp. 306-308; Shaw, Knights of England,
II 134; Berry, Sussex, 192; Hist. of Hampshire, pp. 222-223, 339; Visitations of
Hertfordshire, Harl. Soc. Pub., XXII 43).
16. GOVERNOR ROBERT BROOKE, A.M., of Whitechurch, co. Hampshire,
b. London, England, A.B., Wadham Coll., Oxford, 1620, A.M., 1624; came to
Maryland, 1650, sett. at Brooke Place Manor, Charles Co., 1650; President of the
Provincial Council, 1652, Acting Governor, 1652; d. 20 July 1655; m. (1) 1627, Mary
Baker, d. 1634; m. (2) 1635, Mary Mainwaring, b. London, d. Brooke Place Manor,
Md., 29 Nov. 1663, dau. of Rev. Roger Mainwaring, D.D., Bishop of St. David's,
1636. (Md. Land Office, I folio 165-166).

Line 111

1. SAIER de QUINCY (74-1); m. Margaret de Beaumont.
2. ORABELLA de QUINCY; m. Sir Richard de Harcourt, d. 1228, son of Sir
William de Harcourt, Governor of Tamworth Castle, 1218, and Alice Noell, dau. of
Thomas Noell, Esq., of Ellenhall, co. Stafford.
3. WILLIAM de HARCOURT; m. (1) Alice la Zouche, dau. of Alan la Zouche
(mother of Orabella Harcourt who follows); m. (2) HILLARIA de HASTINGS (7-4),
q.v. (Dudley Pedigree).
4. ORABELLA HARCOURT (by the 1st marriage); m. Henry de Pembrugge,
d. bef. 25 Jan. 1279.
5. FULKE de PEMBRUGGE, fl. 1270-1326, M.P., 1322-1326, d. 1326; m.
Matilda de Bermingham.
6. FULKE de PEMBRUGGE.
7. MARGERY de PEMBRUGGE; m. Sir Ralph Lingen, M.P., 1374-1382.
8. ISABEL LINGEN; m. (1) her cousin, Fulke Pembrugge; m. (2) Sir John
Ludlow; m. (3) Sir Thomas de Petyvine.
9. MARGERY LUDLOW; m. SIR WILLIAM TRUSSELL (131-10), Lord of Elms-
thorpe. (Generations 1 to 9: Adams, Elkington Family, 1945, pp. 16-17; generations
10 to 13: ibid., p. 18).
10. ISABEL TRUSSELL; m. THOMAS WODHULL (59-9), of Warkworth, d.
1441.
11. JOHN WODHULL, of Warkworth, b. 1435, d. 12 Sept. 1490; m. Joan, dau.
of Henry Etwell, LL.D., of London. (See also Line 59.)
12. FULK WODHULL, of Warkworth and Thenford, b. 1459, d. 1508, Sheriff
of Northamptonshire, 1500-1501; m. Anne Newenham, dau. of William Newenham,
of Thenford, co. Northampton. (See also Line 59.)
13. SIR NICHOLAS WODHULL, of Warkworth, b. 1482, d. 5 May 1551, Sheriff
of Northampton, 1516, 1518; m. (1) 1508, Mary Raleigh, dau. of SIR EDWARD RA-
LEIGH, KNT. (34-12) and his wife Margaret Verney; m. (2) ELIZABETH PARR
(118-12), own cousin to Queen Katharine Parr.
14. ANTHONY WODHULL, of Warkworth (by the 1st wife), b. 1518, d. 4 Feb.
1542; m. Anne Smith, dau. of Sir John Smith, Baron of the Exchequer.
15. AGNES WODHULL, only dau., b. 1542, d. 1576/7; m. Sir Richard Chetwode, son of Roger Chetwode.
16. SIR RICHARD CHETWODE, KNT., b. c. 1560, d. aft. 1631; m. DOROTHY
NEEDHAM (24-15), b. 1570, d. aft. 1629.
17. GRACE CHETWODE, b. 1602, d. New London, Connecticut, 21 Apr. 1669;
m. as his 2nd wife, Apr. 1635, the REV. PETER BULKELEY, B.D. (98-16), first
minister at Concord, Massachusetts.
18. THE REVEREND GERSHOM BULKELEY, A.M., b. Cambridge, Mass.,
Jan. 1635/6, d. Glastonbury, Connecticut, 2 Dec. 1713; A.B., Harvard Coll., 1655,
A.M., minister at Wethersfield, Connecticut, 1669-1677.

Line 111A

1. SAIER de QUINCY (74-1); m. Margaret de Beaumont.
2. LORETTE de QUINCY; m. Sir William de Valoniis or Valoynes, d. at Kelso, 1219, Chamberlain of Scotland.
3. CHRISTIAN de VALOYNES, seen 1254; m. bef. 1215, Peter de Maule, d. c. 1254. She brought her husband the baronies of Panmure and Bervie.
4. WILLIAM de MAULE, laird of Panmure, Sheriff of Forfarshire, d. bef. 1312; m. Ethana, dau. of John Vaux or de Vallibus, lord of Dirleton.
5. SIR HENRY de MAULE, laird of Panmure, seen 1312 and 26 May 1325; m. Margaret Hay.
6. SIR WALTER de MAULE, laird of Panmure, seen 31 Dec. 1346 and 17 July 1348, d. bef. Aug. 1348; m. N.
7. WILLIAM MAULE, laird of Panmure, d. bef. 12 Aug. 1407; m. MARION FLEMING (108A-8).
8. SIR THOMAS MAULE, laird of Panmure, slain at the battle of Harlow, 24 July 1411; m. Elizabeth, dau. of Sir Andrew Gray of Foulis, dead in 1441, by his 1st wife, Janet, dau. of Sir Roger de Mortimer and Margaret of Menteith.
9. THOMAS MAULE, laird of Panmure, posthumous son, served heir bef. 31 May 1412, d. 1450; m. 1427, Mary, dau. of Sir Thomas Abercrombie of that Ilk.
10. SIR THOMAS MAULE, "the blind knight," laird of Panmure, d. aft. 16 Jan. 1497/8; m. Elizabeth, dau. of SIR DAVID LINDSAY, 3rd Earl of Crawford (43-10).
11. ALEXANDER MAULE, d.v.p.; m. Elizabeth, d. c. 1526, dau. of Sir David Guthrie of that Ilk.
12. SIR THOMAS MAULE, laird of Panmure, slain at Flodden, 1513; m. (1) bef. 12 Mar. 1490/1, ELIZABETH (41A-13), d. in or bef. 1509, dau. of David Rollock or Rollo of Ballachie.
13. SIR ROBERT MAULE, laird of Panmure, b. c. 1497, d. 3 May 1560, Sheriff of Angus, a prisoner in the Tower of London, 1547-49, "He was a proper comely Gentleman ... letcherous and much given to Hunting and Hawking, the Golf, Foot Ball and other Manly Exercises."; m. as his 2nd wife, in or aft. 1540, ISABEL, d. 1558 (91A-14), dau. of James Arbuthnott of Arbuthnott by JEAN (91A-13), dau. of JOHN STEWART (91A-12), 2nd Earl of Atholl.
14. WILLIAM MAULE of Glaster, 3rd son by his father's 2nd wife, b. c. 1545, d. 19 Apr. 1619; admitted a burgess of Edinburgh, 25 July 1579; Dean of Guild of Edinburgh bef. Nov. 1607; m. Bethia, d. 22 Dec. 1624, dau. of Alexander Guthric.
15. ELEANOR MAULE, b. c. 1585, d. Nov. 1664; m. 6 Sept. 1610, Sir Alexander Morrison of Prestongrange, Haddington, d. 20 Sept. 1631, aged 52, appointed a Lord of Session, 14 Feb. 1626.
16. BETHIA MORRISON, d. 17 Nov. 1639; m. 6 June 1629, SIR ROBERT SPOTSWOOD or SPOTTISWOOD (43A-17), Lord President of the College of Justice, Secretary of State for Scotland, executed 16 Jan. 1646.
16. KATHERINE MORRISON, dau. of Sir Alexander Morrison of Prestongrange by ELEANOR MAULE (111A-15), bp. 16 Feb. 1615; m. (contract 14 Aug. 1635) LT. COL. GEORGE HOME, younger, of Wedderburn (41E-18), slain at the battle of Dunbar, 3 Sept. 1650. (Generations 2-15: SP VII, 5-13; J. M. M'Bain, Eminent Arbroathians (Arbroath, 1897), pp. 116-120; Walter Macfarlane, Genealogical Collections (Edinburgh, 1900), II: 146-9; Generations 15-16: Andrew Ross and Francis J. Grant (eds.), Alexander Nisbet's Heraldic Plates (Edinburgh, 1892), pp. 50, 136; DNB XVIII, 824-5; Spotswood papers (mss.), Colonial Williamsburg, Williamsburg, Virginia; G. E. Cokayne, Complete Baronetage II: 442).

Line 112

6. ISABEL BERKELEY (82-6); m. 1328, ROBERT de CLIFFORD (144-6).
7. ISABELLA CLIFFORD; m. 1361, Sir John de Eure, d. 22 Feb. 1393/4, Constable of Dover Castle, Lord Steward of the King's Household, son of Sir John de Eure and Margaret.
8. SIR RALPH de EURE, d. 10 Mar. 1422, Sheriff of Northumberland, 1389-1397, Governor of the Castle of New Castle, Constable of York Castle; m. (2) CATHARINE de ATON (11-9).

9. CATHARINE EURE, d. bef. 31 Aug. 1459; m. 1401 Sir Alexander Neville, of Thornton Bridge, b. c. 1390, d. 1457.

10. WILLIAM NEVILLE, b. c. 1425/6, d. 1469, of Thornton Bridge; m. Joan.

11. WILLIAM NEVILLE; m. (1) (under age) contract 13 Oct 1457, Joan, dau. of Christopher Boynton; m. (2) Alice.

13. SIR RALPH NEVILLE (by 1st wife), b. c. 1465, d. 24 July 1522, of Thornton Bridge; m. 1500/1, ANNE WARD (102-13), q.v. (Sheppard, op. cit.; see 102-18).

Line 113

7. SIR ROGER de CLIFFORD (82-7), d. 1389; m. Maud, dau. of THOMAS de BEAUCHAMP (5-6) Earl of Warwick. (CP III, 292).

8. THOMAS de CLIFFORD, ae. 26 at father's death, d. 18 Aug. 1391, Lord Clifford, Sheriff of Westmoreland, Governor of Carlisle Castle; m. Elizabeth de Ros, dau. of THOMAS de ROS (1-6) and Beatrice Stafford. (CP III, 292).

9. JOHN de CLIFFORD, K.G., d. 13 Mar. 1421/2, Lord Clifford; m. ELIZABETH de PERCY (36-11), d. 26 Oct. 1437. (CP III, 293).

10. THOMAS de CLIFFORD, b. 25 Mar. 1414, slain at the battle of St. Albans, 22 May 1455; m. aft. Mar. 1424, Joan de Dacre, dau. of Thomas de Dacre, Lord Dacre of Gillesland, and PHILIPPA NEVILLE (8A-10). (CP III, 293).

11. JOAN de CLIFFORD; m. Richard de Musgrave, d. 10 Aug. 1491, son of Thomas de Musgrave and Joan Stapleton of Edenhall.

12. SIR EDWARD de MUSGRAVE, d. 23 May 1542, knighted at Flodden Field, 1513; m. (2) c. 1496, Joan, dau. of Sir Christopher Ward of Givendale.

13. SIR WILLIAM de MUSGRAVE, d. 18 Oct. 1544, knighted at Jedburgh, 25 Sept. 1523; m. Elizabeth Curwen, dau. of Sir Thomas Curwen of Workington.

14. SIR RICHARD de MUSGRAVE, KNT., b. c. 1524, d. at Edenhall, Sept. 1555; m. Anne, dau. of Thomas Wharton, Lord Wharton.

*   *   *   *   *   *

Generations nos. 15-22 encompass only 24 years! This line is NOT an acceptable one. See Line 113A.

*   *   *   *   *   *

15. ELEANOR MUSGRAVE, b. c. 1546, d. 23 July 1623; m. (1) William Thornborough, Esq., of Selside.

16. WILLIAM THORNBOROUGH, ESQ., of Hampsfield, co. Lancaster.

17. ROWLAND THORNBOROUGH, ESQ., of Hampsfield; m. Jane, dau. of Thomas Dalton, Esq., of Turnham.

18. ANNE THORNBOROUGH; m. as his 2nd wife, Thomas Ros.

19. ANNE ROS; m. John Dixon of London.

20. MARGARET DIXON; m. George Sandys, of London and Estwaite Furness, Lancashire, son of William Sandys and Margaret Gerard.

21. EDWIN SANDYS, D.D., b. 1516, d. 1588, Archbishop of York; m. (2) Cicely Wilford, sister of Sir Thomas Wilford.

*   *   *   *   *   *

Edwin Sandys was older than his alleged gt. gt. gt. gt. grandmother, Eleanor Musgrave!

*   *   *   *   *   *

22. ANNE SANDYS, b. c. 21 June 1570; m. Sir William Barne, Knt., of Woolwich, co. Kent, son of Sir George Barne, Knt., Lord Mayor of London, 1586.

23. ANNE BARNE; m. SIR WILLIAM LOVELACE, KNT. (113A-16), of Lovelace, co. Kent.

24. ANNE LOVELACE, b. c. 1611, d. in Virginia, c. 1652; m. c. 1628, the Reverend John Gorsuch, D.D., of Walkerne, co. Hertford, killed 1647, by rebels under Colonel Fairclough of Weston. (v. Redlich and Adams, op. cit., pp. 188-190).

Line 113A

9. PHILIPPA SERGEAUX (134-9), b. 1381; m. (1) Sir Robert Pashley, b. c. 1370; m. (2) William Swynborne.

10. ANNE PASHLEY; m. (1) John Bassingborne; m. (2) Edward Tyrrel, Esq.,

of Downham, Essex, knight of the shire for Essex, 1427, 1432, 1435; Sheriff of Essex
and Herts, 1436; will dated 10 Oct. 1442, I.p.m., 1443.

11. PHILIPPA TYRREL; m. Thomas Cornwallis of Brome, Suffolk, M.P.
1449/50, d. 24 May 1484.

12. WILLIAM CORNWALLIS, ESQ., of Brome and Oakley, Suffolk, London,
Bedfordshire, and Norfolk, d. 1519; m. Elizabeth, dau. of John Stanford, Esq.

13. AFFRA CORNWALLIS (sister of Sir John Cornwallis of Brome, Steward
of the Household of Prince Edward, later Edward VI); m. Sir Anthony Aucher of
Bishopsbourne and Otterden, Kent, b. c. 1500, d. 9 Jan. 1558; marshal of Calais,
governor of Guisnes.

14. EDWARD AUCHER, ESQ., of Bishopsbourne, Kent, b. c. 1539, d. 14
Feb. 1567/8; m. 10 June 1560, Mabel, d. 1597, dau. of Sir Thomas Wroth, M.P.,
by Mary, dau. of Richard, Lord Rich, lord chancellor of England and defamer of
Sir Thomas More.

15. ELIZABETH AUCHER, b. betw. 1561 & 1565, bur. 3 Dec. 1627 at Canter-
bury Cathedral; m. c. 1580/1, Sir William Lovelace of Bethersden, Kent, bp. 30
Sept. 1561 at Canterbury Cathedral, will proved 19 Oct. 1629; member of the Virginia
Company.

16. SIR WILLIAM LOVELACE of Bethersden and Woolwich, Kent, bp. 12 Feb.
1583/4; d. at the siege of Groll, Holland, 12 Aug. 1627; member of the Virginia
Company; m. c. 1610, ANNE (113-23), dau. of Sir William Barne of Woolwich, Kent,
member of the Virginia Company, I.p.m. 22 Oct. 1619, by ANNE (113-22), d. 21 Jan.
1570, dau. of the Rt. Rev. EDWIN SANDYS, D.D., Archbishop of York (113-21).

17. ANNE LOVELACE, b. Woolwich, Kent, c. 1611, d. in Virginia, c. 1652; m.
c. 1628, Rev. John Gorsuch, D.D., rector of Walkern, Herts, d. 1647. (Gen. 9:
Joseph J. Muskett, Suffolk Manorial Families (Exeter, 1908), II, 268: Sir John
Maclean, The Parochial and Family History of the Deanery of Trigg Minor in the
County of Cornwall (London, 1876), II, 507; G.D. Scull, Dorothea Scott of Egerton
House, Kent, 1611-1680 (Oxford, 1883), appendix, chart II. Gen. 10: G. Andrews
Moriarty, "The Early Tyrrels of Heron in East Herndon," NEHGR, CIX, 31; Muskett,
II, 268. Gens. 11-12: Moriarty, op. cit.; Visitation of the County of Nottingham, 1569
and 1614 (Harl. Soc. Pub., vol. IV), p. 161; W.A. Coppinger, The Manors of Suffolk
(Manchester, 1909), III, 239, 241; Va. Mag. of Hist. & Biog., XXVIII, 381; Muskett,
II, 268. Gens. 13-14: Visitation of the County of Nottingham, 1569 and 1614, loc. cit.;
Visitation of Kent, 1574 (Harl. Soc. Pub., vol. LXXIV), p. 25; Visitation of Kent,
1619-1621 (Harl. Soc. Pub., vol. XLII), p. 181; Va. Mag. of Hist. and Biog., XXVIII, 293-
5, 375-80, 382; Coppinger, III, 239, 241. Gens. 15-16: Visitation of Kent, 1619-1621,
pp. 126, 181; Archaeologia Cantiana, X, 204, 208-9; Va. Mag. of Hist. and Biog., XXVIII,
176-82, 380-1; XXIX, 123-4. Gen. 17: Archaeologia Cantiana, X, 208; Visitation of London, 1633-1635 (Harl. Soc. Pub., vol. XV), p. 327; Va. Mag. of Hist. and Biog., XXVIII, 182).

Line 114

1. SAIER de QUINCY (74-1), Magna Charta Surety, 1215.
2. ROBERT de QUINCY, 3rd son, by unkn. mother, of Colne Quincy, co. Essex; m. Helen, widow of John le Scot, Earl of Huntington, and dau. of Llewellyn ap
Iorworth, Prince of Wales, prob. by his wife Joan, natural dau. of King JOHN (161-
12) of England. (CP XII (2), 299).
3. HAWISE de QUINCY, b. c. 1250, d. bef. 27 Mar. 1284/5; m. as his 2nd
wife, bef. 5 Feb. 1267/8, Baldwin Wake, b. 1236, d. sh. bef. 10 Feb. 1281/2, of
Liddell, co. Cumberland. (CP XII (2), 299).
4. SIR JOHN WAKE, Lord Wake, b. prob. late 1268, d. sh. bef. 10 Apr. 1300;
M.P., 1295; m. sh. bef. 24 Sept. 1291, Joan, d. sh. bef. 26 Oct. 1309, perh. dau.
of Sir John Fitz Barnard of Kingsdown, co. Kent, d. 1300. (CP XII (2), 301; Clay,
229).
5. MARGARET WAKE, Lady Wake, b. c. 1309, d. 29 Sept. 1349; m. (1) John
Comyn; m. (2) c. 25 Dec. 1321, Edmund Plantagenet, of Woodstock, Earl of Kent,
executed 19 Mar. 1329/30, son of King EDWARD I (161-14) and Marguerite of France.
(Generations 2 to 6: Clay, pp. 228-229; Gen. 5: CP VII, 142).
6. JOAN PLANTAGENET, Countess of Kent, the "Fair Maid of Kent," ae.
24+ in 1352, b. c. 1328, d. 8 Aug. 1385; m. (1) in or bef. 1339, SIR THOMAS de
HOLAND, K.G. (90-7). (CP VII, 150).

Line 115

6. SIR ROBERT de FERRERS (102-6), Lord Ferrers of Chartley; m. Margaret.
7. SIR JOHN de FERRERS, Lord Ferrers of Chartley, b. Southoe, c. 10 Aug.
1333, slain at Najara, 3 Apr. 1367; m. lic. 19 Oct. 1349, Elizabeth, d. 7 Aug. 1375,
dau. of SIR RALPH de STAFFORD, K.G. (136-6), Earl of Stafford, and MARGARET
de AUDLEY (28-6). (CP V, 313).
8. SIR ROBERT de FERRERS, Lord Ferrers of Chartley, b. 31 Oct. 1357,
d. 12 or 13 Mar. 1412/3; m. (2) MARGARET DESPENSER (13-10), d. 3 Nov. 1415.
(CP V, 315).
9. PHILIPPA de FERRERS, bur. Norton, 5 Nov. 1415; m. SIR THOMAS
GREENE (34-10), q.v. (Generations 6 to 9: CP V, 320 chart).

Line 116

1. ROBERT de ROS, "Furfan," Magna Charta Surety, 1215, a minor 1185, d.
bef. 23 Dec. 1226, of Helmsley in Holderness, co. York, Knight Templar, grandson
of Robert de Ros and Sibyl de Valognes, son & h. of Everard, d. 1183, and Roese,
dau. of Wm. Trussebut, Lord of Warter, by Audrey de Harcourt; m. 1191 Isabel, wid.
of Robert de Brus, natural dau. of William the Lion, King of Scots, by Isabel, dau.
of Richard and Sibyl Avenal. (CP XI, 91-93).
2. SIR WILLIAM de ROS, of Helmsley, d. prob. 1264 in the King's service
at Poitou, 1224, accompanied the King to France, 1230, served in Scotland and
Wales, 1257-1258; m. Lucy Fitz Piers, living 1266, dau. of Piers Fitz Herbert of
Brecknock, Wales.
3. SIR WILLIAM de ROS, of Ingmanthorpe, presumably 3rd son, served in
Scotland, 1257/8, and in Gascony, 1294, d. sh. bef. 28 May 1310; m. c. 1268, Eus-
tache, widow of Sir Nicholas de Cauntelo, dau. of Ralph Fitz Hugh, son and h. of
Hugh Fitz Ralph, by Agnes, dau. and h. of Ralph de Greasley. (CP XI, 94, 117-8).
4. LUCY de ROS, widow in 1332; m. Sir Robert de Plumpton, Knt., of Plumpton, held land at Idle, co. York, 1290, lord of Plumpton, 1315-1325, d. 1325, son of
Sir Robert de Plumpton of Plumpton and Isabella, dau. of Serlo de Westwick, lord
of Grassington in Craven. (CP XI, 118, and note h).
5. SIR WILLIAM de PLUMPTON, KNT., of Plumpton, keeper of Knaresbor-
ough Forest, 1332, Knt., 1340, Knight of the Shire, 1350, High Sheriff of Yorkshire,
1351, d. 1362; m. (1) c. 1330, Alice de Swillington; m. (2) c. 1338, Christian Mowbray, d. 1365, formerly widow of Richard de Emildon, alderman of New Castle.
6. ALICE de PLUMPTON (by the 2nd wife), liv. 21 Mar. 1400; m. (1) 1352,
Sir Richard Shireburne, Knt., of Aighton, d. 1361; m. (2) 1364, Sir John Boteler of
Bewsey in Warrington, Lancashire, M.P., 1366-1380, Knight of the Shire, 1388-
1398, feudal baron of Warrington, 1380-1400, fought in Gascony, 1369, in Aquitaine,
1372, d. 1400, son of William le Boteler and Elizabeth de Havering.
7. ALICE BOTELER, d. 27 Feb. 1441/2; m. John Gerard of Kingsley and
Bryn, b. 1386, d. 6 Nov. 1431, lord of the manors of Kingsley and Bryn, 1416-1431,
son of Sir Thomas and Isabel Gerard of Bryn.
8. CONSTANCE GERARD, b. 1402, liv. 1469; m. c. 1421/3, Sir Alexander
Standish, Knt., of Standish, d. 1445, son of Lawrence Standish and Lora Pilkington.
9. RALPH STANDISH, ESQ., of Standish, b. c. 1424, liv. 1468; m. Margaret
Radcliffe, d. 1476, dau. of Richard Radcliffe of Chadderton.
10. SIR ALEXANDER STANDISH, KNT., of Standish, b. 1452, d. 1507; m.
Sibyl de Bold, widow in 1507, dau. of Sir Henry Bold of Bold.
11. RALPH STANDISH, ESQ., of Standish, b. 1479, d. 1538; m. c. 16 Aug.
1498, ALICE HARINGTON (129-13).
12. ROGER STANDISH, ESQ., of Standish, co. Lancaster, fl. 24 Mar. 1513/4,
3rd son; name of wife unknown.
13. ALICE STANDISH, bur. at Standish, 1564; m. James Prescott, of Standish,
Shevington and Coppull, Standish Parish, b. 1508, d. 1568, son of William and Alice
Prescott.
14. ROGER PRESCOTT, 2nd son, of Shevington, Standish Parish, d. Sept.
1594, will made 26 Sept. 1594; m. (1) Elizabeth; m. (2) 23 Aug. 1568, Ellen Shaw of
Standish.
15. RALPH PRESCOTT, of Shevington in Standish Parish, only son, b. c.

1571/2, d. 1608/9; m. Helen, liv. 1608.

   *   *   *   *   *   *

There is insufficient evidence to identify John Prescott of Lancaster, Mass., with the John, son of Ralph Prescott of Shevington.

   *   *   *   *   *   *

16. JOHN PRESCOTT, founder of Lancaster, Massachusetts, 1645, b. Standish Parish, Lancashire, c. 1604 (named in his father's will, 1608), d. Lancaster, Massachusetts, Dec. 1681; m. Halifax, co. York, 11 Apr. 1629, Mary Platts, bp. Sowerby, Halifax Parish, co. York, 15 Mar. 1607, perh. he who d. Lancaster, Massachusetts, aft. 1678, and left issue: MARY PRESCOTT, m. 1648, Thomas Swayer; HANNAH PRESCOTT, m. 1660, John Rugg; LYDIA PRESCOTT, m. 1658, Jonas Fairbank; SARAH PRESCOTT, m. 1658, Richard Wheeler; CAPTAIN JONATHAN PRESCOTT; CAPTAIN JONAS PRESCOTT, ESQ. Though quite possibly true, evidence of a link between generations 15 and 16 is lacking.

Line 117

2. SIR WILLIAM de ROS (116-2), of Helmsley; m. Lucy Fitz Piers.

3. SIR ROBERT de ROS, d. 17 May 1285, of Helmsley and Belvoir; m. betw. 5 June 1243 & 17 May 1244, ISABEL D'AUBIGNY (1-3), d. 15 June 1301. (CP XI, 95).

4. ISABEL de ROS, m. as his 1st wife, Walter de Fauconberg, 2nd Lord Fauconberg, d. 31 Dec. 1318.

5. JOHN de FAUCONBERG, Lord Fauconberg, b. on or just bef. 24 June 1290, d. 17 or 18 Sept. 1349; m. Eve, dau. of William Bulmer. (Clay, 70).

6. JOAN de FAUCONBERG; m. 1376/7, Sir William Colville, of Arncliffe, d. c. 1380/1.

7. SIR JOHN de COLVILLE, of Arncliffe and Dale, beheaded at Durham, 20 Aug. 1405, with his wife; m. Alice Darcy, dau. of John, Lord Darcy.

8. ISABEL de COLVILLE, liv. 1442/3; m. (1) John Wandesford, of Kirklington, d. c. 1400, son of John de Wandesford.

9. THOMAS WANDESFORD, merchant of London, Sheriff of London, 1443, Alderman, d. 13 Oct. 1448; m. Idonea.

10. ALICE WANDESFORD; m. William Mulso, of Creatingham, co. Suffolk, d. 1495.

11. ANNE MULSO; m. Thomas Louthe, of Sawtry, co. Huntingdon, M.P., d. 1533.

12. EDMUND LOUTHE, killed 1522; m. Edith Stukeley, dau. of John Stukeley of Stukeley, co. Huntingdon.

13. ANNE LOUTHE, d. 1577; m. Simon Throckmorton of Earsham, co. Suffolk, d. 10 July 1527.

14. LIONEL THROCKMORTON, of South Elmham and Bungay, co. Suffolk, d. 1599; m. (2) 1560, Elizabeth Blennerhasset, dau. of John Blennerhasset of Barsham, and his 1st wife, Elizabeth Cornwallis.

15. BASSINGBOURNE THROCKMORTON, ESQ., alderman of Norwich, b. 1564, d. 21 Sept. 1683; m. (1) 1591, Mary Hill, d. 1615, dau. of William Hill, gent., of Bury St. Edmunds, and his wife, Joan Annabel.

16. JOHN THROCKMORTON, of Providence, Rhode Island, bp. 8 May 1601, d. 17 Mar. 1683/4-25 Apr. 1684; m. Rebecca. (Moriarty Notebooks at NEHGS).

Line 118

1. ROBERT de ROS (116-1); m. Isabel of Scotland.

2. ROBERT de ROS, of Wark on Tweed, co. Northumberland, seen 1206/7, Chief Justice of the King's Bench, 1234, Chief Justice of the Forests north of Trent, 1236, d. 1269; m. (2) Christian, dau. of Sir Roger Bertram and Ida. (CP XI, 119-121; Clay, 15).

3. ROBERT de ROS, a younger son, but made h. to father, d. sh. bef. 20 Apr. 1274; m. Margaret de Brus, sister of Piers de Brus of Kendal, d. sh. bef. 30 Jan., 1306/7. She divided her estate between her son William and her nephew Marmaduke de Thwenge. (CP XI, 120-121).

88   [Line 119

4. WILLIAM de ROS, of Kendal Castle, d. bef. 9 May 1310. (Clay, 185).
5. SIR THOMAS de ROS, of Kendal, b. c. 1307, d. c. 1390/1; m. a dau. of
Sir John Preston of Westmoreland. (Clay, 157).
6. JOHN de ROS, of Kendal, d. 1358; m. Katherine, dau. of Sir Thomas
Latimer. (Generations 5 to 10: Clay, 157).
7. ELIZABETH ROS, b. 1356; m. 1383, Sir William Parr, Knt., d. 4 Oct.
1405, of Parr and Kendal.
8. JOHN PARR, of Kendal, b. c. 1383, d. bef. 1407/8; m. Agnes, d. c.
1435/6, dau. of Sir Thomas Crophull. (Gens. 1-9: Sheppard, op. cit.).
9. SIR THOMAS PARR, KNT., of Kendal, Sheriff of Westmoreland, 1461-
1475; attainted; m. Alice, dau. of Sir Thomas Tunstall of Thurland Castle.
10. SIR WILLIAM PARR, K.G., of Kendal, b. c. 1434, d. sh. bef. 26 Feb. 1483/4,
M.P.; m. (2) ELIZABETH FITZ HUGH (94-12); she m. (2) Nicholas Vaux of Harrowden.
11. SIR WILLIAM PARR, d. c. Nov. 1547, Baron Parr of Horton; m. bef. 1511,
Mary Salisbury, d. 10 July 1555, dau. of William Salisbury of Horton and Elizabeth
Wylde. (CP X, 309).
12. ELIZABETH PARR; m. as his 2nd wife, SIR NICHOLAS WODHULL (111-13).

Generations following this in earlier editions are unproven. See TAG, 32: 127.

                                    Line 119

9. SIR THOMAS PARR (118-9); m. Alice Tunstall.
10. AGNES PARR; m. Sir Thomas Strickland, of Sizergh, d. 1467.
11. SIR WALTER STRICKLAND, K.B., d. 1506; m. Elizabeth Pennington.
12. SIR WALTER STRICKLAND, d. 1527/8; m. (2) KATHERINE NEVILLE
(102-14). (Clay, 157; Sheppard, op. cit.).

                                    Line 120

1. ROBERT de VERE (154-3), Magna Charta Surety, 1215, b. prob. aft. 1164,
d. bef. 25 Oct. 1221, 3rd Earl of Oxford, Lord Chamberlain of England; m. Isabel,
d. 13 Feb. 1248, dau. of Hugh de Bolbec. (CP X, 210).
2. HUGH de VERE, b. c. 1210, d. bef. 23 Dec. 1263, 4th Earl of Oxford,
Hereditary Master Chamberlain of England; m. aft. 11 Feb. 1222/3, Hawise, d. 3
Feb., year unkn. but aft. 1263, dau. of SAIER de QUINCY (74-1) and Margaret de
Beaumont. (CP X, 215).
3. ROBERT de VERE, b. c. 1240, d. bef. 7 Sept. 1296, 5th Earl of Oxford,
M.P., 1283-1296; m. by 22 Feb. 1252, Alice, d. bef. 9 Sept. 1312, dau. of Gilbert
de Sanford. (CP X, 216).
4. ALFONSO de VERE, of Great Hormead, co. Hertford, d. c. 20 Dec. 1329;
m. Joan, prob. dau. of Sir Richard Foliot. (CP, loc. cit.)
5. JOHN de VERE, 7th Earl of Oxford, b. c. 12 Mar. 1311/2, d. Rheims, 23
or 24 Jan. 1359/60, Hereditary Chamberlain to the King of England; m. bef. 27 Mar.
1336, Maud de Badlesmere, b. 1308 or 1310, d. prob. 24 May 1366, dau. of Bartholomew de Badlesmere and MARGARET de CLARE (33-6). (CP X, 222).
6. MARGARET de VERE, d. 15 June 1398; m. (1) Henry Beaumont, Lord
Beaumont, b. 1340, d. 25 June 1369; m. (2) as his 2nd wife, Sir Nicholas Louvain,
d. 1375; m. (3) 17 June 1379, Sir John Lord Devereux, d. 22 Feb. 1392/3. (CP II,
61; IV, 296; Gen. Mag. vol. 15: 252-3).
7. JOHN BEAUMONT, K.G., b. 1361, d. Stirling, 9 Sept. 1396, Lord Beaumont, Warden of the Scottish Marches, 1389, 1396, Admiral of the North Sea, Constable of Dover Castle and Lord Warden of the Cinque Ports, 1392, K.G., 1393; m.
Catherine, d. 1426, dau. of Thomas Everingham, of Laxton, co. Nottingham. (CP
II, 61).
8. HENRY BEAUMONT, K.B., b. c. 1380, d. June 1413, Lord Beaumont,
K.B., 1400, Commissioner in France, 1411; m. bef. July 1405, Elizabeth Willoughby,
d. sh. bef. 12 Nov. 1428, dau. of William, Lord Willoughby, and Lucy Strange, dau.
of Roger, Lord Strange of Knockyn. (CP II, 61).
9. SIR HENRY BEAUMONT, b. 1411, d. bef. 1447/8; m. (2) Joan Heronville,

dau. of Henry Heronville.

10. SIR HENRY BEAUMONT, KNT., of Wednesbury, d. 16 Nov. 1471, Sheriff of Stafford co., 1471; m. Eleanor Sutton.

11. CONSTANCE BEAUMONT, b. c. 1467; m. John Mitton, Sheriff of Staffordshire, M.P., son of John Mitton, Esq., and Anne Swinnerton.

12. JOYCE MITTON, b. c. 1487; m. by 1505/6, John Harpersfield of London.

13. EDWARD HARPERSFIELD, alias Mitton, Esq., of Weston-under-Lizard; m. 1530, Anne Skrimshire.

14. KATHERINE MITTON; m. Roger Marshall, merchant of Shrewsbury, d. 4 Aug. 1612.

15. ELIZABETH MARSHALL, d. bef. 1640; m. St. Chad's, Shrewsbury, 29 Aug. 1618, Thomas Lewis, b. Shrewsbury, c. 1590, d. bef. 1640, son of Andrew Lewis and Mary Herring; sett. Saco, Maine, 1631.

16. MARY LEWIS, bp. 28 June 1619; m. aft. 10 May 1638, the Rev. Richard Gibson, A.M., of Portsmouth, N.H.

16. JUDITH LEWIS, bp. 23 Oct. 1626; m. c. 1646, James Gibbins, of Saco, Maine.

Line 121

3. ROBERT de VERE (120-3), b. 1240; m. 1252, Alice de Sanford.

4. JOAN de VERE, d. on or bef. 23 Nov. 1293; m. prob. June 1285, WILLIAM de WARENNE (151-3). (CP XII (2), 507).

5. ALICE de WARENNE, d. bef. 23 May 1338; m. 1305, SIR EDMUND FITZ ALAN, Earl of Arundel (134-6). (CP I, 241).

6. SIR RICHARD FITZ ALAN, b. c. 1313, d. Arundel, 24 Jan. 1375/6, Earl of Arundel and Warenne; m. (1) 9 Feb. 1320/1, ISABEL DESPENSER (34-6), divorced 4 Dec. 1344; m. (2) Ditton, 5 Feb. 1344/5, Eleanor Plantagenet, d. 11 Jan. 1372, dau. of Henry, Earl of Lancaster, and MAUD de CHAWORTH (4-6), wid. of John, 2nd Lord Beaumont. (CP I, 242).

7. SIR JOHN d'ARUNDEL, KNT. (son by the 2nd wife), d. at sea, 15 Dec. 1379, Marshal of England, summ. 1377-9, Lord Arundel; m. 17 Feb. 1358/9, ELEANOR MALTRAVERS (88-8), d. 1405. (CP I, 243; XI, 103).

8. SIR JOHN de ARUNDEL, KNT., of Arundel, b. 30 Nov. 1364, d. 14 Aug. 1390; m. ELIZABETH DESPENSER (14-9). (See Topographer and Genealogist II: 336.) (CP I, 260).

9. MARGARET de ARUNDEL, dau. gen. 7, not of gen. 8, d. 1438; m. lic. 9 Oct. 1394, SIR WILLIAM de ROS, K.G. (1-7) (CP XI, 103).

Line 122

This line not acceptable. See note at Gen. 13. See TAG 52: 216-217 for a royal line for John Davenport.

4. JOAN de VERE (121-4); m. 1283, WILLIAM de WARENNE (151-1).

5. JOHN de WARENNE, 8th and last Earl of Surrey, b. 30 June 1286; died without legitimate issue.

6. SIR EDWARD de WARENNE, KNT., natural son of John de Warenne by Maud of Nerford; living 1347, d. bef. 1368; m. Cicely de Eton, dau. of Sir Nicholas de Eton, Knt., of Poynton and Stockport.

7. SIR JOHN de WARENNE, KNT., b. c. 1343, d. 1387, of Poynton and Stockport; m. 1371, Margaret, d. 6 Apr. 1418, dau. of Sir John de Stafford, Knt., of Wickham.

8. NICHOLAS de WARENNE, b. 1378, d. 1413, of Poynton and Stockport; m. Agnes, liv. 1417, dau. of Sir Richard de Wynnington, Knt., of Wynnington, Cheshire.

9. SIR LAWRENCE de WARENNE, KNT., b. 1394, d. 1444, of Poynton and Stockport; m. Margaret, dau. of Richard Bulkeley and Margery Venables.

10. CICELY de WARENNE; m. c. 4 Jan. 1435, John de Davenport, Esq., bp. Stockport, 3 May 1419, d. Oct. 1478, of Bramhall.

11. MARGARET DAVENPORT, of Bramhall, m. c. 1459/60, her kinsman, NICHOLAS DAVENPORT, ESQ. (130-12).

12. CHRISTOPHER DAVENPORT, of Lowcross in Malpas Parish, founder of the branch of the Davenport family in Coventry; m. Emma, dau. of John Blunt of Stafford.

*   *   *   *   *   *

The parentage of Edward Davenport is not known.

*   *   *   *   *   *

13. EDWARD DAVENPORT, Mayor of Coventry, 1551; m. Margery, dau. of John Harford, alderman of Coventry.

14. HENRY DAVENPORT, Mayor of Coventry, 1613, Alderman for life, 1621, bur. Coventry, Warw., 29 May 1627; m. (1) c. 1585, WINIFRED (122A-15), d. by 1619, dau. of Richard Barnaby.

15. THE REVEREND JOHN DAVENPORT, B.D., bp. Coventry, 9 Apr. 1597, d. Boston, Massachusetts, 15 Mar. 1669/70; Oxford Univ., 1625; a founder of the New Haven Colony in Connecticut, and minister of the First Church there, and later of the First Church in Boston; m. 1619, Elizabeth Wooley.

Line 122A

3. SIR ROBERT de ROS of Helmsley (117-3); m. ISABEL D'AUBIGNY (1-3).

4. MARY de ROS, d. sh. bef. 23 May 1326; m. c. 1271, William de Braose, Lord Braose of Bramber and Gower, of age 15 July 1245, d. sh. bef. 6 Jan. 1290/1, son of John de Braose and Margaret, dau. of Llewellyn ap Iorwerth, Prince of Wales. (CP II, 302; IX, 96 note d; Misc. Gen. et Her. 5 ser. VIII 160).

5. WILLIAM de BRAOSE of Westneston or Wiston, Sussex, d. 1360; m. Eleanor, dau. of Sir Roger de Bavant.

6. SIR PETER de BRAOSE of Westneston or Wiston, Sussex, liv. 1373; m. Joan, dau. of Sir John Weedon, liv. 1378.

7. BEATRIX de BRAOSE, h. of her bro. Sir John de Braose 1426, d. 1440 at advanced age; m. Sir Hugh Shirley of Eatington, Warw., d. 22 July 1403, son of Sir Thomas Shirley and Isabel, a sister (bastard? uterine?) of Ralph, 3rd Lord Basset of Drayton (see CP II, 3-4, and note f). (Gens. 4-7, see Shirley, Stemmata Shirleiana 30; Sussex Arch. Cols. VIII 102-3; Sheppard, op. cit.).

8. SIR RALPH SHIRLEY of Eatington, of age 1392; m. (1) Joan, dau. and h. of Thomas Basset of Frodborough, Notts. and Brailesford, Derby, by Margery, dau. of William Meringe.

9. RALPH SHIRLEY of Eatington, d. 1466; m. (1) Margaret, dau. of John Staunton, (and coh. bro. Thomas) of Staunton Herald.

10. JOHN SHIRLEY of Eatington, d. 1486; m. Eleanor, dau. of Sir Hugh Willoughby of Middleton, Warw. and Margaret de Freville.

11. HUGH SHIRLEY, 4th son, of Stockton, Hereford; m. Anne, dau. and coh. of John Hevyn, Salop., d. 17 Sept. 1510.

12. THOMAS SHIRLEY, d.v.p.; m. Margaret, dau. of John Wroth of Enfield, Middlesex, and Margaret Newdigate.

13. JOYCE SHIRLEY; m. (1) Richard, son of Richard Abington or Habington of Brockhampton, Hereford, and Eleanor Hanley; m. (2) Thomas Blount of Sodington, Worc.

14. MARY ABINGTON or HABINGTON, d. 9 July 1574; m. bef. 1555, Richard Barneby of Acton and The Hull, Worc., son of Thomas, and Joyce, dau. and h. of Walter Acton of Acton, Worc. He bur. Bockleton, Worc. 4 Dec. 1597.

15. WINIFRED BARNABY or BARNEBY, b. by 1569, bur. Coventry, Warw., 12 Apr. 1597; m. c. 1585, as his 1st wife, HENRY DAVENPORT (122-14), draper, alderman, Mayor of Coventry, bur. 29 May 1627. (Stemmata Shirleiana, loc. cit.).

Line 123

Line not sound to Bradbury. See note at Gen. 13.

1. ROBERT de VERE (120-1); m. Isabel de Bolbec.

2. ELEANOR de VERE; m. (2) as his 1st wife, Ralph de Gernon, ae. 30 on 4 Dec. 1258 at father's death, d. 1274, lord of the manors of East Thorpe and Great

Birch, co. Cambridge, son of William. He. m. (2) Hawise Tregoz.

3. WILLIAM GERNON, KNT., of East Thorpe, held the hundred of Lexton, co. Essex, at the time of his death, ae. 24 in 1274, d. 1327, ae. 77. His son was John de Gernon, no. 5.

5. SIR JOHN GERNON, KNT., d. 1333/4, of Lexton Hundred, East Thorpe, and Great Birch; m. (1) Isabella Bygot, d. 1311, ae. 13; m. (2) 1313, Alice, dau. of Sir Roger de Colville of Bytham, co. Lincoln, and his wife Margaret de Braiose, a descendant of Llewellyn ap Iorworth, Prince of Wales, wid. of Guy Gobaud; m. (3) Margaret, dau. of Sir John Wigton.

6. SIR JOHN GERNON, KNT., s. & h. by the 2nd wife, d. 13 Jan. 1383/4; m. 1332, Alice, widow of John Bygot; m. (2) Joan.

7. MARGARET GERNON, ae. 34 at father's death, d. wid. 6 June 1413; m. Sir John de Peyton, Knt., of Peyton Hall, Boxford, co. Essex, son of Sir Robert de Peyton, Knt., a descendant of Reginald de Peyton who held Peyton Hall in Suffolk, in 1135. (See Chester of Chicheley by Waters.)

8. JOHN PEYTON, of Peyton Hall and Wicken, d. 1403/4; m. Joan Sutton, dau. and sole h. of Sir Hamon Sutton, of Wixoe, co. Suffolk. She m. (2) Sir Roger Drury.

9. JOHN PEYTON, ESQ., ae. 12 in 1404, 15 in 1407, d. 6 Oct. 1416, ae. 24 yrs., of East Thorpe; m. Grace, d. 6 May 1439, dau. of John Burgoyne, Esq., of Drayton; she m. (2) Richard Baynard, Esq., of Messing, co. Essex, who d. 1433.

10. THOMAS de PEYTON, b. Dry-Dayton, 14 Feb. 1416/7, d. 30 July 1484, Sheriff of Cambridgeshire and of Huntingdonshire, 1443, 1453; m. (1) Margaret, dau. & h. of Sir John Bernard, Knt.; m. (2) Margaret Francis, dau. of Sir Hugh Fauncis, Knt., of Gifford's Hall, Wickhambrook, co. Suffolk.

11. FRANCIS PEYTON, of Bury St. Edmunds, co. Suffolk, d. 1529, heir to his mother; m. Elizabeth, dau. of Reginald Brooke of Aspall Stoneham.

12. CHRISTOPHER PEYTON, ESQ., of St. Edmunds Bury; m. Joanne Mildmay, sister of Sir Walter Mildmay (1520-1589, founder of Emmanuel College).

13. MARGARET PEYTON; m. Richard Eden, Esq., of Bury St. Edmunds; one of the first publishers of charts of the early voyagers.

      *   *   *   *   *   *

Note: Ann was daughter of Henry Eden, not of Richard Eden. See TAG 52: 176-7, 247; 55: 1-4.

      *   *   *   *   *   *

14. ANN EDEN, bur. at Wicken, 8 Feb. 1611/2, sister of Thomas Eden, LL.D.; m. William Bradbury, Esq., of Wicken Bonhunt, b. 1544, d. Wicken, 30 Nov. 1622, son of Matthew Bradbury and Margaret Rowse.

15. WYMOND BRADBURY, bp. Newport Pond, 16 May 1574, d. 1649/50; m. ELIZABETH WHITGIFT (132-15), b. c. Mar. 1574, d. 26 June 1612, ae. 38 yrs.

16. CAPTAIN THOMAS BRADBURY, gent., 2nd son, bp. Wicken Bonhunt, 28 Feb. 1610/11, d. Salisbury, Massachusetts, 16 Mar. 1695; will made 14 Feb. 1694/5; came to New England, 1634, as agent for SIR FERDINANDO GORGES (See 29-16); m. 1636, Mary Perkins, d. 20 Dec. 1700; their eldest son was Wymond Bradbury. (On Gernon, see Waters, Chester of Chicheley, I pp. 186-203.)

Line 124

1. HUGH de VERE (120-2); m. Hawise de Quincy.

2. ISABEL de VERE; m. Sir John de Courtenay, d. 3 May 1274, of Oakhampton. (CP III, 465).

3. SIR HUGH de COURTENAY, b. 25 Mar. 1248/9 or 1250/1, d. 28 Feb. 1291/2, of Oakhampton; m. Eleanor Despenser, d. 30 Sept. 1328, dau. of Hugh le Despenser and Aline Basset. (CP VI, 124, Moriarty's notes).

4. ELEANOR de COURTENAY; m. Sir Henry de Grey, d. Aylesford, Kent, Sept. 1308, Lord Grey of Codnor, co. Derby, Grey Thurrocks, co. Essex, and Aylesford and Hoo, co. Kent, son of Sir John de Grey and Lucy de Mohun. He m. (2) bef. 6 June 1301, Joan, wid. of Sir Ralf de Cromwell. (CP VI, 123, 124/5).

5. SIR RICHARD de GREY, b. 1281/2, d. sh. bef. 10 Mar. 1334/5; m. Joan Fitz Payn, dau. of Sir Robert Fitz Payn, Lord fitz Payn, and Isabella de Clifford, dau. of Sir John de Clifford of Frampton-on-Severn, Gloucs. (CP, VI, 125/6).

6. JOHN de GREY, KNT., d. Aylesford, 14 Dec. 1392, Lord Grey of Codnor;

m. (1) bef. 4 Sept. 1325, Eleanor; m. (2) bef. 20 Oct. 1330, Alice, dau. of Warin de Lisle and Alice de Tyse. (Generations 6 to 10: Gladys Howard Thompson, The King's Ley, Shrewsbury, England, 1951, chart of the Lee Pedigree; accepted by A. T. Butler, Windsor Herald; Armes, Stratford Hall Lees; CP VI, 125).

7. JANE de GREY, by the 1st wife, of Codnor; m. SIR WILLIAM de HAR-COURT, KNT. (146-6), d. 6 June 1349; m. (2) Sir Ralf de Ferrers. (CP VI, 127).

8. SIR RICHARD de HARCOURT, eldest son, d. 1372; m. Joan, dau. of Sir William Shareshill, Knt., of Shareshill near Wolverhampton, Chief Justice of England.

9. ELIZABETH de HARCOURT; m. Sir Thomas de Astley, Knt., d. 1362, of Astley of Patshull, Shropshire (2nd son of Thomas, Lord Astley, of Astley, and his wife Elizabeth, dau. of GUY de BEAUCHAMP (5-5), and a descendant of Sir Thomas Astley, slain at Evesham, 4 Aug. 1265). (Generations 9 to 17: G.H. Thompson, The King's Ley, Pedigree of Lee; Harl. Soc. Publ., vols. XIII and XIV: Visitations of Essex, I 128; II 542).

10. MARGARET de ASTLEY, d. 1423 (heir to her brother Thomas Astley, of Nordley Regis, Shropshire); m. Roger de Lee (alias Robert de Lee), son of John de Lee of Roden and Stanton; inherited Coton and Nordley Regis, 1376. (The Astley identification is questionable.)

11. JOHN de LEE, b. 1398, resided at Coton, 1405, fl. 1424; m. Jacosa, dau. of Sir John Packington.

12. JOHN LEE, b. c. 1430, of Nordley Regis, Salop, living 1478; m. Elizabeth, dau. of Thomas Corbin, of West Bromwich, co. Stafford.

13. THOMAS LEE, ESQ., of Nordley Regis, d. 16 Mar. 1526 (Inq. p.m., 1526); m. Johanna, dau. of Robert Morton, Esq., of Houghton, Salop, living 1526. (Generations 10 to 13: as above; also Visitation of Shropshire, 1623, p. 18).

14. HUMPHREY LEE, b. 1506, d. 6 Dec. 1588, of Coton Hall, Nordley Regis (Inq. p.m., 12 Mar. 1589), and Le Hay in Alveley Parish, rebuilt Coton Hall, where he resided in 1570; m. Katherine, bur. Alveley, 20 Aug. 1591, dau. of John Blount of Yeo, co. Hereford (son of Sir Humphrey Blount), by Elizabeth, dau. of John Yeo.

15. JOHN LEE, ESQ., of Coton in Nordley Regis in the Parish of Alveley, only son, b. 1530, bur. Chesham, co. Buckingham, 13 June 1605 (will dated 17 May 1605, pr. 14 June 1605); m. (settlement, 24 June 1553), Joyce Romney, only dau. of John Romney, gent., of Lulsley, co. Worcester; she was bur. at Alveley, 4 Dec. 1609; her mother was the dau. of John Berrington of Stock.

16. RICHARD LEE, 6th son, b. Coton, 1563, bp. Alveley, 6 Oct. 1563; mentioned in his father's will, 1605, and in the will of his brother, Gilbert Lee, 1621; m. Alveley, 21 Oct. 1599, Elizabeth Bendy, dau. of John Bendy. (The identification of this generation has been questioned.)

17. COLONEL RICHARD LEE, b. Nordley Regis, c. 1613; of Stratford Langthorne, co. Essex; came to Virginia, 1640; Secretary of State, Virginia, 1649-1652, and of the Council, 1651-1664; will dated, 6 Feb. 1663/4; d. at Dividing Creek in Northampton Co., Va., March 1664; will proved, 10 Jan. 1664/5; m. Jamestown, Virginia, 1641, Anne Constable. (Generations 14 to 17: Va. Mag. of Hist. & Biog., vol. 62, No. 1, pp. 6-14; Hendricks, Lees of Virginia, pp. 24-26; Magazine of the Society of Lees of Virginia, VIII (May 1931), No. 1). (See The Virginia Genealogist, issues 1970 to date, articles on Lee.)

Line 125

3. SIR HUGH de COURTENAY (124-3); m. Eleanor Despenser.

4. SIR HUGH de COURTENAY, d. 23 Dec. 1340, 9th Earl of Devon; m. 1292, Agnes, d. 11 June 1345, dau. of John de St. John by Alice. (CP IV, 323).

5. SIR THOMAS de COURTENAY; m. Muriel, dau. of Sir John de Moels.

6. MURIEL COURTENAY, d. bef. 12 Aug. 1369; m. Sir John de Dinham, Knt., ae. 14+ in 1332, d. 7 Jan. 1382/3, son of Sir John de Dinham and Margaret. (CP IV, 373).

7. SIR JOHN de DINHAM, Lord Dinham, b. 1359/60, d. 25 Dec. 1428; m. (3) aft. 1 Nov. 1402, Philippa, d. 15 May 1465, dau. of Sir John Lovel, Lord Lovel of Titchmarsh, by wife Alianor la Zouche. (CP IV, 374).

8. SIR JOHN DYNHAM, KNT., Lord Dinham, ae. 22+ at father's death, d. 25 Jan. 1457/8; m. bef. 12 July 1434, Joan, d. 1497, dau. of Sir Richard de Arches by wife Lucy. (CP IV, 373-378).

9. JOAN DINHAM, d. aft. 1501; m. bef. 26 Feb. 1486/7, JOHN la ZOUCHE (79-11), q.v.

Line 126

4. SIR HUGH de COURTENAY (125-4); m. Agnes St. John.
5. SIR HUGH de COURTENAY, K.G., b. 12 July 1303, d. 2 May 1377, Earl of Devon; m. 11 Aug. 1325, MARGARET de BOHUN (22-6), d. 1391. (CP IV, 324).
6. SIR PHILIP COURTENAY, d. 29 July 1406, of Powderham, Lord Lieutenant of Ireland, 1383; m. Anne, dau. of Sir Thomas Wake of Blysworth.
7. SIR JOHN COURTENAY; m. Joan Champernoun, dau. of Alexander Champernoun of Beer Ferrers, and Joan, dau. of Martin Ferrers.
8. SIR PHILIP COURTENAY, d. 16 Dec. 1463, of Powderham; m. Elizabeth Hungerford, d. 14 Dec. 1476, dau. of Sir Walter Hungerford, K.G., Lord Treasurer of England.
9. SIR PHILIP COURTENAY, of Molland, Sheriff of Devon, 1471; m. Elizabeth Hingeston.
10. MARGARET COURTENAY; m. Sir John Champernoun, d. 30 Apr. 1503, of Modbury.
11. SIR PHILIP CHAMPERNOUN, d. 2 Aug. 1545, of Modbury; m. KATHERINE CAREW (35-14).

Line 127

5. SIR HUGH de COURTENAY, K.G. (126-5); m. MARGARET de BOHUN (22-6).
6. ELIZABETH de COURTENAY, d. 7 Aug. 1395; m. 1359, Sir Andrew Lutterell, of Chilton, co. Devon.
7. SIR HUGH LUTTERELL, d. 24 Mar. 1428, of Dunster, co. Somerset, Privy Councillor to King Henry V; m. Catherine de Beaumont, d. 28 Aug. 1435, dau. of Sir John de Beaumont, Knt.
8. ELIZABETH LUTTERELL, liv. 1439; m. (2) aft. 1423, John Stratton, Esq., of Lye Hall, Weston, co. Norfolk, liv. 1439.
9. ELIZABETH STRATTON, liv. 1485; m. (1) Sir Thomas Backchurch; m. (2) John Andrews, Esq., of Bayleham, co. Suffolk.
10. ELIZABETH ANDREWS, liv. 1485; m. Sir Thomas Windsor, d. 29 Sept. 1485, of Stanwell, co. Middlesex.
11. SIR ANDREWS WINDSOR, K.B., Lord Windsor, b. 1467, d. 30 Mar. 1543; m. ELIZABETH BLOUNT (88-13). (CP XII (2), 792).

Line 128

10. SIR THOMAS de PEYTON (123-10); m. (2) Margaret (Frauncis) Garneys.
11. ROSE PEYTON, will proved 31 May 1529; m. Robert Freville of Little Shelford, co. Cambridge, d. Apr. 1521, leaving 3 sons and 5 daus. under age.
12. THOMASINE FREVILLE; m. Christopher Burgoyne, of Long Standen, co. Cambridge, son of Thomas Burgoyne and Elizabeth Stafferton.
13. THOMASINE BURGOYNE; m. Robert Shute of Holdrington, Recorder of Cambridge, 1558-1564, M.P., 1571-1572, Baron of the Exchequer and Justice of the Queen's Bench, d. 1590, son of Christopher Shute of Oakington.
14. ANNE SHUTE, liv. 1650; m. John Leete, of Dodington, co. Huntingdon, bp. Oakington, 13 May 1575, d. c. Dec. 1648, but bef. 1654, son of Thomas Leete, of Oakington, and Maria Slade, dau. of Edward Slade of Rushton, co. Northampton.
15. GOVERNOR WILLIAM LEETE, b. Dodington, d. Hartford, Connecticut, 16 Apr. 1683, Governor of Connecticut, 1676-1683; m. Hail Weston, co. Huntingdon, 1 Aug. 1636, Anna Payne, bp. 31 July 1621, d. 1 Sept. 1668, dau. of the Rev. John Payne and Anne Underhill, widow, whom he married, 3 Aug. 1620. (Waters, Chester of Chicheley, 201-203; Harlian Society, 71: 3-4, 25, 96; J. C. Anderson, Family of Leete, London, 1906, pp. 128, 138-139, 141; Edward L. Leete, Family of William Leete, New Haven, Conn., 1884, pp. 9-12; Arthur Adams, Society of Colonial Wars

in the State of Connecticut, 1941, p. 1197; TAG, 31: 144-117).

Line 129

1. WILLIAM D'AUBIGNY, Named in the Magna Charta, 1215, d. nr. Rome, sh.
bef. 30 Mar. 1221, crusader, Earl of Arundel; m. Mabel of Chester, dau. of Hugh, Earl
of Chester. (CP I, 236).
2. CICELY D'AUBIGNY, survived husb.; m. Roger de Mohaut, d. 18 June
1260, 2nd son of Eustace de Arden, Baron of Hawarden, hereditary seneschal of the
co. of Chester. (CP I, 237; IX, 12-13; X, 170).
3. LEUCA de MOHAUT; m. Philip de Orreby, b. c. 1190, d. c. 1230, son of
Sir Philip de Orreby, Knt., Justiciar of Chester, and Emma de Coventre. (CP X,
169-170).
4. AGNES de ORREBY, only dau.; m. Sir Walkelin de Arderne, Knt., d. c.
1265, Justiciar of Chester. (CP X, 170).
5. SIR JOHN de ARDERNE, name of wife unknown. (Generations 5 to 8: G.
Wrottesley, Pedigrees from Plea Rolls, 1905, p. 115).
6. MATILDA de ARDERNE; m. John de Legh of Booths, co. Chester, d.
1323/4, son of John de Legh and Ellen de Corona. (VCH Lanc. IV 211).
7. JOHN de LEGH, of Booths, liv. 1327-1377; m. c. 1337, Elizabeth, only
dau. of Richard de Sandback. (J. P. Earwaker, Sandback, pp. 3-4).
8. MATILDA de LEGH, only dau. and heir; m. Sir Richard Radcliffe of
Ordsall, bailiff of Rochdale, drowned at Rossendale, 19 July 1380, son of Sir John
Radcliffe and Joan de Holand. Sir Richard Radcliffe died possessed of the manors
of Ordsall, Hope, and Shoresworth, part of Flexton, and lands in Salford and Toch-
holes. (VCH Lanc. IV 210-211; Hampson, Book of the Radclyffes, see section and
chart of Radcliffe of Fordenton).
9. SIR JOHN de RADCLIFFE, KNT., of Ordsall, b. Ordsall, 1356, d. 8
Aug. 1422, lord of the manor of Ordsall, 1380-1422; m. 1375, Margaret de Trafford,
d. Aug. 1434, dau. of Sir Henry de Trafford. (VCH Lanc. IV 102, 211, 331; Earwaker, Sandback, pp. 3-4).
10. SIR JOHN de RADCLIFFE, KNT., of Ordsall, b. Ordsall Manor, 1377,
d. Hope Manor, 26 July 1442, lord of the manors of Ordsall and Hope, 1434-1442;
m. c. 13 Mar. 1396, Clemency Standish, dau. of Hugh Standish of Duxbury and Alice
Standish of Standish. (Ibid.).
11. SIR ALEXANDER de RADCLIFFE, KNT., of Ordsall, b. Hope Manor,
1401, d. June 1476, knight of the shire of Lancaster, 1455; held the manors of Hope
and Ordsall, 1442-1476; m. Agnes Harington, d. 1490, dau. of Sir William Harington, K.G. and Margaret Neville, dau. of Sir Robert de Neville of Hornby Castle.
(Hampson, op. cit., pp. 144-146).
12. ISABELLA RADCLIFFE, d. 20 June 1497; m. Sir James Harington, Knt.,
d. 25 June 1479, of Wolfage and Brixworth, son of Sir William Harington and Elizabeth Pilkington.
13. ALICE HARINGTON, b. c. 1480, liv. 1537; m. c. 16 Aug. 1498, RALPH
STANDISH, ESQ. (116-11), of Standish.

Line 130

4. AGNES de ORREBY (129-4); m. Sir Walkelin de Arderne, Knt.
5. SIR PETER de ARDERNE, KNT., of Alford, Alvanley, and Alderley, bore
arms, 1289, d. c. 1292; m. Margery.
6. SIR JOHN de ARDERNE, KNT., of Alford, Alvanley, Alderley, and Elford,
b. 1266, d. 1308; m. bef. 1299, Margery, dau. of Griffin ap Madog, Lord of Brim-
field. (This marriage does not appear in Bartram.)
7. SIR JOHN de ARDERNE, KNT., of Alford and Enford, d. c. 1349; m. (1)
1307/8, Alice, dau. of Hugh de Venables, Baron of Kinderton.
8. PETER de ARDERNE, of Alvanley and Harden, b. 1327, d. bef. 1378/9;
m. Cicely, dau. of Adam de Bredbury, and Cicely his wife.
9. HUGH de ARDERNE, of Harden and Alvanley, d. bef. 1423; m. (2) Cicely,
dau. of Ralph de Hyde.
10. ALICE ARDERNE; m. c. 1414/5, Christopher Davenport, Esq., of Wood-

ford, b. c. 1394, d. c. 1488, son of Nicholas Davenport.

11. JOHN DAVENPORT, of Woodford, d. c. 1480; m. Alice, dau. of Ralph Prestwich.

12. NICHOLAS DAVENPORT, ESQ., of Woodford, succeeded his grandfather, 1488, d. bef. 9 Feb. 1522; m. c. 1459/60, MARGARET DAVENPORT (122-11). (See TAG 52: 216-217 for additional data on Davenport. This line requires further study.)

Line 131

5. SIR PETER de ARDERNE, KNT. (130-5); m. Margery.

6. AGNES ARDERNE; m. Sir Warin Mainwaring, Knt., of Wormingham.

7. MATILDA MAINWARING; m. Sir William Trussell, Knt., Lord of Cubbleston and Wormingham.

8. SIR WARIN TRUSSELL, of Cubbleston; m. Maud, dau. of Sir John de St. Philbert.

9. SIR LAWRENCE TRUSSELL, of Cubbleston; m. Maud, dau. of Thomas Charnells, Lord of Elmesthorpe.

10. SIR WILLIAM TRUSSELL, Lord of Elmesthorpe; m. MARGERY LUDLOW (111-9), q.v.

Line 132

Line requires extra study. See note generation 10, and note at end of line.

1. WILLIAM D'AUBIGNY (129-1); m. Mabel of Chester.

2. MAUD D'AUBIGNY, d. 1238/42; m. bef. 1222, Robert de Tateshal, minor in 1214, d. 16 July 1249, served in Brittany, Scotland, and Wales, 1230, 1244, son of Walter de Tateshal and Iseult, dau. of William Pantulf. (CP I, 237; XII (1), 648-649).

3. ROBERT de TATESHAL, b. 1222, d. 22 July 1273, succeeded to the manor of Buckenham, co. Norfolk, served in Wales, 1260, in Gascony, 1253, captured at the battle of Lewes, 14 May 1264; m. bef. 1249, Nichole, liv. 30 May 1277. (CP I 237; XII (1), 649-650).

4. ROBERT de TATESHAL, Lord Tateshal, b. 5 Dec. 1248, M.P., 1295-1297, d. sh. bef. 8 Sept. 1298; m. perh. bef. 1268, Joan, d. c. 1 Apr. 1310, dau. of Ralph Fitz Randolf of Middleham, co. York, and Anastasia de Percy. (CP XII (1), 650-651; Clay, 159-160).

5. JOAN de TATESHAL; m. Sir Robert de Driby; she received Tateshal for her share of her father's estate. (CP XII (1), 653 note c and d).

6. ALICE de DRIBY; m. Sir William Bernake. (Ibid.).

7. SIR JOHN BERNAKE; m. Joan Marmion. (CP VIII, 516).

8. MAUD BERNAKE, d. 10 Apr. 1419; m. bef. 20 June 1366, SIR RALPH CROMWELL (138-7), Lord Cromwell of Tateshal, co. Lincoln, M.P., 1375-1397, d. 27 Aug. 1398. (CP III, 551-552; V, 519; Clay, 77; Banks I 168-170).

9. MAUD CROMWELL; m. Sir William Fitzwilliam of Sproatsborough, Lord of Emley, d. 8 Apr. 1398. (Ibid.).

10. SIR JOHN FITZWILLIAM, KNT., d. 5 July 1417, Lord of Emley and Sproatsborough; m. Eleanor Greene, dau. of Sir Henry Greene of Drayton. (Ibid.). (Clay, 77-78, says dau. Joan d.y., gives no dau. Jane.)

*   *   *   *   *   *

11. JANE FITZWILLIAM; m. (1) Thomas Bendish, Esq., d. 1477; m. (2) William Bradbury, of Littlebury and Wicken Bonhunt, co. Essex. (NEHGR, 71: 241-242).

*   *   *   *   *   *

No proof that John Barley's wife was Philippa Bradbury (see earlier editions).

12. PHILIPPA BRADBURY, not dau. of No. 11, d. aft. 14 Oct. 1530; m. aft. 7 July 1502, John Josselyn, b. 1460, d. 14 July 1525, of Newell Josselyn in High Roding and Hide Hall in Sawbridgeworth.

*   *   *   *   *   *

13. MARGARET BARLEY, dau. of John Barley, but prob. not by Philippa
Bradbury; m. Edward Bell, Esq., of Writtle, co. Essex.
14. MARGARET BELL; m. William Whitgift of Clavering, gent., d. c. 1615,
brother of John Whitgift, Archbishop of Canterbury.
15. ELIZABETH WHITGIFT, d. 1612; m. (3) WYMOND BRADBURY (123-15),
q.v.

But see TAG 52: 176-177, 247.

Line 133

Line not satisfactory.

12. PHILLIPPA BRADBURY (132-12); m. John Josselyn. (Her parentage not
clear. She was NOT dau. of Jane Fitzwilliam.)
13. SIR THOMAS JOSSELYN, K.B., b. c. 1507, d. 24 Oct. 1562, of Hide Hall,
Sawbridgeworth, and Newell Josselyn; m. 1524, Dorothy Gates, d. 11 Feb. 1582/3,
dau. of Sir Jeffrey Gates.
14. HENRY JOSSELYN, of Willingale-Doe, b. c. 1540, d. bef. 25 Aug. 1587;
m. c. 1562, Anne Torrell, b. c. 12 Dec. 1542, d. 30 May 1589, dau. of Humphrey
Torrell and Alice Leventhorpe.
15. SIR THOMAS JOSSELYN, KNT., of Torrell's Hall, Deputy-Governor of
Maine, 1638; m. (2) c. 1603, Theodora (Cooke) Bere, d. 1635, dau. of Edward Cooke
and Elizabeth Nichols.
16. HENRY JOSSELYN, b. c. 1606, d. Maine, bef. 10 May 1683; Corpus
Christi Coll., Cambridge, 1623; sett. Black Point, Maine, 1634, and at Pemaquid;
Deputy-Governor of Maine, 1645; m. Margaret Cammock, liv. 1680.
16. JOHN JOSSELYN (brother of Henry), b. c. 1608, d.s.p. aft. 1675; traveller,
writer, and naturalist.

But see TAG 52: 176-177, 247.

Line 134

1. WILLIAM D'AUBIGNY (129-1); m. Mabel of Chester.
2. ISABEL D'AUBIGNY, 2nd dau.; m. John Fitz Alan, d. 1240, Lord of Clun
and Oswestry, Salop. (CP I, 237).
3. JOHN FITZ ALAN, d. bef. 10 Nov. 1267; m. Maud le Botiller, d. 27 Nov.
1283, dau. of Theobald le Botiller, Lord Botiller. (CP I, 237, 239-240, 254 chart).
4. JOHN FITZ ALAN, b. 14 Sept. 1246, d. 18 Mar. 1271/2, Earl of Arundel;
m. Isabella, liv. 1300, dau. of Roger de Mortimer of Wigmore and MAUD de BRAI-
OSE (147-3). (CP I, 240).
5. SIR RICHARD FITZ ALAN, KNT., b. 3 Feb. 1266/7, d. 9 Mar. 1301/2,
Earl of Arundel, 1272-1291, M.P.; m. bef. 1285, Alasia di Saluzzo, d. 25 Sept. 1292,
dau. of Thomaso, Marquis of Saluzzo. (CP, loc. cit.; ancestry of both, Sheppard, op. cit.).
6. SIR EDMUND FITZ ALAN, KNT., b. 1 May 1285, beheaded 17 Nov. 1326,
8th Earl of Arundel; m. 1305, ALICE de WARENNE (121-5), d. bef. 23 May 1338.
(CP I, 241-242).
7. SIR RICHARD FITZ ALAN (121-6), d. 24 Jan. 1375/6; m. (1) 9 Feb. 1320/1,
ISABEL DESPENSER (34-6) (CP I, 242); m. (2) 5 Feb. 1344/5, Eleanor, d. 11 Jan.
1372, wid. of John, 2nd Lord Beaumont, dau. of Henry, Earl of Lancaster.
7A. SIR EDMUND FITZ ALAN, KNT., (35-7), 2nd son, by the 1st wife, liv.
1377; m. bef. July 1349, Sibyl, dau. of William de Montagu, d. 30 Jan. 1343/4, Earl
of Salisbury (See 35-7). ALICE (35-8) and PHILIPPA (134-8) are daus. of Sir Edmund Fitz Alan and Sibyl. (CP I, 244 note b, corrected by CP X, 236 note a).
8. PHILIPPA FITZ ALAN; m. Sir Richard Sergeaux, Knt., d. 30 Sept. 1393.
(CP I, 244 note b; Inq.p.m., 1394; Sir John Maclean, ... History of the Deanery of
Trigg Minor, 1876, II 502, 507).
9. PHILIPPA SERGEAUX, b. 1381 (ae. 18 in 1399); m. (1) Sir Robert Pashley,

Knt. (Generations 7 to 15: G.D. Scull, Dorothy Scott of Egerton House, Kent, 1611-
1680, Chart III; Berry, Kent Genealogies, 170, 814, 991; Muskett, Suff. Manorial
Families, II 268).
    10. SIR JOHN PASHLEY; m. Elizabeth Woodville, dau. of Sir Richard Wood-
ville, of the Mote, Maidstone, Constable of the Tower, Sheriff of Kent, 1334, d. 1342.
    11. SIR JOHN PASHLEY; m. Lowys, dau. of Sir Thomas Gower.
    12. ELIZABETH PASHLEY; m. Reginald de Pympe, of Pympe's Court, Nettle-
stead, co. Kent, son of Sir William de Pympe and Elizabeth, dau. of Sir Richard
Whetehill. (Hasted, Kent, II 286, III 292; see Davis, Ancestry of Mary Isaac, p.
273, regarding this marriage, and all statements and dates in this line.)
    13. ANNE (or AMY) PYMPE; m. 1528, Sir John Scott, of Scott's Hall, Knt.,
High Sheriff of Kent, 1528 (Generations 13 to 16, Visitations of Kent, 1530/31, p. 17;
Visit. of Kent, 1574, p. 30; Visitations of Kent, 1619, p. 128; generations 15 to 17,
ibid., p. 168).
    14. SIR REGINALD SCOTT, of Scott's Hall, will dated 4 Sept. 1554, pr. 13
Feb. 1554/5, Sheriff of Kent; m. (2) Mary, dau. of Sir Bryan Tuke, Knt., of Layer
Marney, co. Essex, Secretary to Cardinal Wolsey. (Visitations of Kent, 1663-1668,
p. 145; Visitations of Essex, 1612, I 137, III 612).
    15. MARY SCOTT; m. Richard Argall, Esq., d. 1588, of East Sutton, co.
Kent, son of Thomas Argall, Esq., of London, and Margaret, dau. of John Talla-
karne of Cornwall. (Ibid., I 137; Hasted, Kent, II 418).
    16. ELIZABETH ARGALL, d. 9 Aug. 1638; m. Sir Edward Filmer, Knt.,
d. 1629, of East Sutton, co. Kent, son of Robert Filmer (b. 1525, d. 1585, ae. 60).
(Robert Clutterbuck, History of Hertfordshire, I 172 for Filmer chart).
    17. KATHERINE FILMER; m. aft. 1619, Robert Barham, Jr., b. 1598/9.
(Ibid., 172; Berry, Kent Genealogies, 404; Va. Mag. of Hist. & Biog., 34: 340;
48: 276-280).
    18. CAPTAIN CHARLES BARHAM, b. in England, 1626, d. Surry Co., Va.,
1683, sett. in Virginia as early as 1654, gent., High Sheriff of Surry Co., Va.,
1673, Justice, 1678-1683; m. bef. 2 Feb. 1666, Elizabeth Ridley, dau. of Peter
Ridley of Isle of Wight Co., Va. (Ibid.; James Renat Scott, Scotts of Scott's Hall,
pp. 170-171 (this book should be used with great care). James W.G. MacClamroch,
Esq., of Greensboro, N.C., has done much research on this line).

    16. SIR SAMUEL ARGALL (brother of Elizabeth (No. 16) above), Governor of
Virginia, May 1617-1619, was b. at Bristol, c. 1572, d. 1626; came to Va. as a
trader, 1609. (Waters, Gleanings, etc., II 919-920, gives the will of Sir Samuel
Argall; Visitations of Essex, 1612, I 137).

Line 135

    5. SIR RICHARD FITZ ALAN (134-5); m. Alasia di Saluzzo.
    6. MARGARET FITZ ALAN; m. William Botiller of Wem and Oversley, Lord
Botiller, b. 8 Sept. 1296, d. Dec. 1361, son of William le Botiller. (CP II, 232).
    7. WILLIAM le BOTILLER, Lord Botiller of Wem and Oversley, b. bef.
1331, d. 14 Aug. 1369, M.P., 1368-1369; m. bef. July 1343, Elizabeth. (CP II, 232).
    8. ELIZABETH le BOTILLER, Lady Botiller, ae. 24 at father's death, d.
June 1411; m. (1) betw. 1369 and 1379, SIR ROBERT de FERRERS (102-7).

Line 136

    1. WILLIAM D'AUBIGNY (129-1); m. Mabel of Chester.
    2. NICHOLE D'AUBIGNY, d. bef. 1254; m. as his 1st wife, Roger de Somery,
d. on or bef. 26 Aug. 1273, of Chipping Camden, co. Gloucester, and Sedgley, co.
Stafford, 1247, built Dudley Castle, 1262, son of John de Somery and Hawise de Pay-
nell. (Note: Hawise was the sister, not the dau. of Gervase Paynell.) (CP XII (2),
112).
    3. MARGARET de SOMERY, d. aft. 18 June 1293; m. (1) Ralph Basset, Lord
Basset of Drayton, co. Stafford, slain at Evesham, 4 Aug. 1265, M.P., 1264, son of
Ralph Basset of Drayton; m. (2) bef. 26 Jan. 1270/1, Ralph de Cromwell, d. c. 18
Sept. 1289. (CP III, 551; XII (1), 110-111; II, 1-2).

4. RALPH BASSET, d. 31 Dec. 1299, 1st Lord Basset of Drayton, M.P.,
1295-1299; m. Hawise. (CP II, 2). (This corrects earlier editions.)

5. MARGARET BASSET, d. bef. 17 Mar. 1336/7; m. bef. 1298, Edmund
Stafford, b. 17 July 1273, d. bef. 12 Aug. 1308, Baron Stafford, M.P., 1298-1307,
son of Nicholas de Stafford. (CP XII (1), 173; II, 3-6, note f p. 3).

6. SIR RALPH STAFFORD, K.G., b. 1299, d. 31 Aug. 1372, K.G., 23 Apr.
1349, M.P., 1337-1349, Earl of Stafford; m. (1) Katharine; m. (2) 1335, MARGARET
de AUDLEY (28-6). (CP XII (1), 174-175).

7. SIR HUGH STAFFORD, K.G., son by 2nd wife, b. c. 1342, d. 1386, 2nd
Earl of Stafford; m. PHILIPPA de BEAUCHAMP (5-7), d. 1369.

8. MARGARET STAFFORD, d. 9 June 1396; m. as his 1st wife, SIR RALPH
NEVILLE, K.G. (45-7), 1st Earl of Westmoreland (See 8-9). (Clay, 146).

9. SIR RALPH NEVILLE, 2nd son; m. MARY de FERRERS (102-9).

Line 137

2. NICHOLE D'AUBIGNY (136-2); m. Roger de Somery, d. 1272.

3. JOAN de SOMERY, d. 1282; m. John Lestrange IV, fl. 1255-1265, d. on
or bef. 26 Feb. 1275/6, Lord Strange, Salop. (CP XII (1), 350-351; Le Strange
Records, 154-183).

4. JOHN LESTRANGE V, b. c. 1253, d. c. 8 Aug. 1309, M.P., 1299-1307/8,
of Ness, Kinton, and Midale, Salop, 1st Lord Strange of Knockyn; m. (1) Alienore
de Someri; m. (2) Maud, perh. a de Deyville. (CP XII (1), 352-353; Misc. Gen. et
Her., 5th Series, IX 254-8 says she was dau. of Sir John de Wauton of Wauton Deyville. See also Pedigree and Progress (Wagner) ped. 57; Le Strange Records, 184-
253).

5. ELIZABETH LESTRANGE, b. 1298, liv. 1304/20; m. 1304, Gruffydd of
Rhuddallt, b. 1298, of Glyndfrdwy in Powys Fadog, Wales. (Eyton, Antiquities of
Shropshire, X 262-263; Le Strange Records, 323; Bartram peds Bl. ap. C. 5).

6. GRUFFYDD FYCHAN ab Gruffydd of Rhuddallt, of Glyndyfrdwy; m. Elen
ferch Thomas ab Llywelyn (sister of Margaret, ancestress of the Tudor Kings of
England). (Bartram peds Bl. ap. C. 5).

7. LOWRY ferch Gruffydd Fychan (sister of Owain ab Gruffydd Fychan, i.e.,
Owen Glendower, the Welsh Patriot); m. ROBERT PULESTON, b. c. 1358 (ae. 28
in 1386), liv. 1399, of Emral, co. Flint, Wales. (Do not confuse this Lowri with
Lowri of Yale ancestry, TAG 32: 71-73.) (Tudor 14).

8. ANGHARAD PULESTON ferch Robert Puleston; m. Edward (Trevor) ab
Dafydd, d. 1448, of Bryncinallt (Brynkynalt). (Tudor 14).

9. ROSE ferch Edward (Trevor); m. Otewell Worsley, Lieutenant of the
Castle of Calais. (Tudor 14).

10. MARGARET WORSLEY, d. 1505; m. Adrian Whetehill (or Wheathill), d.
1503, Comptroller of Calais. (See also p. 335, note in Davis, Mary Isaac.)

11. SIR RICHARD WHETEHILL, d. 1536/7, of Calais; m. Elizabeth Muston,
d. 1542/3. (See line 134). (Davis, op. cit.).

12. MARGERY WHETEHILL; m. EDWARD ISAACKE, ESQ. (149-13), d. 1572/3
(will dated 29 Apr. 1572), of Well Court, co. Kent. (Davis, op. cit.).

13. MARY ISAACKE, will dated 18 Feb. 1612; m. c. 1568, Thomas Appleton,
Esq., d. London, 1603 (will made 1 Mar. 1602/3, pr. 16 May 1603), of Waldingfield
Parva, co. Suffolk. (Davis, op. cit.).

14. SAMUEL APPLETON, gent., bp. Little Waldingfield, co. Suffolk, 13
Aug. 1586, d. Rowley, Massachusetts, June 1670, of Ipswich, Mass., 1635, and
Rowley; m. (1) 1616, Judith Everard, d. c. 1628/33. Their children were: CAPTAIN
JOHN APPLETON, of Ipswich; MAJOR SAMUEL APPLETON, of Ipswich; SARAH
APPLETON, m. the Rev. Samuel Phillips of Rowley; JUDITH APLETON, m. Sam-
uel Rogers of Ipswich; and MARTHA APPLETON, m. Richard Jacob of Ipswich.
(Davis, Ancestry of Mary Isaac, p. 41; John Farmer, A Genealogical Register of
the First Settlers of New-England, ..., Lancaster, Mass., 1829, pp. 18-19. Gener-
ations 5 to 14: Bannerman, Visitations of Surrey, 1530, 1572 and 1623 (Harl. Soc.
Publ., vol. 43), p. 21; Bannerman, Visitations of Kent, 1574, 1592 (Harl. Soc. Publ.
vol. 75), Part II, pp. 74 f.; Bridgeman, History of the Princes of South Wales,
Chart IV, p. 249; Bryan Cooke, The Seize Quartiers of the Family of Bryan Cooke;
Lewys Dwnn, Visitations of Wales (ed. of Myrick, 1846), II 151, 310, 317; Visitation
of Shropshire (Harl. Soc. Publ.), II 465; J.E. Lloyd, Owen Glendower, p. 24;

J.Y.W. Lloyd, History of Powys Fadog, I 198, II 119, III 196-197, IV 84-85, V 129-130; Hovenden, Visitation of Kent, 1619-1621 (Harl. Soc. Publ., vol. 42), pp. 153-154; Berry, County Genealogies of Kent, pp. 166-167; Metcalfe, Visitations of Hertfordshire, 1572, 1634 (Harl. Soc. Publ., vol. 22), p. 166; Joseph James Muskett, Suffolk Manorial Families, 1900, I 329-334, cf. 329, Chart of the Appletons of Waldingfield; Genealogist, N.S., IV 5 ff; Walter Goodwin Davis, Ancestry of Phoebe Tilton, pp. 51-57, 61-77, and Ancestry of Mary Isaac; Peter C. Bartram, Welsh Genealogies, 300 to 1400 (U. of Wales Press, 1974). Professor Charles J. Jacobs supplied this line.

Line 137A

3. JOAN de SOMERY (137-3); m. John le Strange IV.

4. HAWISE le STRANGE; m. Sir Robert de Felton of Litcham, Norfolk, cr. Lord Felton, 1312, slain at Bannockburn, 24 June 1314. (CP V, 289-290).

5. SIR JOHN de FELTON of Litcham, Lord Felton, knighted 13 Nov. 1310, Admiral of England, 1325, d. bef. 1346; m. Sibyl. (CP V, 290-291).

6. SIR THOMAS de FELTON, K.G., of Litcham, 2nd son, Inq.p.m. 25 May 1381; m. Joan. (CP V, 292. note e).

7. ELEANOR de FELTON; m. (1) SIR ROBERT de UFFORD, Lord Clavering (49A-7); m. (2) in or bef. Feb. 1394/5, as his 1st wife, Sir Thomas Hoo of Luton-Hoo, Beds., fought at Agincourt. (CP V, 294; VI, 561).

8. SIR THOMAS HOO, K.G., d.s.p.m. 13 Feb. 1454/5, cr. Lord Hoo of Hoo, Beds., 1448; m. (1) Elizabeth, dau. of Nicholas Wychingham of Wychingham, Norfolk. (CP VI, 561-564).

9. ANNE HOO, ae. 30+ in 1454/5; m. Sir Geoffrey Boleyn, Lord Mayor of London, 1457, d. 1463. (CP VI, 565; X, 137, note b; XII (2), 739; DNB II: 783).

10. SIR WILLIAM BOLEYN, K.B., of Blicking, Norfolk; m. MARGARET BUTLER (17-11), dau. of SIR THOMAS BUTLER (17-10), 7th Earl of Ormond, by his 1st wife, ANNE (17B-20), dau. of Sir Richard Hankeford. (CP X, 137, note b; XII (2), 739; DNB II: 783).

Line 138

3. MARGERY de SOMERY (136-3); m. (3) bef. 26 Jan. 1270/1, Ralph de Cromwell.

4. RALPH de CROMWELL, d. sh. bef. 2 Mar. 1298/9.

5. RALPH de CROMWELL, ae. 7 in 1298/9; m. Joan de la Mare, d. 9 Aug. 1348.

6. RALPH de CROMWELL, of Cromwell and West Hallam, d. bef. 28 Oct. 1364; m. 1351, Amice, dau. of Roger de Bellers.

7. RALPH de CROMWELL, Lord Cromwell of Tattershall, co. Lincoln, M.P., 1375-1397, d. 27 Aug. 1398; m. bef. 20 June 1366, MAUD BERNAKE (132-8), d. 10 Apr. 1419. (Generations 3 to 7: CP III, 551-552; V 519).

Line 139

1. ALAN of GALLOWAY, Named in the Magna Charta, 1215, Constable of Scotland, 1215-1234, Lord of Galloway, d. 1234; m. (1) N.N., dau. or sis. of Roger de Lacy, of Pontefract, Constable of Chester (Tr. Dumfrieshire and Galloway Natural History Society 49: 49-55); m. (2) 1209, Margaret de Huntingdon, dau. of David of Huntingdon (son of Henry of Huntingdon and grandson of David I "The Saint," King of Scots) and Maud of Chester. (SP IV, 138-143).

2. HELEN of GALLOWAY (by the first wife), d. aft. 21 Nov. 1245; m. ROGER de QUINCY (74-2, 88-2). (CP XII (2), 751).

Line 140

1. ALAN of GALLOWAY (139-1); m. (2) 1209, Margaret de Huntingdon.
2. DEVORGILLA of GALLOWAY, d. 28 Jan. 1289/90; m. 1233, John de
Balliol, d. 1269, of Barnard Castle; founders of Balliol College.
3. CECILY de BALIOL, d. bef. 1273; m. SIR JOHN de BURGH (55-3), q.v.

Line 141

2. DEVORGILLA of GALLOWAY (140-2); m. 1233, John de Baliol.
3. ALIANORA de BALIOL; m. 1279/83, Sir John Comyn, Black Comyn, d.
c. 1303, Lord of Badenoch.
4. JOHN COMYN, Red Comyn, d. 1306, Lord of Badenoch; m. JOAN de
VALENCE (148-4).
5. ELIZABETH COMYN, b. 1299; m. 1325, Sir Richard Talbot, b. c. 1302,
d. 23 Oct. 1356, Lord Talbot.
6. GILBERT TALBOT, b. c. 1332, d. 24 Apr. 1387, 3rd Lord Talbot, M.P.,
1362; m. (1) bef. 8 Sept. 1352, PETRONELLA BUTLER (26-7). (CP XII (1), 614).
7. SIR RICHARD TALBOT, Lord Talbot, b. c. 1361, d. 7 or 8 Sept. 1396; m.
bef. 23 Aug. 1383, ANKARET le STRANGE (34-8). (CP XII (1), 345, 614).
8. SIR JOHN TALBOT, K.G., b. c. 1384, slain at Castillon, 17 July 1453,
Earl of Shrewsbury; m. (1) 1406/7, Maud de Neville, Lady Furnivall, b. c. 1392,
d. c. 1423, dau. of Thomas Nevill, Lord Furnivall, by his wife Joan Furnivall,
Lady Furnivall.
9. SIR JOHN TALBOT, K.G., b. c. 1413, slain at Battle of Northampton,
10 July 1460, Earl of Shrewsbury; m. bef. 1444/5, ELIZABETH BUTLER (24-10).
(CP XI, 704).

Line 142

1. WILLIAM LONGESPEE, Earl of Salisbury, Named in the Magna Charta,
1215, b. c. 1170-76, d. Salisbury Castle, 7 Mar. 1225/6, natural son of King HENRY II
(161-11); m. 1198, Ela, Countess of Salisbury, b. Amesbury, Wiltshire, c. 1190, d.
1261, dau. of William fitz Patrick, Earl of Salisbury. The mother of William Longespee is unknown. See The Genealogists' Magazine, vol. 14, pp. 361-368.
2. IDA de LONGESPEE; m. (1) WALTER FITZ ROBERT (50-2), q.v.

Line 143

1. WILLIAM LONGESPEE (142-1); m. Ela of Salisbury.
2. SIR WILLIAM LONGESPEE, slain in battle with the Saracens at Mansura
on the Nile, 7 Feb. 1249/50; m. Idoine, d. betw. 1 Jan. 1250/1 and 21 Sept. 1252, dau.
of Richard de Camville and Eustacia, dau. of Gilbert Basset. (CP XI, 382).
3. ELA LONGESPEE, app. d. sh. bef. 22 Nov. 1299; m. 1244, James de
Audley, b. c. 1220, d. c. 11 June 1276, of Heleigh, co. Stafford, Lord Marcher,
Sheriff, 1261-1262, 1270-1271, Justiciar of England. (CP I, 337).
4. NICHOLAS AUDLEY, b. bef. 1258, d. 28 Aug. 1299; m. Catherine Giffard,
b. 1272, liv. 1322, dau. of John Giffard, 1st Lord Giffard of Brimsfield, and Maud,
dau. of Walter de Clifford. (CP I, 338).
5. NICHOLAS AUDLEY, of Heleigh, b. 11 Nov. 1289, d. in 1316, sh. bef. 9
Dec., 1st Lord Audley, M.P., 1312-1316; m. 1312, Joan de Martin, d. betw. Feb.
1319/20 & 1 Aug. 1322, only child of William, Lord Martin. (CP I, 339).
6. SIR JAMES AUDLEY, K.G., b. Knesale, co. Nottingham, 8 Jan. 1312/3,
d. 1 Apr. 1386; m. (1) bef. 13 June 1330, JOAN MORTIMER (12-7), d. 1337/51. (CP
I, 339).

Line 144

1. WILLIAM LONGESPEE (142-1); m. Ela of Salisbury.
2. STEPHEN LONGESPEE, d. 1260, of Sutton, co. Northampton; m. Emmeline de Riddlesford, d. 1276, widow of Hugh de Lacy.
3. ELA LONGESPEE, d. bef. 19 July 1267; m. SIR ROGER la ZOUCHE (90-4).
3. EMMELINE LONGESPEE (sister of Ela above), b. 1252, d. 1291; m. 1276, Maurice Fitz Maurice, d. 1286, Lord of Offaly in Ireland, Justiciar, son of Maurice Fitz Gerald and Eve de Bermingham. (Orpen, Ireland Under the Normans, IV 128-129).
4. JULIANE FITZ MAURICE; m. THOMAS de CLARE (33-4). (Orpen, loc. cit.).
5. MAUD de CLARE, d. betw. 4 Mar. 1326/7 & 24 May 1327; m. (l) 13 Nov. 1295, ROBERT de CLIFFORD, Lord Clifford (8-6). (CP III, 290).
6. ROBERT de CLIFFORD, Lord Clifford, b. 5 Nov. 1305, d. 20 May 1344; m. June 1328, ISABEL BERKELEY (82-6).

Line 145

1. SIR WILLIAM MARSHAL, Named in the Magna Charta, 1215, 3rd Earl of Pembroke, b. prob. 1146, d. 14 May 1219, bur. in the Temple Church, London; Marshal of England, Protector of the Realm, Regent of the Kingdom, 1216-1219, a man of superior ability and exemplary character, son of John Marshal; m. Aug. 1189, Isabel de Clare, d. 1220, dau. of Richard de Clare, "Strongbow," Earl of Pembroke, and Eva, dau. of Dermot MacMurrough, King of Leinster in Ireland. (CP X, 358).
2. ISABEL MARSHAL, d. Berkhampstead, 17 Jan. 1239/40; m. (l) 9 Oct. 1217, SIR GILBERT de CLARE (28-2), Magna Charta Surety, 1215. (CP V, 694).

Line 146

1. SIR WILLIAM MARSHAL (145-1); m. 1189, Isabel de Clare.
2. EVA MARSHAL, d. bef. 1246; m. William de Braiose, d. 2 May 1230, 6th Baron de Braiose, Lord of Abergavenny, 1228-1230. (CP I, 22).
3. EVE de BRAIOSE (or Briouze), d. bef. 28 July 1255; m. aft. 25 July 1238, William de Cantelou, d. 25 Sept. 1254, Lord Abergavenny, of Calne, Wiltshire, and Ashton Cantelou, co. Warwick. (CP I, 22-23).
4. MILICENT de CANTELOU (or Cauntelou), d. sh. bef. 7 Jan. 1298/9; m. (2) EUDO la ZOUCHE (74-4). (CP I, 28-41; XII (2), 937; TAG 49: 1-11).
5. ELLEN la ZOUCHE; m. SIR JOHN de HARCOURT, KNT. (7-6).
6. SIR WILLIAM de HARCOURT, KNT., of Stanton-Harcourt, d. 6 June 1349; m. JANE de GREY (124-7).
7. SIR THOMAS de HARCOURT, KNT., of Stanton-Harcourt, co. Oxford, Market Bosworth, co. Leicester, and Ellenhall, co. Stafford, d. c. 12 Apr. 1417, M.P., for Oxfordshire, 1376; m. c. 1374, MAUD de GREY (50-6).

Line 147

2. EVA MARSHAL (146-2); m. William de Braiose.
3. MAUD de BRAIOSE, d. sh. bef. 23 Mar. 1300/1; m. 1247, Roger de Mortimer, d. sh. bef. 30 Oct. 1282. (CP IX, 276).
4. SIR EDMUND MORTIMER, b. 1261, d. 17 July 1304, 7th Lord Mortimer of Wigmore; m. c. 1285, Margaret de Fienes, d. 7 Feb. 1333/4, dau. of William II de Fienes and Blanche de Brienne. (CP IX, 281).
5. SIR ROGER de MORTIMER, b. 25 Apr. or 3 May 1287, d. 29 Nov. 1330, Earl of March; m. bef. 6 Oct. 1306, JOAN de GENEVILLE (12-6). (CP VIII, 433).
6. KATHERINE de MORTIMER, d. betw. 4 Aug. & 6 Sept. 1369; m. THOMAS de BEAUCHAMP, K.G. (5-6), d. 1369, Earl of Warwick. (CP XII (2), 372).
7. THOMAS de BEAUCHAMP, K.G., Earl of Warwick, b. bef. 16 Mar. 1338/9, d. 8 Apr. 1401; m. bef. Apr. 1381, Margaret de Ferrers, d. 22 Jan. 1406/7, dau. of

WILLIAM de FERRERS (100-7), by Margaret de Ufford. (CP XII (2), 375).
    8. RICHARD de BEAUCHAMP, K.G., Earl of Warwick, b. 25 or 28 Jan.
1381/2, d. 30 Apr. 1439 at Rouen; m. (l) ELIZABETH de BERKELEY (80-9), Lady
Berkeley, Lisle and Teyes. (CP VIII, 54; XII (2), 378).

Line 148

    1. SIR WILLIAM MARSHAL (145-1); m. Isabel de Clare. (CP IV, 196-199).
    2. JOAN MARSHAL, d. bef. Nov. 1234; m. aft. 14 May 1219, as his lst wife,
Warin de Munchensi, Lord of Swanscomb. (CP IX, 421).
    3. JOAN de MUNCHENSI, d. bef. 30 Sept. 1307; m. 13 Aug. 1247, Sir William
de Valence, b. aft. 1225, d. bef. 18 May 1296, Lord of Valence, crusader, 1250,
son of Hugh X de Lusignan and Isabella d'Angouleme, widow of King JOHN (161-12),
of England. (CP X, 377).
    4. JOAN de VALENCE; m. JOHN COMYN (141-4), Lord of Badenoch.

    2. MAUD MARSHAL (sister of Joan above), d. betw. 1 & 7 Apr. 1248; m. (l)
1207, HUGH BIGOD (3-2), Magna Charta Surety, 1215, Earl of Norfolk; m. (2) bef.
13 Oct. 1225, WILLIAM de WARENNE (151-1), Named in the Magna Charta, 1215.
(CP IX, 589; XII (l), 500).

Line 149

    1. SIR WILLIAM MARSHAL (145-1); m. Isabel de Clare. (CP IV, 196-199).
    2. SIBYL MARSHAL (one of five daughters), childless wid. of Sir Gilbert Bas-
set; m. as his lst wife, bef. 14 May 1219, William de Ferrers, 5th Earl of Derby, d.
24 or 28 Mar. 1254, Sheriff of Lancashire and Keeper of the Honour of Lancaster,
1223-1228. (CP IV, 199).
    3. MAUD de FERRERS (one of seven daughters), d. 12 Mar. 1298/9; m. (l)
Simon de Kyme, d.s.p. 30 July 1248; m. (2) William Fort de Vivonne (or Vivonia) in
Poitou, of Chewton, d. 22 May 1259, son of Hugh de Vivonia and MABEL MALET
(59-2, q.v. (Gens. 1 to 3: CP IV, 194-199; II, 48; Turton, charts 119 and 134).
    4. CICELY de VIVONIA (one of four daughters), b. 1257, d. 10 Jan. 1320;
m. John de Beauchamp of Hatch, co. Somerset, b. c. 1248, d. Hatch, 24 Oct. 1283.
(CP II, 48, 49; IV, 199; Somerset Arch. & Natural History Soc., Proceedings,
XXXVI 34-38).
    5. JOHN de BEAUCHAMP, KNT., Lord Beauchamp, of Hatch, M.P., 1299-
1336, Governor of Bridgewater Castle, 1325, b. 27 July 1274, d. aft. 1 Jan. 1336/7;
m. c. 1301, Joan Chenduit, d. 9 Feb. 1327. (CP II, 48-49; IV, 199; Somerset Arch.
& Natural History Soc., Proceedings, XXXVI 36-40).
    6. WILLIAM BEAUCHAMP, b. c. 1302, of Wellington, co. Somerset, d.v.p.
(Somerset, XXXVI 40; Turton, chart 162; ment. in footnote CP II, 49).

  *   *   *   *   *   *
The editor would like a better referance than Turton for the existance of the dau.
Mary, not in Somerset, loc. cit.

  *   *   *   *   *   *

    7. MARY BEAUCHAMP; m. John Bodulgate, of Grafton. (Ibid., charts 3 and
162).
    8. ELIZABETH BODULGATE; m. Sir Richard Wydeville (or Woodville), d.
1441. (Turton, chart 3; John Batten, "The Barony of Beauchamp of Somerset," in
Somersetshire Archaeological and Natural History Society, vol. 34 (1890), pp. 20-59;
Excerpta Historica, p. 249; CP XI, 17).
    9. JOAN WYDEVILLE; m. William Haute (Haut, Hawte), of Bishopsbourne,
co. Kent. (James Gardiner, The Paston Letters, Introduction, p. ccc, footnote,
calls her Joan, not Matilda.)

  *   *   *   *   *   *
William Haute was m. two times: (l) Margaret (Berwick) Butler; (2) Joan Wydeville.
Uncertain which wife was mother of No. 10. (See Davis, Mary Isaac, pp. 152, 156-8.)

    *   *   *   *   *   *

10. WILLIAM HAUTE, of Bishopsbourne, co. Kent, liv. 1473; m. Joan, dau. of Henry Horne.

11. SIR THOMAS HAUTE, K.B., knighted, 1501; m. Isabel, dau. of Sir Thomas Frowick.

12. MARGERY HAUTE; m. William Isaacke.

13. EDWARD ISAACKE, ESQ., d. 1572/3, of Well Court, co. Kent; m. MARGERY WHETEHILL (137-12), q.v. (Generations 8 to 13: DNB 42: 414; Baker, Northamptonshire, II 166; Hasted, Hist. of Kent, IV 17; Hovenden, Visitation of Kent, 1619-1621 (Harl. Soc. Publ., vol. 42) pp. 212-214; see Walter Goodwin Davis, Ancestry of Mary Isaac, 1955, carries the line back to Richard Wydeville but does not name his wife or give her ancestry.)

Line 149A

2. SIBYL MARSHAL (149-2); m. William de Ferrers, Earl of Derby. (CP IV, 199).

3. ISABEL de FERRERS, d. by 26 Nov. 1260; m. as his 2nd wife, Sir Reynold de Mohun of Dunster, Somerset, a minor 1228, d. 20 Jan. 1257/8, Justice of Common Pleas, Chief Justice. (CP IX, 19-21).

4. ISABEL de MOHUN; m. Sir Edward Deincourt, 1st Lord Deincourt, d. 6 Jan. 1326/7; son of Sir John Deincourt by Agnes Neville, widow and 2nd wife of Richard de Percy who d. bef. 18 Aug. 1244; Agnes, who d. bef. 20 July 1293, was the dau. of Sir Geoffrey de Neville of Raby, co. Durham. (CP IV, 118-20; IX, 494-5).

5. JOHN DEINCOURT, d.v.p.; m. unidentified wife. (CP IV, 120).

6. SIR WILLIAM DEINCOURT, 2nd Lord Deincourt, ae. 26+ in 1326/7, d. 2 June 1364; m. bef. 26 Mar. 1326, MILICENT la ZOUCHÉ (74-6), d. 22 June 1379, dau. of SIR WILLIAM la ZOUCHE, 1st Lord Zouche (74-5) of Harryngworth, by Maud Lovel, dau. of John Lovel, 1st Lord Lovel of Titchmarsh by his 1st wife, Isabel de Bois. (CP IV, 120-22; XII (2), 97, 938-40).

7. MARGARET DEINCOURT (74-8), d. 2 Apr. 1380; m. by Trinity, 13 Apr. 1372, Sir Robert de Tibetot, 3rd Lord Tibetot (2-7), b. 1341, d. 13 Apr. 1372. (CP XII (2), 97).

8. MARGARET de TIBETOT, ae. 6+ in 1372, d. betw. 13 Apr. & 14 May 1431; m. (1) bef. 23 Apr. 1385, Sir Roger le Scrope, 2nd Lord Scrope, b. bef. 1373, knighted bef. 23 Nov. 1385, d. 3 Dec. 1403. (CP XI, 541 2; XII (2), 97 note i).

9. SIR RICHARD le SCROPE, 3rd Lord Scrope, b. 31 May 1394, present at Agincourt, 25 Oct. 1415, d. 29 Aug. 1420; m. bef. 31 Dec. 1413, MARGARET NEVILLE (46-8), dau. of RALPH NEVILLE (45-7), 1st Earl of Westmoreland by his 1st wife, MARGARET STAFFORD (136-8); d. 3 Edw. IV. (CP XI, 542-3).

Line 149B

2. SIBYL MARSHAL (149-2); m. William de Ferrers, 5th Earl of Derby.

3. SIBYL de FERRERS, seen 5 Oct. 1273, 4th dau.; m. bef. 21 Sept. 1247, as his 1st wife, Sir Francis de Bohun of Midhurst, Sussex, d. 14 Sept. 1273, son of Savary de Bohun of Midhurst by Cicely, dau. of Geoffrey Fitz Piers, Earl of Essex. (CP II, 199; IV, 199; V, 122-4; The Genealogist (New Series), XXVIII: 1-2, XXIX: 64).

4. SIR JOHN de BOHUN of Midhurst, Sussex, and Ballymadden, Kildare, ae. 26 on 14 Sept. 1273, d. 28 Sept. 1284, summoned to attend Edward I at Shrewsbury, 28 June 1283; m. c. 1274, Joan, b. Dec. 1256, d. sh. bef. 23 Mar. 1327/8, only dau. and heir of Bartholomew de la Chapelle of Waltham, co. Lincoln, d. bef. 17 July 1258, Serjeant of the King's Chapel. (CP II, 199-200, 303-4; The Genealogist (N.S.), XXVIII: 2-4).

5. JAMES de BOHUN, 2nd son, of Ballymadden, Kildare, b. Ford, 3 Feb. 1280/1, d. sh. bef. 30 May 1306; had seizin of the manor Midhurst, Sussex, on the death s.p. of his brother, John de Bohun; m. as her 1st husb. Joan, d. betw. 8 Dec. 1321 & 23 June 1324, dau. and coheir of Sir William de Braiose of Bamber and Gower, d. 1326, 2nd Lord Braiose, a descendant of Llewelyn ap Iorwerth, Prince of North Wales, presumably by his wife Joan, illeg. dau. of King John. (CP II, 200, 302-4; The Genealogist (N.S.), XXVIII: 5-6; I.J. Saunders, English Baronies (Oxford, 1960),

104

p. 108).

6. SIR JOHN de BOHUN of Midhurst, b. Todham, 14 Nov. 1301, d. 5 Dec. 1367, accompanied Edward III to Ireland, 1331, and to France, 1346, cr. by writ, 10 Oct. 1359, Lord Bohun; m. (1) bef. 1326, Isabel, d. bef. 1342, perhaps dau. of Sir Henry de Tregoz of Goring, Sussex. (CP II, 200-1; The Genealogist (N.S.), XXVIII: 7-8).

7. JOAN de BOHUN, seen 24 Sept. 1349; m. John de Lisle of Gatcombe in the Isle of Wight, b. 13 June 1324, d. 31 Mar. 1349. (The Genealogist (N.S.), XXVIII: 8-9).

8. ELIZABETH de LISLE, seen 13 Sept. 1369, heir of her brother, John de Lisle, who d.s.p. 3 Sept. 1369; m. John de Bramshot. (The Genealogist (N.S.), XXVIII: 9).

9. WILLIAM BRAMSHOT, lord of the manor of Gatcombe in the Isle of Wight, b.c. 1370; m. c. 1395, Joan. (Visitation of the County of Sussex, 1530 and 1633-4 (Harl. Soc. Publ., vol. LIII), p. 44).

10. JOHN BRAMSHOT, b. c. 1400, d. 1468, lord of the manors of Gatcombe, Calbourne, and Whitwell, in the Isle of Wight; m. 1444, as her 1st husband, Katherine, dau. of Sir John Pelham, Chamberlain to Queen Katherine, consort of Henry V, by Joan de Courcy, member of the Queen's Household. (CP IV, 480 note a; John Comber, Sussex Genealogical Collections (Cambridge, 1933), III: 204-5; Sussex Archaeological Collections, LXIX: 67-8).

11. ELIZABETH BRAMSHOT; m. John Dudley, Esq., of Altherington, Sussex, d. bef. 26 June 1501, Sheriff of Sussex and Surrey, 1484-5, 2nd son of Sir John de Sutton, K.G., 1st Lord Dudley, by ELIZABETH BERKELEY (80A-8). (CP IV, 480 note a).

12. EDMUND DUDLEY, ESQ., b. c. 1462, beheaded 18 Aug. 1510, M.P., Speaker of the House of Commons, 1504, Privy Councillor, Chancellor of the Exchequer; m. Elizabeth, dau. of Edward Grey, Lord Lisle, by whom he was the father of John Dudley, Duke of Northumberland. By an unknown mistress, Edmund Dudley left illegitimate issue. (CP IV, 480 note a; DNB VI, 100-102).

13. SIMON DUDLEY, natural son, b. 1505, d. 1555, of Elmley Lovett, co. Worcestershire, and Hackney, co. Middlesex, member of the Household of Henry VIII, he was an officer at the coronation of Queen Anne Boleyn, and in 1544 accompanied the King to France; m. (1) bef. 1533, Emme, seen 5 Sept. 1543, dau. of Thomas Saunders. (TAG, 44: 129-30).

14. JOHN DUDLEY, Gent., of Hackney, Middlesex, b. c. 1528, d. bef. 15 Feb. 1592/3, Serjeant of the Pastry to Queen Elizabeth I, had a grant of arms, 1588. By an unknown mistress, he left illegitimate issue. (TAG, 44: 130-1, 135).

15. CAPT. ROGER DUDLEY, natural son, b. c. 1552, d. 1585; m. before 1576, SUSANNAH THORNE (50-13), bp. 5 Mar. 1559/60, seen 29 Oct. 1588. (TAG, 44: 131-132). This identification of Roger's (No. 15) father is probable; it is not proven.

Line 150

4. SIR EDMUND MORTIMER (147-4), d. 17 June 1304, 7th Baron Mortimer of Wigmore; m. Margaret de Fienes, d. 7 Feb. 1333/4. (NEHGR, 116: 16-17).

5. ISOLDE de MORTIMER, liv. 1336 (widow of Sir Walter de Balan); m. Hugh de Audley, Lord Audley, b. c. 1267, d. betw. Nov. 1325 & Mar. 1325/6, Ambassador to France, son of James de Audley and ELA LONGESPEE (143-3). (CP I 346-347; IX, 499-501).

6. HUGH de AUDLEY, d. 10 Nov. 1347, 8th Earl of Gloucester; m. Windsor, 28 Apr. 1317, MARGARET de CLARE (28-5), d. 9 Apr. 1342. (CP V, 715).

6. ALICE de AUDLEY (sister of Hugh 6 above), d. 12 Jan. 1373/4; m. c. 14 Jan. 1326/7, RALPH de NEVILLE (44-5), b. c. 1291, d. 5 Aug. 1367, Lord Neville of Raby, q.v. (CP IX, 499-501).

Line 151

1. WILLIAM de WARENNE, Named in the Magna Charta, 1215, 6th Earl of Surrey, d. London, 27 May 1240, son of Hamelin (bastard son of Geoffrey Plantagenet (see 161-10)) and Isabella de Warenne; m. (2) bef. 13 Oct. 1225, MAUD MARSHAL

(148-2, 155-3). (CP XII (1), 500).

2. JOHN de WARENNE, b. in or aft. Aug. 1231, d. aft. Michaelmas 1304, Earl of Surrey; m. Aug. 1247, Alice de Lusignan, d. 9 Feb. 1255/6, dau. of Hugh X de Lusignan and Isabella d'Angouleme. (CP XII (1), 503).

3. WILLIAM de WARENNE, b. c. 1256, killed in a tournament at Croydon, 15 Dec. 1286; m. prob. in June 1285, JOAN de VERE (121-4). (CP XII (1), 507).

Line 152

2. JOHN de WARENNE (151-2); m. Alice de Lusignan.

3. ELEANOR de WARENNE, b. 1251, liv. 1282; m. York, 8 Sept. 1268, Sir Henry de Percy, Knt., b. c. 1235, d. 29 Aug. 1272, Lord Percy. (CP X, 455).

4. SIR HENRY de PERCY, Lord Percy, b. posthumous at Petworth, c. 25 Mar. 1273, d. betw. 2 and 10 Oct. 1314; m. Eleanor Fitz Alan, d. July or Aug. 1328. (See note at end of line.) (CP X, 456).

5. HENRY de PERCY, K.G., b. c. 1299, d. end of Feb. 1351/2, Lord Percy of Alnwick, M.P., 1322-1352; m. IDOINE de CLIFFORD (8-7).

6. HENRY de PERCY, ae. 30+ at father's death, b. c. 1320, d. c. 18 May 1368, fought at Crecy, 1346; m. (1) Sept. 1334, Mary Plantagenet, d. 1 Sept. 1362, dau. of Henry, Earl of Lancaster and MAUD de CHAWORTH (4-6). (CP X, 462).

The parentage of Eleanor Fitz Alan, wife of Sir Henry Percy (No. 4) is not clear. CP X p. 458 note k says she was sister of "Richard de Arundel, the King's batchelor, and his executor when he died, Mar. 1314." Richard and Eleanor might be Children of Richard, Earl of Arundel b. 1266/7, but are not mentioned by him or by other Arundel chroniclers. Clay, p. 161, says she was the dau. of John, Earl of Arundel (father of Richard, d. 1266/7) and received Leconfield in dower. But CP I p. 240 shows John's IPM, Hen. III file 42, no. 5, which says only one son Richard, b. 3 Feb. 1266/7, his heir. John's widow Isabel, dau. of Roger Mortimer, m. (2) 1273 Ralph d'Arderne. It seems likely Eleanor was of the family of Fitz Alans, Earls of Arundel, but exact connection is not established.

Line 153

1. ADELIZA (or ADELAIDE) de CLAREMONT; m. (1) Gilbert Fitz Richard, b. bef. 1066, d. 1114/7,"Earl of Clare" and Lord of Tunbridge, founder of the Priory of Clare, 1090, Lord of Cardigan, 1107-1111, son of Richard Fitz Gilbert of Clare and Rohese, dau. of William Giffard, the Elder.

2. RICHARD FITZ GILBERT de CLARE, slain by the Welsh near Abergavenny, 15 Apr.1136; m. Adeliza, sister of Ranulph de Guernons, Earl of Chester.

3. ROGER de CLARE, d. 1173, Earl of Hertford, 1156-1173; m. Maud, dau. of James de St.Hilary. (CP III, 243; VI, 499).

4. RICHARD de CLARE (28-1), Magna Charta Surety, 1215, d. c. 27 Nov. 1217, 6th Earl of Clare, Earl of Hertford and Gloucester; m. Amice, Countess of Gloucester, dau. & h. of William fitz Robert, Earl of Gloucester. (See lines 28 to 43).

5. SIR GILBERT de CLARE (28-2), Magna Charta Surety, 1215, b. c. 1180, d. Penros, Brittany, 25 Oct. 1230, 7th Earl of Clare, Earl of Hertford, 1217-1230, and of Gloucester; m. 9 Oct. 1217, ISABEL MARSHAL (145-2), d. Berkhampstead, 17 Jan. 1239/40; she m. (2) 30 Mar. 1231, Richard (Plantagenet), Earl of Cornwall. (CP III, 242-244; Michael Altschul, The Clares, 1217-1314).

Line 154

1. ALICE de CLARE, d. c. 1163; m. Aubrey de Vere II, b. prob. bef. 1090, slain in London, 15 May 1141, of Great Addington and Drayton, Sheriff of London and Middlesex, Justice and Master Chamberlain of England, 1133. (CP X, 195).

2. AUBREY de VERE, b. prob. c. 1110, d. 26 Dec. 1194, 1st Earl of Oxford; m. (3) 1162/3, Agnes, b. 1151 or 1152, surv. husb., dau. of Henry of Essex, Lord of

Rayleigh and Haughley. (CP X, 199).
    3. ROBERT de VERE (120-1), Magna Charta Surety, 1215, b. bef. 1164, d.
bef. 23 Oct. 1221; m. Isabel; d. 3 Feb. 1245, dau. of Hugh de Bolbec.

Line 155

    1. JULIANA de VERE (dau. of ALICE (154-1) and Aubrey de Vere II), liv.
1185; m. (1) Hugh Bigod, 1st Earl of Norfolk, b. c. 1095, Lord of Framlingham,
1120, Royal Steward, 1123 (son of Roger Bigod, d. Sept. 1107, and his wife Alice,
liv. 1130, dau. of Robert de Toeni, Lord of Belvoir). (The marriage of Juliana and
Hugh was annulled.) JULIANA m. (2) Walkelin Maminot, d. 1182. Hugh m. (2)
Gundred de Warenne, d. 1200/8, and she m. (2) William de Lancaster, Baron of
Kendal. (CP IX, 579).
    2. ROGER BIGOD (3-1) (son of Hugh and Juliana), Magna Charta Surety, 1215,
Royal Steward, 1186, 2nd Earl of Norfolk, 1189, Baron of the Exchequer, 1195-1196,
b. c. 1150, d. bef. 2 Aug. 1121; m. Ida.
    3. HUGH BIGOD (3-2), Magna Charta Surety, 1215, d. Feb. 1224/5, 3rd Earl
of Norfolk; m. 1207, MAUD MARSHAL (148-2), d. 27 Mar. 1248, dau. of SIR WIL-
LIAM MARSHAL, Named in the Magna Charta, 1215; she m. (2) 1225, WILLIAM de
WARENNE (151-1), Named in the Magna Charta, 1215, q.v.

Line 156

    1. ALICE de VERE (dau. of ALICE (154-1) and Aubrey de Vere II), b. bef.
1141, liv. 1185; m. (1) Robert of Essex, Lord of Rayleigh; m. (2) Roger Fitz Richard,
1st Lord of Warkworth, co. Northumberland, d. 1178, son of Richard and Jane, dau.
of Roger Bigod.
    2. ROBERT FITZ ROGER, b. bef. 1178, d. 1212, 2nd Baron of Warkworth,
Lord of Clavering, Sheriff of Northumberland; m. Margaret, dau. of William de
Chesney.
    3. JOHN FITZ ROBERT (44-1), Magna Charta Surety, 1215, lord of Wark-
worth, d. 1240; m. (2) Ada de Baliol, d. Stokesley, 29 July 1251, dau. of Hugh de
Baliol of Barnard Castle and Cicely de Fountaines. (See Sir Charles Clay, "Ancestry of the Earls of Warkworth," Archaeologia Aeliana, 4th Ser. vol. 32).

Line 157

    1. MAUD de ST. LIZ, d. 1140; m. Robert Fitz Richard, d. 1134, son of Richard
Fitz Gilbert de Clare and grandson of Gilbert, Count of Brionne, who was son of
Godfrey, Count of Brionne, illegitimate son of Richard I, the Fearless, Duke of
Normandy.
    2. MAUD FITZ ROBERT, b. bef. 1134; m. William II (called le Breton)
D'Aubigny, son of William D'Aubigny of Belvoir (d. 1155/6) and grandson of Robert
de Toeni, Lord of Belvoir.
    3. WILLIAM D'AUBIGNY (1-1), Lord of Belvoir, Magna Charta Surety, 1215,
succeeded to his father's estates 1167/8; d. 1 May 1236.

Line 158

    1. GUNDRED (dau. of Gherbod the Fleming), d. 27 May 1085; m. bef. 1077, Wil-
liam de Warenne, d. Lewes, 24 June 1088, cr. 1st Earl of Surrey, son of Rodolf
de Warenne and Beatrice.
    2. EDITH de WARENNE; m. (2) Gerold de Gournay, Lord of Gournay-en-
Bray.
    3. GUNDRED de GOURNAY; m. as his 2nd wife, June 1118, Nele D'Aubigny
(son of Roger and Amice), d. 21/26 Nov. 1129, who was granted the English lands of
Robert de Stuteville after the battle of Tinchebrai, 1106. (Nele m. (1) c. 1107, Maud

de Laigle, former wife of Robert de Mowbray, Earl of Northumbria, whose surname, Mowbray, was taken by a son of the 2nd wife.) (CP IX, 367).

4. ROGER de MOWBRAY (son of Gundred and Nele D'Aubigny), d. in Palestine, c. 1188, went on the 2nd crusade, 1147; m. Alice de Gaunt, widow of Ilbert de Lacy, and dau. of Walter de Gaunt and Maud of Brittany. (CP IX, 369).

5. NELE de MOWBRAY, of Thirsk, went on a crusade with King Richard, 1189, d. at Acre, 1191; m. 1170, Mabel, d. c. 1203.

6. WILLIAM de MOWBRAY (63-1), Magna Charta Surety, 1215, of Thirsk and Slingsby, crusader, 1193, d. Axholme, bef. Mar. 1223/4; m. Avice. (Greenway, Charters of the Honour of Mowbray, esp. pp. 260-261).

Line 159

1. ROHESE de VERE (dau. of ALICE de CLARE (154-1) and Aubrey de Vere II), liv. Oct. 1166; m. Geoffrey de Mandeville, d. Mildenhall, co. Suffolk, c. Sept. 1144.

2. MAUD de MANDEVILLE; m. (1) Piers de Lutegareshale; m. (2) Hugh de Boclande of Buckland, liv. 1176.

3. HAWISE de BOCLANDE, d. bef. 19 July 1233; m. William de Lanvallei, of Wakerly, d. bef. 18 May 1205, son of William de Lanvallei and Gunnora, dau. of Hubert St. Clare. (Wrottesley, Pedigrees from Plea Rolls, p. 486).

4. WILLIAM de LANVALLEI (55-1), Magna Charta Surety, 1215, d. 1217, of Wakerly and Great Bromley, co. Essex; m. a dau. of ALAN BASSET, of Wycome, co. Buckingham, Named in the Magna Charta, 1215.

Line 160

3. GEOFFREY FITZ PIERS (son of MAUD de MANDEVILLE (159-2) and Piers de Lutegareshale), d. 14 Oct. 1213, Earl of Essex, Justiciar of England, 1198-1213, Sheriff of the Shires of Northampton, Essex, and Hertford; m. (1) bef. 25 Jan. 1184/5, Beatrix de Say, d. bef. 19 Apr. 1197, dau. of William de Say; m. (2) Avelina de Clare, d. bef. 4 June 1225. (CP V, 122).

4. MAUD FITZ GEOFFREY (by the 1st wife), Countess of Essex, d. 27 Aug. 1236; m. (1) HENRY de BOHUN (18-1), Magna Charta Surety, 1215. (CP V, 134).

Line 161

1. ALFRED the GREAT, King of England, 871-901, b. Wantage 849, d. 26 Oct. 899, son of Aethelwulf, King of Wessex; m. 868, Alswitha, d. c. 905, dau. of Earl Aethelred of Mercia.

2. EDWARD I, the Elder, King of England, 901-924, b. 875, d. 924; m. (3) 919, Eadgifu, d. 961, dau. of Sigehelm, Earl of Kent.

3. EDMUND I, the Magnificent, King of England, 940-946, b. 920, d. 946; m. St. Alfgifu.

4. EDGAR, the Peaceful, King of England, 959-975, b. 943, d. 975; m. 965, Elfrida, b. 945, d. 1000, dau. of Earl Ordgar.

5. AETHELRED II, the Redeless, King of England, 979-1016, b. 968, d. 1016; m. (1) 985, Alffaed, dau. of Thored.

6. EDMUND II, Ironside, King of England, 1016, b. 989, d. 30 Nov. 1016; m. Ealgyth.

7. EDWARD, the Atheling, b. 1016, d. 1057; m. Agatha of Hungary.

8. MARGARET (St. Margaret of Scotland), b. 1045, d. 16 Nov. 1093; m. 1068/9, Malcolm III Canmore, King of Scots, b. 1031, d. 13 Nov. 1093.

9. MARGARET (or MATHILDA) of SCOTLAND, b. 1079, d. 1 May 1118; m. 11 Nov. 1100, HENRY I Beauclerc, King of England, 1100-1135, son of William the Conqueror and Maud of Flanders.

10. MATILDA of ENGLAND, b. 1104, d. 10 Sept. 1167; m. 3 Apr. 1127, Geoffrey V Plantagenet, Count of Anjou, Duke of Normandy.

11. HENRY II, Curt Mantel, King of England, 1154-1189, b. 5 Mar. 1132/3, d. 6 July 1189; m. 18 May 1153, Eleanor of Poitou.

12. JOHN, Lackland, who signed the Magna Charta in 1215, King of England, 1199-1216, b. 24 Dec. 1166, d. 19 Oct. 1216; m. (2) 24 Aug. 1200, Isabella of Angouleme.

13. HENRY III, King of England, 1216-1272, b. 1 Oct. 1207, d. 16 Nov. 1272; m. 14 Jan. 1437, Eleanor of Provence.

14. EDWARD I, King of England, 1272-1307, b. 17 June 1239, d. 7 July 1307; m. (1) Oct. 1254, Eleanor of Castile; m. (2) 8 Sept. 1299, Marguerite of France.

15. EDWARD II, King of England, 1307-1327, b. 25 Apr. 1284, d. 21 Sept. 1327; m. Isabella of France.

16. EDWARD III, King of England, 1327-1377, b. 13 Nov. 1312, d. 21 June 1377; m. 24 Jan. 1328, Philippa of Hainaut. They had (in order given) 1. Edward, "the Black Prince," Prince of Wales, father of Richard II who d. s. p.; 2. William of Hatfield d. y.; 3. LIONEL of Antwerp, Duke of Clarence; 4. JOHN of Gaunt, Duke of Lancaster; 5. EDMUND of Langley, Duke of York; and 6. Thomas of Woodstock, Duke of Gloucester. They also had 5 daus. of whom Isabel who m. Ingelram de Couci, Earl of Bedford, and Mary who m. John V de Montfort, Duke of Brittany, left issue.

17. LIONEL, Duke of Clarence, K.G., b. Antwerp, 29 Nov. 1338, d. Piedmont, 17 Oct. 1368; m. (1) 9 Sept. 1312, Elizabeth, d. 1363, Countess of Ulster, dau. & h. of William de Burgh, 3rd Earl of Ulster; m. (2) 28 May 1368, Violante, d. s. p., dau. of Galeazzo Visconti, Prince of Milan.

18. PHILIPPA PLANTAGENET, only child, by 1st wife, Countess of Ulster, b. 16 Aug. 1355, d. 5 Jan. 1381/2; m. 1368 EDMUND MORTIMER (36-9), d. 27 Dec. 1381, 3rd Earl of March.

19. ROGER MORTIMER, Earl of March, b. 11 Apr. 1374, d. 20 July 1398; m. ELEANOR (94-9), d. 23 Oct. 1405, eldest dau. of THOMAS HOLAND (94-8), 2nd Earl of Kent. (She m. (2) as 1st wife, EDWARD, Lord Cherleton de Powys (30-8).

20. ANNE MORTIMER, dau. & h. Countess of March and Ulster; m. bef. June 1408 (Papal disp. to remain in mar.), RICHARD PLANTAGENET, Earl of Cambridge (161-18).

17. EDMUND, Duke of York, K.G., b. 5 June 1341, d. 1 Aug. 1402; m. (1) Mar. 1371/2 Isabel, d. 23 Nov. 1392, yst. dau. & coh. of Pedro I the Cruel, King of Castile and Leon; m. (2) 4 Nov. 1393, Joan, b. 12 Apr. 1434, d. s. p., 2nd dau. of THOMAS HOLAND (94-8), 2nd Earl of Kent. She m. (2) Mar. 1406, William, Lord Willoughby de Eresby, d. 30 Nov. 1409; m. (3) 6 Sept. 1410, Henry, 1st Lord Scrope de Masham, d. s. p. 3 June 1415; m. (4) Henry Brounflete, Lord Vesci, d. 6 Jan. 1467/8.

18. RICHARD (2nd son, event. h.), Earl of Cambridge, b. 1375, beheaded 5 Aug. 1415; m. (1) bef. June 1408 (Papal disp. to remain in mar.), ANNE MORTIMER (161-20), Countess of March; m. (2) Maud, dau. of Thomas, Lord Clifford.

19. RICHARD, 3rd Duke of York, K.G., b. 21 Sept. 1411, killed 31 Dec. 1460; m. bef. 18 Oct. 1424, Cecily (d. 31 May 1495), dau. of RALPH NEVILL (45-7), 1st Earl of Westmoreland.

20. EDWARD IV (4th Duke of York, K.G.), b. Rouen, 28 Apr. 1441, d. 9 Apr. 1483, proclaimed King, 4 Mar. 1461; m. Grafton, Northants., 1 May 1464, Elizabeth, bur. 10 June 1492, wid. of Sir John Grey of Groby, dau. of Sir Richard Wydville.

21. PRINCESS ELIZABETH PLANTAGENET, eldest dau., b. 11 Feb. 1465, d. 1503; m. 18 Jan. 1486, HENRY VII (161-21).

17. JOHN, Duke of Lancaster, K.G., titular King of Castile and Leon, b. 24 June 1340, d. 3 Feb. 1398/9; m. (1) 19 May 1359, Blanche, d. 31 Sept. 1369, yst. dau. & coh. of Henry Plantagenet, Duke of Lancaster (by whom he was father of Henry IV); m. (2) June 1371, Constance, d. June 1394, eldest dau. & coh. of Pedro I the Cruel, King of Castile and Leon (by whom, a dau. Katharine who m. Henry III of Trastamara, King of Castile and Leon); m. (3) 13 Jan. 1396/7 Katharine, formerly his mistress, wid. of Sir Hugh Swynford, dau. & coh. of Sir Payn Roet of Hainault, Guienne King of Arms.

18. JOHN BEAUFORT, Earl of Somerset, Marquis of Dorset, K.G. (see 90-9), b. c. 1372, d. 16 Mar. 1410. He was legitimated with the 3 other chn. of Katharine by Act of Parliament 20 Rich. II (1397) for all purposes except the royal succession. He m. as her 1st husb., c. 1399, Margaret, d.c. 30 Dec. 1439, 3rd dau. and event. coh. of THOMAS HOLAND (90-8), 2nd Earl of Kent, K.G. She m. (2) 1411, Thomas, Duke of Clarence, K.G., 2nd son of Henry IV.

19. JOHN BEAUFORT, Duke of Somerset, K.G., b. 25 Mar. 1404, d. 27 May

1444; m. 1439, MARGARET (57-11), wid. of Sir Oliver St. John, Knt., sole dau. & h. of John, Lord Beauchamp of Bledsoe. She m. (3) as his 2nd wife, LIONEL, Lord Welles, K.G. (82-10).

20. MARGARET BEAUFORT, b. Apr. 1441, d. 5 July 1509; m. (1) 1455, Edmund Tudor, Earl of Richmond, d. 1 Nov. 1456, son of Sir Owen Tudor & Katharine, Princess of France, Queen-Dowager of England, & wid. of Henry VI; m. (2) c. 1459, Henry Stafford, d.s.p., 1481, 3rd son of Humphrey, Duke of Buckingham, K.G.; m. (3) 1482/3, as his 2nd wife, Thomas Stanley, d. 5 July 1509, Earl of Derby.

21. HENRY (TUDOR) VII, (Earl of Richmond), b. Pembroke Castle, 28 Jan. 1457 d. 5 Apr. 1509, proclaimed King, 22 Aug. 1485; m. 18 Jan. 1486, PRINCESS ELIZABETH PLANTAGENET (161-21), d. 11 Feb. 1503.

22. PRINCESS MARGARET TUDOR, b. 29 Nov. 1489, d. 18 Oct. 1541; m. (1) 8 Aug. 1503, JAMES IV, King of Scotland (92-13), d. 9 Sept. 1513; m. (2) as his 2nd wife, 6 Aug. 1514, Archibald Douglas, 6th Earl of Angus, divorced 11 Mar. 1527/8 (by whom she had a dau. Margaret, b. 1515, d. 1577/8, m. 1544, Matthew Stuart, Earl of Lennox, d. 4 Sept. 1571, parents of Henry Stuart, Lord Darnley (see 92-15)); m. (3) bef. 1528, Henry Stewart, Lord Methven.

Line 162

This line does not connect with Fitz Randolph (Line 164).

9. MARGARET de GREY (26-9) (a descendant of Edward I (161-14) and Eleanor of Castile); m. JOHN DARCY (33-11).

10. SIR PHILIP DARCY, b. c. 1398, d.s.p.m. 2 Aug. 1418; m. bef. 28 Oct. 1412, Alianor Fitz Hugh, d. 30 Sept. 1457, dau. of Sir Henry Fitz Hugh of Ravensworth and Elizabeth, dau. of Sir Robert Grey. (CP IV, 66-68).

11. MARGERY DARCY, b. Ravensworth, 1 Sept. 1418, d. bef. 20 Apr. 1469; m. bef. 20 Nov. 1431, Sir John Conyers of Hornby Castle, co. York, d. 14 Mar. 1489/90. (CP IV, 66-68).

Line 163

1. SIR THOMAS GIFFARD, KNT., of Twyford, co. Buckingham, b. c. 1345, d. 25 Sept. 1394; m. c. 1361, Elizabeth de Missenden, d.c. 1367.

2. ROGER GIFFARD, ESQ., of Twyford, b. c. 1367, d. 14 Apr. 1409; m. (3) c. 1407, Isabel Stretle.

3. THOMAS GIFFARD, of Twyford, 1408-1469; m. Eleanor Vaux. (See Notes below.)

4. JOHN GIFFORD, ESQ., of Twyford, 1431-1506; m. Agnes Winslowe.

5. THOMAS GIFFORD, of TWYFORD, co. Buckingham, d. 10 Oct. 1511; m. Jane Langston, who survived him, dau. of John Langston.

6. AMY GIFFORD, b. c. 1485/90; m. bef. 1511, Richard Samwell, d. 3 May 1519, of Cotesford, co. Oxford, son of John Samwell, of co. Cornwall.

7. SUSANNA SAMWELL, b. c. 1510/15; m. bef. 1535, Peter Edwards, b. c. 1490, d. c. 1552, of Peterborough, son of Peter Edwards.

8. EDWARD EDWARDS, gent., of Alwalton, co. Huntington, b. c. 1537, d. 1592; m. Ursula Coles, bur. Alwalton, 2 Feb. 1606, dau. of Richard Coles and Jane Bond of Preston-over-Hill.

9. MARGARET EDWARDS, m. bef. 25 Dec. 1591, Henry Freeman, of Cranford, co. Northampton, b. c. 1560, son of Thomas Freeman, of Irchester, co. Northampton.

10. ALICE FREEMAN, d. New London, Connecticut, 11 Feb. 1664/5; m. (1) c. 1615, as his 2nd wife, John Tompson, gent., of Little Preston, Preston Capes, b. c. 1580/90, d. London, 6 Nov. 1626, son of Thomas Tompson; m. (2) Roxbury, Mass., bef. 30 May 1644, Robert Parke.

11. MARY TOMPSON, bp. Preston Capes, co. Northampton, England, 14 Nov. 1619, d. Roxbury, Mass., 4 Aug. 1693; m. Roxbury, 3 Dec. 1641, Joseph Wise, of Roxbury, 1640, d. Roxbury, 12 Sept. 1684. Their distinguished son, the Reverend John Wise, Harvard College, 1673, was the great apostle of liberty.

11. BRIDGET TOMPSON, bp. Preston Capes, 11 Sept. 1622, d. Aug. 1643; m.

Mar. 1640/1, Captain George Denison, gent., bp. Bishop's Stortford, co. Hertford, 10 Dec. 1620, d. Hartford, Conn., 23 Oct. 1694, son of William Denison and Margaret (Chandler) Monck. He. m. (2) Ann Borodell.

11. DOROTHY TOMPSON, bp. Preston Capes, 5 July 1624, d. aft. 1709; m. by 28 Oct. 1644, Thomas Parke, d. Preston, Conn., 30 July 1709, son of Robert Parke and Martha Chaplin. (George Andrews Moriarty, in NEHGR, 75: 135-136; Clarence A. Torrey, in TAG, 13: 1-8: 14: 145 f.: Walter Metcalfe, Visitations of Northamptonshire, 1564, 1618/9, London, 1887, p. 195; Sir Henry Ellis, Visitations of Huntingdon, 1613 (Camden Soc.), p. 113; Robert L. Sttenrod, in TAG, 29: 215-218; Winifred Lovering Holman, Stevens and Allied Families, 419-426, 431; Lechford's ms. Note-Book, 1638-1641 (American Antiquarian Society), p. 381 (22 Mar. 1640/1); Aspinwall Notarial Records (Boston Pub. Doc., No. 32), 1903, p. 186. For the Reverend John Wise, see Sibley's Harvard Graduates, II 428-441. There may be a connection in gen. 3 to Vaux of Harrowden.

Notes: Thomas Tompson, No. 11 in earlier editions, must be dropped. See Ernest Flagg, Founding of New England, 349-50. For Vaux, see Moriarty in Misc. Gen. et Her. 5 series VI especially pp. 126-7, 226-7, 129, 135.

Line 164

1. ROGER BIGOD (3-1), 2nd Earl of Norfolk, Magna Charta Surety, 1215, b. c. 1140/45, d. 1221; m. Ida. (CP IX, 586-589).

2. MARY BIGOD, heiress of Menethorpe, co. York, prob. m. Ranulf fitz Robert, lord of Middleham, co. York, to which he succeeded by 1206, d. bef. 7 Dec. 1252, bur. at Coverham Abbey, co. York; held 6 knights' fees in the honour of Richmond, co. York, and 6 in Norfolk, the latter acquired presumably from the Bigods. (Clay, Early Yorkshire Charters, V: 303; Genealogist, N.S., 3:33; Feudal Aids, 6: 156; VCH, North Riding of York, 1: 254).

3. RANULF fitz RANULF, lord of Spennithorne, co. York, b. c. 1220/5, d. bef. 1294; m. Bertrama, widow of Sir Roger de Ingoldsby. (Ibid., 1: 258).

4. RALPH fitz RANULF, lord of Spennithorne, b. c. 1250/60, d. bef. 1316; m. Theophania (or Tiffany) de Lascelles, dau. and coheiress of Sir Roger de Lascelles (IV) of Kirkby-under-Knowle, co. York, who is now considered by legal fiction to have been 1st Baron Lascelles. (Ibid., 1: 258: "Lascelles Fee," Clay, Early Yorkshire Charters, V 182-186; CP VII, 446-449).

5. RANULF fitz RALPH, lord of Spennithorne, sometimes called Ranulf de Lascelles, b. c. 1300, d. aft. 1343; m. Isabel. (VCH op. cit., 1: 258; Feet of Fines for co. of York, 1327-1347, p. 166).

6. JOHN fitz RANULF, lord of Spennithorne, b.c. 1325, d. bef. 1369; m. by Oct. 1343, Maud "de Campania," who m. (2) Robert de Hilton, lord of Swine. (VCH op. cit., 1: 259; Feet of Fines for co. of York, loc. cit.; Yorks. Archaeol. Journal, 25: 174).

7. RANDALL (or RANULF) fitz JOHN, lord of Spennithorne, b. c. 1345, d. aft. 1388. (VCH North Riding, 1: 259).

8. SIR JOHN FITZ RANDALL (or FitzRandolph), Knt., lord of Spennithorne, b. c. 1374, beheaded, 1405, for taking part in the rebellion of Henry Percy, 1st Earl of Northumberland, Richard Scrope, Archbishop of York, and other northern magnates. (VCH North Riding, 1: 259; C.W.C. Oman, Political History of England, 1377-1485, pp. 194-198; see Close Rolls, 17 Feb. 1407, for lands of which Sir John was seised at time of his death).

9. SIR RALPH FITZ RANDALL (or FitzRandolph), Knt., lord of Spennithorne, b. c. 1398, under age in 1407, will dated 20 Jan. 1457/8, pr. ult. Jan. 1457/8; m. Elizabeth. (VCH North Riding, 1: 259; Sir Ralph's will is printed in Surtees Soc. Publ., 26: 4).

10. JOHN FITZ RANDOLPH (or FitzRandall), Esq., lord of Spennithorne, b. c. 1420, d. 5 Mar. 1474/5; m. Joan Conyers, eldest dau. of Sir Christopher Conyers, Knt., of Hornby Castle, co. York, b. c. 1380, d. aft. 1462 m. (1) bef. Sept. 1415, Ellen, b. c. 1399, d. 6 Aug. 1444, dau. of Thomas Rolleston of Mablethorp, co. Lincoln, Esq., by Beatrice Haulay his wife, heiress of Ingleton, co. York. (VCH North Riding, 1: 259; J. W. Clay, Extinct & Dormant Peerages of the Northern

Counties of England, 32-33; Yorks. Arch. Soc. Record Series, 59: 105, Inq.p.m. of
Thomas Rolleston).

11. JOHN FITZ RANDOLPH, b. perhaps 1455/60, prob. d. bef. 1514, presumed to have been third or fourth son of John FitzRandolph and Joan Conyers, and
brother of Sir Ralph FitzRandolph of Spennithorne (c. 1444-1517) and of Christopher
FitzRandolph, parson of Kirkby-in-Ashfield, co. Nottingham (d. 1516). (See note to
this pedigree; FitzRandolph pedigree in British Museum Add. Mss. 6705, f58b,
begins with this John).

12. CHRISTOPHER FITZ RANDOLPH, b.c. 1495, d. sh. bef. 26 Apr. 1570
(administration granted on that date to his widow Jane and eldest son Thomas;
doubtless came to Kirkby-in-Ashfield, co. Nottingham, because of his uncle Christopher FitzRandolph, parson of that place, who d. 1516 leaving a will dated 1 June
1516 of which the nephew Christopher was named as one of the executors; m. by contract dated 1514 to Jane (or Joan) Langton, dau. and heiress of Cuthbert Langton
of Langton Hall in the parish of Kirkby-in-Ashfield. Jane was b. c. 1499, d. betw.
30 July 1573 (date of will) and 2 Apr. 1574 (probate). (NEHGR, 97: 296, 99: 335-336;
Brit. Museum Add. Mss. 6705: f58b; Add. Mss. 6707: f102; Harl. Mss. 1400: 58,
58b; Thoroton, Antiquities of Nottinghamshire, 2: 296; Harl. Soc. Publ., 4: 187.
L. V. F. Randolph, FitzRandolph Traditions, mentions Christopher FitzRandolph and
Jane Langton many times, but this book regrettably contains many errors, Whitaker,
Richmondshire II p. 46).

13. CHRISTOPHER FITZ RANDOLPH, b. c. 1530, bur. at Sutton-in-Ashfield,
co. Nottingham, 28 June 1588 (this is the correct date of burial from original paper
Parish Register of Sutton-in-Ashfield. The date was incorrectly copied as "7 June
1589" in late parchment copy of original Register, and wrong date from the copy was
unfortunately printed in the NEHGR, 97: 298). Christopher was his parents' fourth
son, and was named in his mother's will, dated 30 July 1573. His own will, dated
20 June 1588, was proved 1 Apr. 1589 in the Peculiar Court of the Manor of Mansfield (Notts. County Record Office, D.D.P. 17/69). Christopher's wife, who pre-
deceased him, was not named in his will. He had four sons, James, Anthony, Edward, and Christopher, named in the will.

14. EDWARD FITZ RANDOLPH, b. c. 1565, d. betw. 13 Aug. 1647 (date of
will) and 27 Oct. 1647 (probate). He was prob. b. at Hucknall-under-Huthwaite in
the parish of Sutton-in-Ashfield, Notts, and moved aft. 1621 to Kirsall in the parish
of Kneesall, Notts, where he died. He was the 3rd son named in his father's will,
and was prob. the nephew Edward named in the will of his uncle Thomas FitzRandolph, 21 May 1600. (NEHGR, 97: 297). He m. (1) at Sutton-in-Ashfield, 16 Nov.
1589, Alice Tompson, bur. there 27 Dec. 1604. He m. (2) at Sutton-in-Ashfield,
17 Dec. 1605, Frances Howis, apparently a native of the parish of Kneesall, Notts,
bur. at Kneesall 7 June 1631 (NEHGR, 97: 298; Transcript of the Parish Registers
of Kneesall; original will of Edward FitzRandolph at York Probate Registry, in which
he bequeathed ten pounds sterling to his son Edward "if he cum to demand it.")

15. EDWARD FITZ RANDOLPH (son of the 2nd marriage), the emigrant to New
England and eventual settler in New Jersey, bp. at Sutton-in-Ashfield, Notts, 5
July 1607, emigrated 1630 to Scituate, Mass., then moved to Barnstable, Cape Cod,
and finally to Piscataway, N.J., where he d. c. 1684/5. He m. at Scituate, 10 May
1637, Elizabeth Blossom, b. at Leyden, Netherlands, 1620, d. at Piscataway, c.
1713, having remarried, 30 June 1685, Capt. John Pike. (NEHGR, 97: 275-276,
298; 99: 335-336; Louise Aymar Christian and Howard Stelle Fitz Randolph, Fitz
Randolph Genealogy, 5).

Note: Although this line is probably sound, attention should be drawn to differing
evidences. C. T. Clay, Early Yorkshire Charters, 5: 303, says that Ranulf fitz
Robert "is said to have married Mary daughter of Roger Bigod earl of Norfolk"
(see above, Generation 2). But Mary definitely brought the lands of Menethorpe, co.
York, to her husband in gift of frank-marriage, which lands had previously been
held by Roger Bigod (ibid., footnote 4 and authorities there cited). Moreover, the
careful pedigree in the Genealogist, N.S., 3: 33, gives Mary as daughter of Roger
Bigod.

The weakest link is that which connects Generations 10 and 11 (above). John
FitzRandolph (Generation 10) was succeeded at Spennithorne by his eldest son Sir
Ralph FitzRandolph (b.c. 1444, d. 1517) who married Elizabeth Scrope, daughter
of Sir Thomas Scrope, 5th Lord Scrope of Masham. They had a son John FitzRandolph (who d. in 1517 shortly after his father, and was the last of the FitzRandolphs
of Spennithorne), and five daughters, Elizabeth, Alice, Mary, Dorothy, and Agnes,

who were coheiresses of their brother John at his death in 1517 (Surtees Soc. Publ.,
133: 24). In 1514, Christopher FitzRandolph (Generation 12) was married by contract
to Jane Langton. Two of the feoffees of the marriage contract were John FitzRandolph, heir of Spennithorne, mentioned above, and his brother-in-law Sir Nicholas
Strelley of Linby, co. Notts, husband of Elizabeth FitzRandolph, the eldest of the
five Spennithorne coheiresses. It is presumed that John FitzRandolph and Strelley
were feoffees because the bridegroom, Christopher FitzRandolph, was John's first
cousin and Strelley's first-cousin-in-law (see discussion by Anthony R. Wagner,
Richmond Herald, in NEHGR, 99: 335-336).

   We also know that Christopher FitzRandolph (Generation 12) had an uncle,
Christopher FitzRandolph, parson of Kirkby-in-Ashfield, co. Notts, who was presented to that living 3 Mar. 1489/90 by Sir John Conyers of Hornby Castle, co. York,
Knt., who had acquired the advowson. Christopher FitzRandolph the parson made a
will dated 1 June 1516, proved 17 July 1516, of which his nephew Christopher (Generation 12) was one of the executors. Christopher the parson unfortunately did not
mention his kinsmen of the Spennithorne line in this will.

   We further know that John FitzRandolph (Generation 10) married Joan Conyers,
eldest daughter of Sir Christopher Conyers, Knt., lord of Hornby Castle, co. York
(Raine, Testamenta Eboracenses, 3: 228; Conyers pedigree in J.W. Clay, Extinct
and Dormant Peerages of the Northern Counties of England, 32-33). Joan (Conyers)
FitzRandolph was living, a widow, 22 June 1483, when she was named in the will of
that date of her brother Christopher Conyers, Rector of Rudby, co. York (Raine,
Test. Ebor., 3: 287). We think (but cannot prove) that John FitzRandolph (Generation 10) and his wife Joan Conyers had, in addition to their eldest son and heir Sir
Ralph, younger sons named Richard, John, and Christopher, and a daughter Margery who married John Burgh of East Hawkswell, co. York (for the Burghs, see
Whitaker, Richmondshire, 347). Of the above-named three younger sons, we sup-
pose that John was the John FitzRandolph (Generation 11), while Christopher was
the parson of Kirkby-in-Ashfield, named for his grandfather and uncle, the two
Christopher Conyerses. If this connection be correct, as we believe, it would
explain why Sir John Conyers of Hornby (eldest son of Sir Christopher and brother
of Joan (Conyers) FitzRandolph) acquired the advowson of Kirkby-in-Ashfield and
presented Christopher FitzRandolph (whom we believe to have been Sir John's nephew) to that living. It may be noted in passing that the given name Christopher
entered the FitzRandolph family through the marriage to Joan Conyers in the fif-
teenth century and continued as a given name in that family for over two centuries.
Edward[1] FitzRandolph's (Generation 15) eldest surviving son Nathaniel[2] had an eldest
son John[3] who had an eldest son Christopher[4], b. at Woodbridge, N.J., 23 Feb. 1682
(L.A. Christian and H.S.F. Randolph, FitzRandolph Genealogy, 9).

   Bearing in mind the possibilities that Mary Bigod (Generation 2) may not have
been the wife of Ranulph fitz Robert, and that John FitzRandolph (Generation 11) may
not have been a younger son of John FitzRandolph (Generation 10), even though we
think that those connections are correct, we have presented the above pedigree.

                                                            John Insley Coddington

                                         Line 165

   8. ROBERT III STEWART, King of Scots (41-8); m. in or sh. bef. 1367 Annabella Drummond.
   9. MARGARET STEWART, d. bef. Sept. 1465; m. bef. 1390, Archibald Douglas, 4th Earl of Douglas and Duke of Touraine, b. c. 1370, slain at the battle of
Verneuil, 17 Aug. 1424, bur. in the cathedral at Tours, son of Sir Archibald Douglas, "The Grim," (see 41C-8), 3rd Earl of Douglas, by Joanna Moray; Lord Warden
of the Marches, 1400, commanded the Scots at Homildon Hill, 14 Sept. 1402, cr.
14 Apr. 1424 Duke of Touraine in the Peerage of France by King Charles VII. (CP
IV, 433-4; SP III, 157-61, 165-7).
   10. ELIZABETH DOUGLAS, d. c. 1451; m. (3) as his 1st wife, WILLIAM SIN-
CLAIR (41C-10), d. 1480, Lord Sinclair, Earl of Orkney, which earldom he resigned
into the hands of King James III, 1470, cr. 28 Aug. 1455 Earl of Caithness, which
earldom he resigned to his 2nd son by his 2nd wife, 7 Dec. 1476. (CP XI, 737; SP
II, 332; IX, 50).
   11. WILLIAM SINCLAIR, "The Waster," 2nd Lord Sinclair, d. sh. aft. 14
July 1487 (although the eldest son, he was set aside by his father from succession to

the Earldom of Caithness after a jury of nobles found him <u>incompos mentis et fatuus</u>); m. (dispensation 29 Apr. 1458) CHRISTIAN (41H-12), d. bef. 16 Mar. 1500/1, dau. of GEORGE LESLIE (41H-11), 1st Earl of Rothes. (<u>CP</u> XI, 737-8; <u>SP</u> II, 333-4: VII, 569-70).

      12. HENRY SINCLAIR, 3rd Lord Sinclair, slain at Flodden, 9 Sept. 1513; m. bef. 4 Dec. 1488, Margaret, d. sh. aft. 11 June 1542, dau. of Adam Hepburn, Master of Hailes, sister of Patrick Hepburn, 1st Earl of Bothwell. (<u>CP</u> XI, 738; <u>SP</u> VII, 572-3).

Chaplin 163
Charlton (see Cherleton)
Charnells 131
Chaumpaigne 16A
Chauncy 3, 89A
Chaworth 2, 4, 18, 33, 44, 121, 152
Chedworth 63, 73
Chenduit 149
Cheney (Cheyne) 5, 37, 89, 108
Cherleton 30, 31, 32, 63, 94, 94A, 98, 98A, 161
Chester 7, 41, 107, 129, 132, 134, 136, 139, 153
Chetwode 24, 59, 98, 111
Cholmley 76
Church 16B
Claiborne 61
Clapham 95
CLARE (MC) 2, 8, 13, 14, 17A, 17C, 28, 28A, 33, 34, 36, 40, 41, 54, 63, 80, 100, 107, 120, 144, 145, 146, 148, 149, 150, 153, 154, 157, 160
Claremont 153
Clark (Clarke, Clerke) 41, 76, 100
Clavering 49
Clayton 87
Clifford 8, 11, 36, 37, 39, 76, 82, 87, 100, 101, 112, 113, 124, 143, 144, 152, 161
Clifton 52, 53
Cliveden 80
Clinton 16
Clopton 5, 57, 89
Cobham 9
Cockburn 41
Cocke 101
Cockram 75
Codd 47
Cogan 15, 88
Coke 94A
Cole 22, 163
Collier 96
Colville 28A, 43, 78A, 117, 123
Comyn 108, 108A, 108B, 114, 141, 148
Conningsby 6, 51
Constable 76, 77, 109, 124
Conyers 109, 162, 164
Cook (Cooke) 133
Cope 34
Copely (Copley) 4, 95
Corbet 98
Corbin 124
Cornwall 4
Cornwallis 16B, 113A, 117
Corona 129
Cosynton 63
Cotton 24
Couci 161
Courcy 88A, 149A
Courtenay 22, 35, 63, 124, 125, 126, 127
Coventry 129
Covert 65
Coytmore 103, 104
Cox 72

Cranage 39
Cranston 41, 100
Crichton 41, 91C
Crispin 105
Cromwell 21, 62, 124, 132, 136, 138
Crophull 118
Crosse 79
Crowne 39
Culcheth 65
Culpeper 47, 48, 63, 69
Cunningham 41
Curtis 30
Curwen 113
Curzon 55
Cutts 23

--- D ---

Dacre 8A, 16C, 36, 49A, 113
Dalmahoy 92B
Dalton 113
Dalyngruge 18
Dammartin 16A
Damory 40
Danby 47
Darcy 24, 25, 33, 117, 162
Darnell 63
Darrell 21
Daundelyn 46
Dauney 22
Davenport 98A, 122, 130
Dawes 32
Dean 6
Deighton 28, 50
Deincourt 2, 74, 149A
Deiville 137
de la Mare 138
de la Mote 102
de la Pole 10
Delaval 81
De la Warre (Delaware) 4, 55, 56, 80, 90
Delves 101
Denison 50, 163
Denmark 17C, 92
Dennis (or Dennys) 22, 29, 51, 66, 69, 70
Desmond 1
Despenser 4, 9, 10, 13, 14, 34, 35, 37, 47, 74, 76, 79, 80, 100, 115, 121, 124, 125, 134
Devereux 120
Devon (see Courtenay)
Digby 55
Digges (Digge) 16B, 48
Dineley 87
Dinham (see Dynham)
Dixon 113
Douglas 41, 41A, 41C, 41E, 41G, 42, 43B, 92, 92A, 92B, 93, 165
Drake 22, 27
Driby 132
Drummond 41, 41E, 41F, 43D, 92, 165
Drury 5, 37, 74, 75, 123
Dryden 34